STAR TREK

DEATH BEFORE DISHONOR

PETER DAVID

JAMES W. FRY

ARNE STARR

TITAN BOOKS

STAR TREK: DEATH BEFORE DISHONOR

ISBN 1 84576 154 5

Published by Titan Books
A division of Titan Publishing Group Ltd.
144 Southwark St
London SE1 0UP

Originally published by DC Comics as *Star Trek* Vol. 2 #1–6.

A CIP catalogue record for this title is available from the British Library.

This edition first published: December 2005
2 4 6 8 10 9 7 5 3 1

Printed in Italy.

Other titles of interest available from Titan Books:

Star Trek: To Boldly Go (ISBN: 1 84576 084 0)
Star Trek – The Next Generation: The Hero Factor (ISBN: 1 84576 153 7)
Alien Legion: On the Edge (ISBN: 1 84023 765 1)
Alien Legion: Tenants of Hell (ISBN: 1 84023 811 9)
Battlestar Galactica: Saga of a Star World (ISBN: 1 84023 930 1)
Battlestar Galactica: The Memory Machine (ISBN: 1 84023 945 X)

What did you think of this book?
We love to hear from our readers.
Please email us at readerfeedback@titanmail.com,
or write to us at the above address.

www.titanbooks.com

CONFESSIONS OF A FORMER VULCAN

*I*n a 1967 article for *TV Guide* titled, 'Mr Spock Is Dreamy!', legendary SF author Isaac Asimov said it had never occurred to him that *Star Trek*'s pointy-eared, half-human/half-Vulcan science officer might be sexy. According to Asimov, he never realised that "...girls palpitate over the way one eyebrow goes up a fraction; that they squeal with passion when a little smile quirks his lip. And all because he's smart! If only I had known," laments the author, tongue firmly in cheek, "If only I had known!"

Leonard Nimoy interviewed
by Joe Nazzaro

The fact that Mr Spock may have exuded a certain degree of on-screen sex appeal would probably not have come as a surprise to Leonard Nimoy, who has played the character off and on for almost three decades. In fact, Nimoy once admitted that after the *Star Trek* episode *Amok Time* – in which Spock is possessed by *pon far*, a Vulcan mating drive – his fan mail jumped from a few hundred letters to 10,000 a week.

The prospect of becoming a household name was several light years from Nimoy's mind in 1949, when he began his career in show business at the age of eighteen. As the actor now recalls, he literally walked up and down LA's Sunset Boulevard knocking on any door that said, 'Agency'. To make ends meet between acting jobs, he worked in an ice cream parlour, drove a cab, sold vacuum cleaners and even delivered newspapers. When *Star Trek* eventually came along, it was the first steady job he'd had in seventeen years.

In the early '50s, Nimoy began to get work in such films as *Kid Monk Baroni*, playing a would-be boxer; *Seven Days In May*; *The Balcony*, with future Columbo Peter Falk; and *Death Watch*, which Nimoy produced with the late Vic Morrow. He also made an appearance in the schlocky 1952 SF serial, *Zombies of the Stratosphere*, also distributed under the equally lurid title, *Satan's Satellites*. Nimoy, well-concealed in a silly, *Buck Rogers*-type costume, plays a Martian named Narab – an omen of things to come, perhaps?

The actor also made numerous television appearances, including such programmes as *Profiles In Courage* and *The Outer Limits*. In the early '60s, he guested in an episode of *The Lieutenant*, where he caught the eye of producer Gene Roddenberry. Already a veteran television writer by that time, Roddenberry reportedly said of Nimoy, "If I ever do a science fiction show, I'm going to put pointy ears on him and use him."

The writer/producer was as good as his word, and cast Nimoy in the pilot for a new series to be called *Star Trek*. The 1964 pilot *The Cage* was financed by NBC,

needed bargaining chip when it became time to negotiate.

"That's absolutely true," Nimoy recalls, "and I think that's precisely what happened. Because they wanted me to consider working in the film, we were able to quickly settle the suit. It was dragging on until we came to the point where they came to me and said, 'We want you to act in this film.'

"What I told them was, 'I will talk to you about that as soon as this suit is settled,' and as soon as that word got to the proper people, they moved quickly on the suit."

Rediscovering Spock's long-disused persona was a major challenge for Nimoy, who remembers having a tough time working on *Star Trek: The Motion Picture*. "It was strange, it was complicated, and it was somewhat schizophrenic for a while. Jumping back into Spock's skin wasn't easy, particularly because there were writing issues.

"The script I originally read for the film did not even contain the Spock character, so it was a case of them describing to me what Spock would be doing in the next draft of the script. That took a little time and a little fine-tuning to finally get it to fruition, but I was never totally satisfied with that film."

After finishing *Star Trek: The Motion Picture*, Nimoy was ready to put his Spock ears back into mothballs again. What he didn't foresee was the studio's decision to green-light a second *Star Trek* film. "At that time, there was really no reason for anybody to believe there were going to be any more *Star Trek* films. I thought when that picture was done, in more ways than one, it really finished the issue.

"Frankly, I was shocked when I got the call from [Executive Producer] Harve Bennett, saying he had just signed a deal for another picture. I knew Harve somewhat, although I was surprised to hear that he had just signed a deal with Paramount Pictures, and part of that deal was to explore the possibility of making another *Star Trek* film."

While Nimoy may have been less than enthusiastic about doing another *Star Trek* film, Bennett was able to overcome the actor's trepidation by promising to kill his character off. The promise of a memorable death scene for Spock was just too good to pass up.

"That's about right," Nimoy chuckles. "I was not anxious to go back, because I had been disillusioned on the first picture, and secondly it was known that the next picture was going to be done on a very tight budget, so it felt as if they were going to try to get one last squeeze out of the cow. I really wasn't anxious to participate in that but when Harve said what he did about a death scene, I thought, 'Well, maybe this is the way to finish it!' It worked extremely well, and I had a good time doing the second film.

who were less than enthusiastic about the final product. Among their criticisms were the presence of a female first officer (played by Roddenberry's future wife, Majel Barrett) and that Vulcan fellow, who was just too… well, alien for their tastes.

In the end, a second pilot was commissioned with William Shatner playing the new captain. Roddenberry agreed to lose his female Number One, but stuck to his guns with Mr Spock, ears and all. This time, *Star Trek* was picked up as a series, ensuring its cast a place in folk history.

For Nimoy, playing Spock meant a degree of recognisability he had never felt before. He soon began receiving more fan mail than any of his co-stars, and was even able to parlay his new-found fame into a brief but successful music career. Unfortunately, such fame was not without its price. When *Star Trek* was finally cancelled, the actor had difficulty shaking the shadow of Spock. As the actor remembers, his theatrical work was often overlooked by members of the press, who were more interested in asking questions about *Star Trek* in general and Mr Spock in particular.

In the late '70s, rumours of a big-budget *Star Trek* film began to circulate, especially after the unexpected success of *Star Wars* in 1977. While most of the original cast members expressed interest in a big-screen version of *Star Trek*, Nimoy had some reservations. Compounding the problem was the actor's disagreement with the studio regarding merchandising royalties, which had yet to be settled.

On the other hand, Nimoy says that it was Spock's popularity that actually helped resolve his long-standing grievance. Doing *Star Trek: The Motion Picture* without everyone's favourite Vulcan would have been highly illogical, as Spock might say, giving the actor a much-

"The actual death scene was difficult, and I didn't enjoy playing it. The scene was well-written, and I thought we played it well but it was still very difficult to do."

Spock's actual demise turned out to be more of a problem than anyone thought. When rumours of the scene were leaked prematurely, Paramount Pictures was deluged with letters protesting Spock's death. Bennett decided to use the adverse publicity to his advantage, and staged a mock death scene early in the film, as part of a training exercise. The real moment of truth would come at the end of the film, when Spock sacrifices his life to save the *U.S.S. Enterprise* and its crew.

Not surprisingly, preview audiences were stunned by the film's tragic denouement, and sensing a potential lynching by angry *Star Trek* fans, the filmmakers added a final coda, suggesting that Spock might not be dead after all. The last-minute addition helped restore the film's emotional balance, and *Star Trek II: The Wrath of Khan* became a financial and critical success.

"It was okay with me," says Nimoy of the film's now-ambiguous ending. "I could understand that the audience was really depressed without it, and then I thought, 'I don't know what they're going to do about the follow-up in the next film, but it might be interesting to explore what that could be about.'"

The actor decided that the best place to explore Spock's return was from behind the camera. When filming began on *Star Trek III: The Search for Spock*, it was with Leonard Nimoy as director.

Helming the latest entry in Paramount Pictures' *Star Trek* film franchise also became a political lesson for Nimoy, who not only had to deal with the studio in a new light, but also his co-stars. "I was really surprised," he admits. "I had no idea how to play at that level, so I had a lot to learn.

"I guess I was naïve, but I was very surprised at the mixed emotions the cast had about my doing the job. I have still not ferreted out all the issues that were involved. Perhaps they thought it was a frivolous gesture on my part – an 'if you want me, then give me the baton' sort of thing. I'm not sure they knew if I was qualified or not, what my position would be as a director towards them, and maybe being elevated out of the ranks from their point of view. I just thought it was another way of working with my colleagues."

Nimoy's skilful direction of *Star Trek III: The Search for Spock* resulted in his being offered *Star Trek IV: The Voyage Home*, still regarded by many fans as the best of the *Star Trek* films. This time, it was smoother sailing for the actor/director, who also contributed some of the film's major story elements.

Even though *Star Trek IV: The Voyage Home* was Nimoy's last directing credit on the film series, his involvement with *Star Trek* was far from over. In addition to appearing in the fifth film (directed by William Shatner), he produced and provided story input for *Star Trek VI: The Undiscovered Country*. Nimoy also saw the character of Spock – now an ambassador – cross over into *Star Trek: The Next Generation*, in the two-part 1991 adventure *Unification*.

More recently, Nimoy's efforts have taken him away from the *Star Trek* universe, into other SF-related projects. He's now working on the comedy/virtual reality series *Deadly Games*, as well as a new comic book series, *Primortals*. Ironically, the ideas are based on a series of discussions he once had with Isaac Asimov, the man who wrote the 'Mr Spock Is Dreamy' essay almost thirty years ago.

"I'm on a consultant basis with *Primortals*, and it's moving very smoothly," says Nimoy. "We have storylines in place for the next several issues, and the response so far has been wonderful. I've had a number of enquiries from film companies about moving into other media with *Primortals*, and I'm delighted with the way it's going."

Looking ahead, Nimoy has confirmed that he will be starring in an episode of *The Outer Limits* revival, currently being screened on BBC2. The remake of *I, Robot* – a story Nimoy guest-starred in for the original series – will be directed by the actor's son, Adam, who helmed a pair of episodes for *Star Trek: The Next Generation*.

The older Nimoy has also reportedly been signed to direct a half-hour segment of an SF anthology for Miramax Films. It's another step into the unknown for the man who travelled to Hollywood in 1949, and then spent a good part of his career exploring the Final Frontier. Later this year his second autobiography will be published in Britain. After trying to divest himself of his famous alter ego in his first title, *I Am Not Spock*, Nimoy told an interested interviewer, with a wry smile on his face, that he was considering calling this volume *Maybe I Am Spock After All...*

[Editor's note: This interview first appeared in *Star Trek Monthly* #2, cover date August 1995, published in the UK by Titan Magazines.]

GREAT SCOTT!

James Doohan interviewed
by Ian Spelling

James Doohan smiles.

"I was at the airport in Los Angeles and I was sitting on a bench waiting for a limo to come and pick me up. All of a sudden, this fellow walked by. He was about ten yards away and he said, 'Scotty!' I looked over at him and smiled and said, 'Hi there.' He came back over to me and said, 'I just came off the plane from Scotland.' It was a marvellous moment. He didn't talk forever; he didn't bother me. He just thought it was amusing, and so did I. But his accent was real."

James Doohan smiles again. There's a glint in his eyes.

"I have so many of those stories from over the years," he says. "So many."

How could Doohan not? After all, he's the man who brought to life possibly the world's favourite fictional Scotsman, none other than miracle worker Montgomery Scott, chief engineer of the *U.S.S. Enterprise NCC-1701* of the original series of *Star Trek*. Millions of people know Doohan, love Doohan, as Scotty. And he's recounted just about every one of his countless stories at the many *Star Trek* and science fiction conventions he's attended over the last 20-something years. He told even more of them, and revealed far more about himself, in his recent autobiography, *Beam Me Up, Scotty*, from Pocket Books.

The old news, however, gets older: Doohan dislikes William Shatner; always did, always will. He's had his well-publicised battles with Paramount Pictures. He loves *Star Trek* and appreciates everything it and the fans have done for him, but the actor within feels he's never, ever, had the chance to shine in anything but *Star Trek* – that his *Star Trek* association forever left him typecast as a 23rd Century engineer with a Scottish accent. And the new news grows increasingly sparse. As he ages, Doohan finds himself working just a bit less and spending more time at home in Washington State with his wife and family.

So what to discuss when paths cross and Doohan agrees to sit for an impromptu conversation? "Well," Doohan proudly offers, "my son is an entrepreneur who has signed a contract with a London firm to create a science fiction café. It was originally called 'Scotty's Pub and Sci-Fi Café'. We dropped that because we wanted to bring in more celebrities. We've got a number of the original cast members of *Star Trek*, as well as people from *Battlestar Galactica* and other science fiction series. The first café will be in

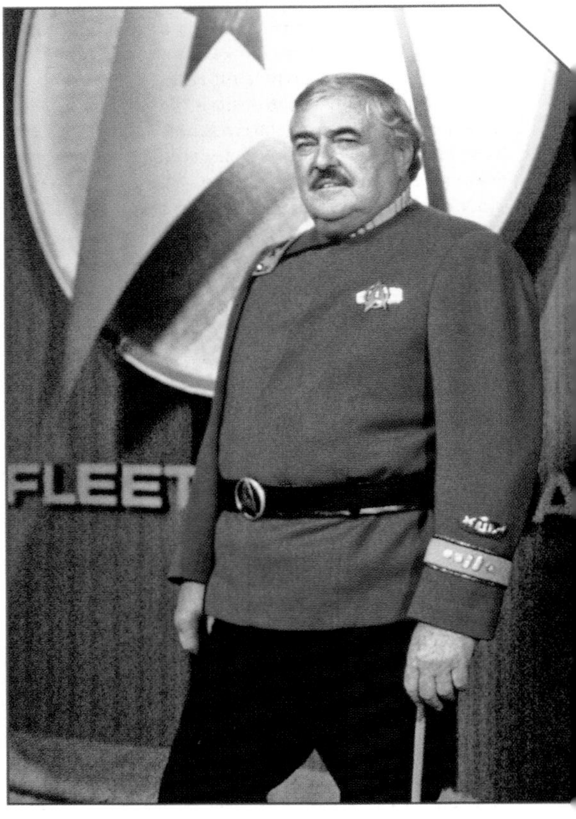
FLEET

Seattle, not too far from where I live. I think it will be a lot of fun. The first one should open in late 1998 or early 1999."

Just as Doohan finishes his sentence, a woman who must be in her late twenties approaches him, bearing a piece of paper and a pen. "Can I have your autograph, Mr Doohan?" she wonders politely. Doohan asks the woman's name and obliges her request. "Nice to meet you," he says as she wanders off, quite obviously satisfied by her positive brush with a *Star Trek* legend. Does Doohan still get a lot of this? "Oh, people still recognise me," he says, laughing. "It's funny. I know I don't look the same as I did all those years ago, but I look pretty much now the way I did in the last few movies [the original cast] did. So, people still say, 'Scotty!' or 'Aren't you Scotty?' Occasionally, someone will actually call me 'Mr Doohan...' That's always refreshing!

"Back home, everyone knows me pretty well, I guess. If I go into the same supermarket we usually go to, no one says anything. Or they just smile at me as I go by. If I go to a different supermarket for whatever reason, I get asked all the questions all over again. It's all right, though. It's nice to be recognised. If I go to a convention, it's another matter. The fans are there to see me and whoever else the organisers have brought in. That's even more interesting, of course. You see some of the same people over and over; so they know you. Some people are kids just discovering the show or me, so it's all new to them and they ask questions and ask for autographs as if I've never been asked before. The conventions are a whole other world."

As it inevitably must, the conversation turns to *Star Trek*. Doohan, who most likely suited up as Scotty for the very last time in *Star Trek Generations*, dives into it like a real trooper. "We did a good show. We did several good movies," he asserts. "We never saw enough of Scotty, never got a real idea of who he was. But who isn't going to say that? We all know that George [Takei], Walter [Koenig], Nichelle [Nichols] and I would have preferred to do more. We all wanted to do more. We all asked to do more – that wasn't a secret. As an actor, *Star Trek* was a mixed blessing because it was work, but I never had enough to do. I like [specific] scenes or episodes, but an actor always wants more.

"It was fun to come back one more time [in *Star Trek Generations*], but I don't get any feelings of sadness about it all being over. I felt a bit the same way doing *Generations* that I did doing *Relics* for *Star Trek: The Next Generation*. It was a chance to play a role I like. *Relics* was more touching in a certain way for me because it was more about Scotty than my scenes in *Generations* were. But we lost the captain in *Generations* and there was emotion to that, too. Nevertheless, I wouldn't be being honest if I didn't say that *Relics* was the better experience. That was the most Scotty had probably ever gotten to do in one episode! Look, Scotty was created so long ago with love by Gene Roddenberry, and I always played him with love. To me, that's good enough. That's enough to last me the rest of my life."

Doohan says he never grows bored of talking about *Star Trek*. "It's just hard sometimes," he remarks. "I don't know what to say all the time. So much of it has been said so many times. The stories don't change because they're true. They're what people ask me to talk about, so I do. I don't have too many new *Star Trek* stories to tell now. It's much easier for me to be asked a direct question. Something too general can get me rambling on. But I would also like to think that my life story is far more interesting than just my *Star Trek* experiences."

Doohan shared much of his life story in *Beam Me Up, Scotty*. Still, he's not exactly enamoured of his autobiography. And the reason? Too much *Star Trek*. "Paramount Pictures wanted fifty percent of the book to be about *Star Trek*," he explains. "I said, 'My life with *Star Trek* wasn't that interesting,' so we filled up the book with some *Star Trek* stories that weren't that exciting or that had already been told by the other [*Star Trek*] actors in their books. I think it would have been more interesting if I only had *Star Trek* stories people hadn't heard before. But I did get to tell how I became an actor, and I also got to talk about my war experiences, which were horrendous. I went through a lot during the war. I got slightly wounded and I survived to tell about it. Those parts of the book were very enjoyable for me to look back on. I hope people found them interesting.

"My favourite story in the book," Doohan continues, "is the one about my learning to fly, which was after I got wounded on D-Day. I was hit by eight machine gun bullets and five weeks later got out of the hospital, returned to the reinforcement depot and saw a notice on the notice board the very first hour there asking artillery officers to volunteer for air observation. I said, 'Whoops! They're gonna teach me to fly,' and they did! Later, when I only had about eighteen hours of flying time to my name, I was up at 10,000 feet and I broke through a cloud. And there, coming right at me, were thirty-six B-17s. I tell you, in four seconds, everything flashed before me!"

While Doohan does spend more time at home these days, his rather intense schedule would still wear out a lesser person in a matter of weeks. He remains a convention favourite, criss-crossing the United States and sometimes the world to make close encounters with *Star Trek* fans. Producers still seek out his acting skills, too. "I just did a movie called *Bugbusters* with George Takei, Randy Quaid, June Lockhart, Bernie [*The Love Boat*] Kopell and Katherine [*Under Siege 2*] Heigl," he says. "George is great in it. Randy is great in it, and I'm supposed to be great in it, too. I play a local sheriff who turns out to not be such a good guy.

"I also do a lot of in-house work for companies – sort of in-house training films. I've done things for Hitachi. I've done work for Digital. I've done work for other computer companies that are not such big names. They have me come in and they call me the world's greatest engineer, and it's a lot of fun. The films are never seen by the public. Also, a few years ago now, I did the [on-camera] narration for a film thrill ride at the Empire State Building in New York City which they're still using. I do the occasional guest spot or whatever on television, as well as the occasional movie."

All in all, then, life is pretty good for James Doohan.

"Life *is* good. Life is *very* good," he says. "I love to work. When I'm not working I'm looking for work. I'm very fortunate. People like to see me work and they like to see me work for them. Sometimes it's something big and sometimes it's something small or, like I said, not ever seen by the public. That's OK. Sometimes it's a convention or a public appearance, and those things are fun, too. People are still seeing Scotty, as well, and there are people still discovering *Star Trek*.

"Millions of people have seen *Star Trek*. Millions and millions. I've met many of them. *Star Trek* has had a great influence on young people. So, while Scotty may not have been the most fulfilling role, I'm very proud to have played him. I'm still proud to be associated with him and with *Star Trek*. I think I'm a very lucky man."

[Editor's note: This interview first appeared in *Star Trek Monthly* #40, cover dated June 19, published in the UK by Titan Magazines. *Star Trek Generations* was released in 1994.]

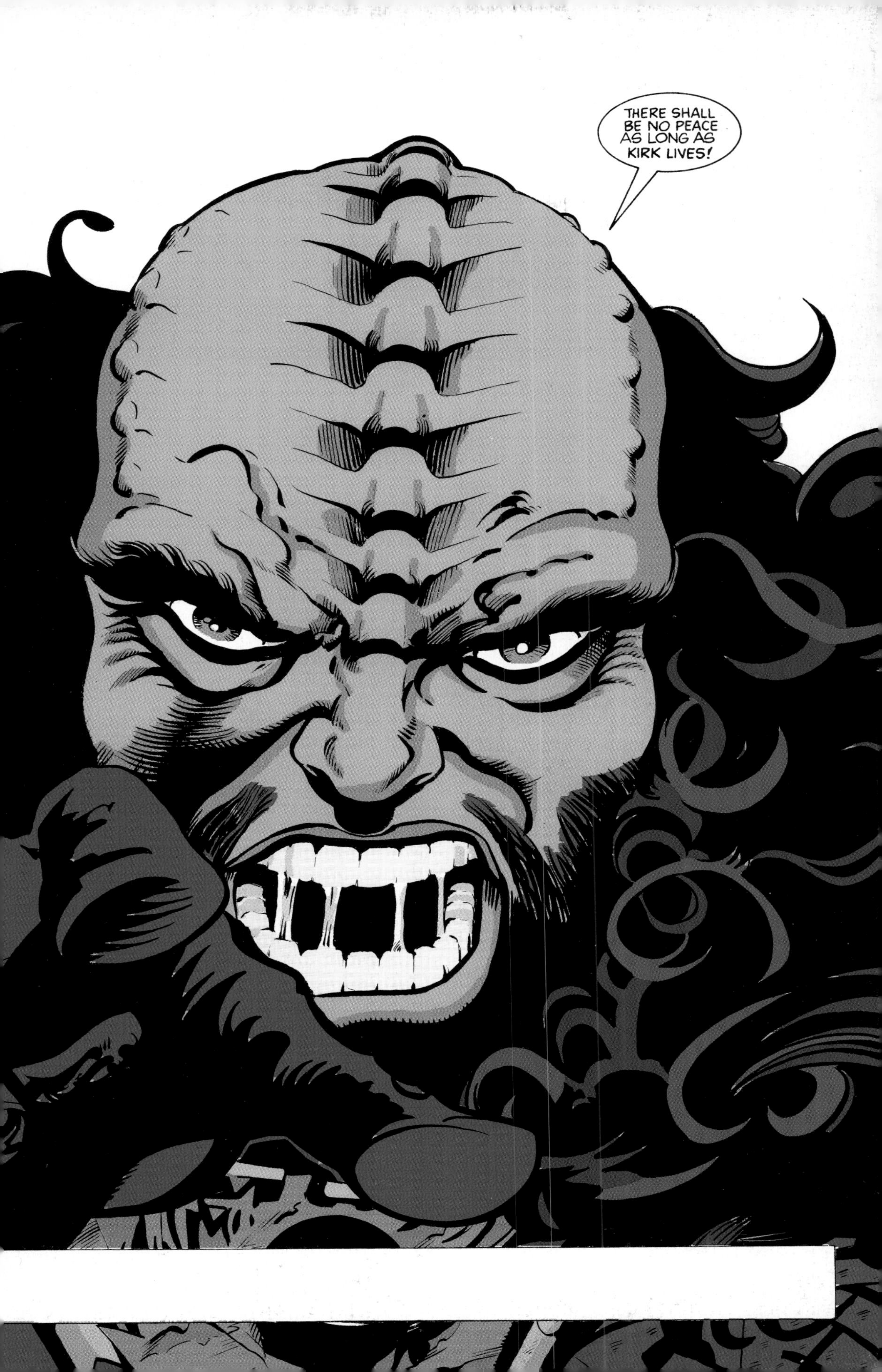
THERE SHALL BE NO PEACE AS LONG AS KIRK LIVES!

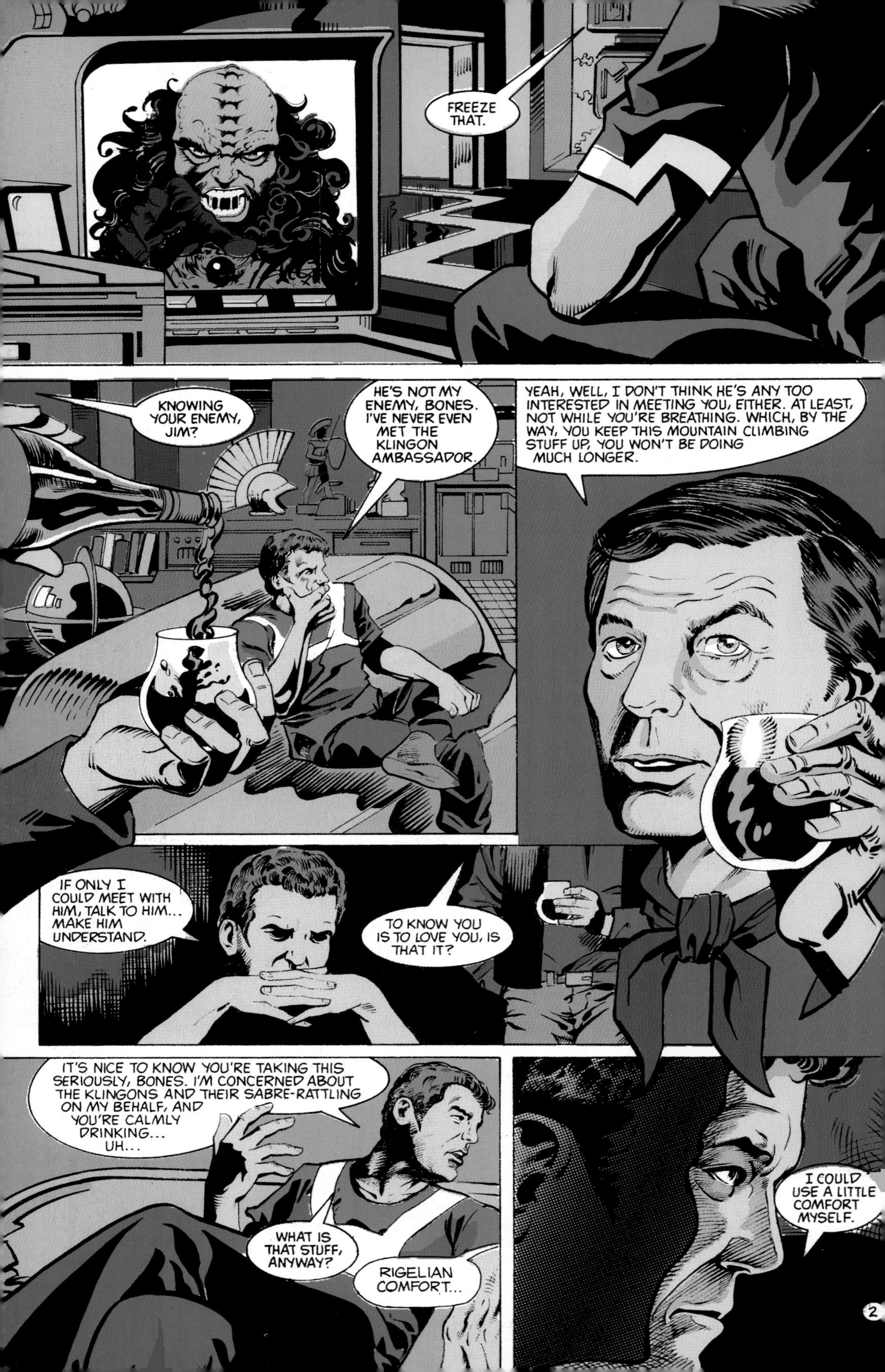
FREEZE THAT.
KNOWING YOUR ENEMY, JIM?
HE'S NOT MY ENEMY, BONES. I'VE NEVER EVEN MET THE KLINGON AMBASSADOR.
YEAH, WELL, I DON'T THINK HE'S ANY TOO INTERESTED IN MEETING YOU, EITHER. AT LEAST, NOT WHILE YOU'RE BREATHING. WHICH, BY THE WAY, YOU KEEP THIS MOUNTAIN CLIMBING STUFF UP, YOU WON'T BE DOING MUCH LONGER.
IF ONLY I COULD MEET WITH HIM, TALK TO HIM... MAKE HIM UNDERSTAND.
TO KNOW YOU IS TO LOVE YOU, IS THAT IT?
IT'S NICE TO KNOW YOU'RE TAKING THIS SERIOUSLY, BONES. I'M CONCERNED ABOUT THE KLINGONS AND THEIR SABRE-RATTLING ON MY BEHALF, AND YOU'RE CALMLY DRINKING... UH...
WHAT IS THAT STUFF, ANYWAY?
RIGELIAN COMFORT...
I COULD USE A LITTLE COMFORT MYSELF.

COMFORT OF THE FEMALE KIND?

OH, YES. THE FEMALE KIND.

EXACTLY WHAT I WAS THINKING.

WERE YOU?

SURE. ALTHOUGH WE HAVE TO BE CAREFUL. THESE OLD "BONES" AREN'T GETTING ANY YOUNGER, Y'KNOW.

BUT BEING WITH HER... THE YEARS MELT AWAY.

A SPECIFIC "HER"?

OH, YES. A VERY SPECIFIC "HER."

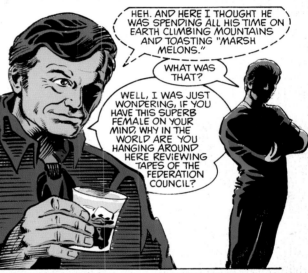

HEH. AND HERE I THOUGHT HE WAS SPENDING ALL HIS TIME ON EARTH CLIMBING MOUNTAINS AND TOASTING "MARSH MELONS."

WHAT WAS THAT?

WELL, I WAS JUST WONDERING, IF YOU HAVE THIS SUPERB FEMALE ON YOUR MIND, WHY IN THE WORLD ARE YOU HANGING AROUND HERE REVIEWING TAPES OF THE FEDERATION COUNCIL?

YOU'RE RIGHT. COME ON. LET'S GO TO HER.

"COME ON"? JIM... YOU DON'T NEED ME ALONG.

OF COURSE I DO. IT WOULDN'T BE THE SAME WITHOUT YOU.

3

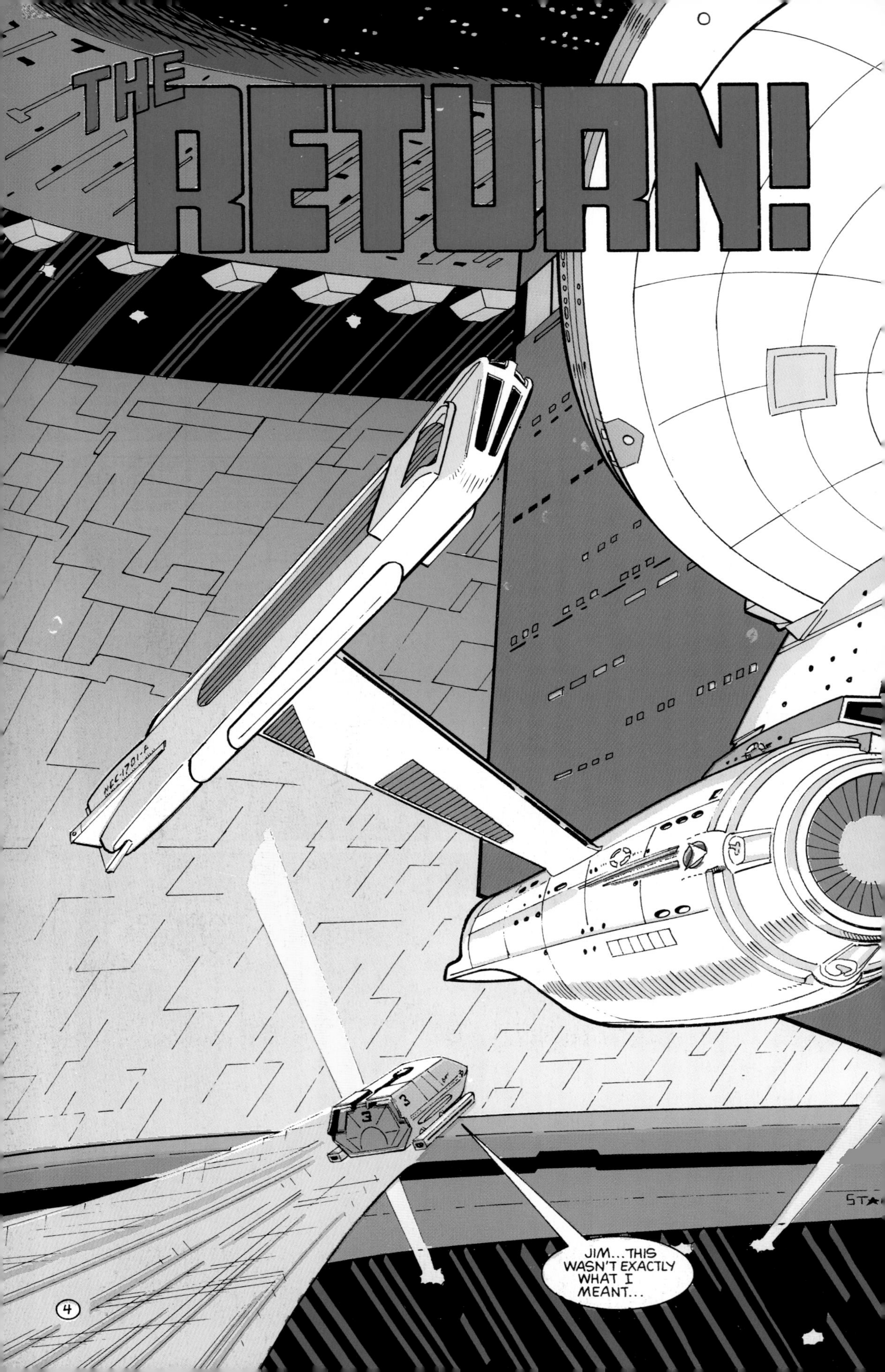
THE RETURN!
NCC-1701-A
JIM... THIS WASN'T EXACTLY WHAT I MEANT...
ST
4

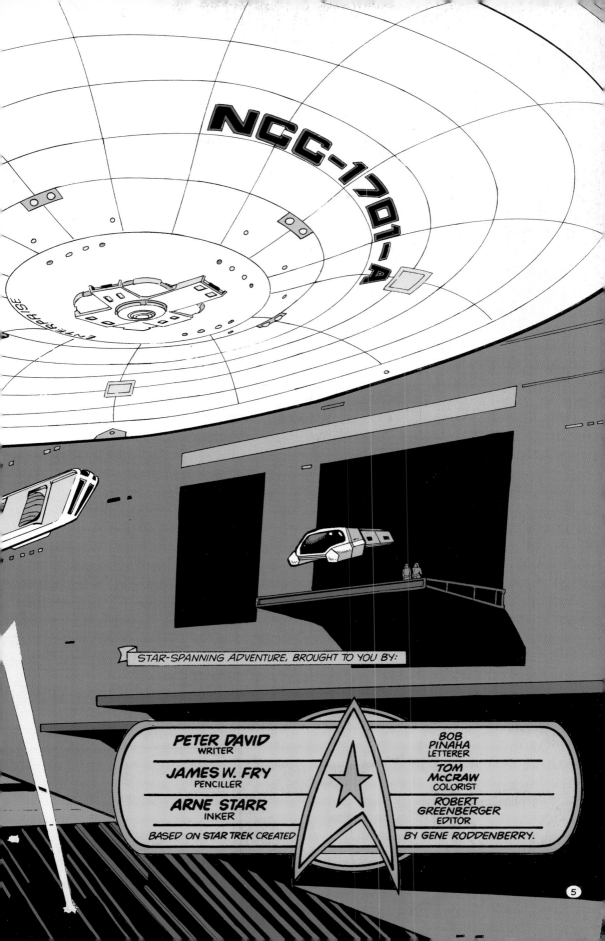

STAR-SPANNING ADVENTURE, BROUGHT TO YOU BY:

PETER DAVID
WRITER

JAMES W. FRY
PENCILLER

ARNE STARR
INKER

BOB PINAHA
LETTERER

TOM McCRAW
COLORIST

ROBERT GREENBERGER
EDITOR

BASED ON STAR TREK CREATED BY GENE RODDENBERRY.

WHY? WHAT WERE YOU TALKING ABOUT?

NOTHING. FORGET IT.

BEFORE YOU CAME OVER I GOT WORD THAT THE ENTERPRISE WOULD BE READY FOR SPACE SHORTLY. SO I FIGURED...

...WHY WAIT?

WHY INDEED?

I JUST HOPE THEY GOT THE DAMNED THING FIXED. IT'S NOWHERE UP TO THE QUALITY OF THE ORIGINAL ENTERPRISE.

DON'T REMIND ME.

ALL THIS TIME, AND I STILL, IN MY NIGHTMARES...

...I SEE HER FLAMING WRECKAGE, A COMET OVER THE GENESIS PLANET.

I SHOULD HAVE BEEN ON HER, BONES.

JIM...FOR ALL THE HUMAN ATTRIBUTES WE GIVE INANIMATE OBJECTS... THAT'S STILL ALL THEY ARE. YOU DIDN'T BETRAY OR MURDER THE ENTERPRISE.

I WISH I COULD BELIEVE THAT.

ALL RIGHT. HOW ABOUT THIS, THEN...

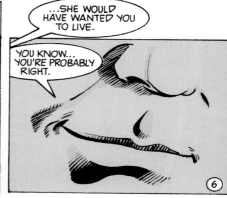

...SHE WOULD HAVE WANTED YOU TO LIVE.

YOU KNOW... YOU'RE PROBABLY RIGHT.

6

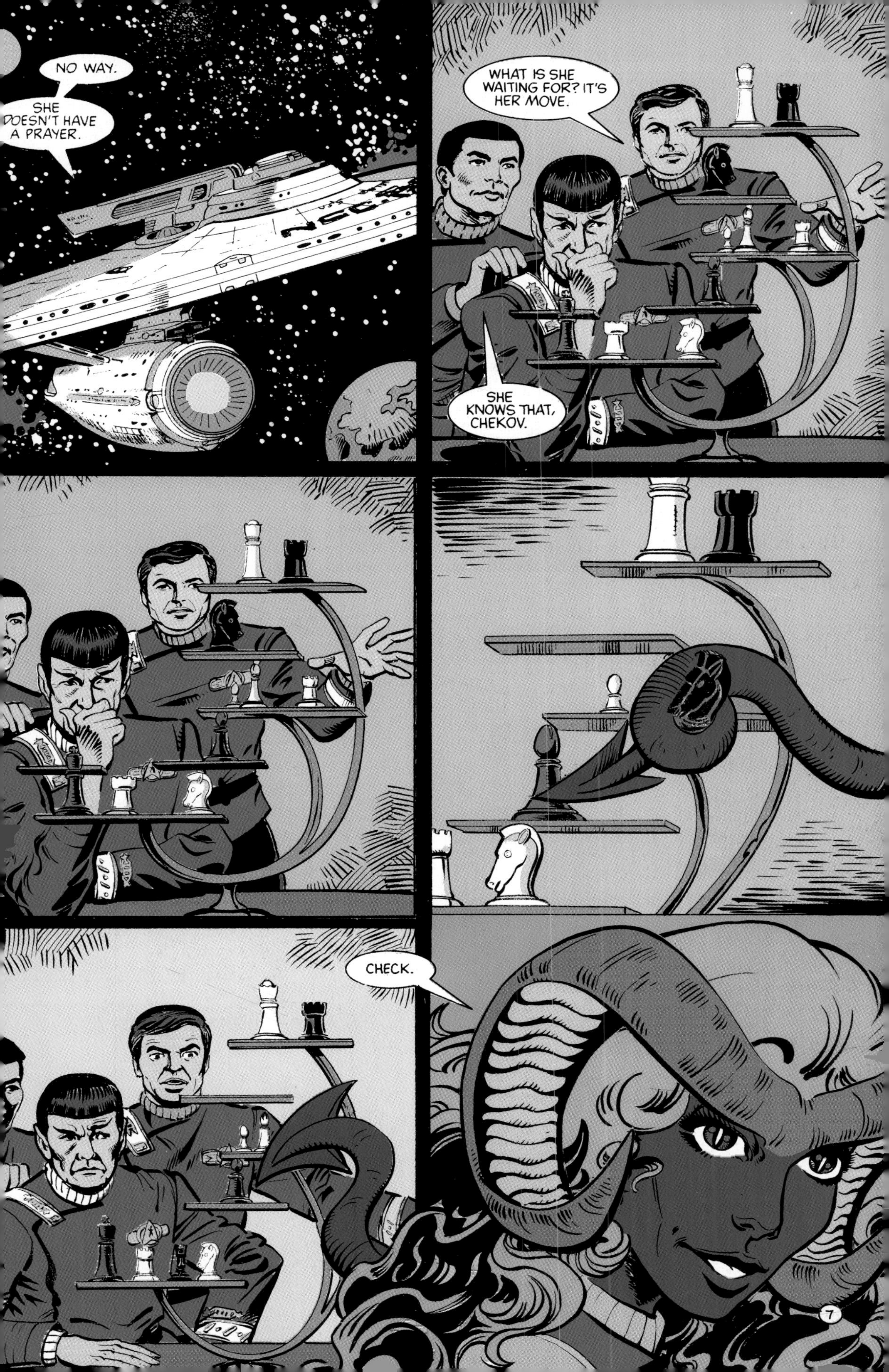
NO WAY.
SHE DOESN'T HAVE A PRAYER.
WHAT IS SHE WAITING FOR? IT'S HER MOVE.
SHE KNOWS THAT, CHEKOV.
CHECK.
7

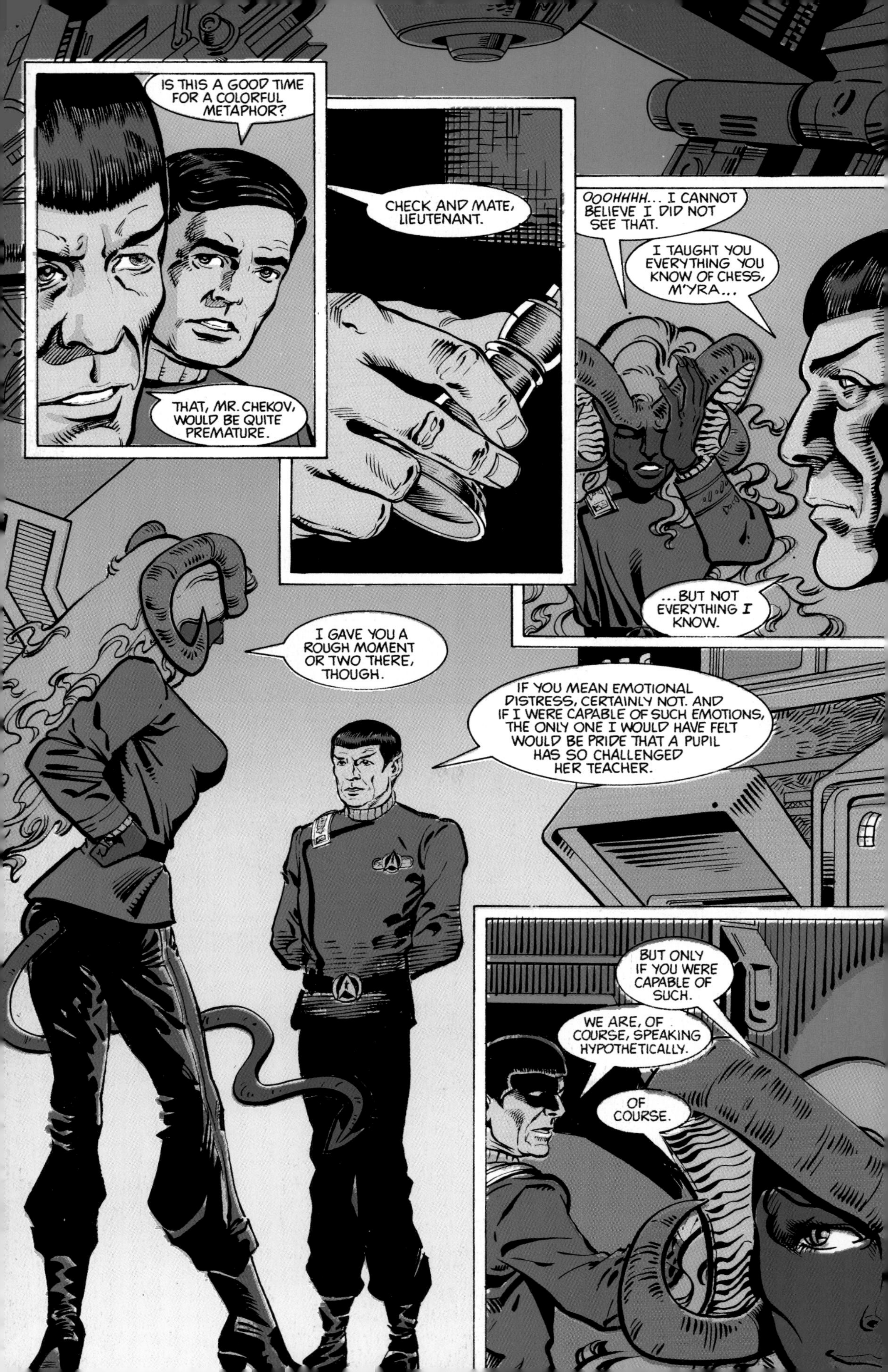
IS THIS A GOOD TIME FOR A COLORFUL METAPHOR?
THAT, MR. CHEKOV, WOULD BE QUITE PREMATURE.
CHECK AND MATE, LIEUTENANT.
OOOHHHH... I CANNOT BELIEVE I DID NOT SEE THAT.
I TAUGHT YOU EVERYTHING YOU KNOW OF CHESS, M'YRA...
...BUT NOT EVERYTHING I KNOW.
I GAVE YOU A ROUGH MOMENT OR TWO THERE, THOUGH.
IF YOU MEAN EMOTIONAL DISTRESS, CERTAINLY NOT. AND IF I WERE CAPABLE OF SUCH EMOTIONS, THE ONLY ONE I WOULD HAVE FELT WOULD BE PRIDE THAT A PUPIL HAS SO CHALLENGED HER TEACHER.
BUT ONLY IF YOU WERE CAPABLE OF SUCH.
WE ARE, OF COURSE, SPEAKING HYPOTHETICALLY.
OF COURSE.

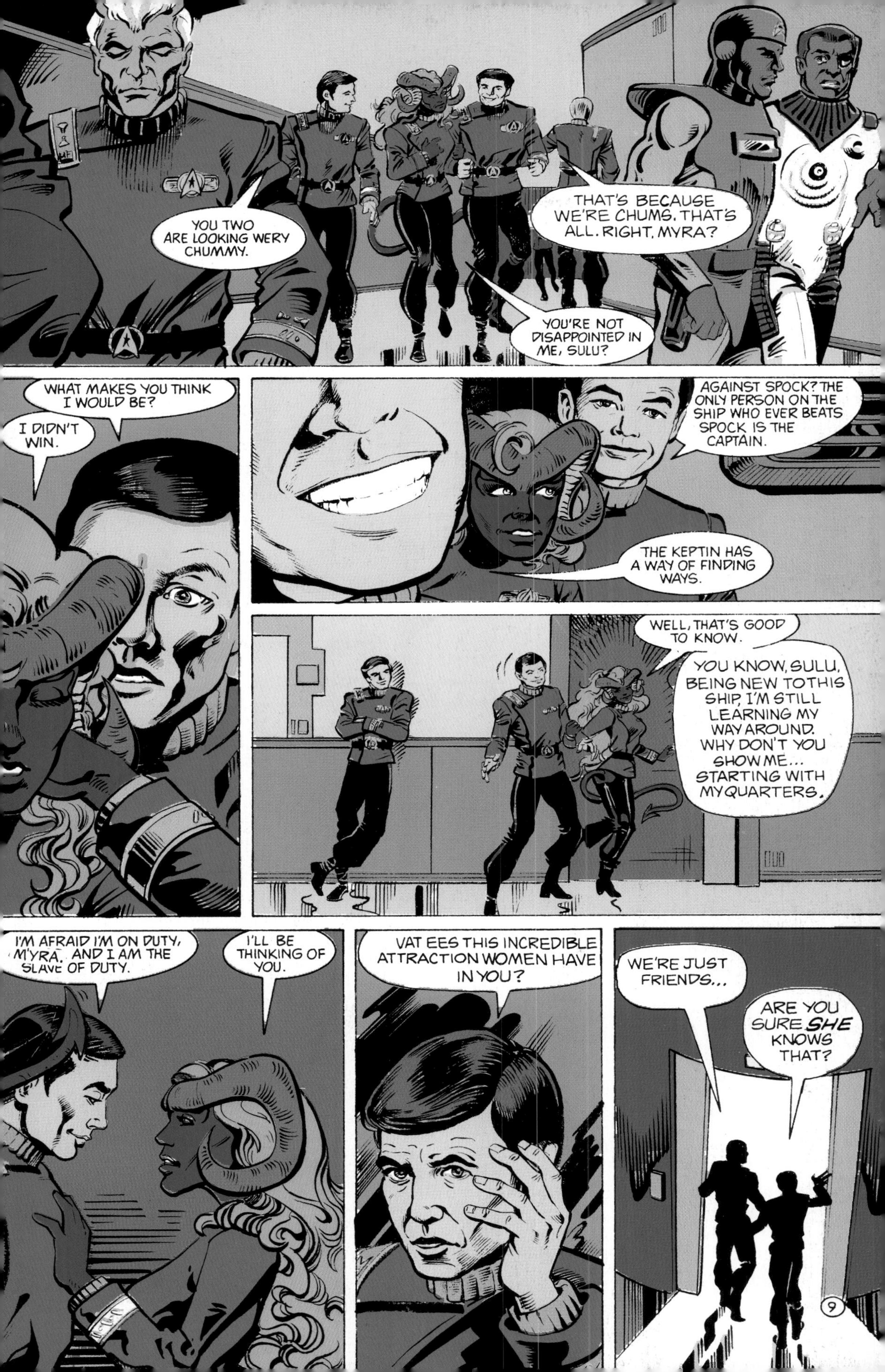
YOU TWO ARE LOOKING WERY CHUMMY.
THAT'S BECAUSE WE'RE CHUMS. THAT'S ALL. RIGHT, MYRA?
YOU'RE NOT DISAPPOINTED IN ME, SULU?
WHAT MAKES YOU THINK I WOULD BE?
I DIDN'T WIN.
AGAINST SPOCK? THE ONLY PERSON ON THE SHIP WHO EVER BEATS SPOCK IS THE CAPTAIN.
THE KEPTIN HAS A WAY OF FINDING WAYS.
WELL, THAT'S GOOD TO KNOW.
YOU KNOW, SULU, BEING NEW TO THIS SHIP, I'M STILL LEARNING MY WAY AROUND. WHY DON'T YOU SHOW ME... STARTING WITH MY QUARTERS.
I'M AFRAID I'M ON DUTY, M'YRA. AND I AM THE SLAVE OF DUTY.
I'LL BE THINKING OF YOU.
VAT EES THIS INCREDIBLE ATTRACTION WOMEN HAVE IN YOU?
WE'RE JUST FRIENDS...
ARE YOU SURE SHE KNOWS THAT?
9

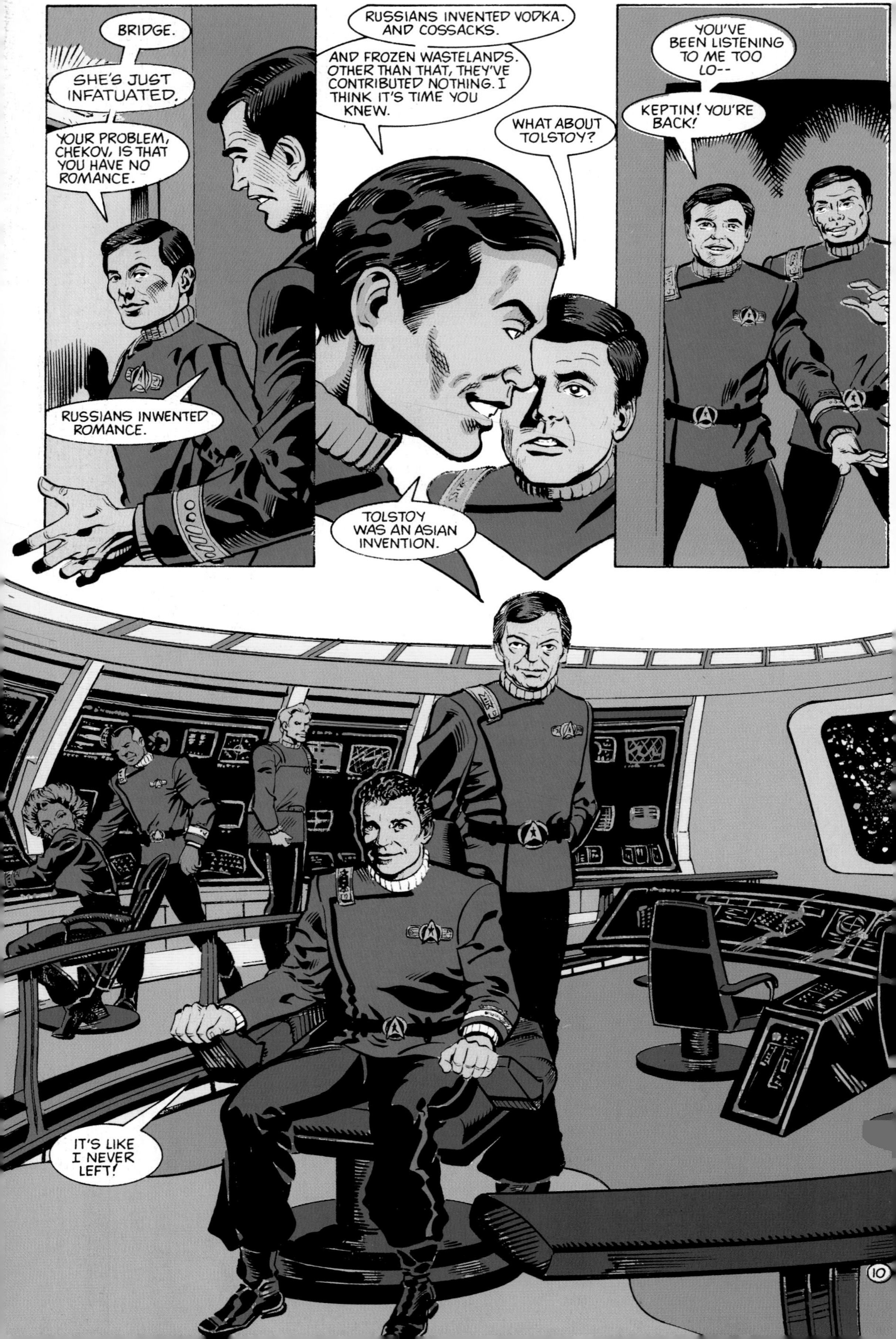

BRIDGE.
SHE'S JUST INFATUATED.
YOUR PROBLEM, CHEKOV, IS THAT YOU HAVE NO ROMANCE.
RUSSIANS INWENTED ROMANCE.
RUSSIANS INVENTED VODKA. AND COSSACKS.
AND FROZEN WASTELANDS. OTHER THAN THAT, THEY'VE CONTRIBUTED NOTHING. I THINK IT'S TIME YOU KNEW.
WHAT ABOUT TOLSTOY?
TOLSTOY WAS AN ASIAN INVENTION.
YOU'VE BEEN LISTENING TO ME TOO LO--
KEPTIN! YOU'RE BACK!
IT'S LIKE I NEVER LEFT!

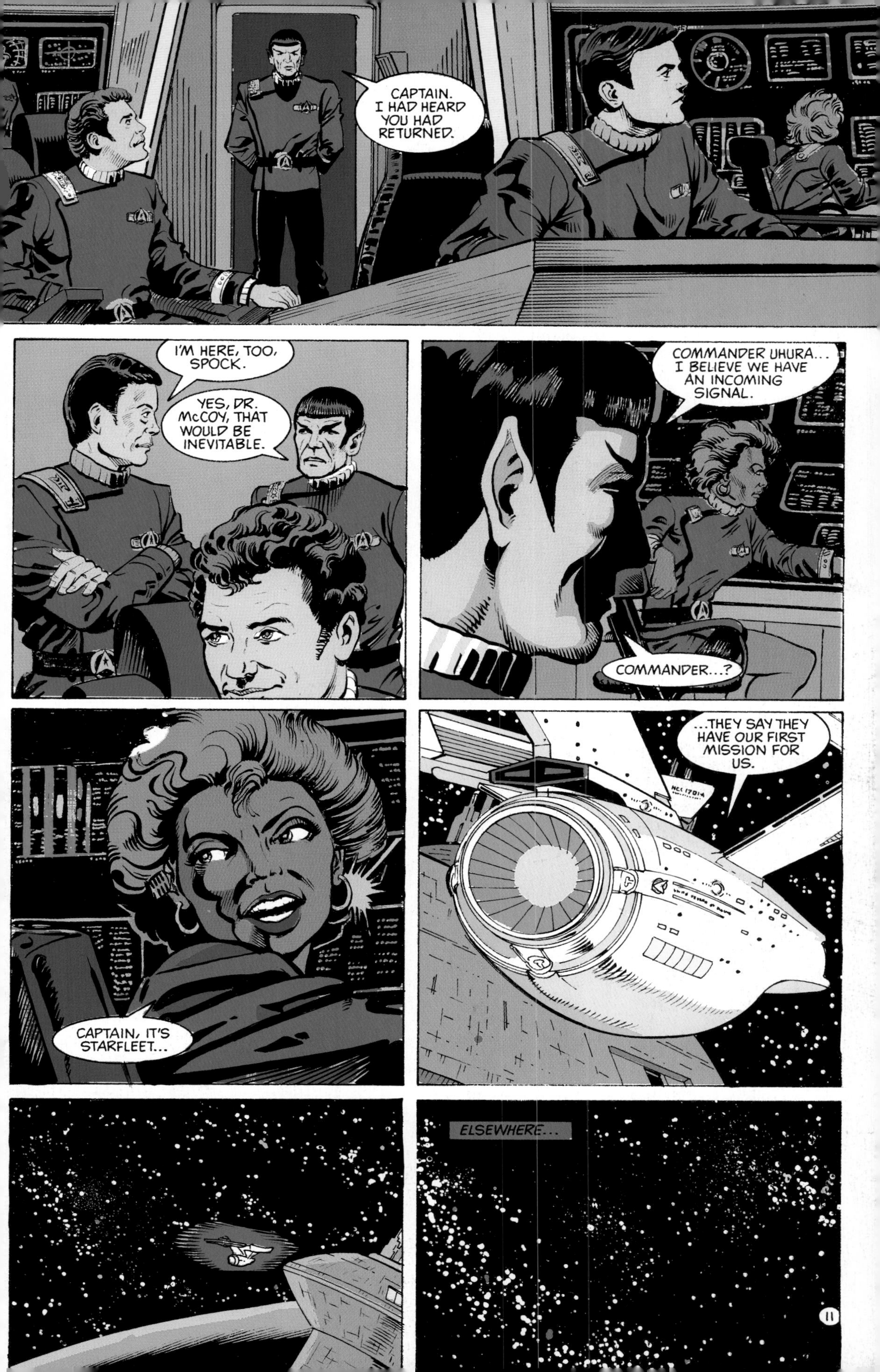
CAPTAIN. I HAD HEARD YOU HAD RETURNED.
I'M HERE, TOO, SPOCK.
YES, DR. McCOY, THAT WOULD BE INEVITABLE.
COMMANDER UHURA... I BELIEVE WE HAVE AN INCOMING SIGNAL.
COMMANDER...?
CAPTAIN, IT'S STARFLEET...
...THEY SAY THEY HAVE OUR FIRST MISSION FOR US.
NCC 1701-A
ELSEWHERE...
11

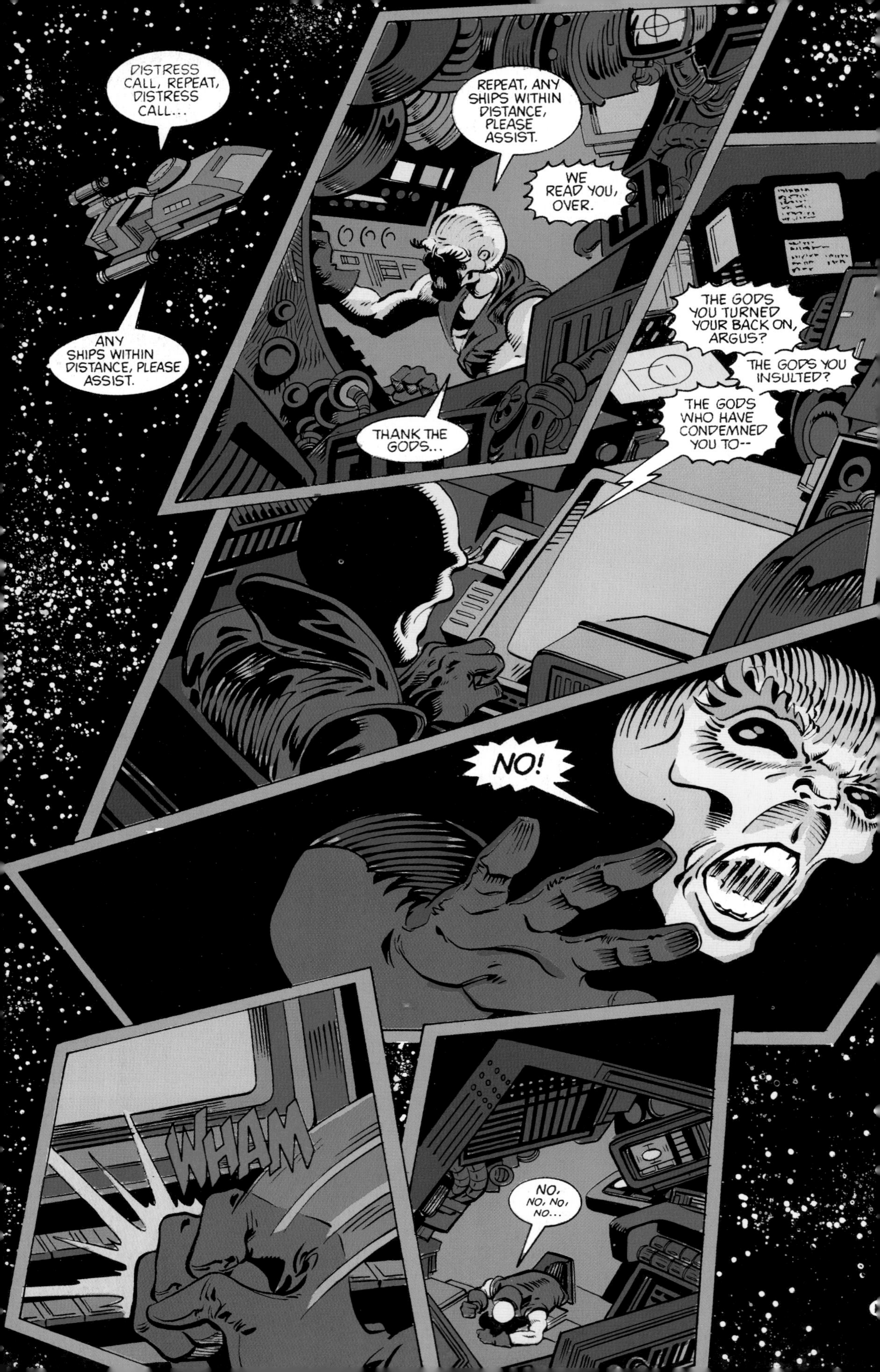
DISTRESS CALL, REPEAT, DISTRESS CALL...
ANY SHIPS WITHIN DISTANCE, PLEASE ASSIST.
REPEAT, ANY SHIPS WITHIN DISTANCE, PLEASE ASSIST.
WE READ YOU, OVER.
THANK THE GODS...
THE GODS YOU TURNED YOUR BACK ON, ARGUS?
THE GODS YOU INSULTED?
THE GODS WHO HAVE CONDEMNED YOU TO--
NO!
WHAM
NO, NO, NO, NO...

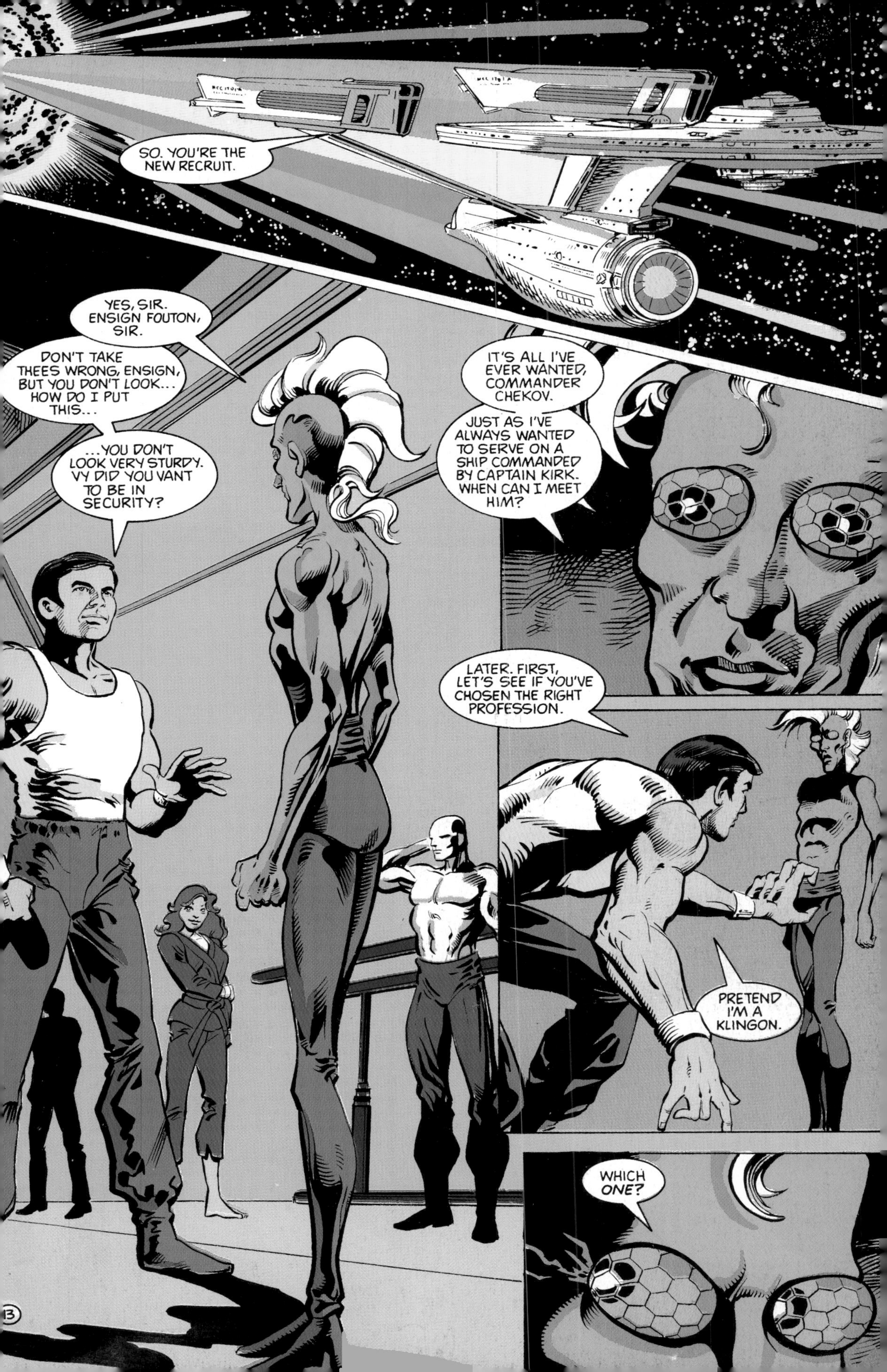
SO. YOU'RE THE NEW RECRUIT.
YES, SIR. ENSIGN FOUTON, SIR.
DON'T TAKE THEES WRONG, ENSIGN, BUT YOU DON'T LOOK... HOW DO I PUT THIS...
...YOU DON'T LOOK VERY STURDY. VY DID YOU VANT TO BE IN SECURITY?
IT'S ALL I'VE EVER WANTED, COMMANDER CHEKOV.
JUST AS I'VE ALWAYS WANTED TO SERVE ON A SHIP COMMANDED BY CAPTAIN KIRK. WHEN CAN I MEET HIM?
LATER. FIRST, LET'S SEE IF YOU'VE CHOSEN THE RIGHT PROFESSION.
PRETEND I'M A KLINGON.
WHICH ONE?
13

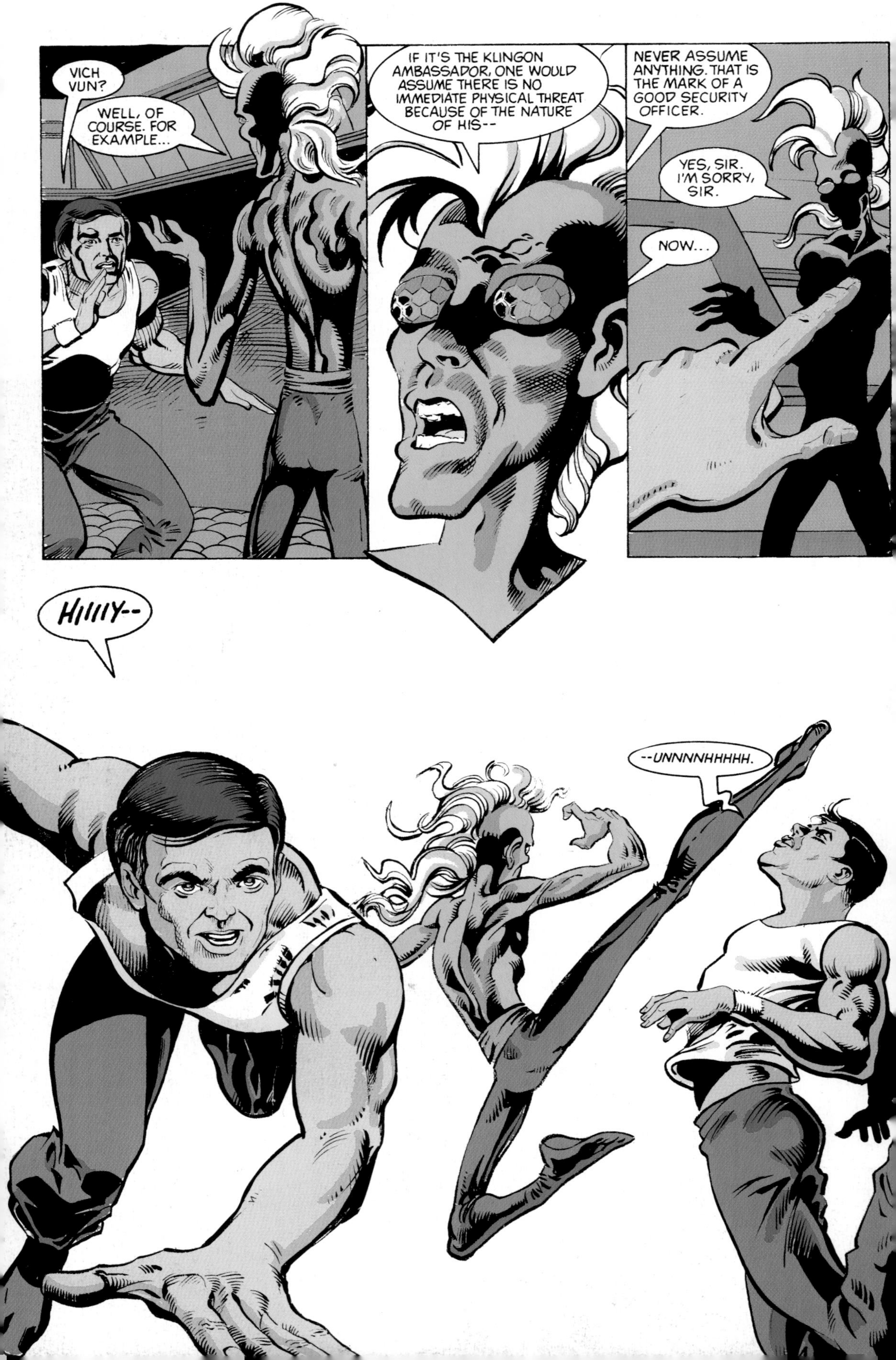
VICH VUN?
WELL, OF COURSE. FOR EXAMPLE...
IF IT'S THE KLINGON AMBASSADOR, ONE WOULD ASSUME THERE IS NO IMMEDIATE PHYSICAL THREAT BECAUSE OF THE NATURE OF HIS--
NEVER ASSUME ANYTHING. THAT IS THE MARK OF A GOOD SECURITY OFFICER.
YES, SIR. I'M SORRY, SIR.
NOW...
HIIIIY--
--UNNNNHHHHH.

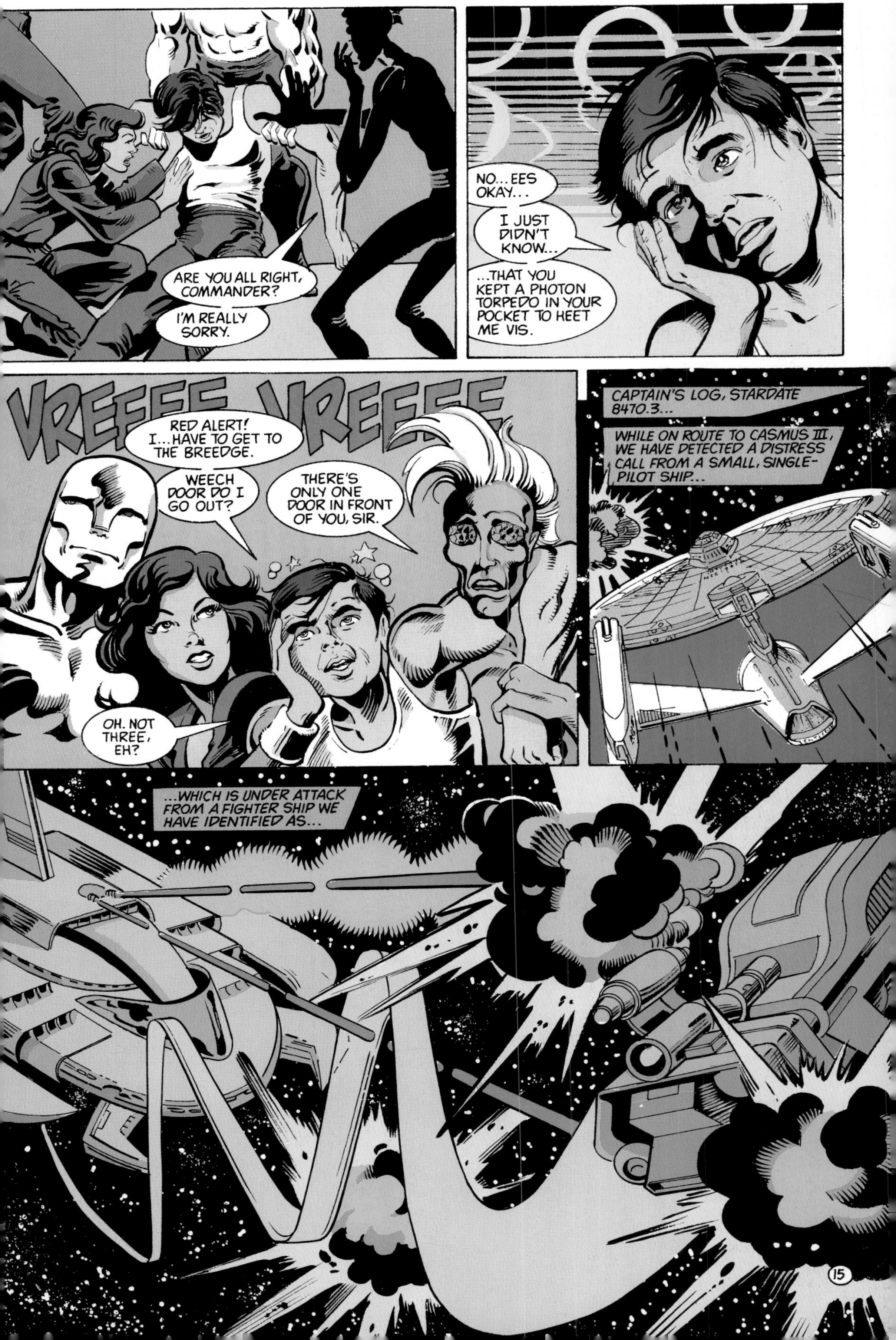
ARE YOU ALL RIGHT, COMMANDER?
I'M REALLY SORRY.
NO... EES OKAY...
I JUST DIDN'T KNOW...
...THAT YOU KEPT A PHOTON TORPEDO IN YOUR POCKET TO HEET ME VIS.
VREEEE VREEEE
RED ALERT! I... HAVE TO GET TO THE BREEDGE.
WEECH DOOR DO I GO OUT?
THERE'S ONLY ONE DOOR IN FRONT OF YOU, SIR.
OH. NOT THREE, EH?
CAPTAIN'S LOG, STARDATE 8470.3...
WHILE ON ROUTE TO CASMUS III, WE HAVE DETECTED A DISTRESS CALL FROM A SMALL, SINGLE-PILOT SHIP...
...WHICH IS UNDER ATTACK FROM A FIGHTER SHIP WE HAVE IDENTIFIED AS...

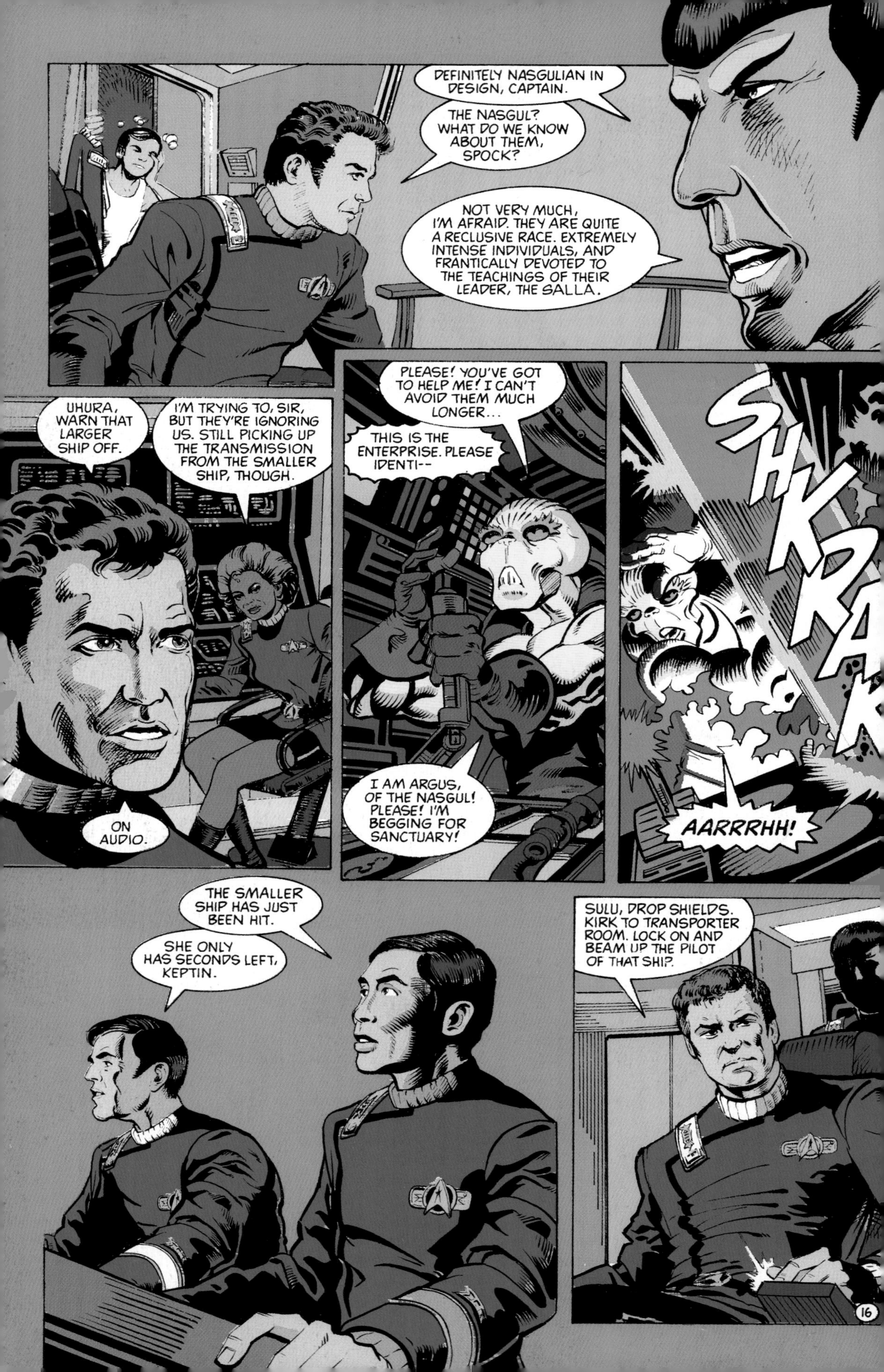
DEFINITELY NASGULIAN IN DESIGN, CAPTAIN.
THE NASGUL? WHAT DO WE KNOW ABOUT THEM, SPOCK?
NOT VERY MUCH, I'M AFRAID. THEY ARE QUITE A RECLUSIVE RACE. EXTREMELY INTENSE INDIVIDUALS, AND FRANTICALLY DEVOTED TO THE TEACHINGS OF THEIR LEADER, THE SALLA.
UHURA, WARN THAT LARGER SHIP OFF.
I'M TRYING TO, SIR, BUT THEY'RE IGNORING US. STILL PICKING UP THE TRANSMISSION FROM THE SMALLER SHIP, THOUGH.
ON AUDIO.
PLEASE! YOU'VE GOT TO HELP ME! I CAN'T AVOID THEM MUCH LONGER...
THIS IS THE ENTERPRISE. PLEASE IDENTI--
I AM ARGUS, OF THE NASGUL! PLEASE! I'M BEGGING FOR SANCTUARY!
SHKRAK
AARRRHH!
THE SMALLER SHIP HAS JUST BEEN HIT.
SHE ONLY HAS SECONDS LEFT, KEPTIN.
SULU, DROP SHIELDS. KIRK TO TRANSPORTER ROOM. LOCK ON AND BEAM UP THE PILOT OF THAT SHIP.

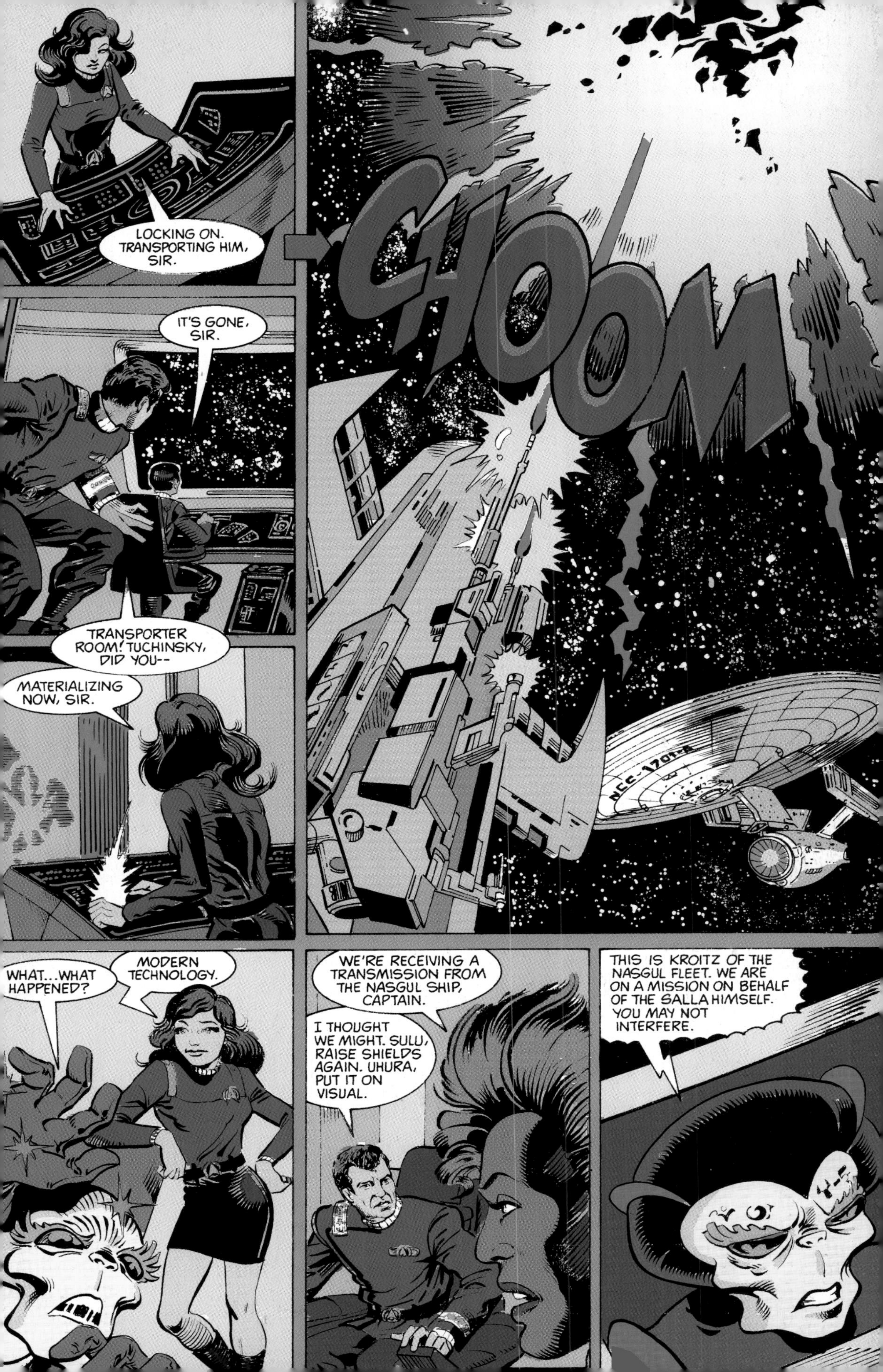
LOCKING ON. TRANSPORTING HIM, SIR.
CHOOOM
IT'S GONE, SIR.
TRANSPORTER ROOM! TUCHINSKY, DID YOU--
MATERIALIZING NOW, SIR.
NCC-1701-A
WHAT...WHAT HAPPENED?
MODERN TECHNOLOGY.
WE'RE RECEIVING A TRANSMISSION FROM THE NASGUL SHIP, CAPTAIN.
I THOUGHT WE MIGHT. SULU, RAISE SHIELDS AGAIN. UHURA, PUT IT ON VISUAL.
THIS IS KROITZ OF THE NASGUL FLEET. WE ARE ON A MISSION ON BEHALF OF THE SALLA HIMSELF. YOU MAY NOT INTERFERE.

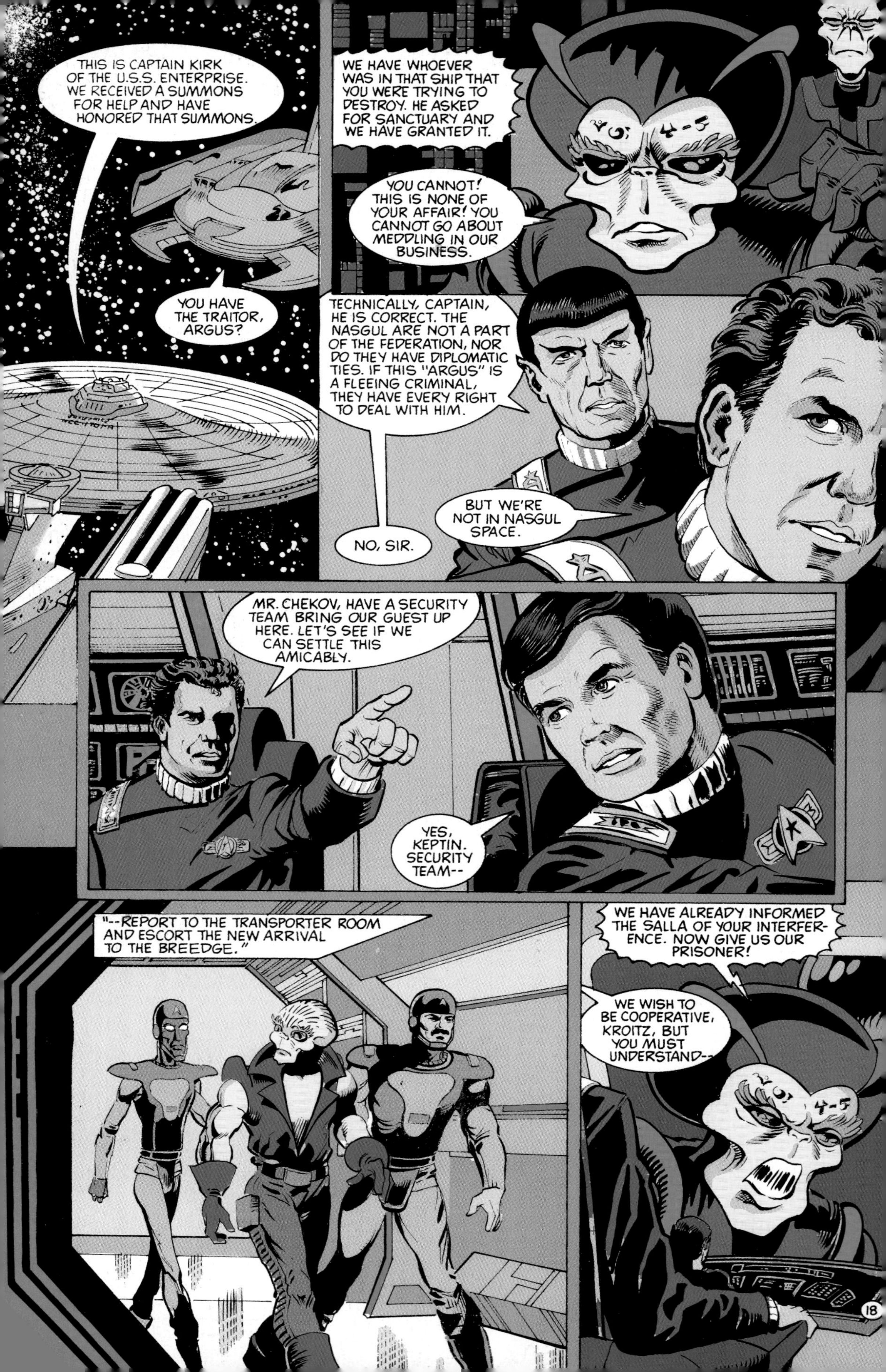
THIS IS CAPTAIN KIRK OF THE U.S.S. ENTERPRISE. WE RECEIVED A SUMMONS FOR HELP AND HAVE HONORED THAT SUMMONS.
YOU HAVE THE TRAITOR, ARGUS?
WE HAVE WHOEVER WAS IN THAT SHIP THAT YOU WERE TRYING TO DESTROY. HE ASKED FOR SANCTUARY AND WE HAVE GRANTED IT.
YOU CANNOT! THIS IS NONE OF YOUR AFFAIR! YOU CANNOT GO ABOUT MEDDLING IN OUR BUSINESS.
TECHNICALLY, CAPTAIN, HE IS CORRECT. THE NASGUL ARE NOT A PART OF THE FEDERATION, NOR DO THEY HAVE DIPLOMATIC TIES. IF THIS "ARGUS" IS A FLEEING CRIMINAL, THEY HAVE EVERY RIGHT TO DEAL WITH HIM.
BUT WE'RE NOT IN NASGUL SPACE.
NO, SIR.
MR. CHEKOV, HAVE A SECURITY TEAM BRING OUR GUEST UP HERE. LET'S SEE IF WE CAN SETTLE THIS AMICABLY.
YES, KEPTIN. SECURITY TEAM--
"--REPORT TO THE TRANSPORTER ROOM AND ESCORT THE NEW ARRIVAL TO THE BREEDGE."
WE HAVE ALREADY INFORMED THE SALLA OF YOUR INTERFERENCE. NOW GIVE US OUR PRISONER!
WE WISH TO BE COOPERATIVE, KROITZ, BUT YOU MUST UNDERSTAND--

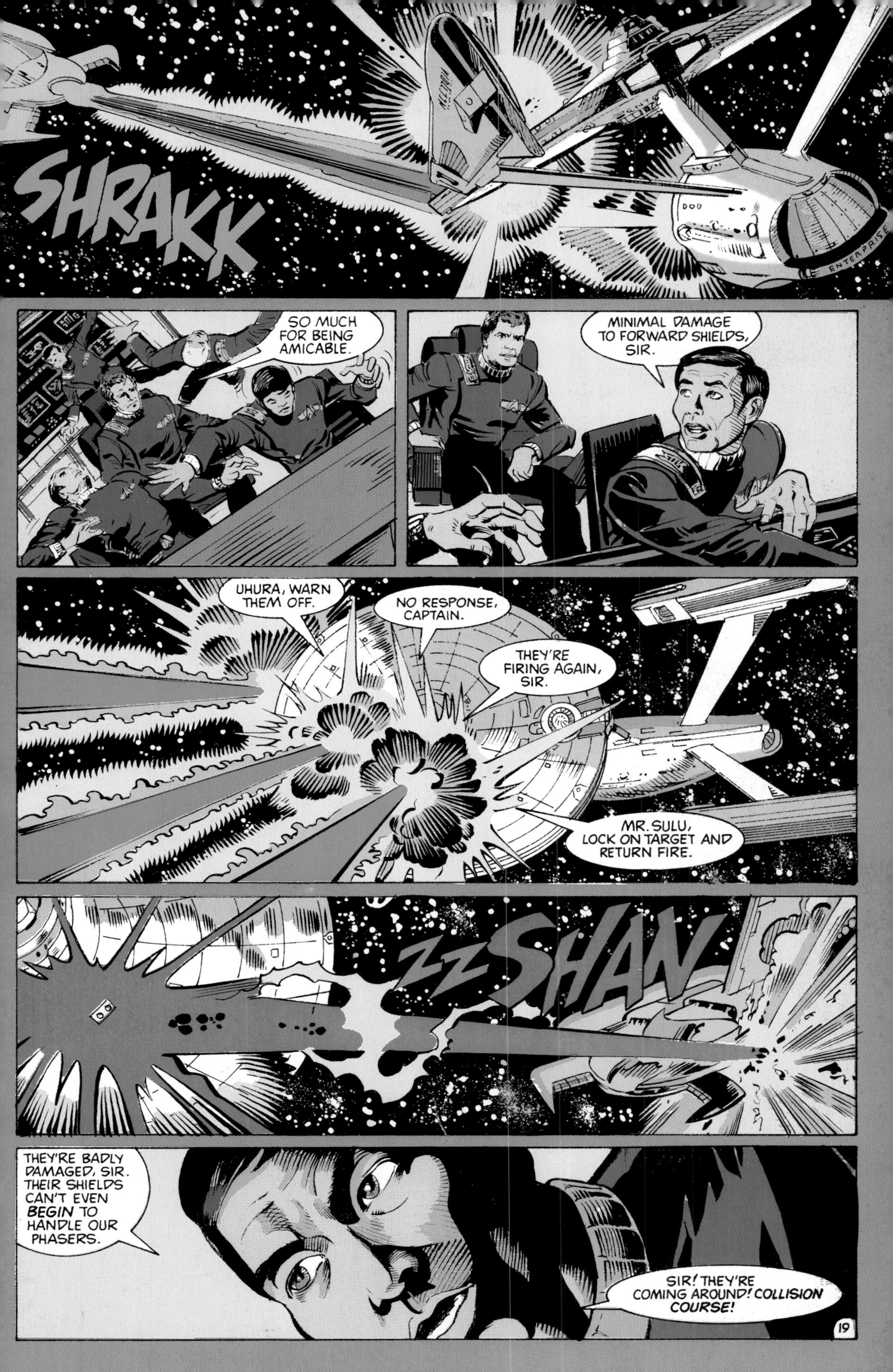
SHRAKK
ENTERPRISE
SO MUCH FOR BEING AMICABLE.
MINIMAL DAMAGE TO FORWARD SHIELDS, SIR.
UHURA, WARN THEM OFF.
NO RESPONSE, CAPTAIN.
THEY'RE FIRING AGAIN, SIR.
MR. SULU, LOCK ON TARGET AND RETURN FIRE.
ZZSHAN
THEY'RE BADLY DAMAGED, SIR. THEIR SHIELDS CAN'T EVEN BEGIN TO HANDLE OUR PHASERS.
SIR! THEY'RE COMING AROUND! COLLISION COURSE!

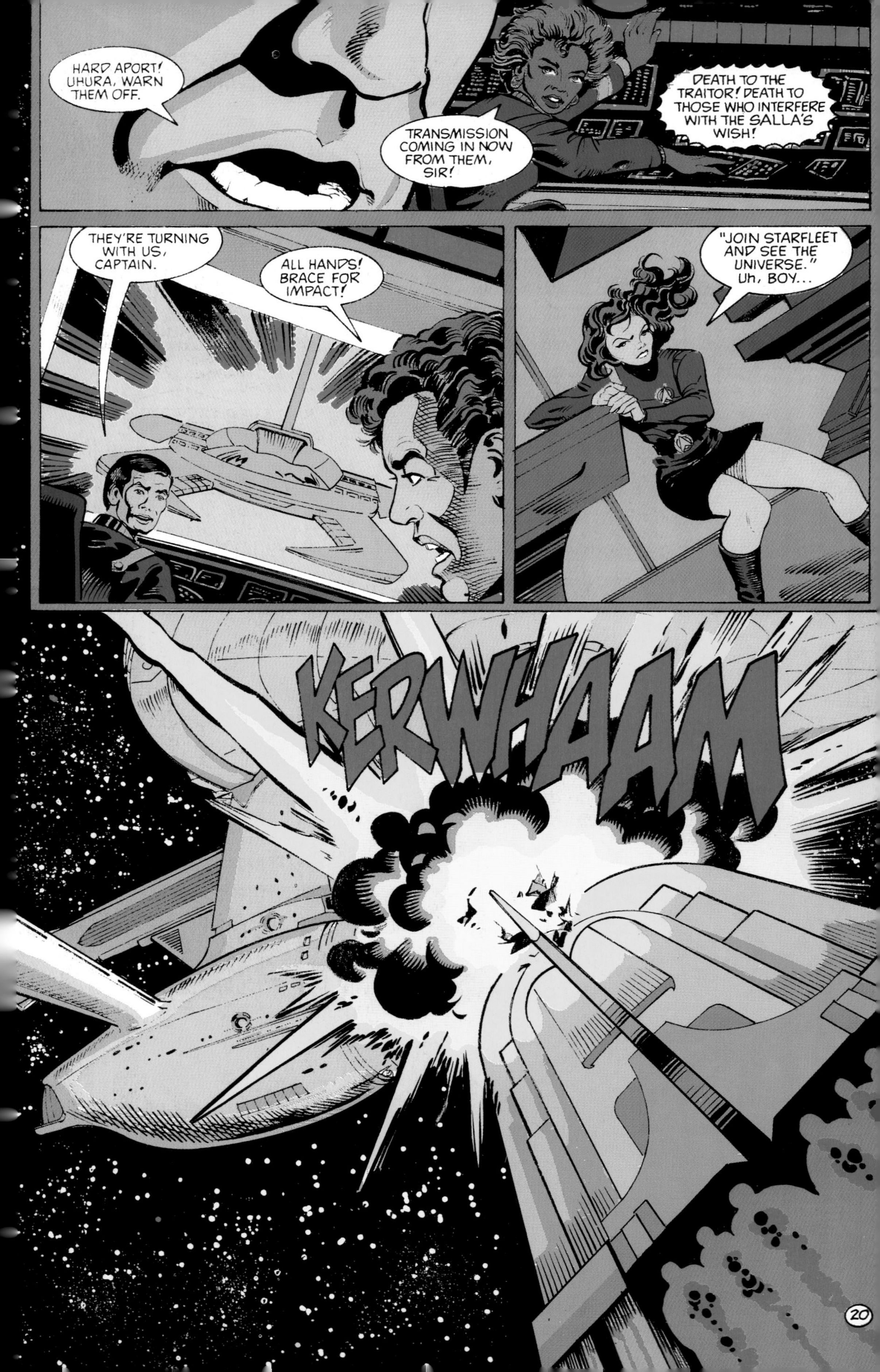
HARD APORT! UHURA, WARN THEM OFF.
TRANSMISSION COMING IN NOW FROM THEM, SIR!
DEATH TO THE TRAITOR! DEATH TO THOSE WHO INTERFERE WITH THE SALLA'S WISH!
THEY'RE TURNING WITH US, CAPTAIN.
ALL HANDS! BRACE FOR IMPACT!
"JOIN STARFLEET AND SEE THE UNIVERSE." Uh, BOY...
KERWHAAM
20

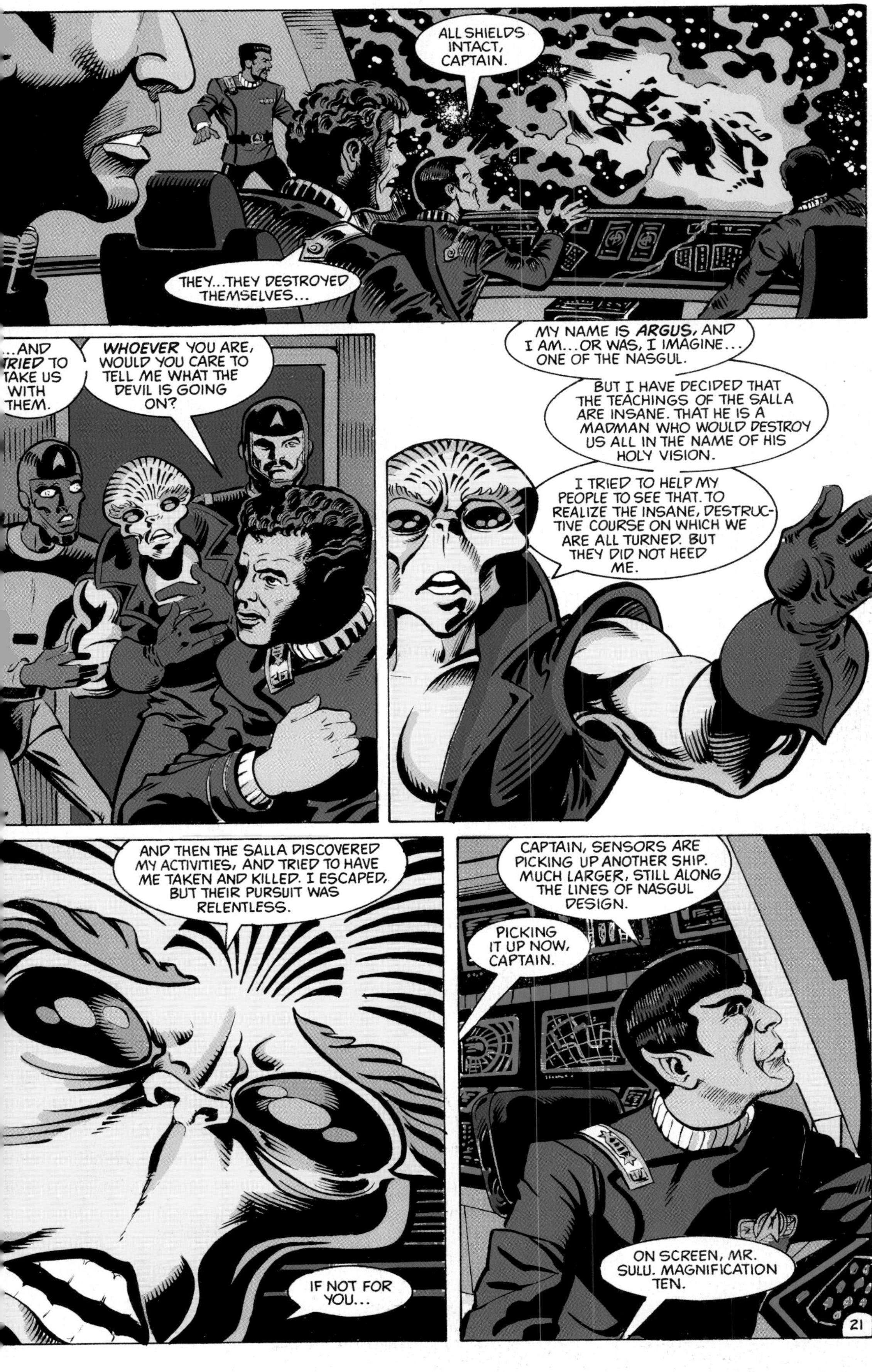
ALL SHIELDS INTACT, CAPTAIN.
THEY...THEY DESTROYED THEMSELVES...
...AND TRIED TO TAKE US WITH THEM.
WHOEVER YOU ARE, WOULD YOU CARE TO TELL ME WHAT THE DEVIL IS GOING ON?
MY NAME IS ARGUS, AND I AM...OR WAS, I IMAGINE... ONE OF THE NASGUL.
BUT I HAVE DECIDED THAT THE TEACHINGS OF THE SALLA ARE INSANE. THAT HE IS A MADMAN WHO WOULD DESTROY US ALL IN THE NAME OF HIS HOLY VISION.
I TRIED TO HELP MY PEOPLE TO SEE THAT. TO REALIZE THE INSANE, DESTRUCTIVE COURSE ON WHICH WE ARE ALL TURNED. BUT THEY DID NOT HEED ME.
AND THEN THE SALLA DISCOVERED MY ACTIVITIES, AND TRIED TO HAVE ME TAKEN AND KILLED. I ESCAPED, BUT THEIR PURSUIT WAS RELENTLESS.
IF NOT FOR YOU...
CAPTAIN, SENSORS ARE PICKING UP ANOTHER SHIP. MUCH LARGER, STILL ALONG THE LINES OF NASGUL DESIGN.
PICKING IT UP NOW, CAPTAIN.
ON SCREEN, MR. SULU. MAGNIFICATION TEN.

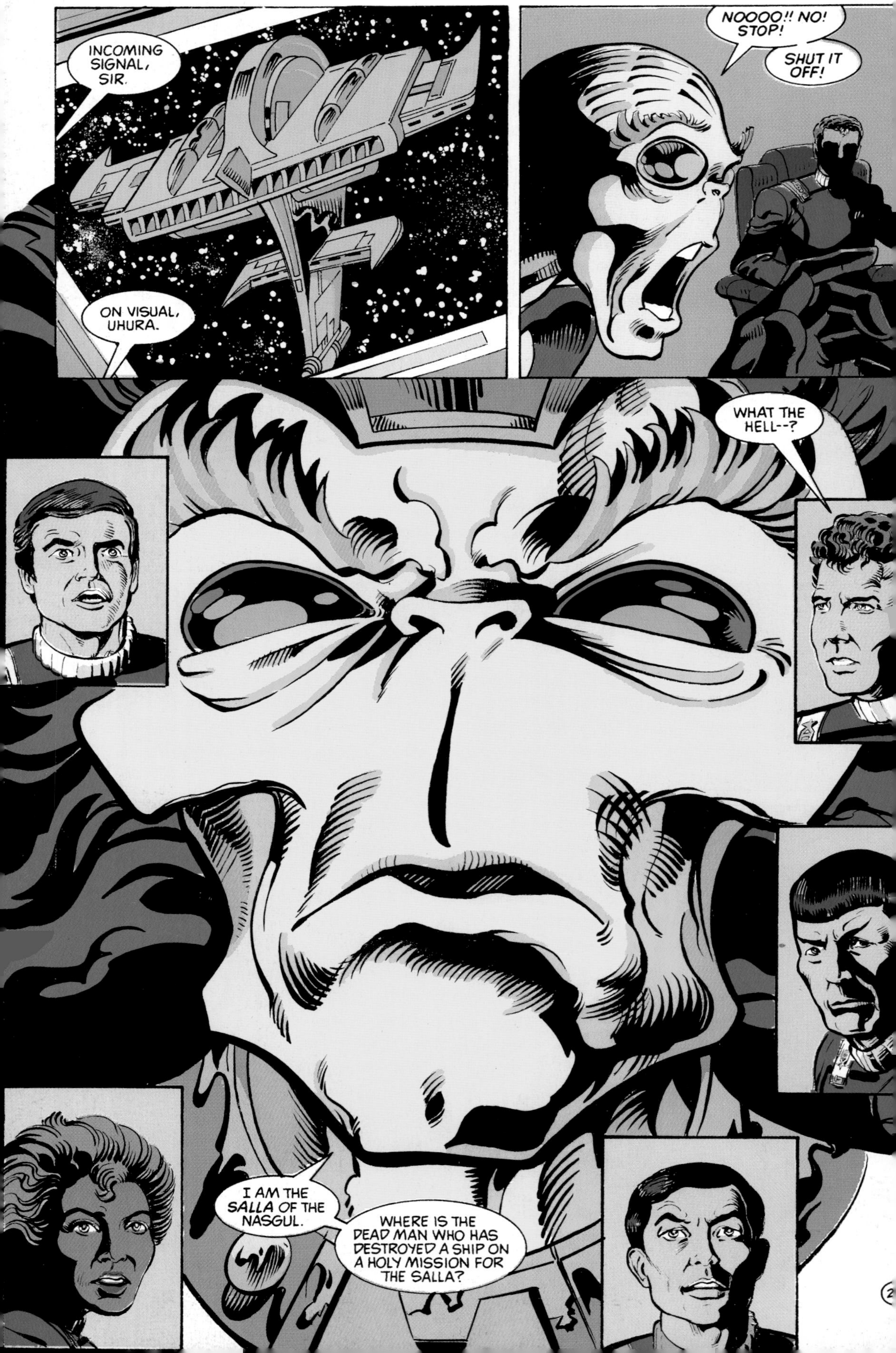
INCOMING SIGNAL, SIR.
ON VISUAL, UHURA.
NOOOO!! NO! STOP!
SHUT IT OFF!
WHAT THE HELL--?
I AM THE SALLA OF THE NASGUL.
WHERE IS THE DEAD MAN WHO HAS DESTROYED A SHIP ON A HOLY MISSION FOR THE SALLA?

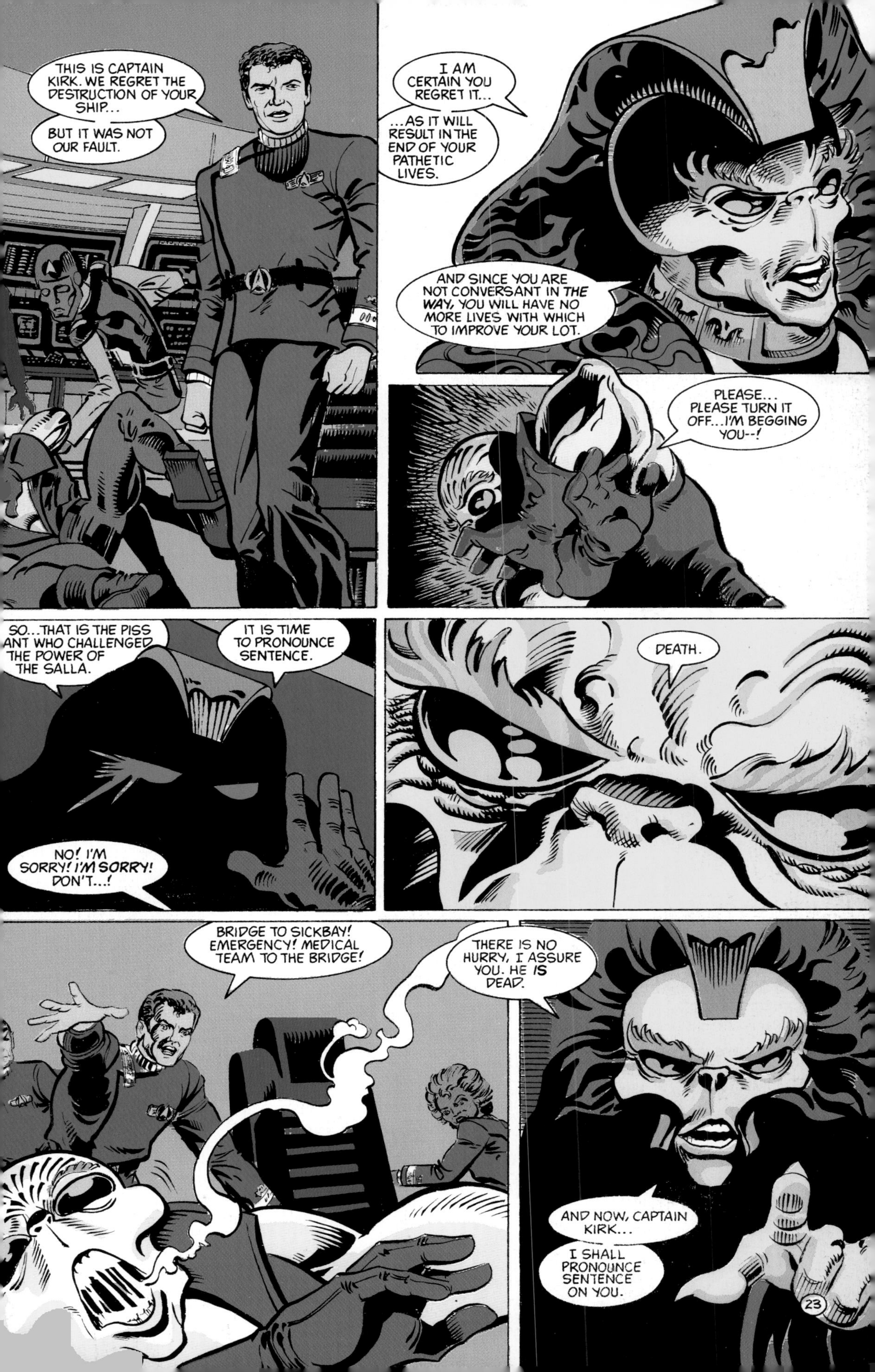
THIS IS CAPTAIN KIRK. WE REGRET THE DESTRUCTION OF YOUR SHIP...
BUT IT WAS NOT OUR FAULT.
I AM CERTAIN YOU REGRET IT...
...AS IT WILL RESULT IN THE END OF YOUR PATHETIC LIVES.
AND SINCE YOU ARE NOT CONVERSANT IN THE WAY, YOU WILL HAVE NO MORE LIVES WITH WHICH TO IMPROVE YOUR LOT.
PLEASE... PLEASE TURN IT OFF...I'M BEGGING YOU--!
SO...THAT IS THE PISS ANT WHO CHALLENGED THE POWER OF THE SALLA.
IT IS TIME TO PRONOUNCE SENTENCE.
NO! I'M SORRY! I'M SORRY! DON'T...!
DEATH.
BRIDGE TO SICKBAY! EMERGENCY! MEDICAL TEAM TO THE BRIDGE!
THERE IS NO HURRY, I ASSURE YOU. HE IS DEAD.
AND NOW, CAPTAIN KIRK...
I SHALL PRONOUNCE SENTENCE ON YOU.
23

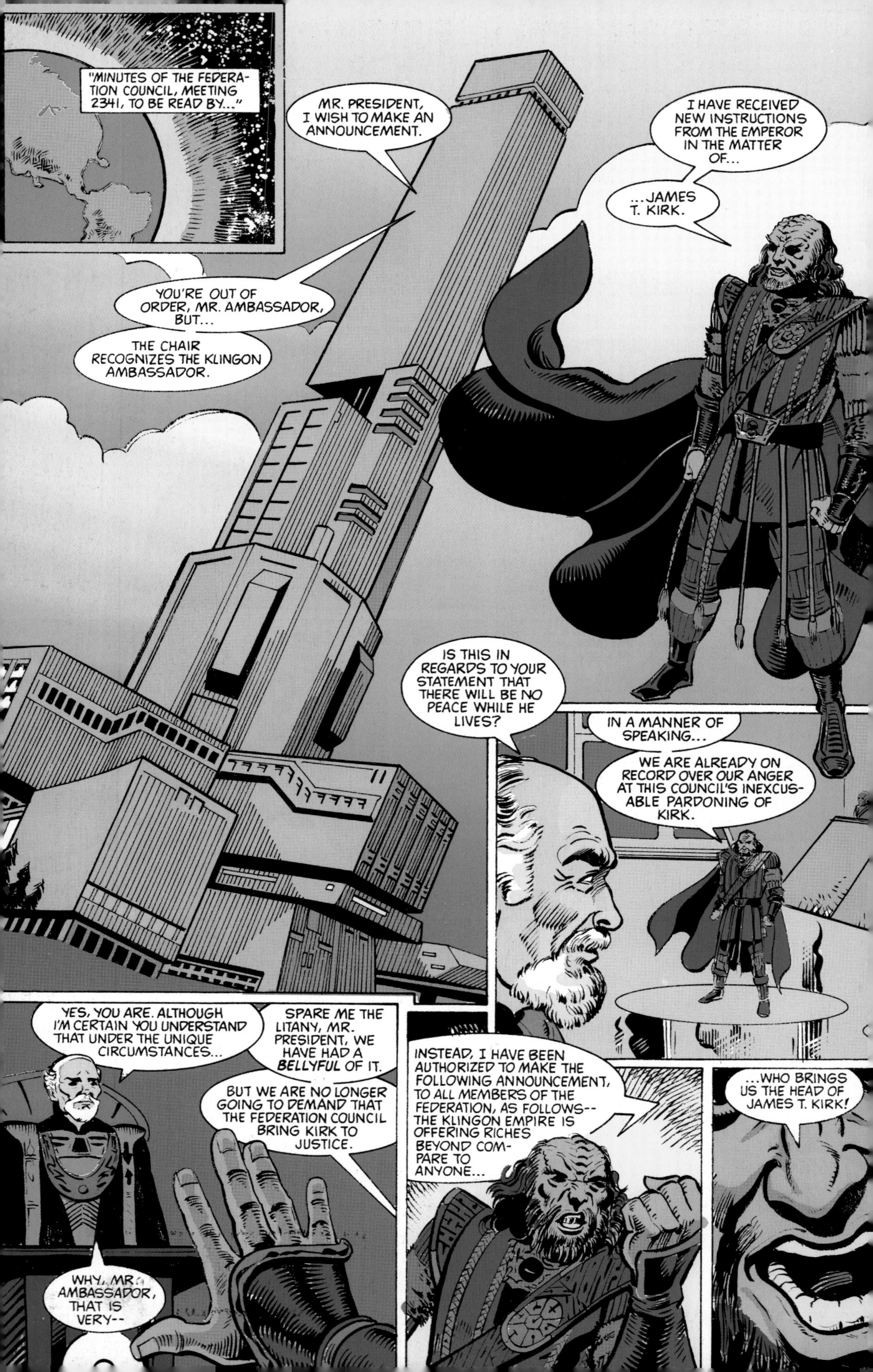
"MINUTES OF THE FEDERATION COUNCIL, MEETING 2341, TO BE READ BY..."
MR. PRESIDENT, I WISH TO MAKE AN ANNOUNCEMENT.
YOU'RE OUT OF ORDER, MR. AMBASSADOR, BUT...
THE CHAIR RECOGNIZES THE KLINGON AMBASSADOR.
I HAVE RECEIVED NEW INSTRUCTIONS FROM THE EMPEROR IN THE MATTER OF...
...JAMES T. KIRK.
IS THIS IN REGARDS TO YOUR STATEMENT THAT THERE WILL BE NO PEACE WHILE HE LIVES?
IN A MANNER OF SPEAKING...
WE ARE ALREADY ON RECORD OVER OUR ANGER AT THIS COUNCIL'S INEXCUSABLE PARDONING OF KIRK.
YES, YOU ARE. ALTHOUGH I'M CERTAIN YOU UNDERSTAND THAT UNDER THE UNIQUE CIRCUMSTANCES...
SPARE ME THE LITANY, MR. PRESIDENT, WE HAVE HAD A BELLYFUL OF IT.
BUT WE ARE NO LONGER GOING TO DEMAND THAT THE FEDERATION COUNCIL BRING KIRK TO JUSTICE.
WHY, MR. AMBASSADOR, THAT IS VERY--
INSTEAD, I HAVE BEEN AUTHORIZED TO MAKE THE FOLLOWING ANNOUNCEMENT, TO ALL MEMBERS OF THE FEDERATION, AS FOLLOWS-- THE KLINGON EMPIRE IS OFFERING RICHES BEYOND COMPARE TO ANYONE...
...WHO BRINGS US THE HEAD OF JAMES T. KIRK!

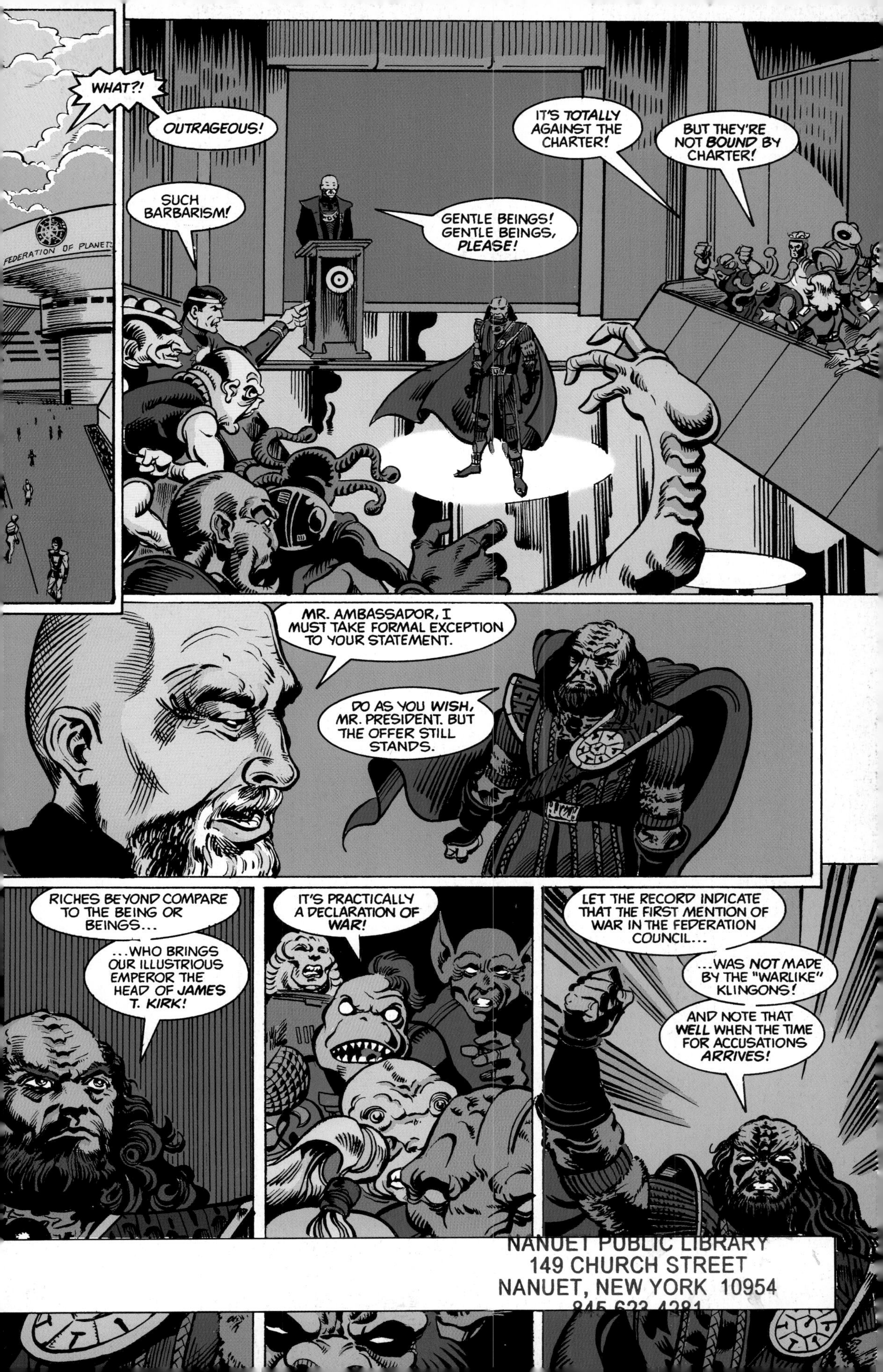
WHAT?!
OUTRAGEOUS!
SUCH BARBARISM!
FEDERATION OF PLANETS
GENTLE BEINGS! GENTLE BEINGS, PLEASE!
IT'S TOTALLY AGAINST THE CHARTER!
BUT THEY'RE NOT BOUND BY CHARTER!
MR. AMBASSADOR, I MUST TAKE FORMAL EXCEPTION TO YOUR STATEMENT.
DO AS YOU WISH, MR. PRESIDENT. BUT THE OFFER STILL STANDS.
RICHES BEYOND COMPARE TO THE BEING OR BEINGS...
...WHO BRINGS OUR ILLUSTRIOUS EMPEROR THE HEAD OF JAMES T. KIRK!
IT'S PRACTICALLY A DECLARATION OF WAR!
LET THE RECORD INDICATE THAT THE FIRST MENTION OF WAR IN THE FEDERATION COUNCIL...
...WAS NOT MADE BY THE "WARLIKE" KLINGONS!
AND NOTE THAT WELL WHEN THE TIME FOR ACCUSATIONS ARRIVES!

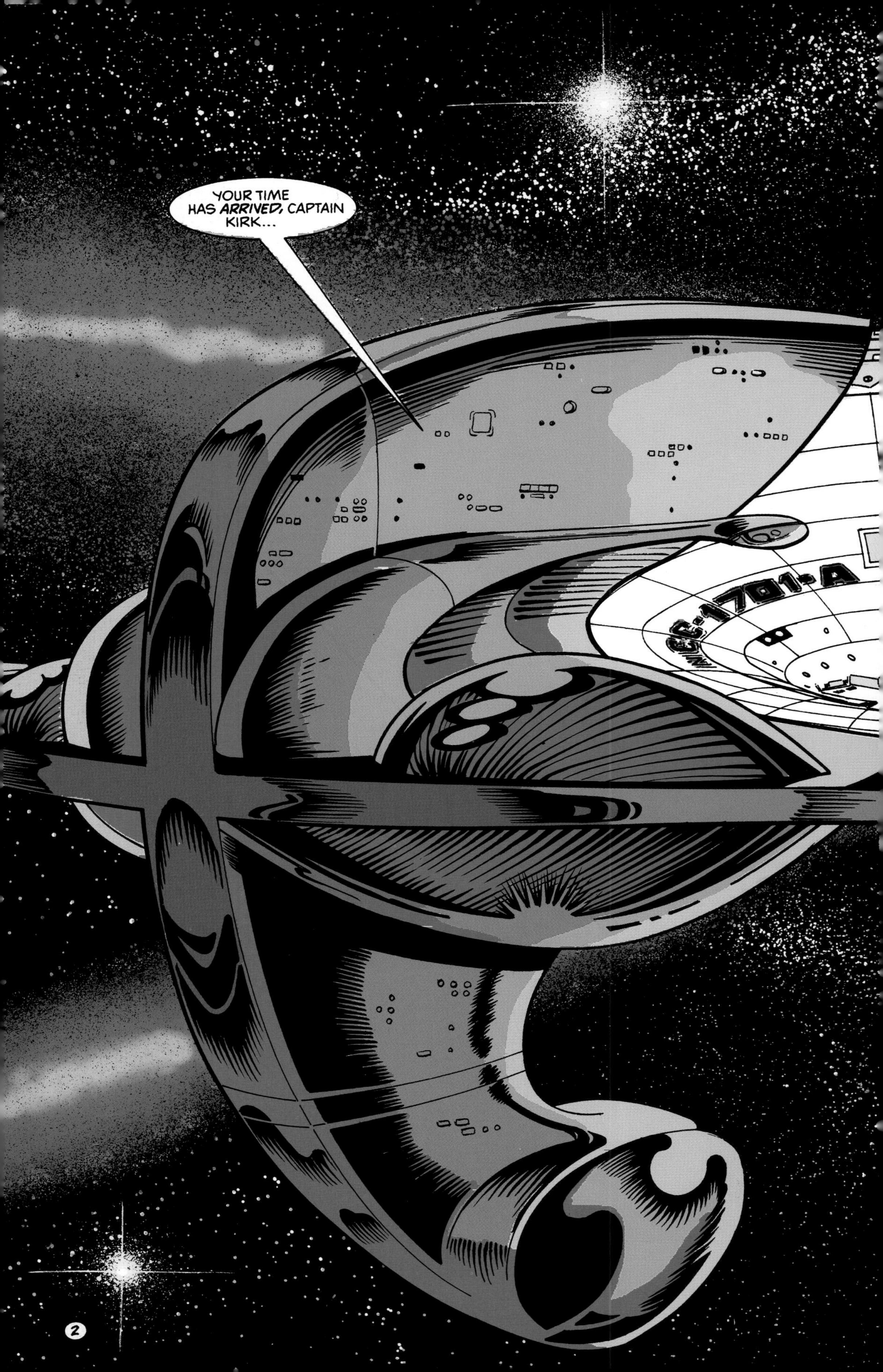
YOUR TIME HAS ARRIVED, CAPTAIN KIRK...
NCC-1701-A

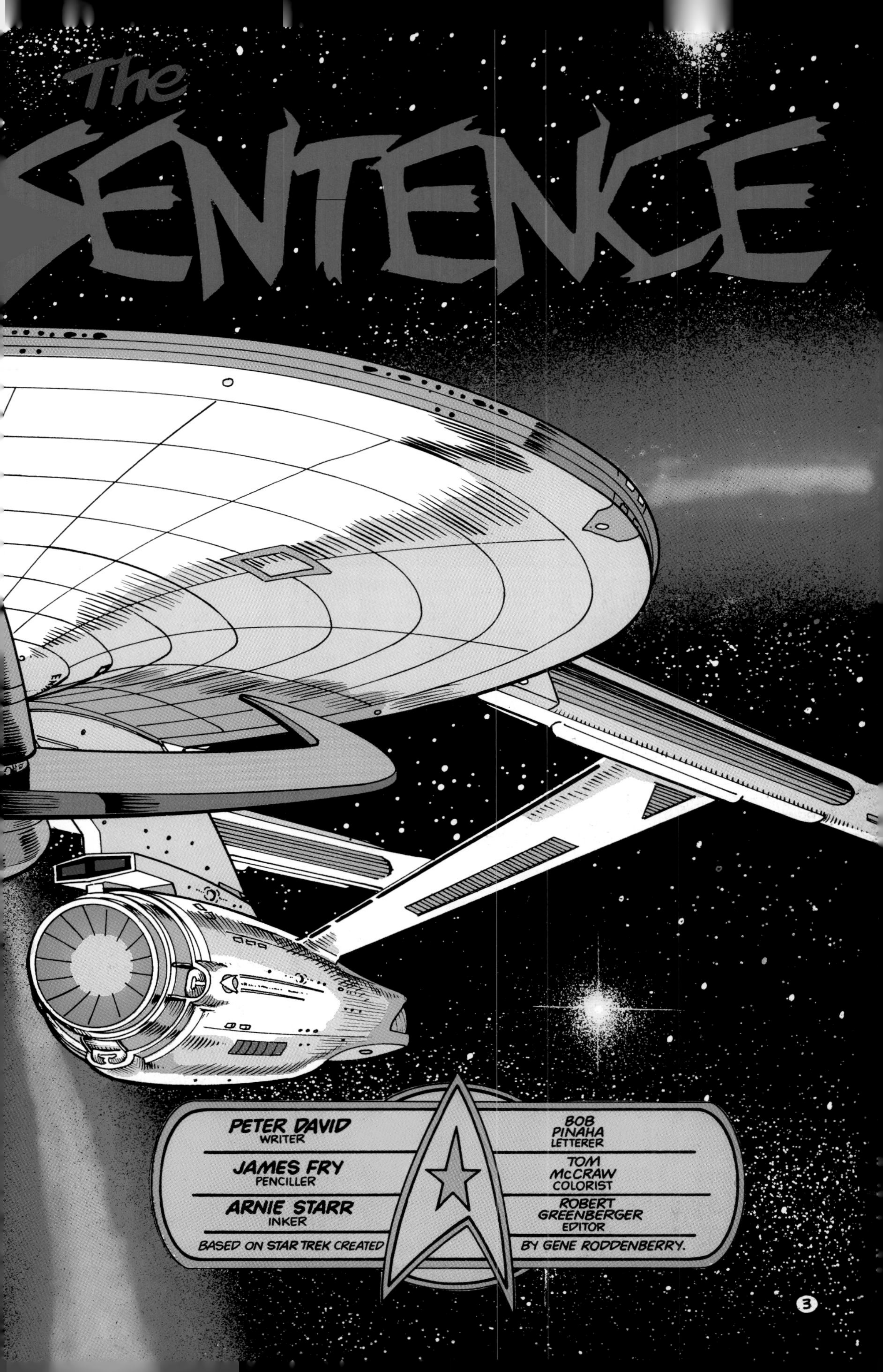

The SENTENCE
PETER DAVID WRITER
JAMES FRY PENCILLER
ARNIE STARR INKER
BOB PINAHA LETTERER
TOM McCRAW COLORIST
ROBERT GREENBERGER EDITOR
BASED ON STAR TREK CREATED BY GENE RODDENBERRY.

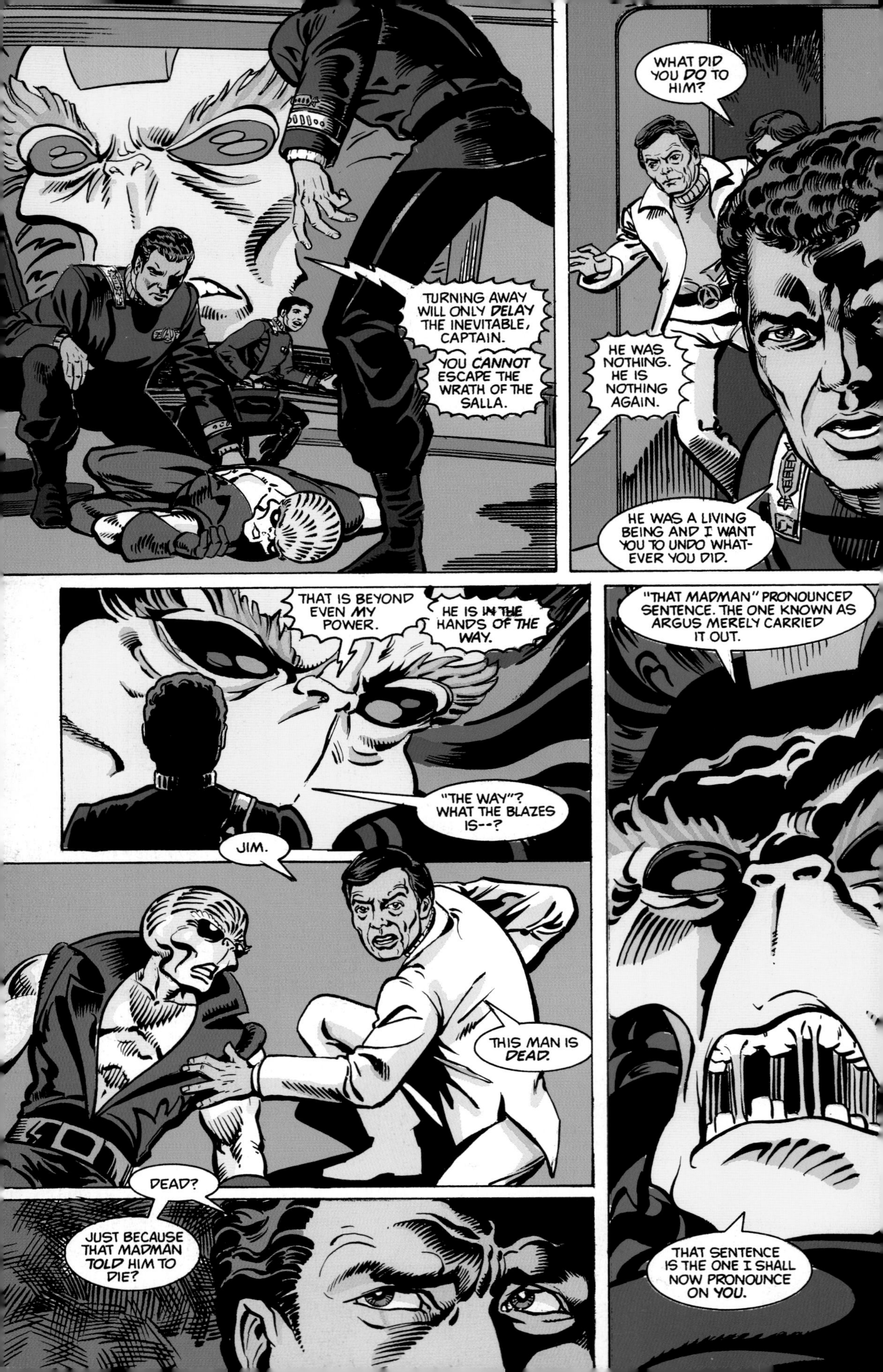
TURNING AWAY WILL ONLY DELAY THE INEVITABLE, CAPTAIN.
YOU CANNOT ESCAPE THE WRATH OF THE SALLA.
WHAT DID YOU DO TO HIM?
HE WAS NOTHING. HE IS NOTHING AGAIN.
HE WAS A LIVING BEING AND I WANT YOU TO UNDO WHATEVER YOU DID.
THAT IS BEYOND EVEN MY POWER.
HE IS IN THE HANDS OF THE WAY.
"THE WAY"? WHAT THE BLAZES IS--?
JIM.
THIS MAN IS DEAD.
DEAD?
JUST BECAUSE THAT MADMAN TOLD HIM TO DIE?
"THAT MADMAN" PRONOUNCED SENTENCE. THE ONE KNOWN AS ARGUS MERELY CARRIED IT OUT.
THAT SENTENCE IS THE ONE I SHALL NOW PRONOUNCE ON YOU.

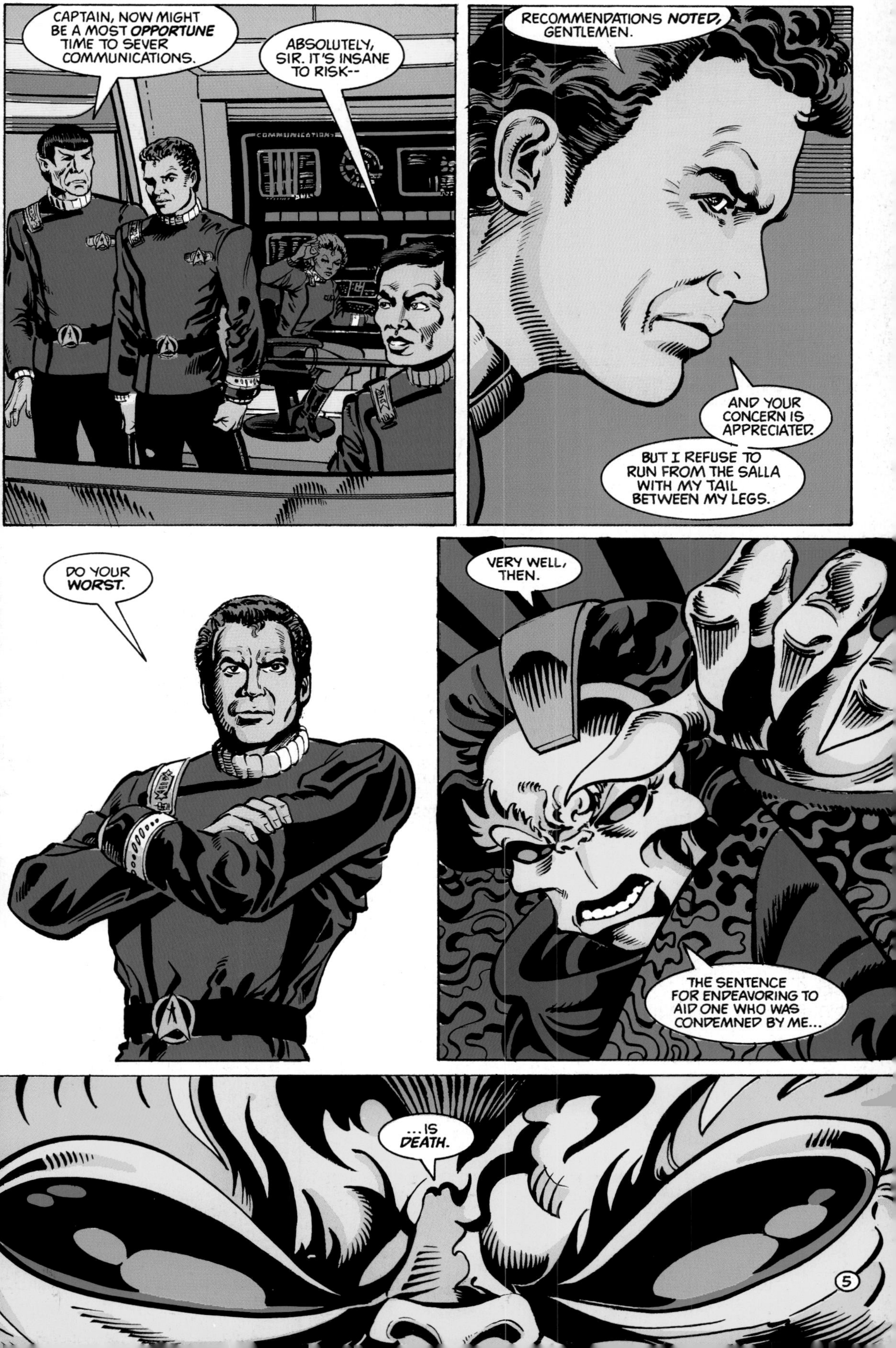
CAPTAIN, NOW MIGHT BE A MOST OPPORTUNE TIME TO SEVER COMMUNICATIONS.
ABSOLUTELY, SIR. IT'S INSANE TO RISK--
COMMUNICATIONS
RECOMMENDATIONS NOTED, GENTLEMEN.
AND YOUR CONCERN IS APPRECIATED.
BUT I REFUSE TO RUN FROM THE SALLA WITH MY TAIL BETWEEN MY LEGS.
DO YOUR WORST.
VERY WELL, THEN.
THE SENTENCE FOR ENDEAVORING TO AID ONE WHO WAS CONDEMNED BY ME...
...IS DEATH.

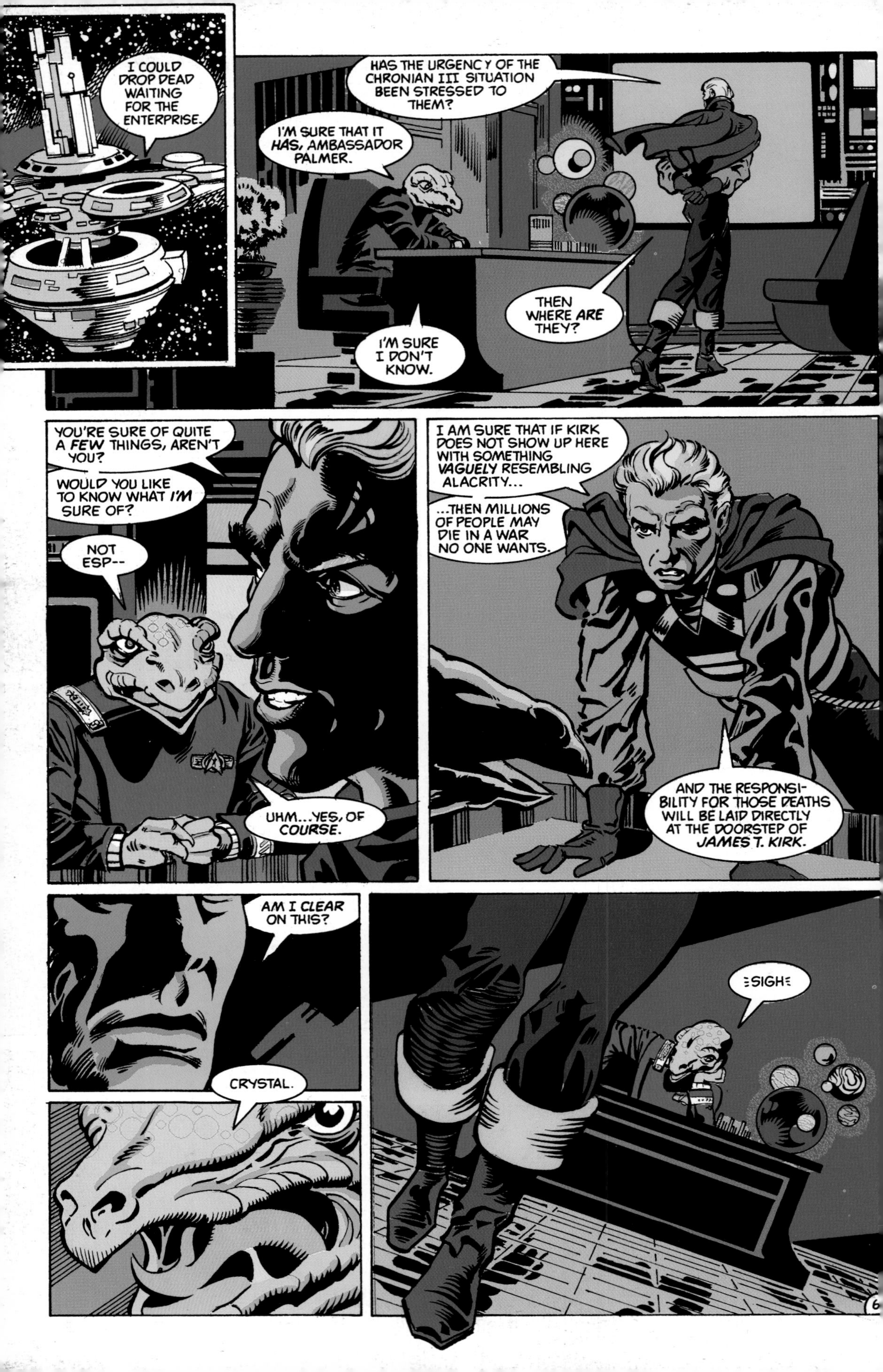

I COULD DROP DEAD WAITING FOR THE ENTERPRISE.
HAS THE URGENCY OF THE CHRONIAN III SITUATION BEEN STRESSED TO THEM?
I'M SURE THAT IT HAS, AMBASSADOR PALMER.
THEN WHERE ARE THEY?
I'M SURE I DON'T KNOW.
YOU'RE SURE OF QUITE A FEW THINGS, AREN'T YOU?
WOULD YOU LIKE TO KNOW WHAT I'M SURE OF?
NOT ESP--
UHM...YES, OF COURSE.
I AM SURE THAT IF KIRK DOES NOT SHOW UP HERE WITH SOMETHING VAGUELY RESEMBLING ALACRITY...
...THEN MILLIONS OF PEOPLE MAY DIE IN A WAR NO ONE WANTS.
AND THE RESPONSI-BILITY FOR THOSE DEATHS WILL BE LAID DIRECTLY AT THE DOORSTEP OF JAMES T. KIRK.
AM I CLEAR ON THIS?
CRYSTAL.
SIGH

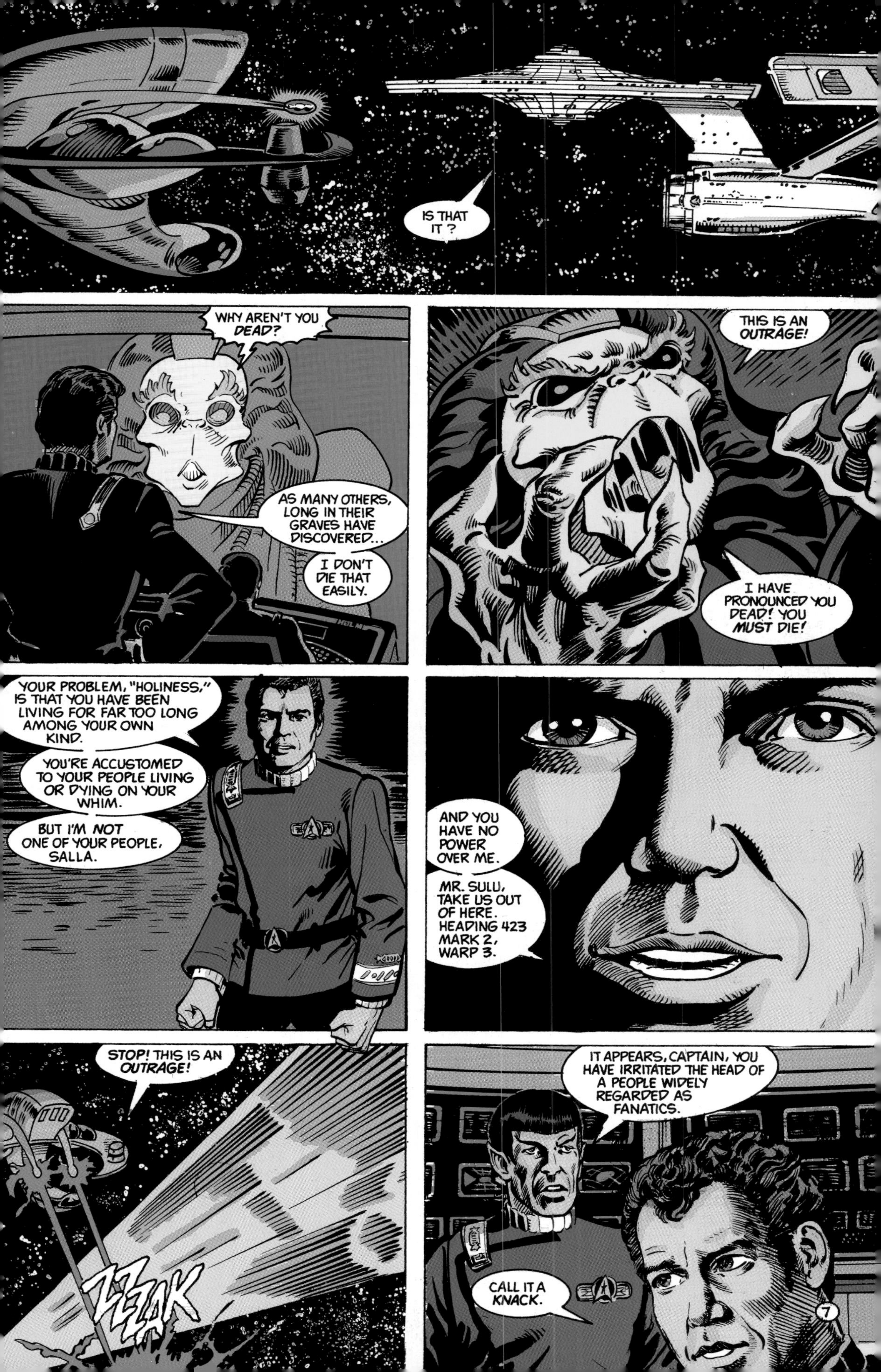
IS THAT IT ?
WHY AREN'T YOU DEAD?
AS MANY OTHERS, LONG IN THEIR GRAVES HAVE DISCOVERED...
I DON'T DIE THAT EASILY.
THIS IS AN OUTRAGE!
I HAVE PRONOUNCED YOU DEAD! YOU MUST DIE!
YOUR PROBLEM, "HOLINESS," IS THAT YOU HAVE BEEN LIVING FOR FAR TOO LONG AMONG YOUR OWN KIND.
YOU'RE ACCUSTOMED TO YOUR PEOPLE LIVING OR DYING ON YOUR WHIM.
BUT I'M NOT ONE OF YOUR PEOPLE, SALLA.
AND YOU HAVE NO POWER OVER ME.
MR. SULU, TAKE US OUT OF HERE. HEADING 423 MARK 2, WARP 3.
STOP! THIS IS AN OUTRAGE!
ZZZAK
IT APPEARS, CAPTAIN, YOU HAVE IRRITATED THE HEAD OF A PEOPLE WIDELY REGARDED AS FANATICS.
CALL IT A KNACK.
7

"CAPTAIN'S LOG, STARDATE--"

ZLIIIIX PHWEEEET

"WILL SOMEONE GET THIS DAMNED THING FIXED?!"

YOU SEEM MOST DISTRESSED OVER THE "DAMNED THING" AND--

SPOCK...COLORFUL METAPHORS ARE USED TO EXPRESS IRRITATION.

IRRITATION, SIR?

MY POINT EXACTLY.

THIS IS DAMNED IRRITATING.

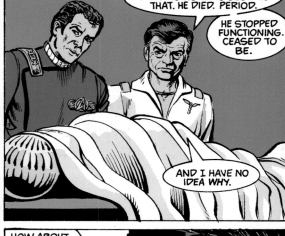

THERE IS NOTHING BESIDES THAT. HE DIED. PERIOD.

HE STOPPED FUNCTIONING. CEASED TO BE.

AND I HAVE NO IDEA WHY.

WHAT IS, BONES? DID YOU FIND OUT WHAT HAPPENED TO HIM?

YES. HE DIED.

BESIDES THAT.

HOW ABOUT BECAUSE THE SALLA TOLD HIM TO?

I LIKE THAT IDEA LEAST OF ALL.

8

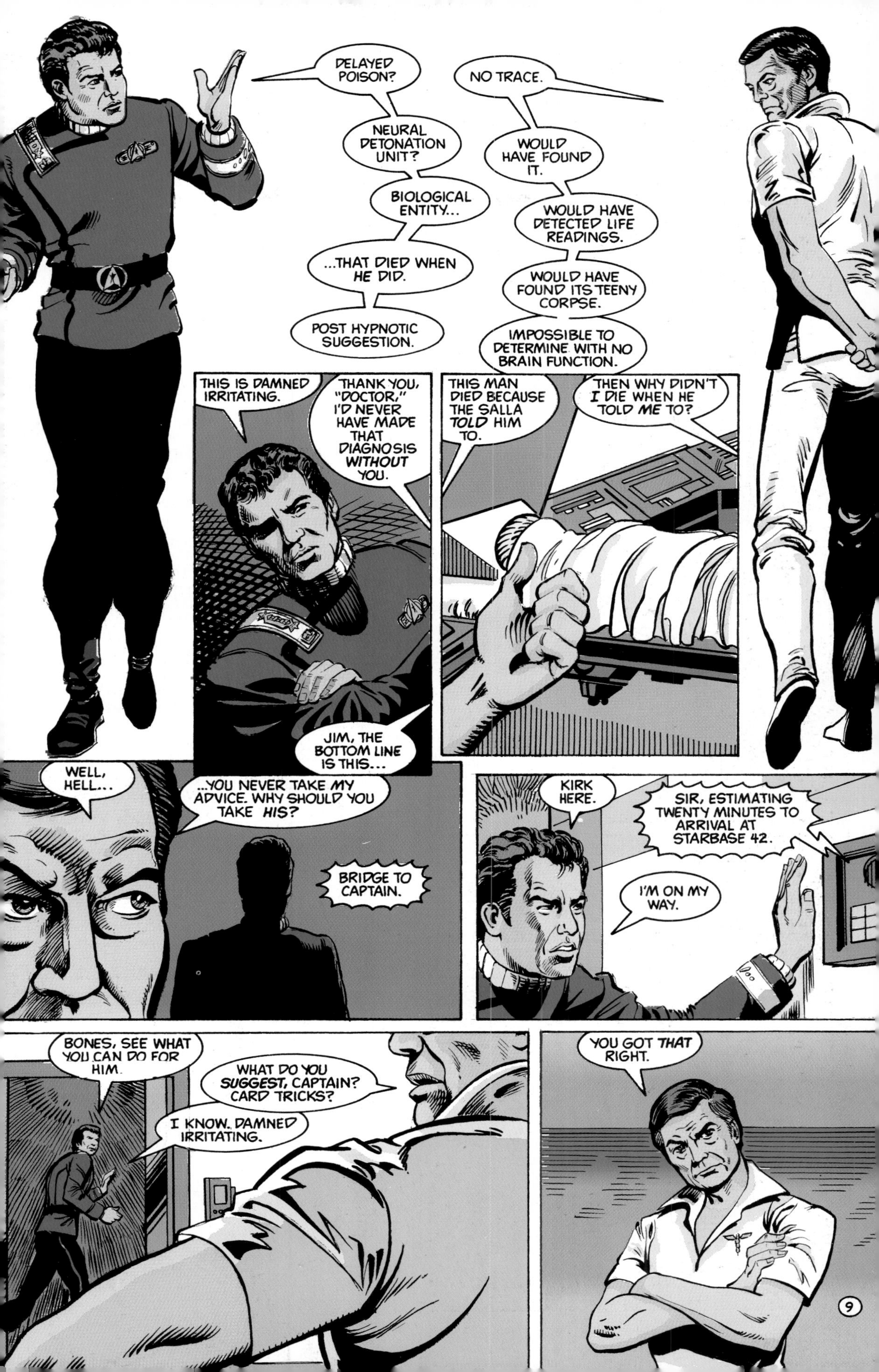

DELAYED POISON?
NO TRACE.
NEURAL DETONATION UNIT?
WOULD HAVE FOUND IT.
BIOLOGICAL ENTITY...
WOULD HAVE DETECTED LIFE READINGS.
...THAT DIED WHEN HE DID.
WOULD HAVE FOUND ITS TEENY CORPSE.
POST HYPNOTIC SUGGESTION.
IMPOSSIBLE TO DETERMINE WITH NO BRAIN FUNCTION.
THIS IS DAMNED IRRITATING.
THANK YOU, "DOCTOR," I'D NEVER HAVE MADE THAT DIAGNOSIS WITHOUT YOU.
THIS MAN DIED BECAUSE THE SALLA TOLD HIM TO.
THEN WHY DIDN'T I DIE WHEN HE TOLD ME TO?
JIM, THE BOTTOM LINE IS THIS...
WELL, HELL...
...YOU NEVER TAKE MY ADVICE. WHY SHOULD YOU TAKE HIS?
BRIDGE TO CAPTAIN.
KIRK HERE.
SIR, ESTIMATING TWENTY MINUTES TO ARRIVAL AT STARBASE 42.
I'M ON MY WAY.
BONES, SEE WHAT YOU CAN DO FOR HIM.
WHAT DO YOU SUGGEST, CAPTAIN? CARD TRICKS?
I KNOW. DAMNED IRRITATING.
YOU GOT THAT RIGHT.

CAPTAIN KIRK, SIR?

YES, ENSIGN... *FOUTON*, IS IT?

YES, SIR.

WHAT *IS* IT, FOUTON?

I WANTED TO *APOLOGIZE*, SIR.

APOLOGIZE? WHATEVER *FOR?*

FOR LETTING YOU DOWN.

MR. FOUTON, WHAT ARE YOU *TALKING* ABOUT?

I WAS ONE OF THE MEN WHO ESCORTED THE NASGULIAN TO THE BRIDGE. HE DIED WHILE HE WAS UNDER MY CHARGE.

I'D UNDERSTAND IF YOU WANTED MY RESIGNATION, SIR.

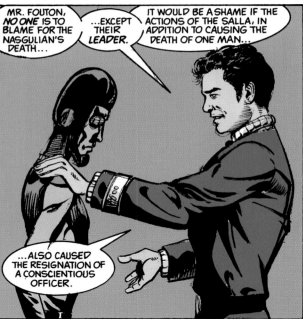

MR. FOUTON, *NO ONE* IS TO BLAME FOR THE NASGULIAN'S DEATH...

...EXCEPT THEIR *LEADER.*

IT WOULD BE A SHAME IF THE ACTIONS OF THE SALLA, IN ADDITION TO CAUSING THE DEATH OF ONE MAN...

...ALSO CAUSED THE RESIGNATION OF A CONSCIENTIOUS OFFICER.

YES, SIR!

SALUTES AREN'T NECESSARY, ENSIGN. IN FACT, THEY'RE SOME-WHAT *PASSÉ.*

"YES, SIR," "HELLO, CAPTAIN"... THESE HAVE ALWAYS BEEN *MORE* THAN SUFFICIENT ON THE ENTERPRISE.

YES, SIR, CAPTAIN. HELLO, CAPTAIN.

CARRY ON, ENSIGN.

YES, SIR.

GOODBYE, CAPTAIN.

10

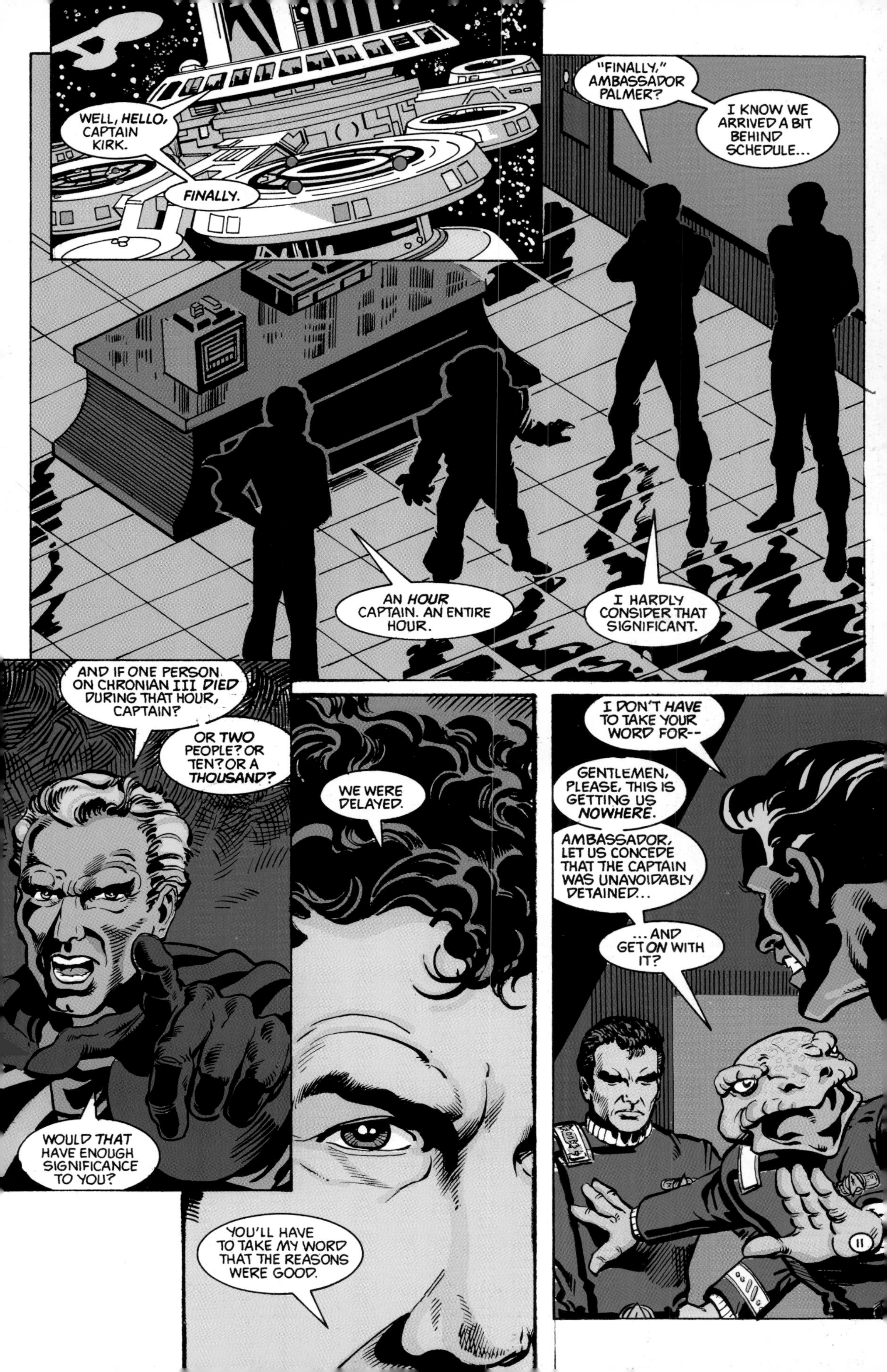

WELL, HELLO, CAPTAIN KIRK.
FINALLY.
"FINALLY," AMBASSADOR PALMER?
I KNOW WE ARRIVED A BIT BEHIND SCHEDULE...
AN HOUR CAPTAIN. AN ENTIRE HOUR.
I HARDLY CONSIDER THAT SIGNIFICANT.
AND IF ONE PERSON ON CHRONIAN III DIED DURING THAT HOUR, CAPTAIN?
OR TWO PEOPLE? OR TEN? OR A THOUSAND?
WOULD THAT HAVE ENOUGH SIGNIFICANCE TO YOU?
WE WERE DELAYED.
YOU'LL HAVE TO TAKE MY WORD THAT THE REASONS WERE GOOD.
I DON'T HAVE TO TAKE YOUR WORD FOR--
GENTLEMEN, PLEASE, THIS IS GETTING US NOWHERE.
AMBASSADOR, LET US CONCEDE THAT THE CAPTAIN WAS UNAVOIDABLY DETAINED...
...AND GET ON WITH IT?
11

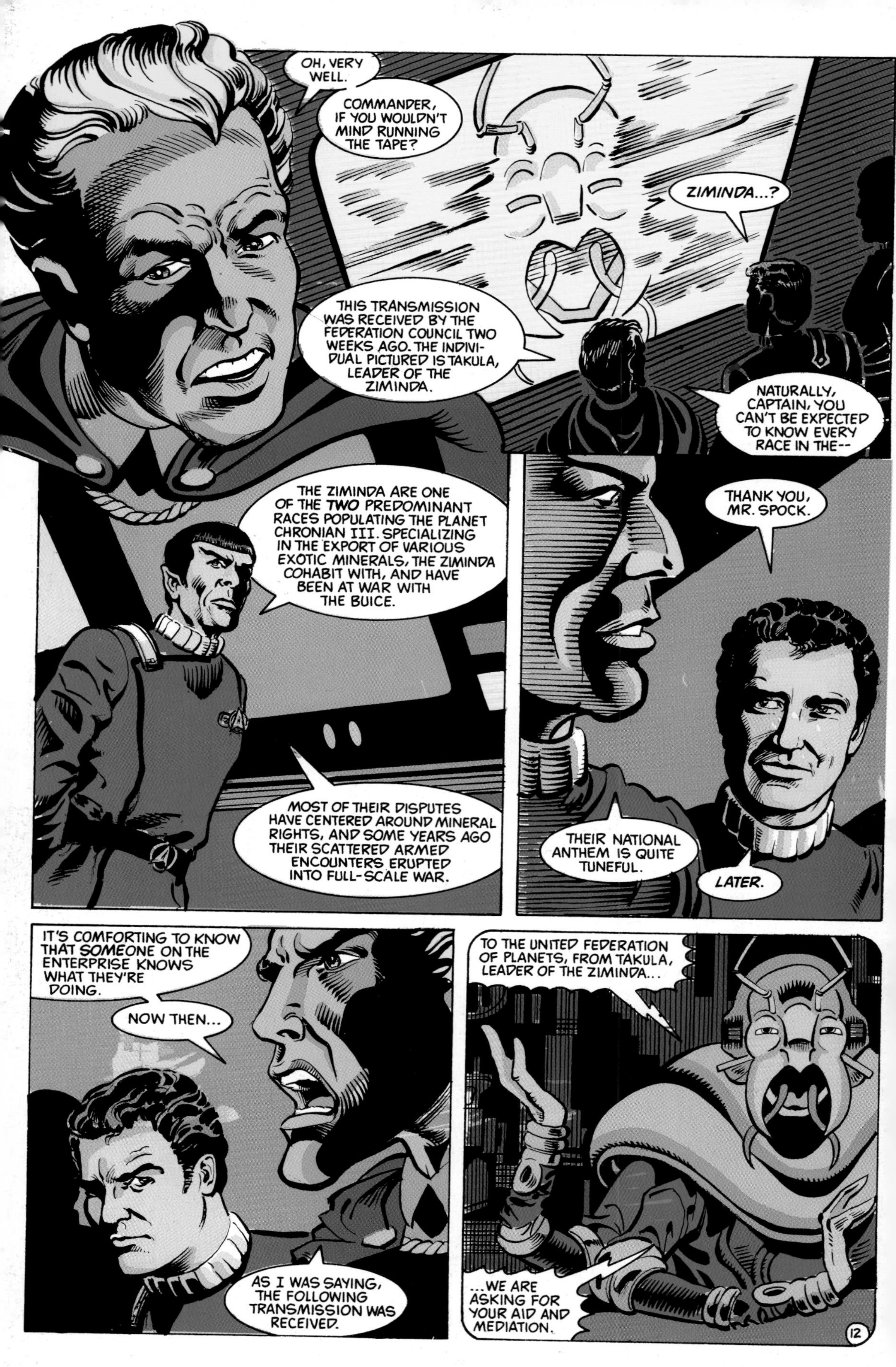

OH, VERY WELL.
COMMANDER, IF YOU WOULDN'T MIND RUNNING THE TAPE?
ZIMINDA...?
THIS TRANSMISSION WAS RECEIVED BY THE FEDERATION COUNCIL TWO WEEKS AGO. THE INDIVIDUAL PICTURED IS TAKULA, LEADER OF THE ZIMINDA.
NATURALLY, CAPTAIN, YOU CAN'T BE EXPECTED TO KNOW EVERY RACE IN THE--
THE ZIMINDA ARE ONE OF THE TWO PREDOMINANT RACES POPULATING THE PLANET CHRONIAN III. SPECIALIZING IN THE EXPORT OF VARIOUS EXOTIC MINERALS, THE ZIMINDA COHABIT WITH, AND HAVE BEEN AT WAR WITH THE BUICE.
MOST OF THEIR DISPUTES HAVE CENTERED AROUND MINERAL RIGHTS, AND SOME YEARS AGO THEIR SCATTERED ARMED ENCOUNTERS ERUPTED INTO FULL-SCALE WAR.
THANK YOU, MR. SPOCK.
THEIR NATIONAL ANTHEM IS QUITE TUNEFUL.
LATER.
IT'S COMFORTING TO KNOW THAT SOMEONE ON THE ENTERPRISE KNOWS WHAT THEY'RE DOING.
NOW THEN...
AS I WAS SAYING, THE FOLLOWING TRANSMISSION WAS RECEIVED.
TO THE UNITED FEDERATION OF PLANETS, FROM TAKULA, LEADER OF THE ZIMINDA...
...WE ARE ASKING FOR YOUR AID AND MEDIATION.
12

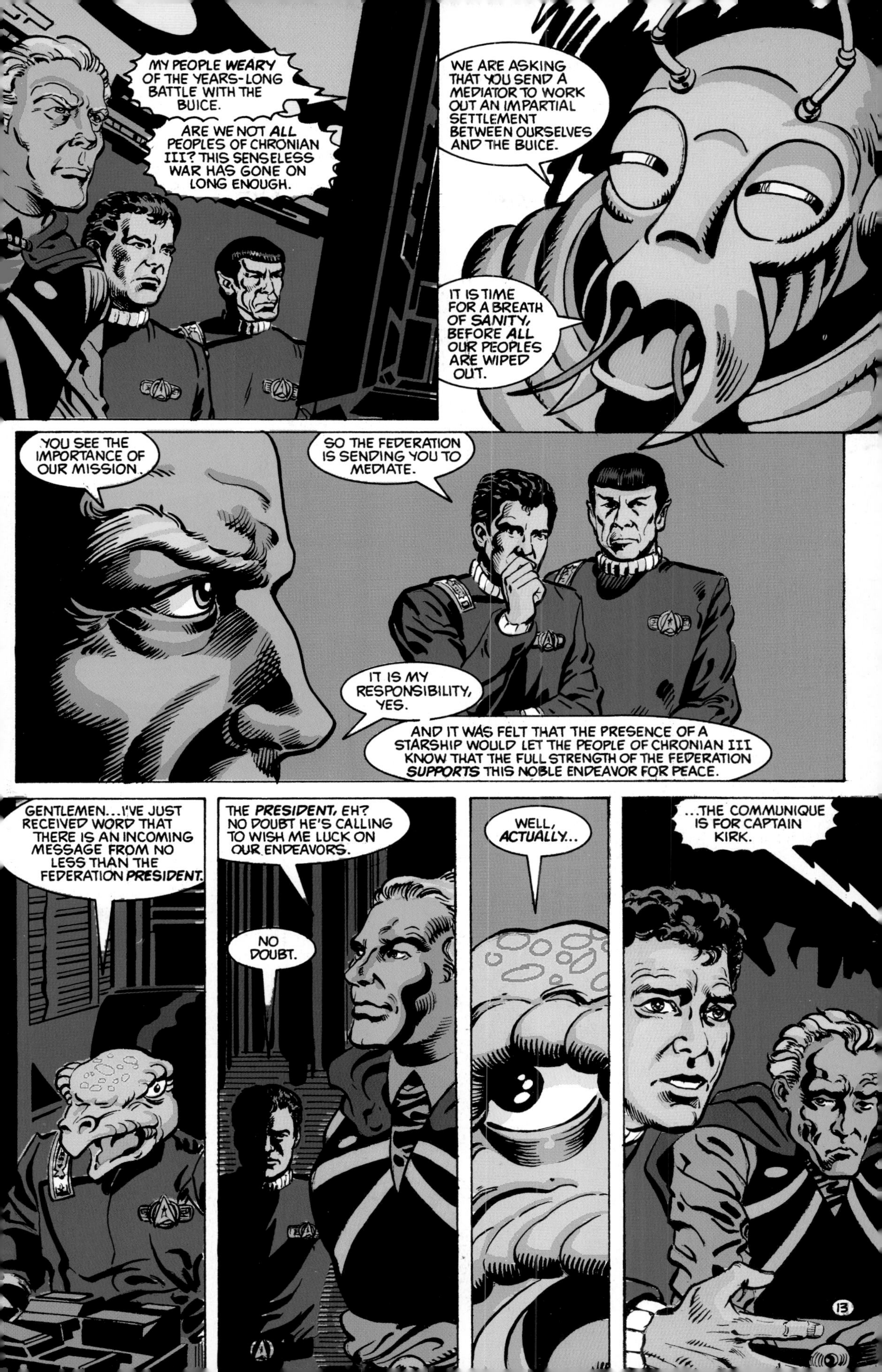
MY PEOPLE WEARY OF THE YEARS-LONG BATTLE WITH THE BUICE.
ARE WE NOT ALL PEOPLES OF CHRONIAN III? THIS SENSELESS WAR HAS GONE ON LONG ENOUGH.
WE ARE ASKING THAT YOU SEND A MEDIATOR TO WORK OUT AN IMPARTIAL SETTLEMENT BETWEEN OURSELVES AND THE BUICE.
IT IS TIME FOR A BREATH OF SANITY, BEFORE ALL OUR PEOPLES ARE WIPED OUT.
YOU SEE THE IMPORTANCE OF OUR MISSION.
SO THE FEDERATION IS SENDING YOU TO MEDIATE.
IT IS MY RESPONSIBILITY, YES.
AND IT WAS FELT THAT THE PRESENCE OF A STARSHIP WOULD LET THE PEOPLE OF CHRONIAN III KNOW THAT THE FULL STRENGTH OF THE FEDERATION SUPPORTS THIS NOBLE ENDEAVOR FOR PEACE.
GENTLEMEN... I'VE JUST RECEIVED WORD THAT THERE IS AN INCOMING MESSAGE FROM NO LESS THAN THE FEDERATION PRESIDENT.
THE PRESIDENT, EH? NO DOUBT HE'S CALLING TO WISH ME LUCK ON OUR ENDEAVORS.
NO DOUBT.
WELL, ACTUALLY...
...THE COMMUNIQUE IS FOR CAPTAIN KIRK.
13

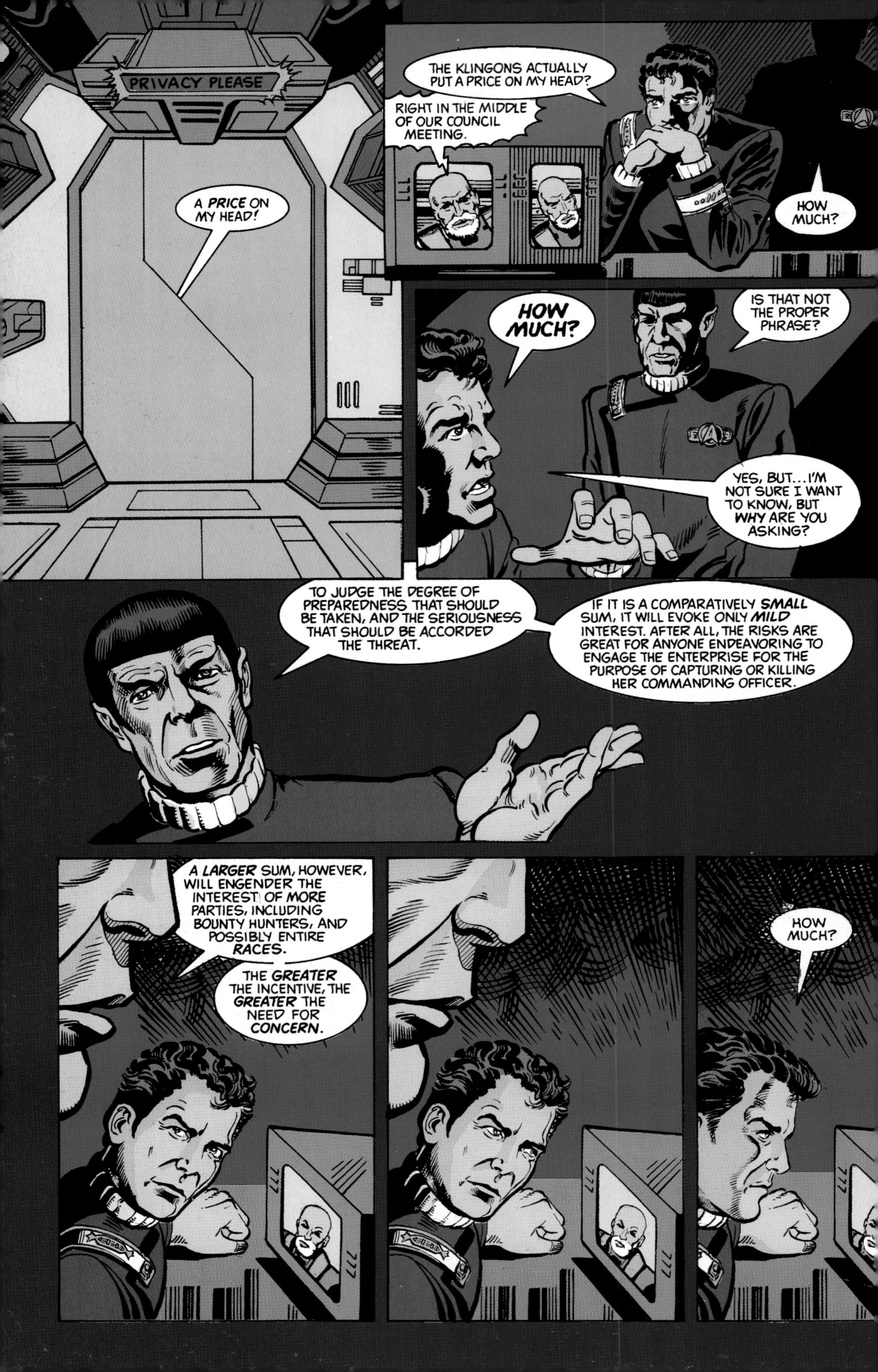
PRIVACY PLEASE
A PRICE ON MY HEAD!
THE KLINGONS ACTUALLY PUT A PRICE ON MY HEAD?
RIGHT IN THE MIDDLE OF OUR COUNCIL MEETING.
HOW MUCH?
HOW MUCH?
IS THAT NOT THE PROPER PHRASE?
YES, BUT...I'M NOT SURE I WANT TO KNOW, BUT WHY ARE YOU ASKING?
TO JUDGE THE DEGREE OF PREPAREDNESS THAT SHOULD BE TAKEN, AND THE SERIOUSNESS THAT SHOULD BE ACCORDED THE THREAT.
IF IT IS A COMPARATIVELY SMALL SUM, IT WILL EVOKE ONLY MILD INTEREST. AFTER ALL, THE RISKS ARE GREAT FOR ANYONE ENDEAVORING TO ENGAGE THE ENTERPRISE FOR THE PURPOSE OF CAPTURING OR KILLING HER COMMANDING OFFICER.
A LARGER SUM, HOWEVER, WILL ENGENDER THE INTEREST OF MORE PARTIES, INCLUDING BOUNTY HUNTERS, AND POSSIBLY ENTIRE RACES.
THE GREATER THE INCENTIVE, THE GREATER THE NEED FOR CONCERN.
HOW MUCH?

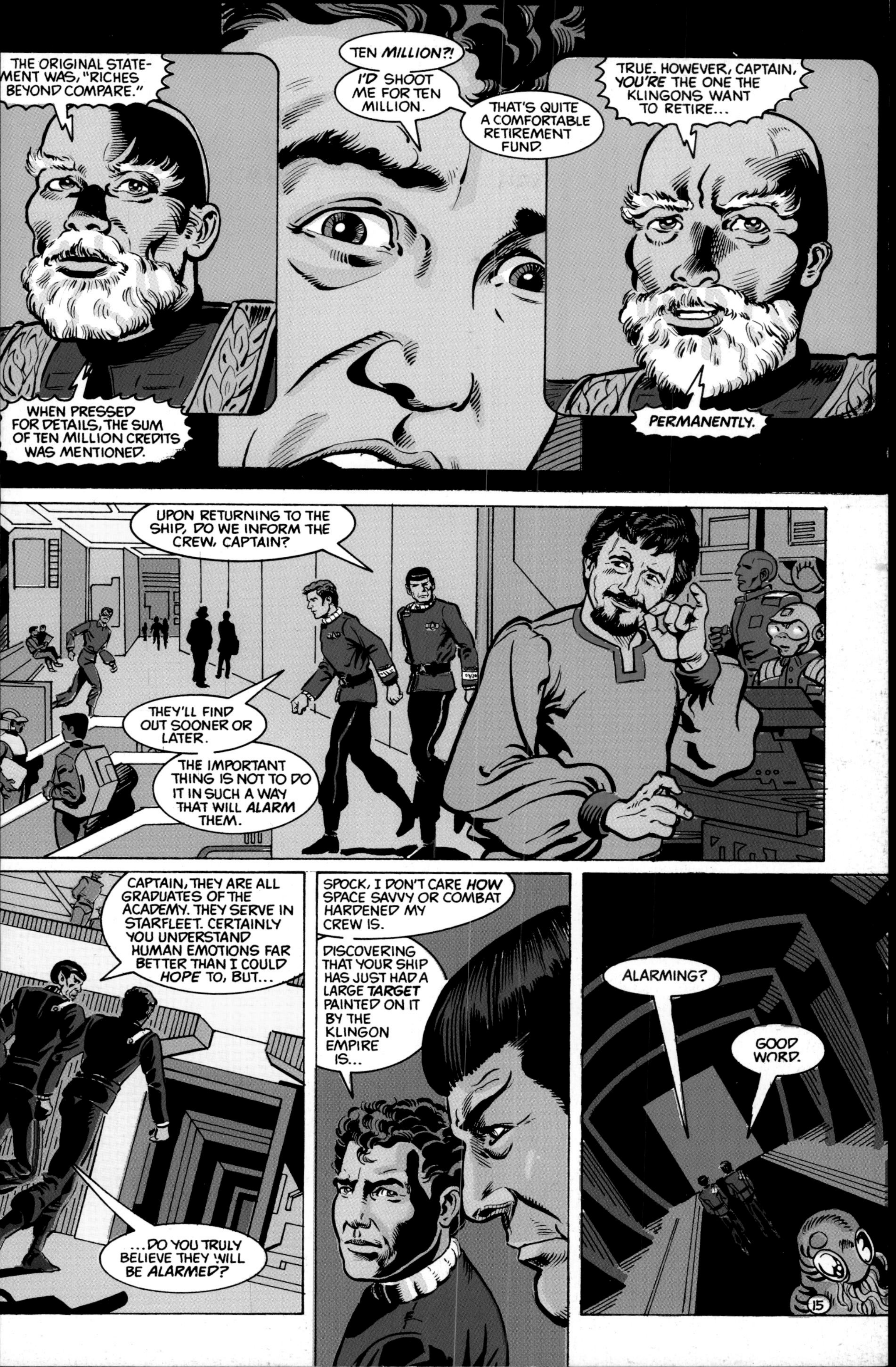
THE ORIGINAL STATEMENT WAS, "RICHES BEYOND COMPARE."
WHEN PRESSED FOR DETAILS, THE SUM OF TEN MILLION CREDITS WAS MENTIONED.
TEN MILLION?!
I'D SHOOT ME FOR TEN MILLION.
THAT'S QUITE A COMFORTABLE RETIREMENT FUND.
TRUE. HOWEVER, CAPTAIN, YOU'RE THE ONE THE KLINGONS WANT TO RETIRE...
PERMANENTLY.
UPON RETURNING TO THE SHIP, DO WE INFORM THE CREW, CAPTAIN?
THEY'LL FIND OUT SOONER OR LATER.
THE IMPORTANT THING IS NOT TO DO IT IN SUCH A WAY THAT WILL ALARM THEM.
CAPTAIN, THEY ARE ALL GRADUATES OF THE ACADEMY. THEY SERVE IN STARFLEET. CERTAINLY YOU UNDERSTAND HUMAN EMOTIONS FAR BETTER THAN I COULD HOPE TO, BUT...
...DO YOU TRULY BELIEVE THEY WILL BE ALARMED?
SPOCK, I DON'T CARE HOW SPACE SAVVY OR COMBAT HARDENED MY CREW IS.
DISCOVERING THAT YOUR SHIP HAS JUST HAD A LARGE TARGET PAINTED ON IT BY THE KLINGON EMPIRE IS...
ALARMING?
GOOD WORD.
15

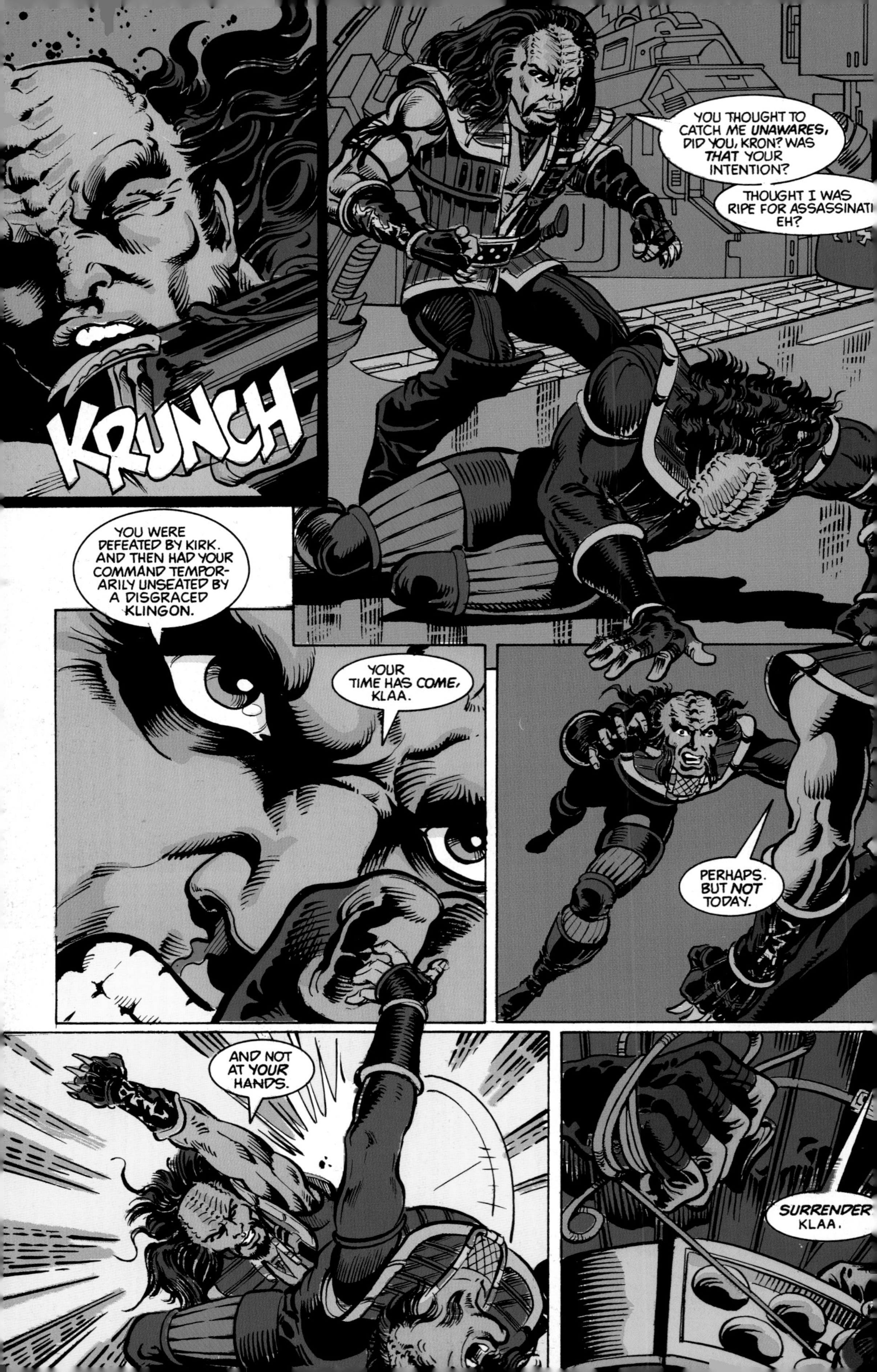
KRUNCH
YOU THOUGHT TO CATCH ME UNAWARES, DID YOU, KRON? WAS THAT YOUR INTENTION?
THOUGHT I WAS RIPE FOR ASSASSINATI EH?
YOU WERE DEFEATED BY KIRK. AND THEN HAD YOUR COMMAND TEMPORARILY UNSEATED BY A DISGRACED KLINGON.
YOUR TIME HAS COME, KLAA.
PERHAPS. BUT NOT TODAY.
AND NOT AT YOUR HANDS.
SURRENDER KLAA.

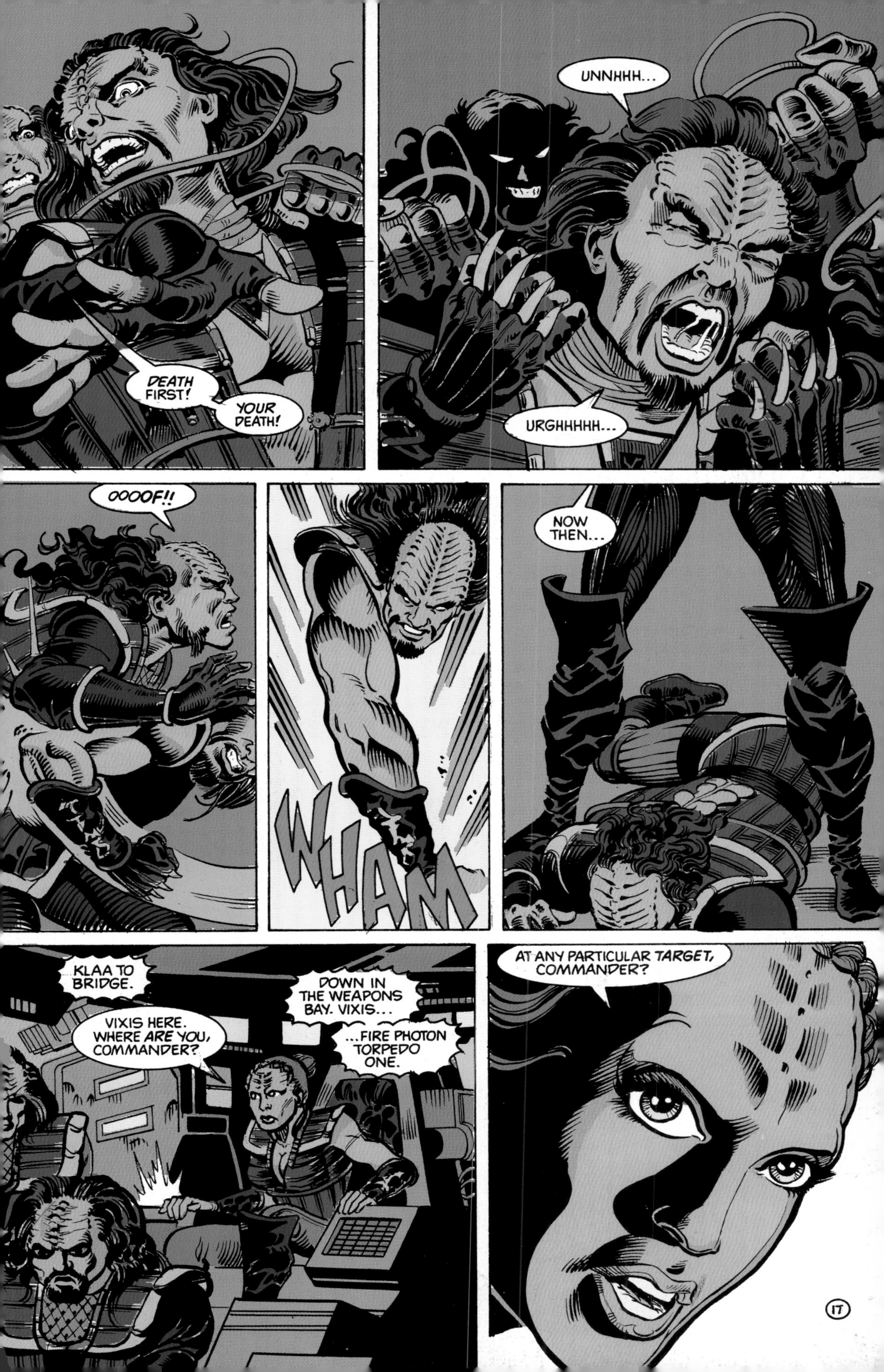

DEATH FIRST!
YOUR DEATH!
UNNHHH...
URGHHHHH...
OOOOF!!
WHAM
NOW THEN...
KLAA TO BRIDGE.
VIXIS HERE. WHERE ARE YOU, COMMANDER?
DOWN IN THE WEAPONS BAY. VIXIS...
...FIRE PHOTON TORPEDO ONE.
AT ANY PARTICULAR TARGET, COMMANDER?

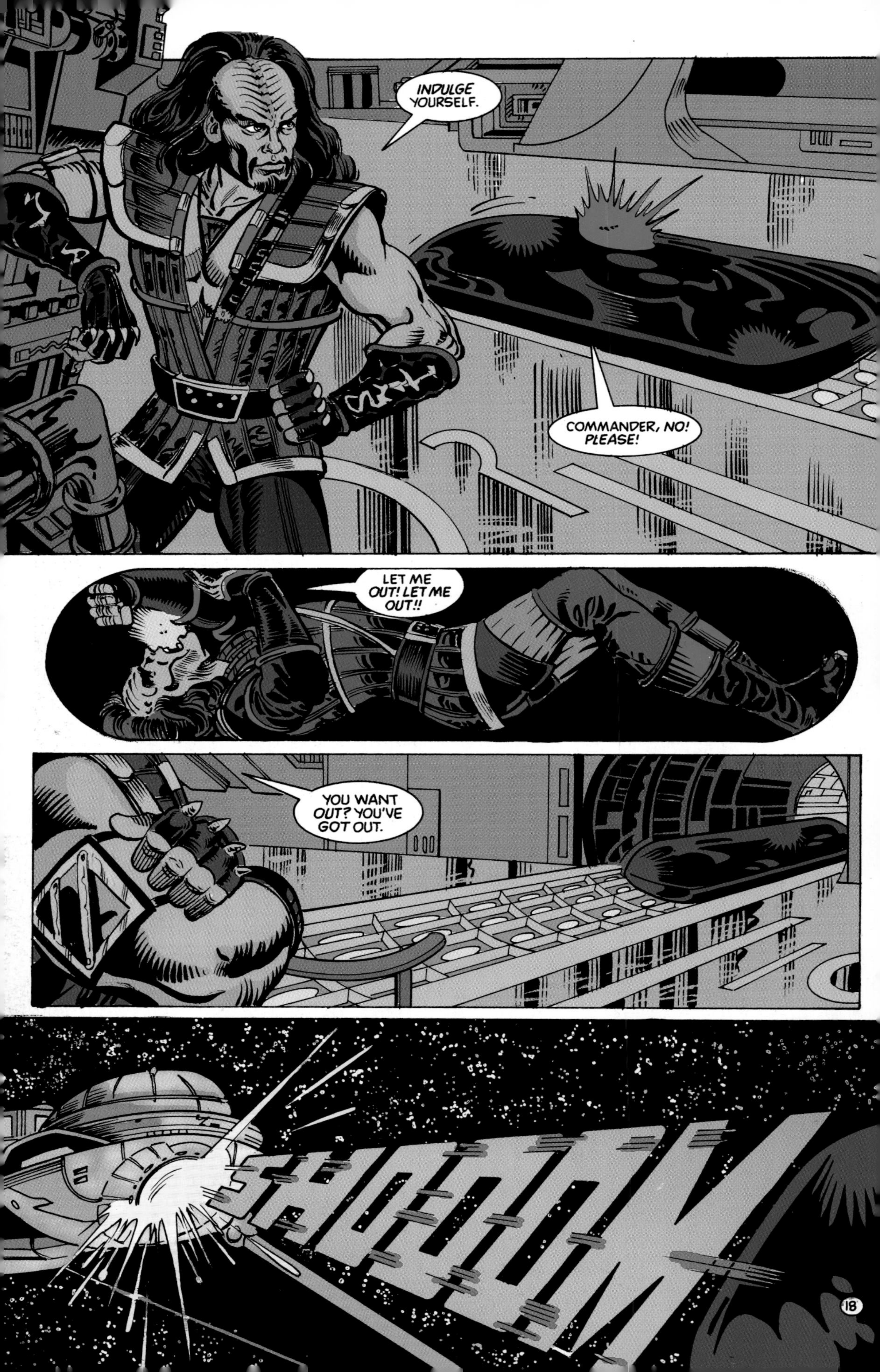
INDULGE YOURSELF.
COMMANDER, NO! PLEASE!
LET ME OUT! LET ME OUT!!
YOU WANT OUT? YOU'VE GOT OUT.

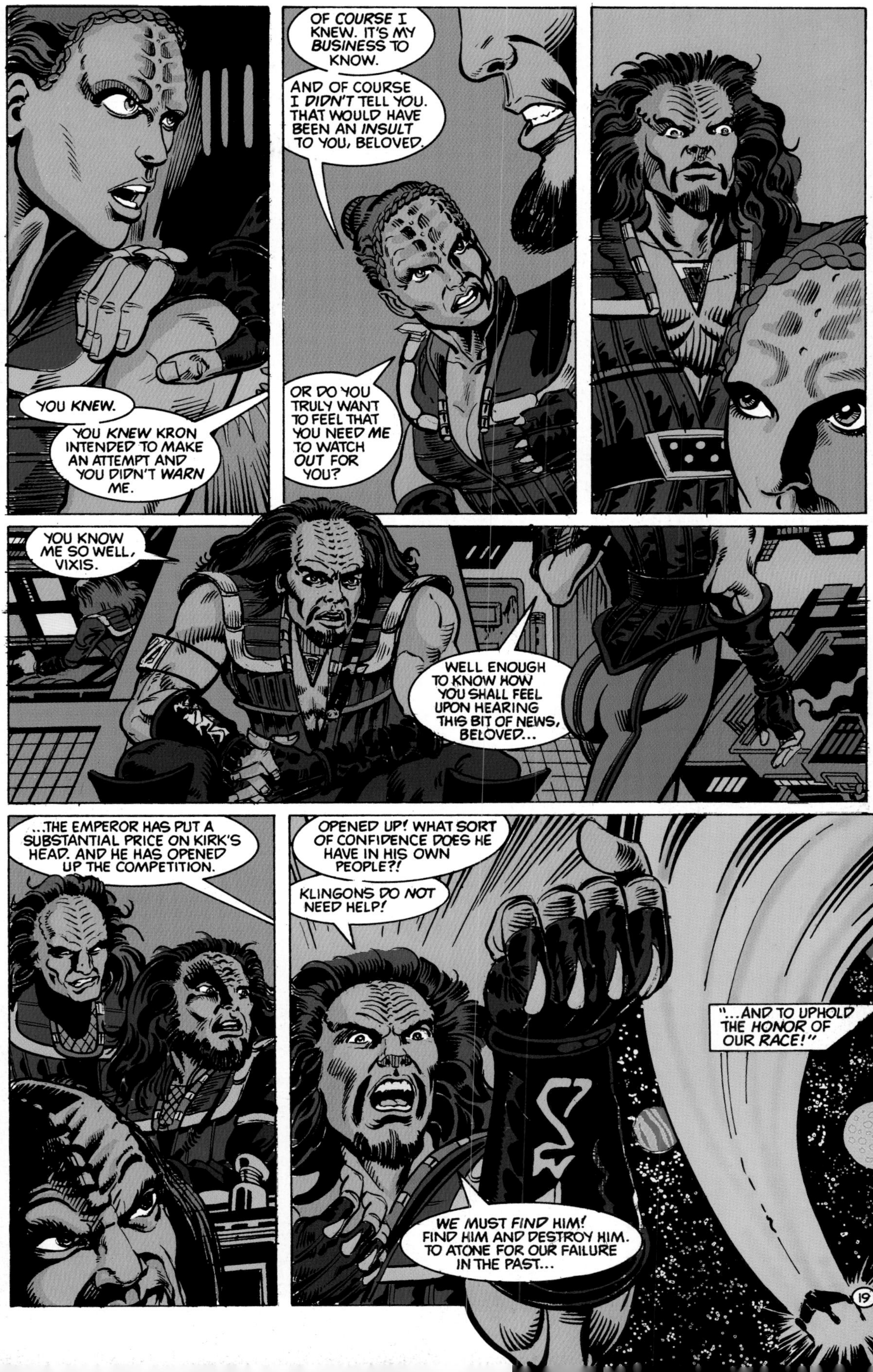
YOU KNEW.
YOU KNEW KRON INTENDED TO MAKE AN ATTEMPT AND YOU DIDN'T WARN ME.
OF COURSE I KNEW. IT'S MY BUSINESS TO KNOW.
AND OF COURSE I DIDN'T TELL YOU. THAT WOULD HAVE BEEN AN INSULT TO YOU, BELOVED.
OR DO YOU TRULY WANT TO FEEL THAT YOU NEED ME TO WATCH OUT FOR YOU?
YOU KNOW ME SO WELL, VIXIS.
WELL ENOUGH TO KNOW HOW YOU SHALL FEEL UPON HEARING THIS BIT OF NEWS, BELOVED...
...THE EMPEROR HAS PUT A SUBSTANTIAL PRICE ON KIRK'S HEAD. AND HE HAS OPENED UP THE COMPETITION.
OPENED UP! WHAT SORT OF CONFIDENCE DOES HE HAVE IN HIS OWN PEOPLE?!
KLINGONS DO NOT NEED HELP!
WE MUST FIND HIM! FIND HIM AND DESTROY HIM. TO ATONE FOR OUR FAILURE IN THE PAST...
"...AND TO UPHOLD THE HONOR OF OUR RACE!"
19

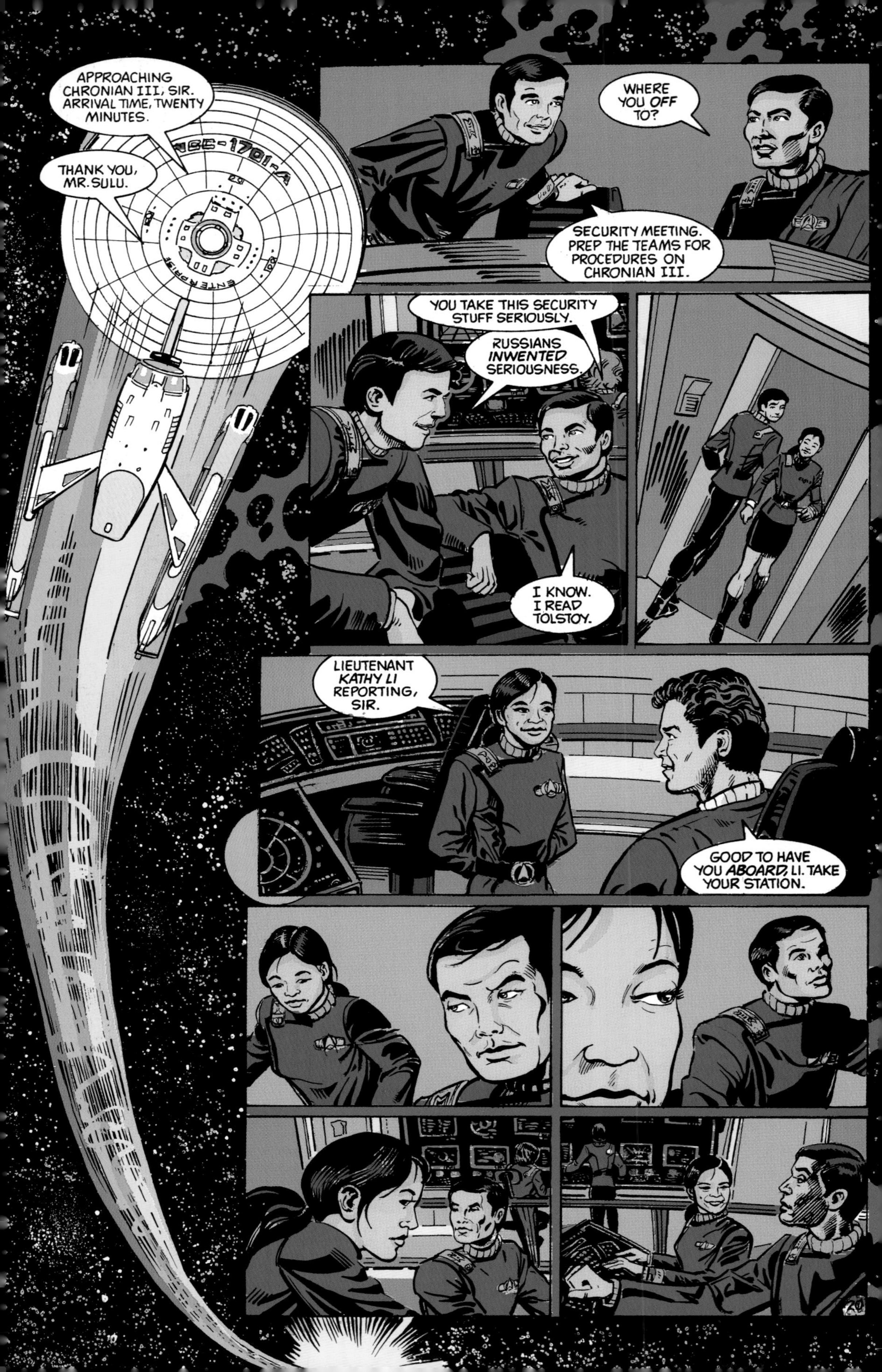
APPROACHING CHRONIAN III, SIR. ARRIVAL TIME, TWENTY MINUTES.
THANK YOU, MR. SULU.
NCC-1701-A
ENTERPRISE
WHERE YOU OFF TO?
SECURITY MEETING. PREP THE TEAMS FOR PROCEDURES ON CHRONIAN III.
YOU TAKE THIS SECURITY STUFF SERIOUSLY.
RUSSIANS INWENTED SERIOUSNESS.
I KNOW. I READ TOLSTOY.
LIEUTENANT KATHY LI REPORTING, SIR.
GOOD TO HAVE YOU ABOARD, LI. TAKE YOUR STATION.
20

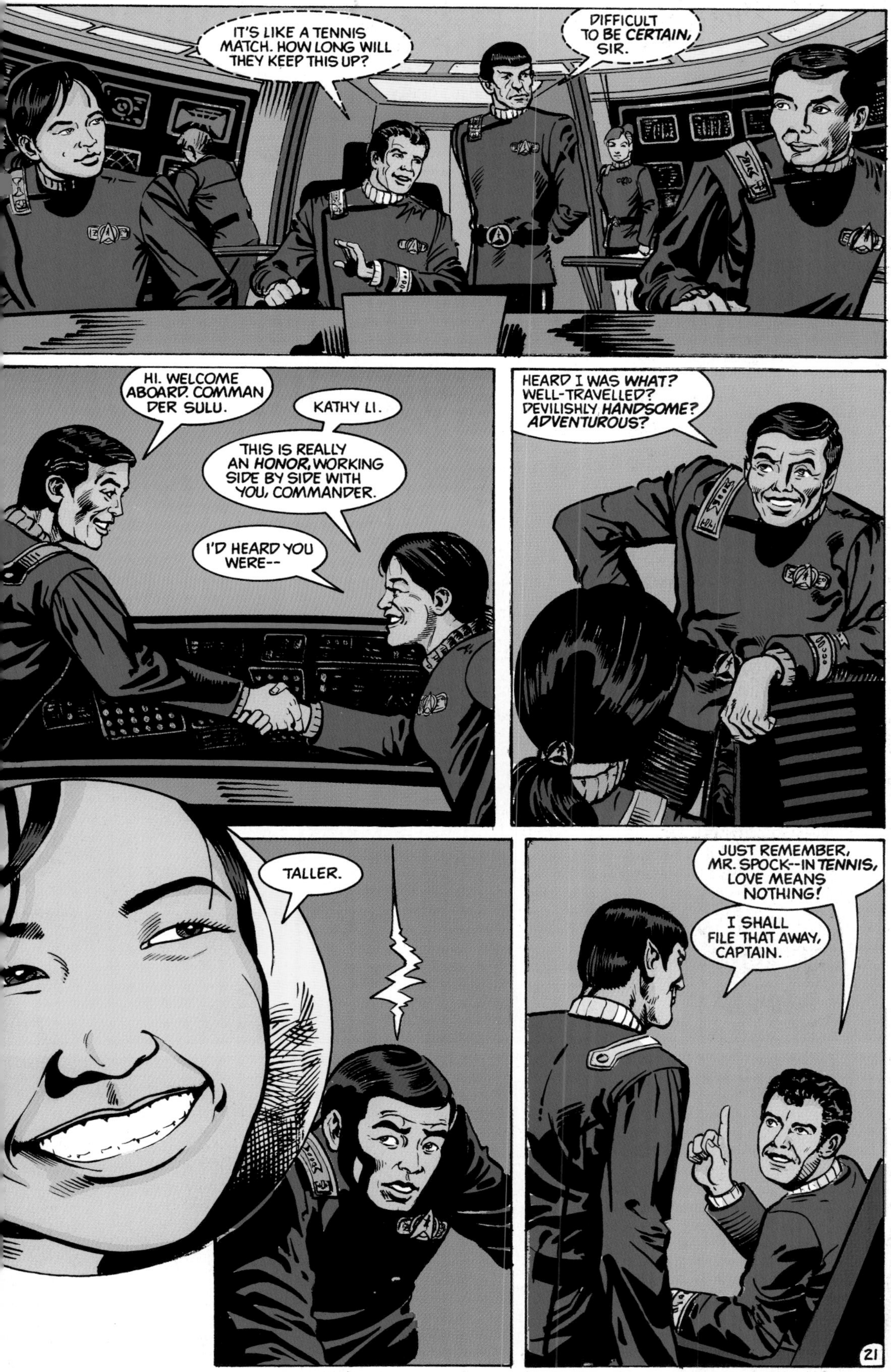
IT'S LIKE A TENNIS MATCH. HOW LONG WILL THEY KEEP THIS UP?
DIFFICULT TO BE CERTAIN, SIR.
HI. WELCOME ABOARD. COMMAN DER SULU.
KATHY LI.
THIS IS REALLY AN HONOR, WORKING SIDE BY SIDE WITH YOU, COMMANDER.
I'D HEARD YOU WERE--
HEARD I WAS WHAT? WELL-TRAVELLED? DEVILISHLY HANDSOME? ADVENTUROUS?
TALLER.
JUST REMEMBER, MR. SPOCK--IN TENNIS, LOVE MEANS NOTHING!
I SHALL FILE THAT AWAY, CAPTAIN.
21

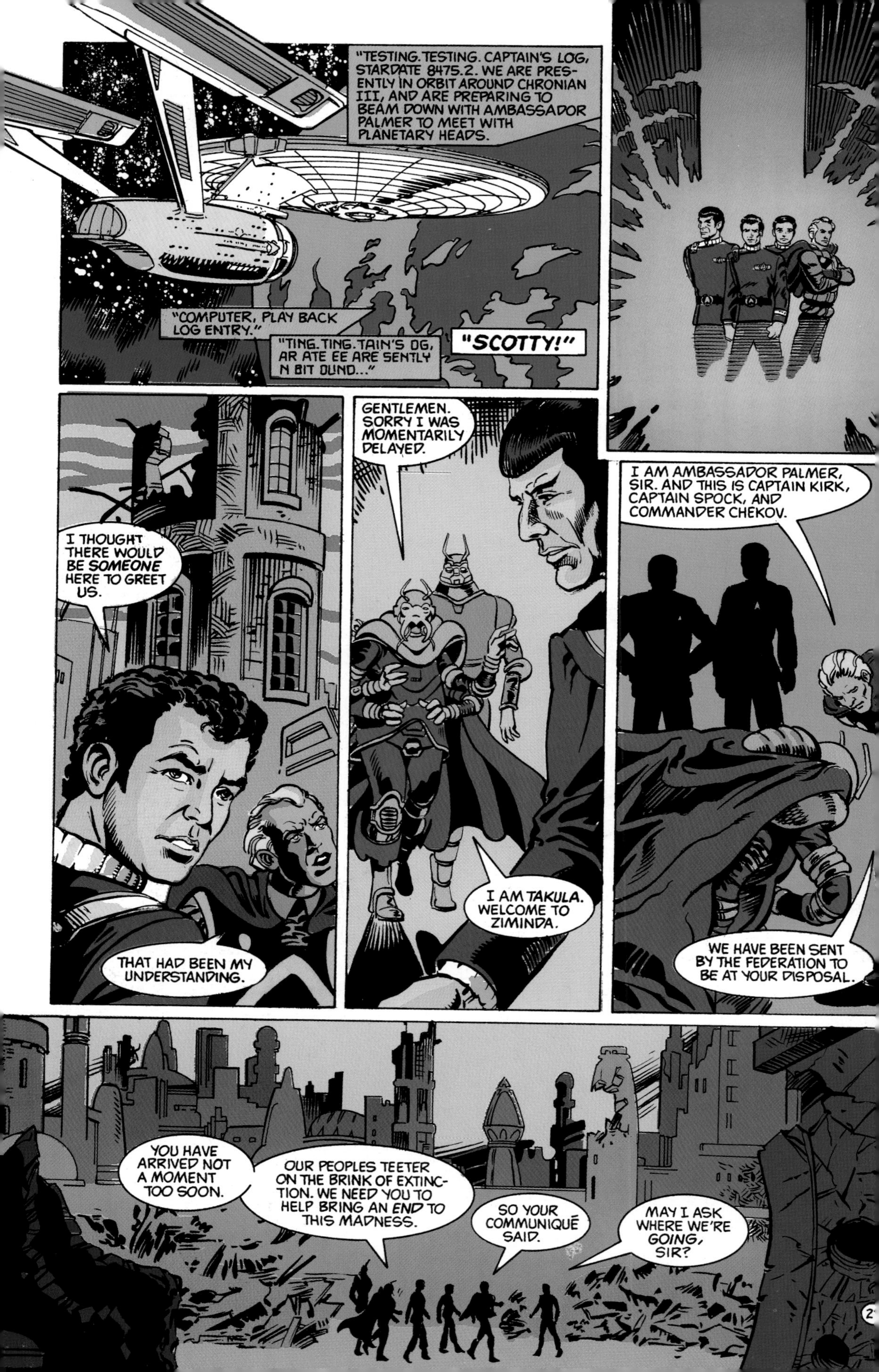
"TESTING. TESTING. CAPTAIN'S LOG, STARDATE 8475.2. WE ARE PRESENTLY IN ORBIT AROUND CHRONIAN III, AND ARE PREPARING TO BEAM DOWN WITH AMBASSADOR PALMER TO MEET WITH PLANETARY HEADS.
"COMPUTER, PLAY BACK LOG ENTRY."
"TING. TING. TAIN'S OG, AR ATE EE ARE SENTLY N BIT OUND..."
"SCOTTY!"
I THOUGHT THERE WOULD BE SOMEONE HERE TO GREET US.
THAT HAD BEEN MY UNDERSTANDING.
GENTLEMEN. SORRY I WAS MOMENTARILY DELAYED.
I AM TAKULA. WELCOME TO ZIMINDA.
I AM AMBASSADOR PALMER, SIR. AND THIS IS CAPTAIN KIRK, CAPTAIN SPOCK, AND COMMANDER CHEKOV.
WE HAVE BEEN SENT BY THE FEDERATION TO BE AT YOUR DISPOSAL.
YOU HAVE ARRIVED NOT A MOMENT TOO SOON.
OUR PEOPLES TEETER ON THE BRINK OF EXTINCTION. WE NEED YOU TO HELP BRING AN END TO THIS MADNESS.
SO YOUR COMMUNIQUÉ SAID.
MAY I ASK WHERE WE'RE GOING, SIR?

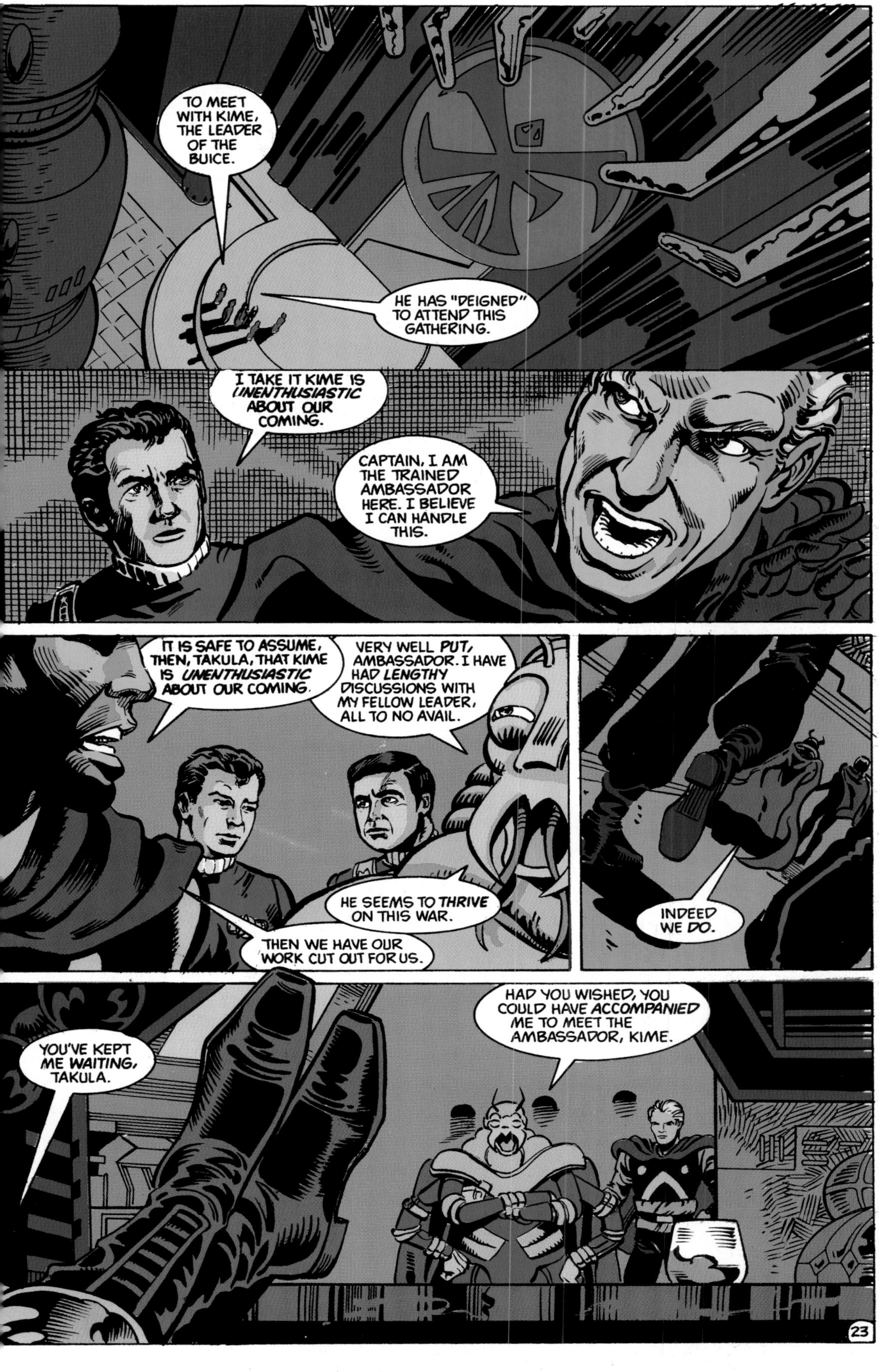
TO MEET WITH KIME, THE LEADER OF THE BUICE.
HE HAS "DEIGNED" TO ATTEND THIS GATHERING.
I TAKE IT KIME IS UNENTHUSIASTIC ABOUT OUR COMING.
CAPTAIN, I AM THE TRAINED AMBASSADOR HERE. I BELIEVE I CAN HANDLE THIS.
IT IS SAFE TO ASSUME, THEN, TAKULA, THAT KIME IS UNENTHUSIASTIC ABOUT OUR COMING.
VERY WELL PUT, AMBASSADOR. I HAVE HAD LENGTHY DISCUSSIONS WITH MY FELLOW LEADER, ALL TO NO AVAIL.
HE SEEMS TO THRIVE ON THIS WAR.
THEN WE HAVE OUR WORK CUT OUT FOR US.
INDEED WE DO.
YOU'VE KEPT ME WAITING, TAKULA.
HAD YOU WISHED, YOU COULD HAVE ACCOMPANIED ME TO MEET THE AMBASSADOR, KIME.

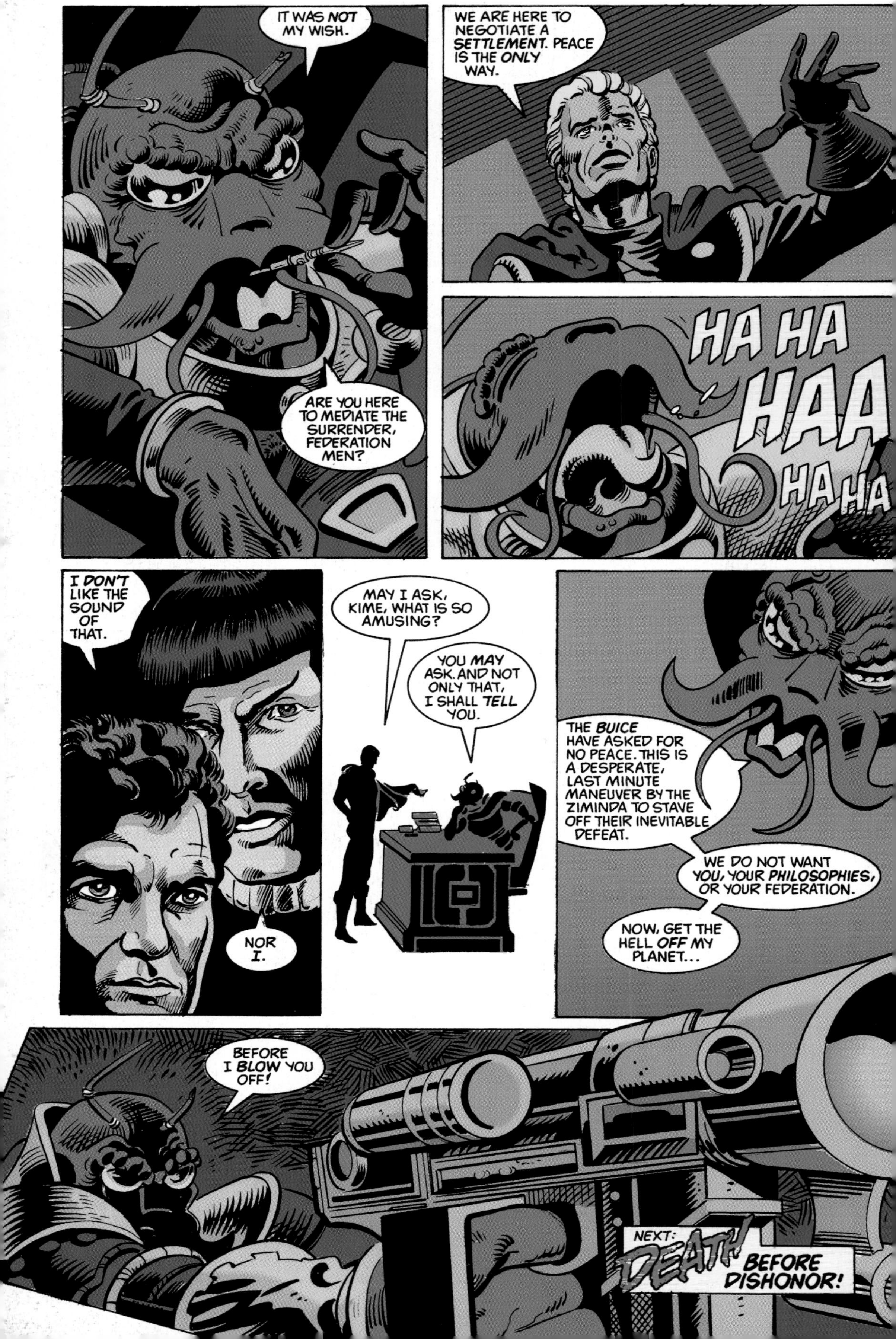
IT WAS NOT MY WISH.
ARE YOU HERE TO MEDIATE THE SURRENDER, FEDERATION MEN?
WE ARE HERE TO NEGOTIATE A SETTLEMENT. PEACE IS THE ONLY WAY.
HA HA HAA HA HA
I DON'T LIKE THE SOUND OF THAT.
NOR I.
MAY I ASK, KIME, WHAT IS SO AMUSING?
YOU MAY ASK. AND NOT ONLY THAT, I SHALL TELL YOU.
THE BUICE HAVE ASKED FOR NO PEACE. THIS IS A DESPERATE, LAST MINUTE MANEUVER BY THE ZIMINDA TO STAVE OFF THEIR INEVITABLE DEFEAT.
WE DO NOT WANT YOU, YOUR PHILOSOPHIES, OR YOUR FEDERATION.
NOW, GET THE HELL OFF MY PLANET...
BEFORE I BLOW YOU OFF!
NEXT: DEATH BEFORE DISHONOR!

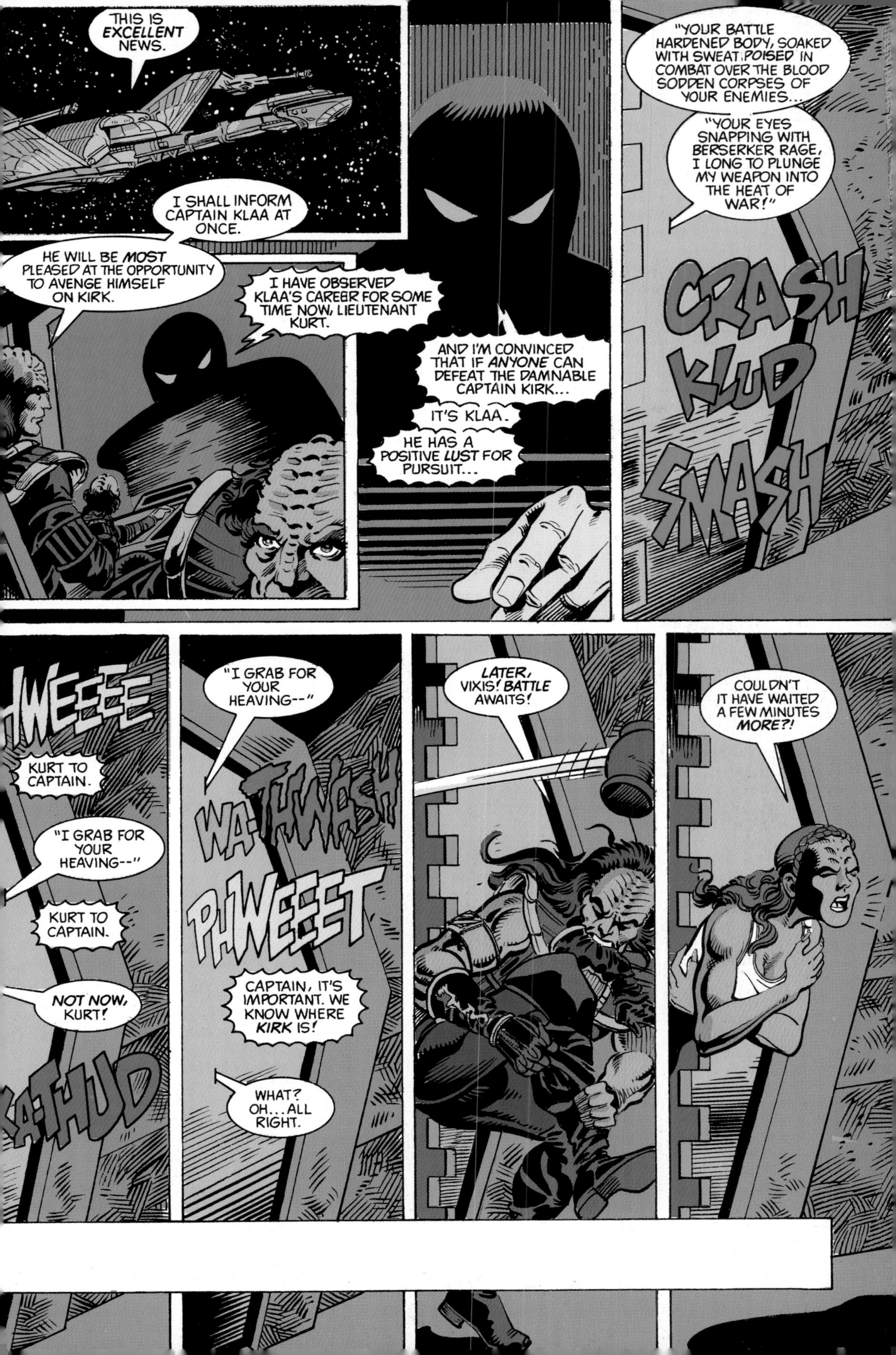

THIS IS EXCELLENT NEWS.
I SHALL INFORM CAPTAIN KLAA AT ONCE.
HE WILL BE MOST PLEASED AT THE OPPORTUNITY TO AVENGE HIMSELF ON KIRK.
I HAVE OBSERVED KLAA'S CAREER FOR SOME TIME NOW, LIEUTENANT KURT.
AND I'M CONVINCED THAT IF ANYONE CAN DEFEAT THE DAMNABLE CAPTAIN KIRK...
IT'S KLAA.
HE HAS A POSITIVE LUST FOR PURSUIT...
"YOUR BATTLE HARDENED BODY, SOAKED WITH SWEAT, POISED IN COMBAT OVER THE BLOOD SODDEN CORPSES OF YOUR ENEMIES...
"YOUR EYES SNAPPING WITH BERSERKER RAGE, I LONG TO PLUNGE MY WEAPON INTO THE HEAT OF WAR!"
CRASH
KLUD
SMASH
HWEEEE
KURT TO CAPTAIN.
"I GRAB FOR YOUR HEAVING--"
KURT TO CAPTAIN.
NOT NOW, KURT!
A-THUD
"I GRAB FOR YOUR HEAVING--"
WA-THWASH
PHWEEET
CAPTAIN, IT'S IMPORTANT. WE KNOW WHERE KIRK IS!
WHAT? OH...ALL RIGHT.
LATER, VIXIS! BATTLE AWAITS!
COULDN'T IT HAVE WAITED A FEW MINUTES MORE?!

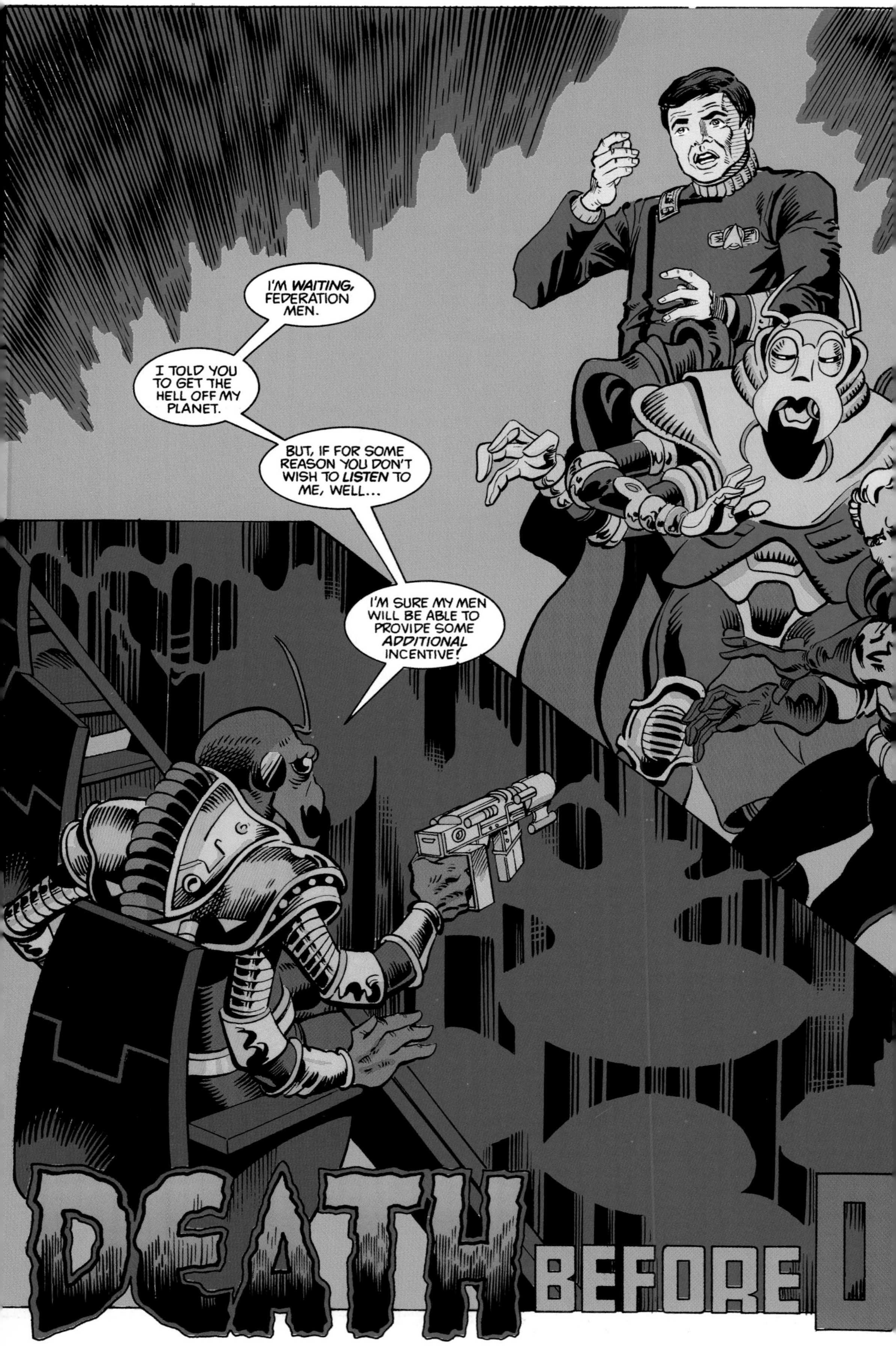
I'M WAITING, FEDERATION MEN.
I TOLD YOU TO GET THE HELL OFF MY PLANET.
BUT, IF FOR SOME REASON YOU DON'T WISH TO LISTEN TO ME, WELL...
I'M SURE MY MEN WILL BE ABLE TO PROVIDE SOME ADDITIONAL INCENTIVE!
DEATH BEFORE

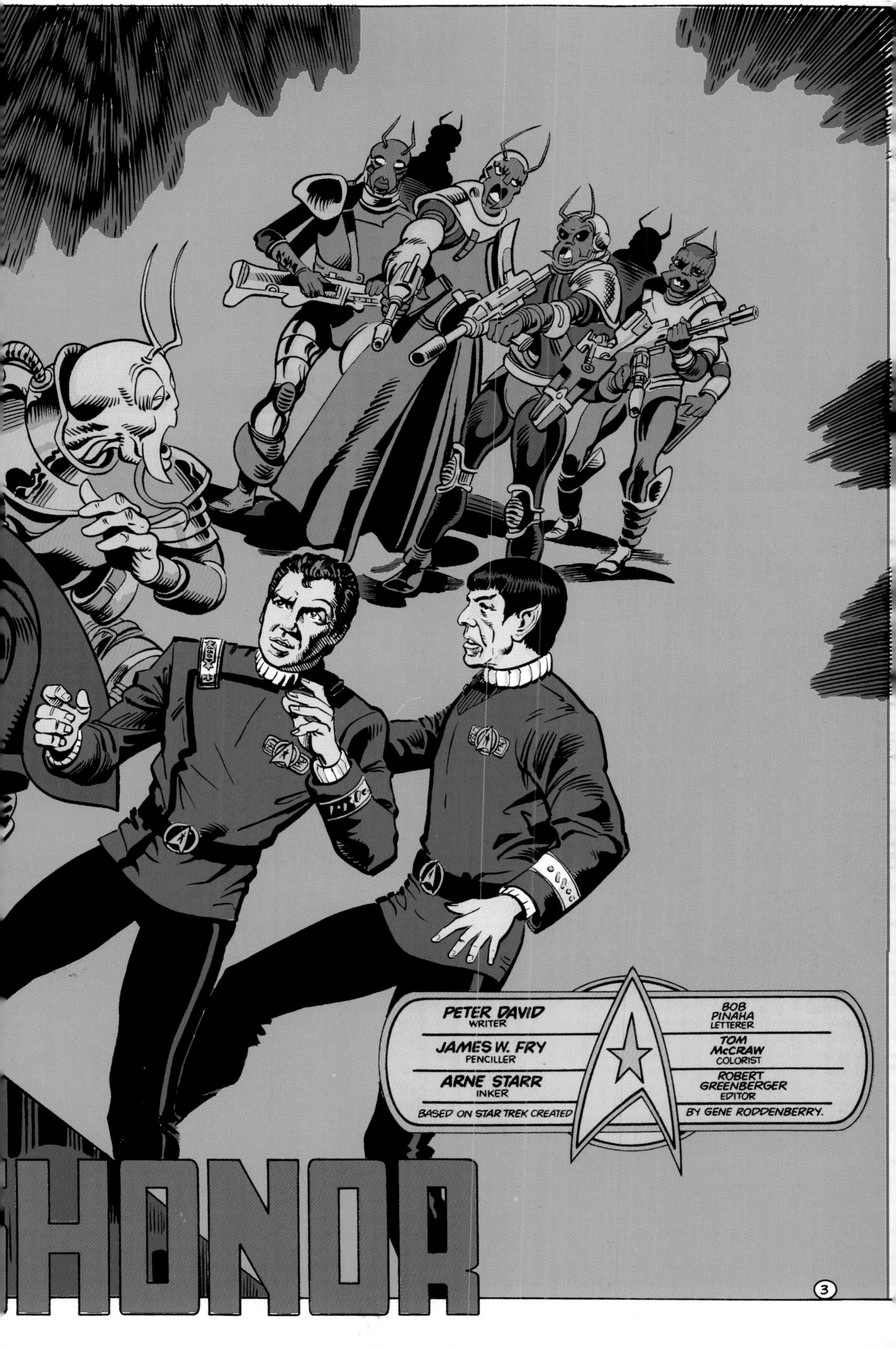
PETER DAVID
WRITER
JAMES W. FRY
PENCILLER
ARNE STARR
INKER
BOB PINAHA
LETTERER
TOM McCRAW
COLORIST
ROBERT GREENBERGER
EDITOR
BASED ON STAR TREK CREATED BY GENE RODDENBERRY.
HONOR

DAMN YOU, KIME! THIS IS SUPPOSED TO BE A *PEACEFUL* MEETING!

WHAT ARE THESE ARMED BULLIES OF YOURS *DOING* HERE?

IF I WEREN'T INTENDING THIS AS PEACE, MY MEN WOULD HAVE REDUCED YOU TO *JELLY* BY NOW.

BELAY IT, CHEKOV.

THIS IS A *DANGEROUS* SITUATION, KEPTIN.

BEING THE *FIRST* TO FIRE *WON'T* HELP.

THESE REPRESENTATIVES OF THE FEDERATION ARE HERE TO HELP US.

I'VE SOUGHT THEIR AID TO AVOID FURTHER POINTLESS WAR BETWEEN OUR PEOPLES.

IF *THAT* IS YOUR ONLY CONCERN, THE ANSWER IS SIMPLE.

SURRENDER. TOTALLY...

...AND UNCONDITIONALLY.

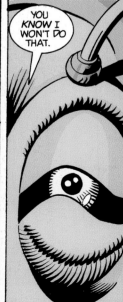

YOU *KNOW* I WON'T DO THAT.

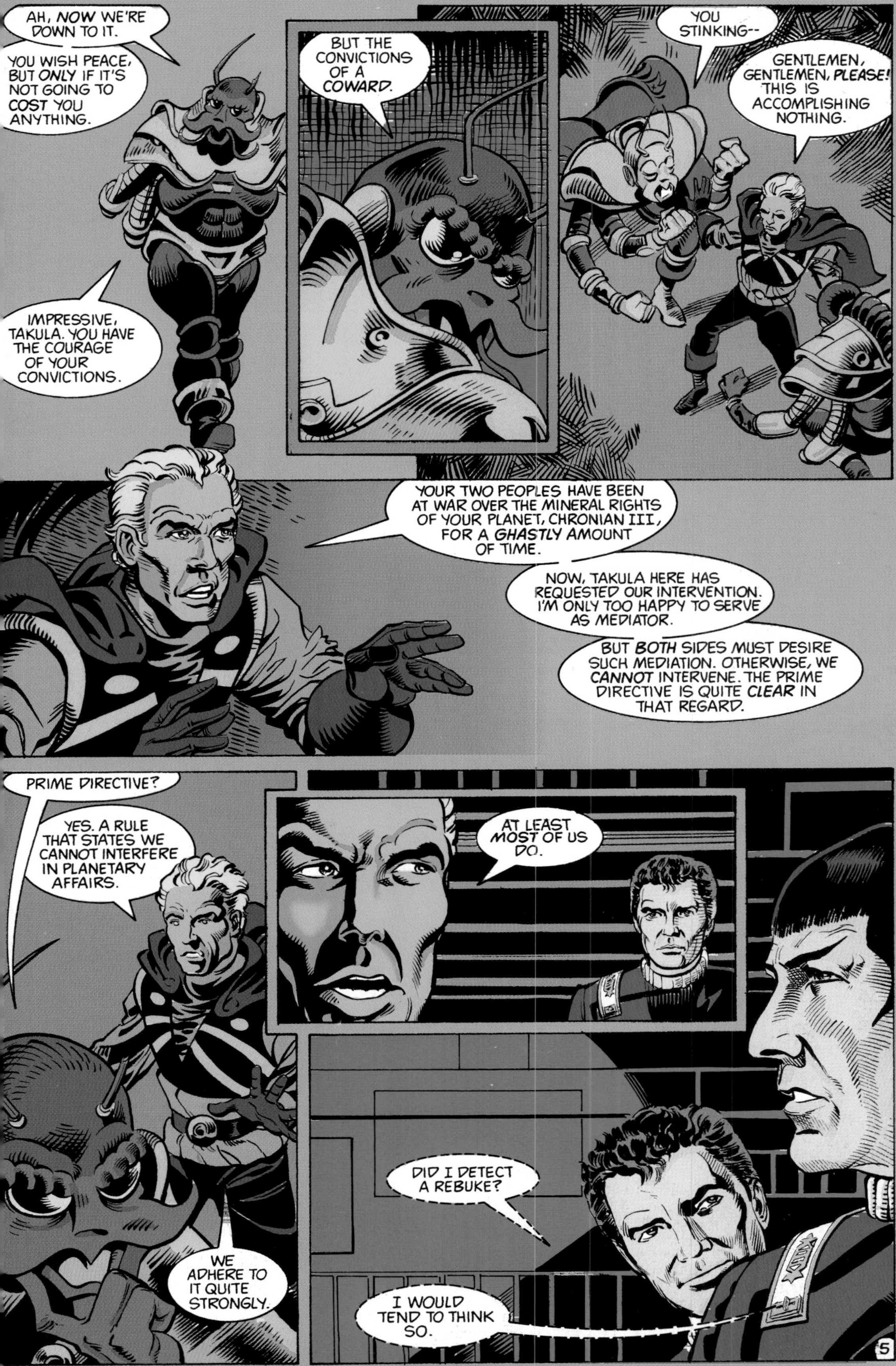
AH, NOW WE'RE DOWN TO IT.
YOU WISH PEACE, BUT ONLY IF IT'S NOT GOING TO COST YOU ANYTHING.
IMPRESSIVE, TAKULA. YOU HAVE THE COURAGE OF YOUR CONVICTIONS.
BUT THE CONVICTIONS OF A COWARD.
YOU STINKING--
GENTLEMEN, GENTLEMEN, PLEASE! THIS IS ACCOMPLISHING NOTHING.
YOUR TWO PEOPLES HAVE BEEN AT WAR OVER THE MINERAL RIGHTS OF YOUR PLANET, CHRONIAN III, FOR A GHASTLY AMOUNT OF TIME.
NOW, TAKULA HERE HAS REQUESTED OUR INTERVENTION. I'M ONLY TOO HAPPY TO SERVE AS MEDIATOR.
BUT BOTH SIDES MUST DESIRE SUCH MEDIATION. OTHERWISE, WE CANNOT INTERVENE. THE PRIME DIRECTIVE IS QUITE CLEAR IN THAT REGARD.
PRIME DIRECTIVE?
YES. A RULE THAT STATES WE CANNOT INTERFERE IN PLANETARY AFFAIRS.
WE ADHERE TO IT QUITE STRONGLY.
AT LEAST MOST OF US DO.
DID I DETECT A REBUKE?
I WOULD TEND TO THINK SO.
5

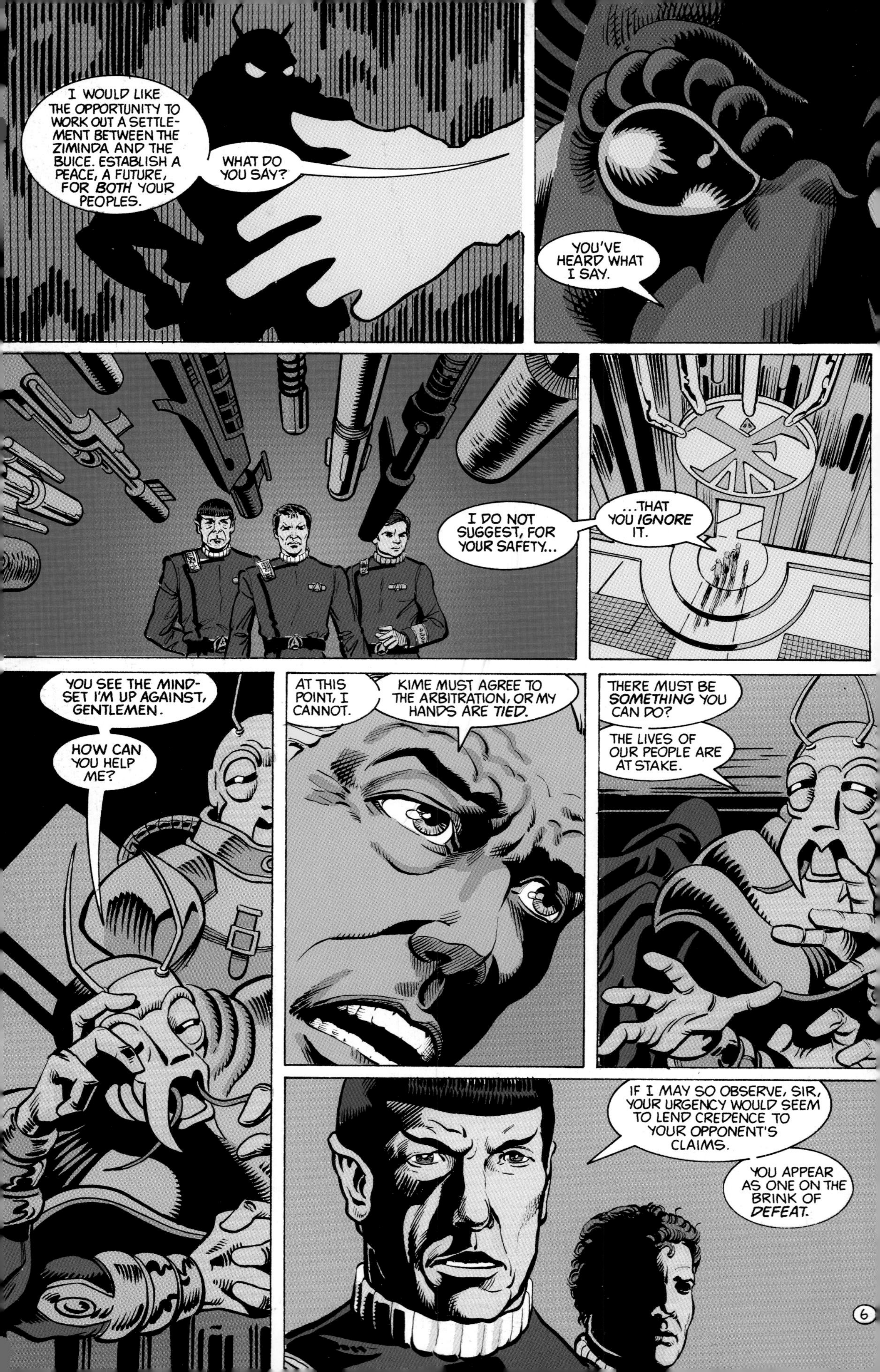
I WOULD LIKE THE OPPORTUNITY TO WORK OUT A SETTLE-MENT BETWEEN THE ZIMINDA AND THE BUICE. ESTABLISH A PEACE, A FUTURE, FOR BOTH YOUR PEOPLES.
WHAT DO YOU SAY?
YOU'VE HEARD WHAT I SAY.
I DO NOT SUGGEST, FOR YOUR SAFETY...
...THAT YOU IGNORE IT.
YOU SEE THE MIND-SET I'M UP AGAINST, GENTLEMEN.
HOW CAN YOU HELP ME?
AT THIS POINT, I CANNOT.
KIME MUST AGREE TO THE ARBITRATION, OR MY HANDS ARE TIED.
THERE MUST BE SOMETHING YOU CAN DO?
THE LIVES OF OUR PEOPLE ARE AT STAKE.
IF I MAY SO OBSERVE, SIR, YOUR URGENCY WOULD SEEM TO LEND CREDENCE TO YOUR OPPONENT'S CLAIMS.
YOU APPEAR AS ONE ON THE BRINK OF DEFEAT.

NO, MR. SPOCK IS QUITE CORRECT. WE ARE *INDEED* ON THE BRINK OF DEFEAT.

WHEN YOU'VE BEEN WITH HIM AS LONG AS I HAVE, YOU LEARN *NOT* TO SET YOURSELF UP.

MR. SPOCK, YOU ARE SPEAKING ON MATTERS THAT YOU HAVE NO KNOWLEDGE OF.

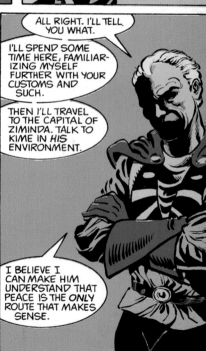

INDEED, IT HAS TAKEN THE CAPTAIN *MANY* OCCASIONS TO FULLY REALIZE THE--

THANK YOU, SPOCK. AMBASSADOR PALMER GETS MY DRIFT.

WHO KNOWS? IF IT *WERE* THE BUICE STARING INTO THE ABYSS OF EXTINCTION, IT MIGHT BE KIME ASKING FOR HELP AND I *MYSELF* MIGHT BE THE HARDLINER.

AS IT IS... IT IS I WHO ASK FOR YOUR HELP.

ALL RIGHT. I'LL TELL YOU WHAT.

I'LL SPEND SOME TIME HERE, FAMILIARIZING MYSELF FURTHER WITH YOUR CUSTOMS AND SUCH.

THEN I'LL TRAVEL TO THE CAPITAL OF ZIMINDA. TALK TO KIME IN *HIS* ENVIRONMENT.

I BELIEVE I CAN MAKE HIM UNDERSTAND THAT PEACE IS THE *ONLY* ROUTE THAT MAKES SENSE.

I WON'T BE NEEDING YOU MEN FOR A WHILE. YOU CAN RETURN TO YOUR SHIP.

7

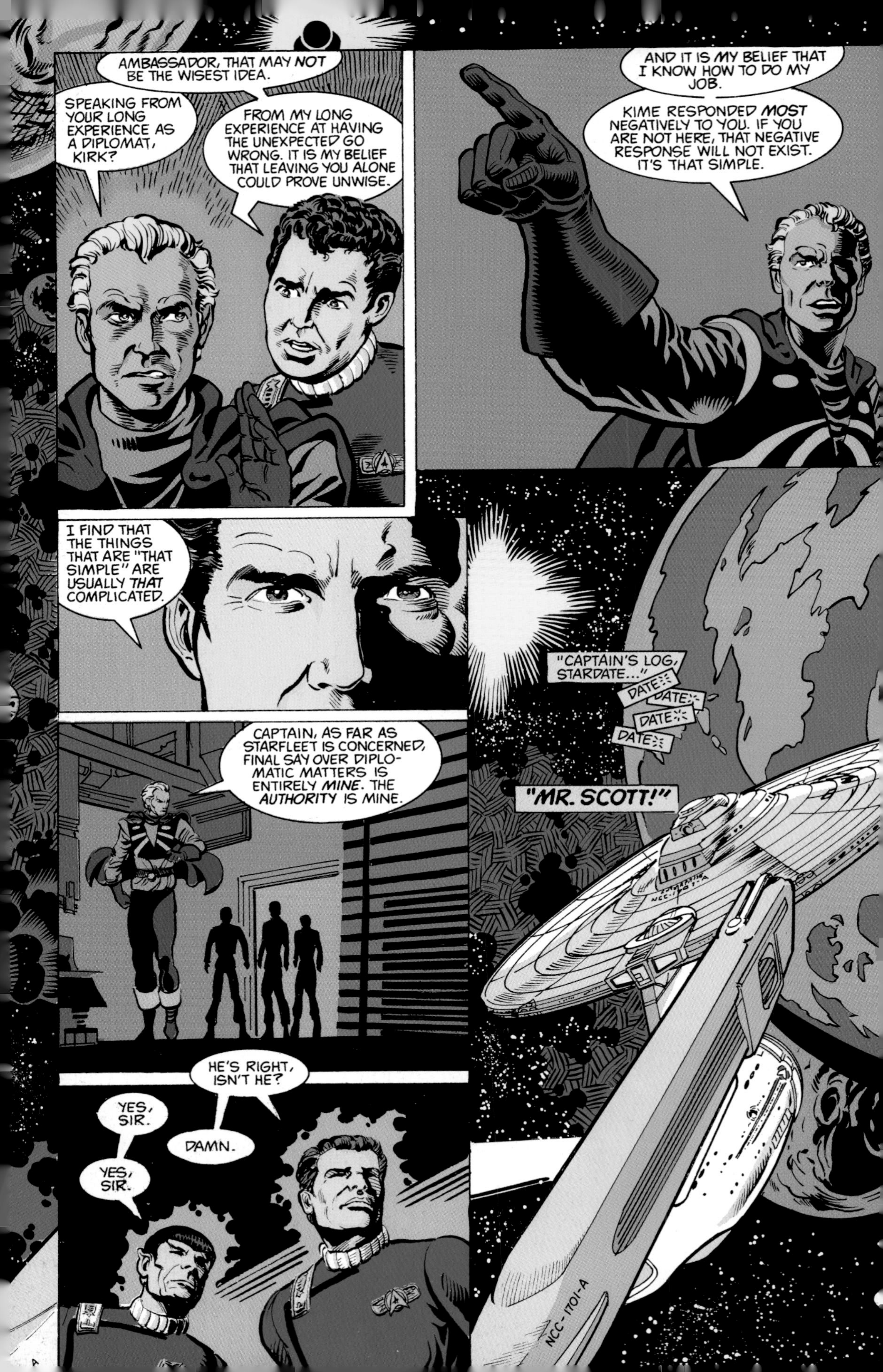
AMBASSADOR, THAT MAY NOT BE THE WISEST IDEA.
SPEAKING FROM YOUR LONG EXPERIENCE AS A DIPLOMAT, KIRK?
FROM MY LONG EXPERIENCE AT HAVING THE UNEXPECTED GO WRONG. IT IS MY BELIEF THAT LEAVING YOU ALONE COULD PROVE UNWISE.
AND IT IS MY BELIEF THAT I KNOW HOW TO DO MY JOB.
KIME RESPONDED MOST NEGATIVELY TO YOU. IF YOU ARE NOT HERE, THAT NEGATIVE RESPONSE WILL NOT EXIST. IT'S THAT SIMPLE.
I FIND THAT THE THINGS THAT ARE "THAT SIMPLE" ARE USUALLY THAT COMPLICATED.
CAPTAIN, AS FAR AS STARFLEET IS CONCERNED, FINAL SAY OVER DIPLOMATIC MATTERS IS ENTIRELY MINE. THE AUTHORITY IS MINE.
HE'S RIGHT, ISN'T HE?
YES, SIR.
DAMN.
YES, SIR.
"CAPTAIN'S LOG, STARDATE..."
DATE
DATE
DATE
DATE
"MR. SCOTT!"
NCC-1701-A

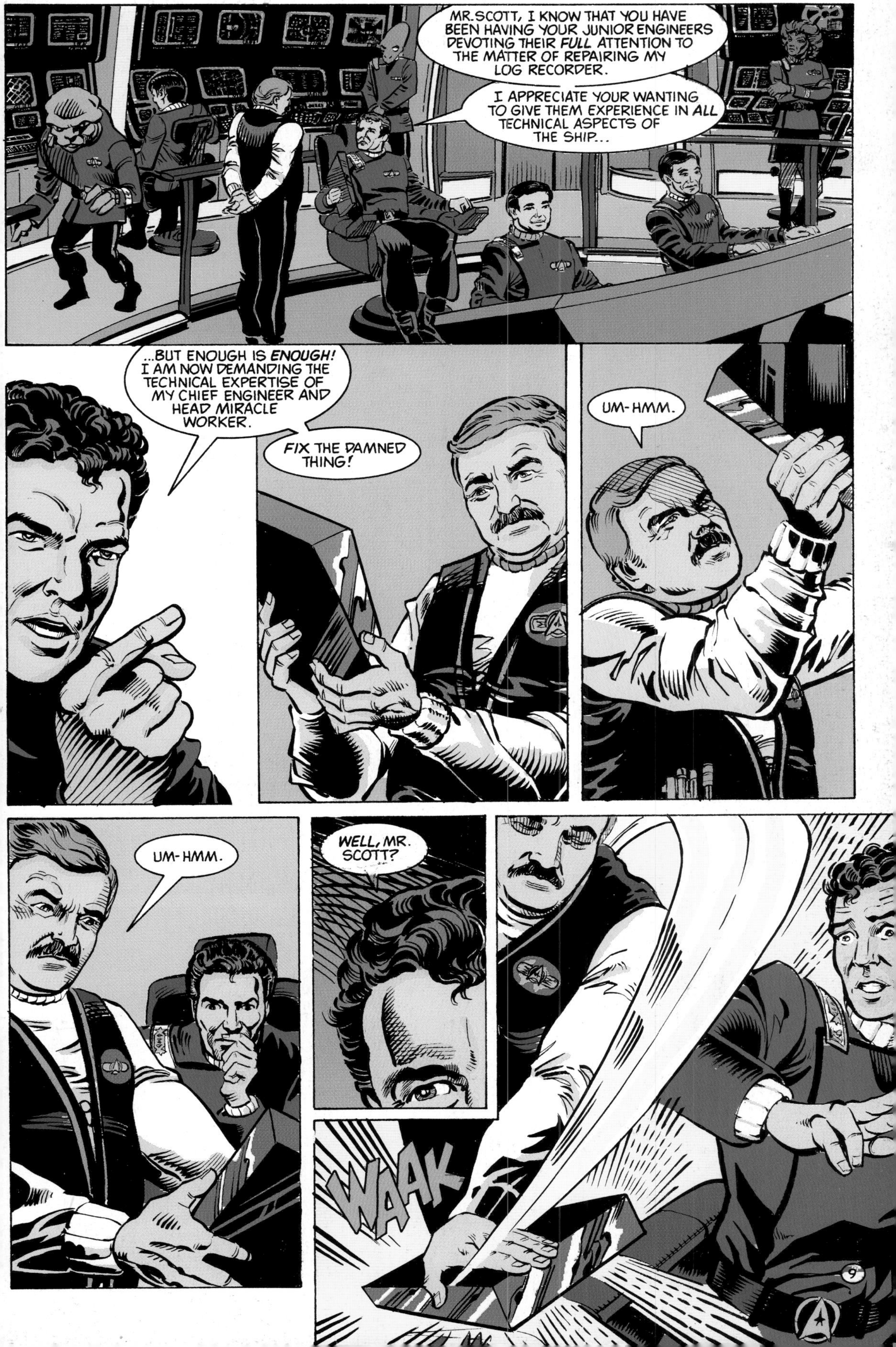
MR. SCOTT, I KNOW THAT YOU HAVE BEEN HAVING YOUR JUNIOR ENGINEERS DEVOTING THEIR FULL ATTENTION TO THE MATTER OF REPAIRING MY LOG RECORDER.
I APPRECIATE YOUR WANTING TO GIVE THEM EXPERIENCE IN ALL TECHNICAL ASPECTS OF THE SHIP...
...BUT ENOUGH IS ENOUGH! I AM NOW DEMANDING THE TECHNICAL EXPERTISE OF MY CHIEF ENGINEER AND HEAD MIRACLE WORKER.
FIX THE DAMNED THING!
UM-HMM.
UM-HMM.
WELL, MR. SCOTT?
WAAK

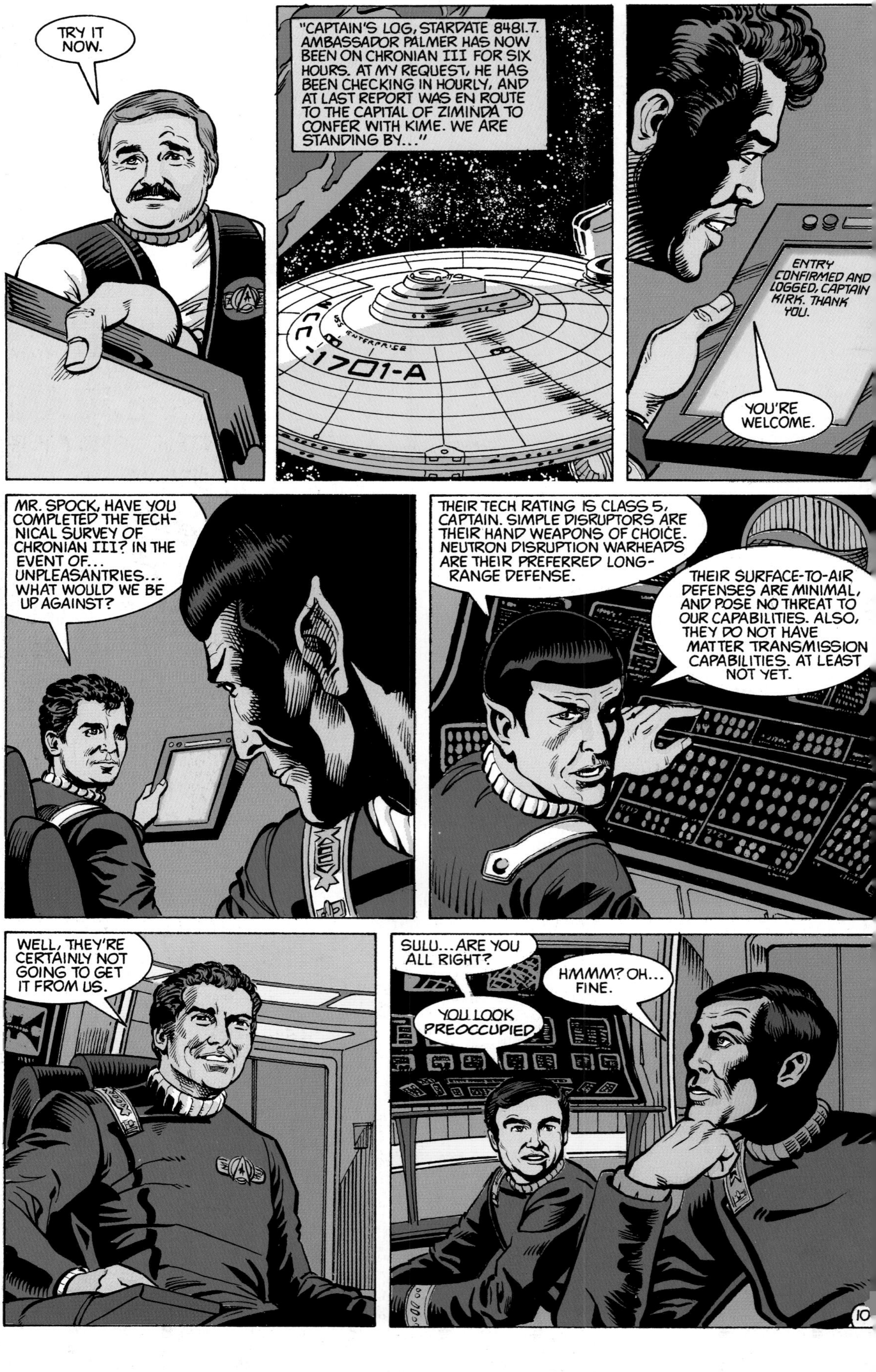

TRY IT NOW.
"CAPTAIN'S LOG, STARDATE 8481.7. AMBASSADOR PALMER HAS NOW BEEN ON CHRONIAN III FOR SIX HOURS. AT MY REQUEST, HE HAS BEEN CHECKING IN HOURLY, AND AT LAST REPORT WAS EN ROUTE TO THE CAPITAL OF ZIMINDA TO CONFER WITH KIME. WE ARE STANDING BY..."
NCC-1701-A
USS ENTERPRISE
ENTRY CONFIRMED AND LOGGED, CAPTAIN KIRK. THANK YOU.
YOU'RE WELCOME.
MR. SPOCK, HAVE YOU COMPLETED THE TECHNICAL SURVEY OF CHRONIAN III? IN THE EVENT OF... UNPLEASANTRIES... WHAT WOULD WE BE UP AGAINST?
THEIR TECH RATING IS CLASS 5, CAPTAIN. SIMPLE DISRUPTORS ARE THEIR HAND WEAPONS OF CHOICE. NEUTRON DISRUPTION WARHEADS ARE THEIR PREFERRED LONG-RANGE DEFENSE.
THEIR SURFACE-TO-AIR DEFENSES ARE MINIMAL, AND POSE NO THREAT TO OUR CAPABILITIES. ALSO, THEY DO NOT HAVE MATTER TRANSMISSION CAPABILITIES. AT LEAST NOT YET.
WELL, THEY'RE CERTAINLY NOT GOING TO GET IT FROM US.
SULU... ARE YOU ALL RIGHT?
YOU LOOK PREOCCUPIED.
HMMM? OH... FINE.
10

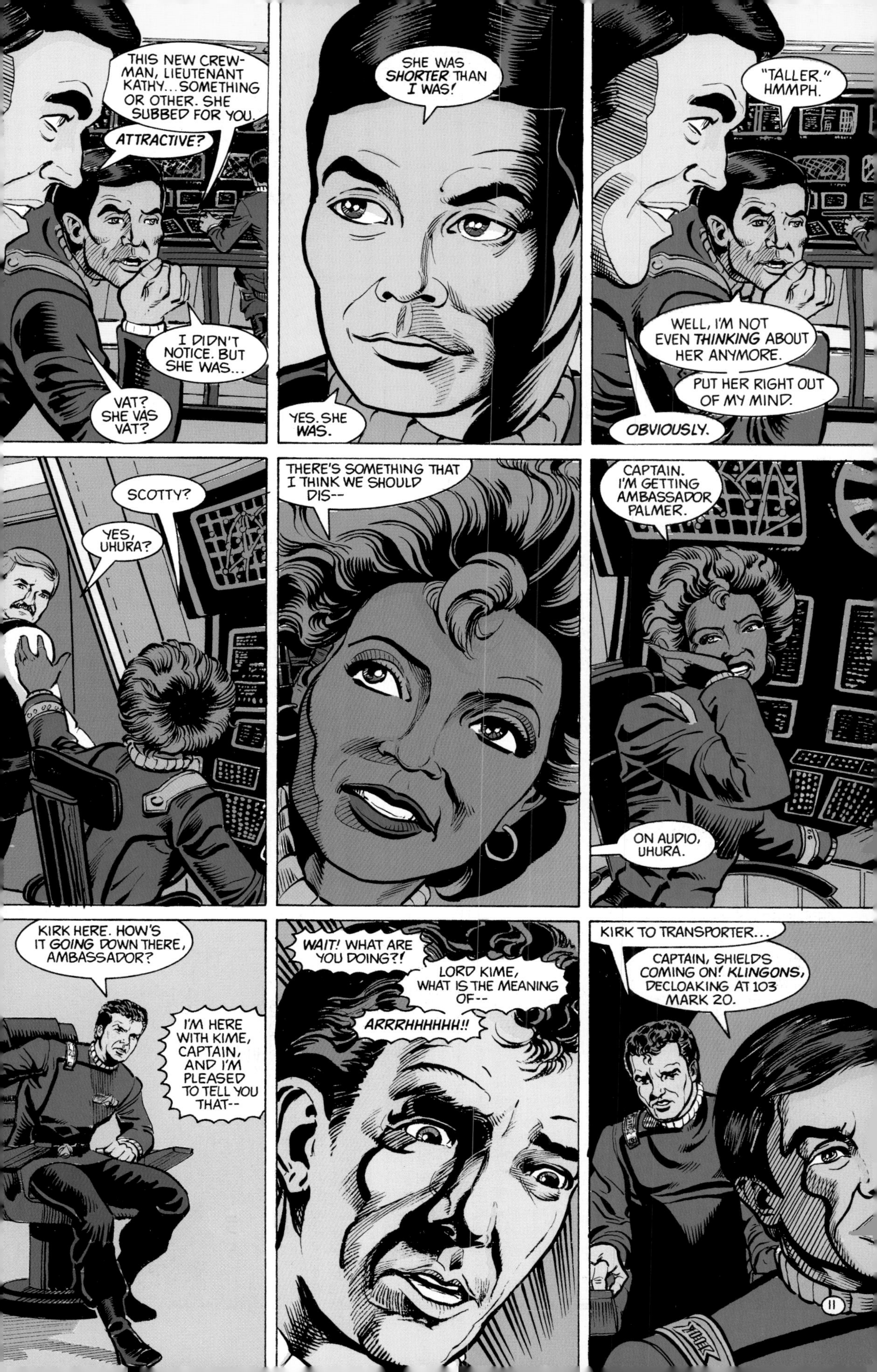
THIS NEW CREW-MAN, LIEUTENANT KATHY... SOMETHING OR OTHER. SHE SUBBED FOR YOU.
ATTRACTIVE?
I DIDN'T NOTICE. BUT SHE WAS...
VAT? SHE VAS VAT?
SHE WAS SHORTER THAN I WAS!
YES. SHE WAS.
"TALLER." HMMPH.
WELL, I'M NOT EVEN THINKING ABOUT HER ANYMORE.
PUT HER RIGHT OUT OF MY MIND.
OBVIOUSLY.
SCOTTY?
YES, UHURA?
THERE'S SOMETHING THAT I THINK WE SHOULD DIS--
CAPTAIN. I'M GETTING AMBASSADOR PALMER.
ON AUDIO, UHURA.
KIRK HERE. HOW'S IT GOING DOWN THERE, AMBASSADOR?
I'M HERE WITH KIME, CAPTAIN, AND I'M PLEASED TO TELL YOU THAT--
WAIT! WHAT ARE YOU DOING?!
LORD KIME, WHAT IS THE MEANING OF--
ARRRHHHHHH!!
KIRK TO TRANSPORTER...
CAPTAIN, SHIELDS COMING ON! KLINGONS, DECLOAKING AT 103 MARK 20.
11

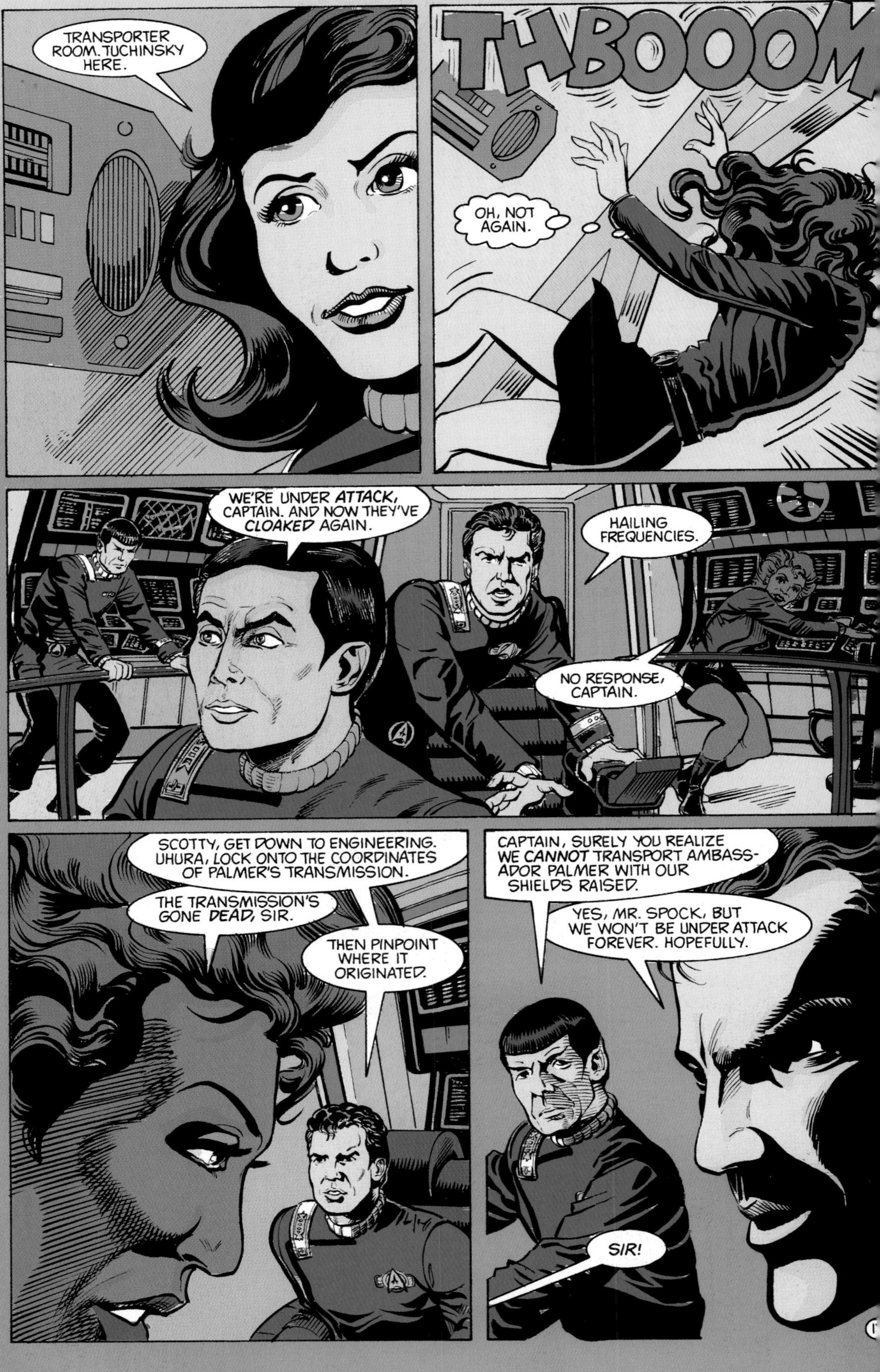
TRANSPORTER ROOM. TUCHINSKY HERE.
THBOOOM
OH, NOT AGAIN.
WE'RE UNDER ATTACK, CAPTAIN. AND NOW THEY'VE CLOAKED AGAIN.
HAILING FREQUENCIES.
NO RESPONSE, CAPTAIN.
SCOTTY, GET DOWN TO ENGINEERING. UHURA, LOCK ONTO THE COORDINATES OF PALMER'S TRANSMISSION.
THE TRANSMISSION'S GONE DEAD, SIR.
THEN PINPOINT WHERE IT ORIGINATED.
CAPTAIN, SURELY YOU REALIZE WE CANNOT TRANSPORT AMBASS-ADOR PALMER WITH OUR SHIELDS RAISED.
YES, MR. SPOCK, BUT WE WON'T BE UNDER ATTACK FOREVER. HOPEFULLY.
SIR!

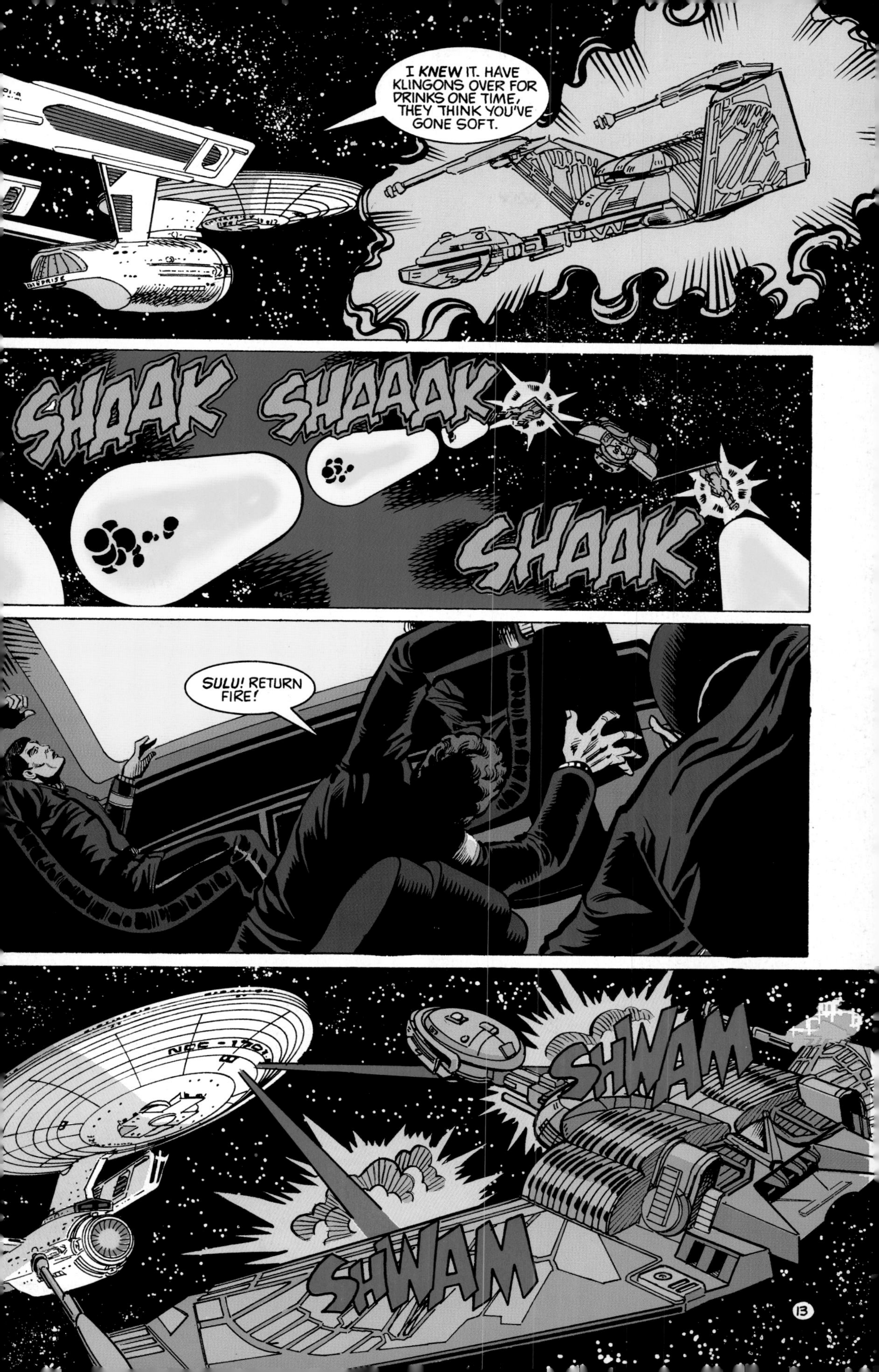
I KNEW IT. HAVE KLINGONS OVER FOR DRINKS ONE TIME, THEY THINK YOU'VE GONE SOFT.
SHAAK
SHAAAK
SHAAK
SULU! RETURN FIRE!
SHWAM
SHWAM

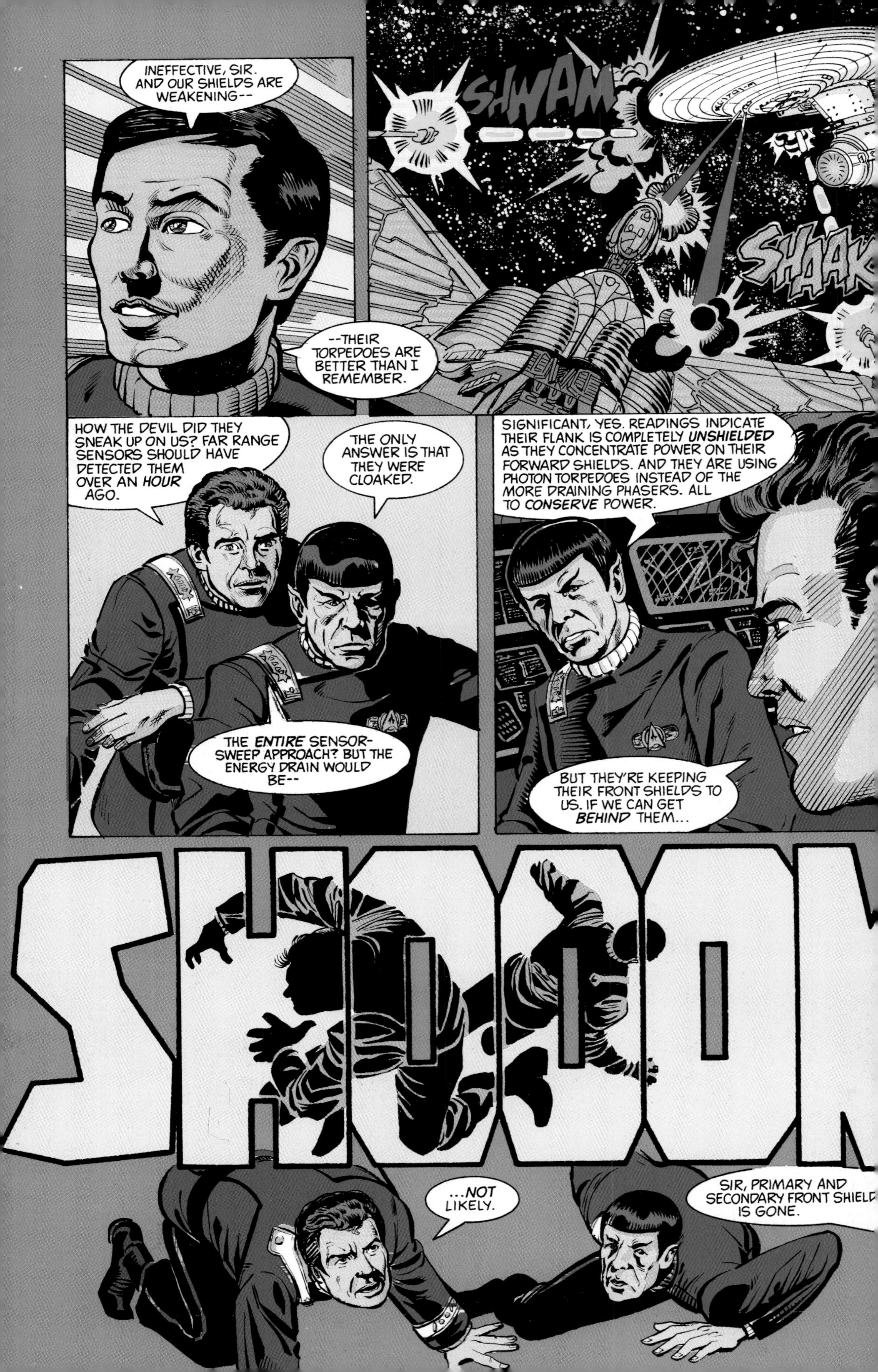

INEFFECTIVE, SIR. AND OUR SHIELDS ARE WEAKENING--
SHWAM
SHAAK
--THEIR TORPEDOES ARE BETTER THAN I REMEMBER.
HOW THE DEVIL DID THEY SNEAK UP ON US? FAR RANGE SENSORS SHOULD HAVE DETECTED THEM OVER AN HOUR AGO.
THE ONLY ANSWER IS THAT THEY WERE CLOAKED.
THE ENTIRE SENSOR-SWEEP APPROACH? BUT THE ENERGY DRAIN WOULD BE--
SIGNIFICANT, YES. READINGS INDICATE THEIR FLANK IS COMPLETELY UNSHIELDED AS THEY CONCENTRATE POWER ON THEIR FORWARD SHIELDS. AND THEY ARE USING PHOTON TORPEDOES INSTEAD OF THE MORE DRAINING PHASERS. ALL TO CONSERVE POWER.
BUT THEY'RE KEEPING THEIR FRONT SHIELDS TO US. IF WE CAN GET BEHIND THEM...
...NOT LIKELY.
SIR, PRIMARY AND SECONDARY FRONT SHIELD IS GONE.

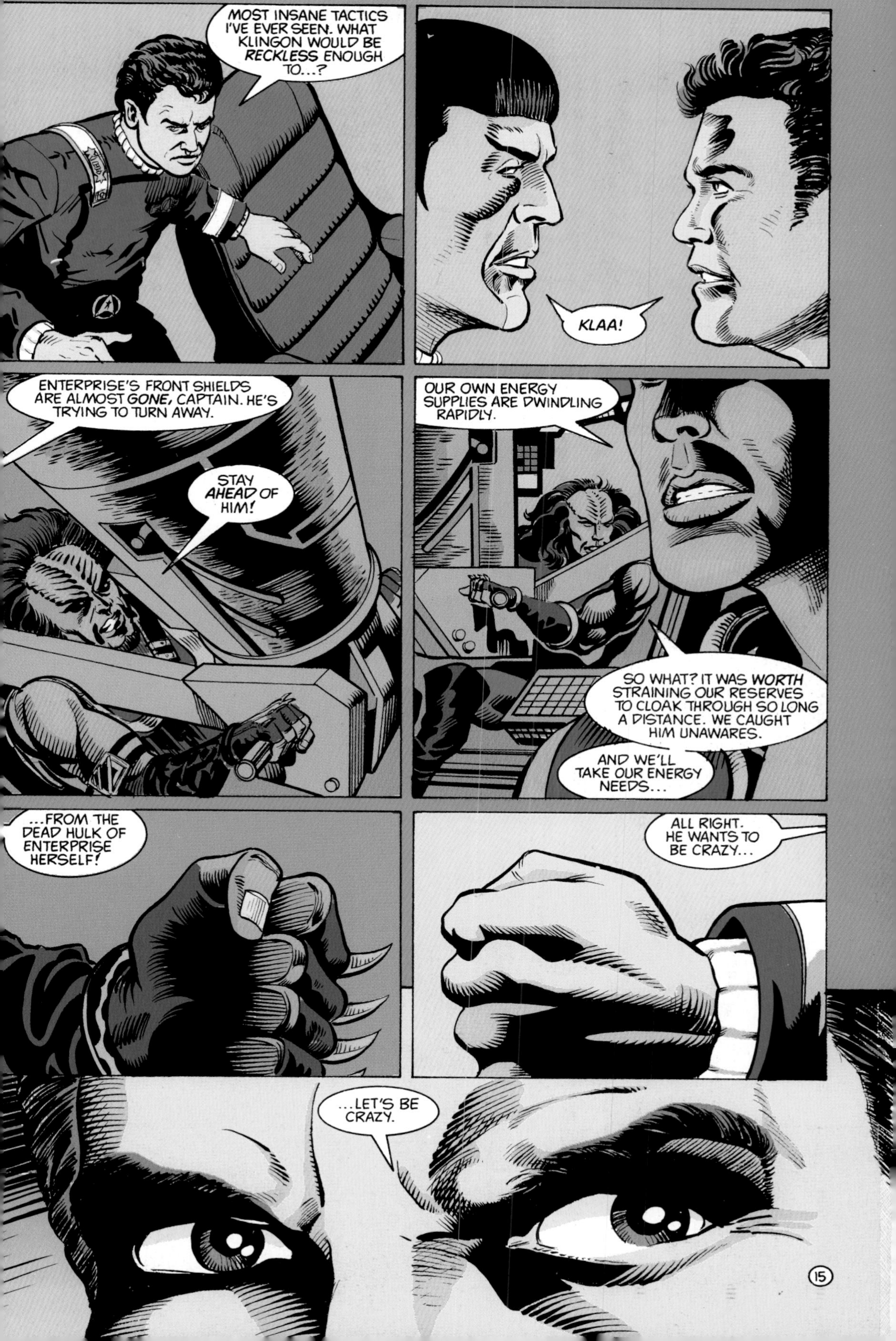

MOST INSANE TACTICS I'VE EVER SEEN. WHAT KLINGON WOULD BE RECKLESS ENOUGH TO...?
KLAA!
ENTERPRISE'S FRONT SHIELDS ARE ALMOST GONE, CAPTAIN. HE'S TRYING TO TURN AWAY.
STAY AHEAD OF HIM!
OUR OWN ENERGY SUPPLIES ARE DWINDLING RAPIDLY.
SO WHAT? IT WAS WORTH STRAINING OUR RESERVES TO CLOAK THROUGH SO LONG A DISTANCE. WE CAUGHT HIM UNAWARES.
AND WE'LL TAKE OUR ENERGY NEEDS...
...FROM THE DEAD HULK OF ENTERPRISE HERSELF!
ALL RIGHT. HE WANTS TO BE CRAZY...
...LET'S BE CRAZY.

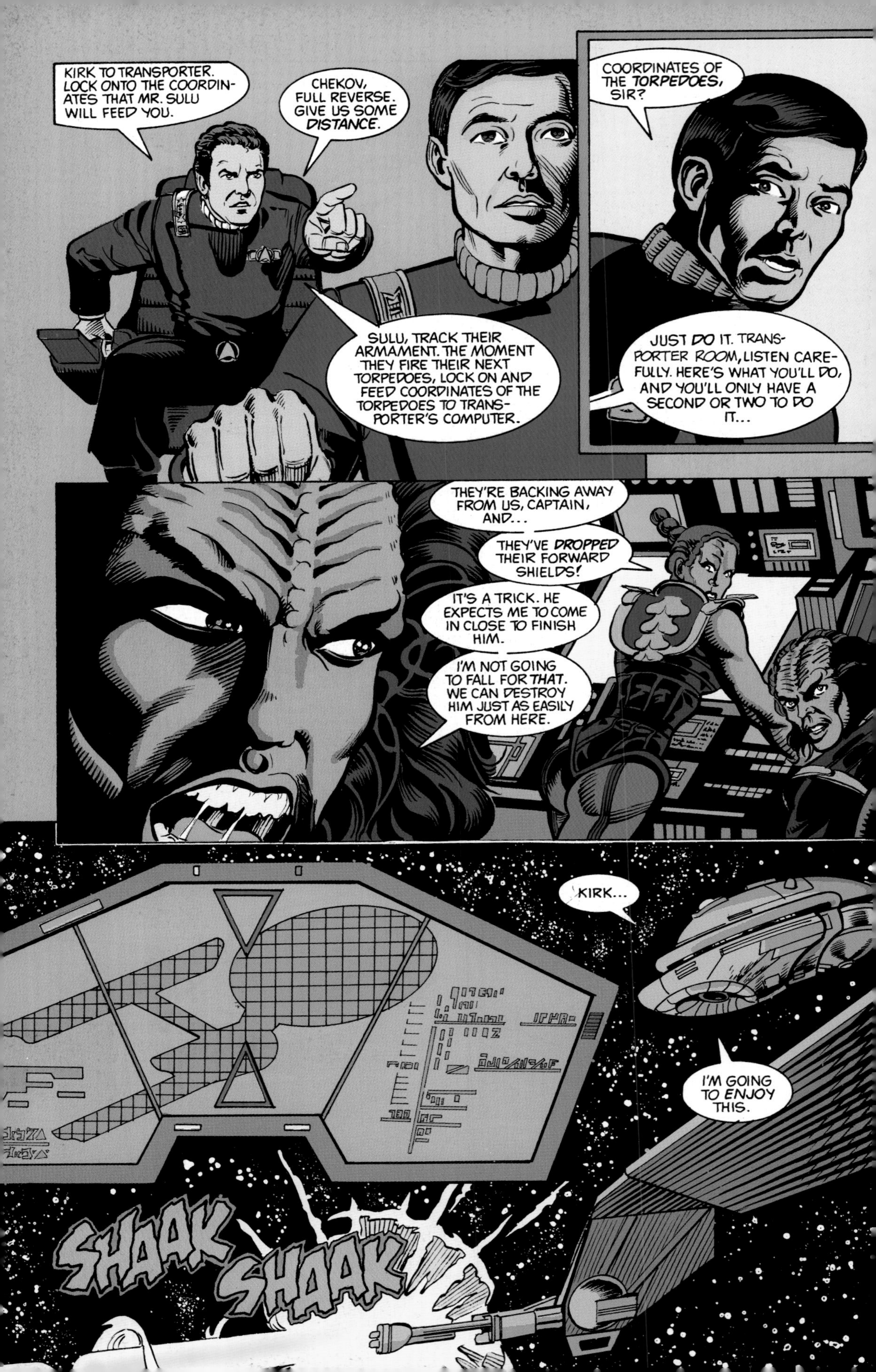
KIRK TO TRANSPORTER. LOCK ONTO THE COORDINATES THAT MR. SULU WILL FEED YOU.
CHEKOV, FULL REVERSE. GIVE US SOME *DISTANCE*.
SULU, TRACK THEIR ARMAMENT. THE MOMENT THEY FIRE THEIR NEXT TORPEDOES, LOCK ON AND FEED COORDINATES OF THE TORPEDOES TO TRANSPORTER'S COMPUTER.
COORDINATES OF THE *TORPEDOES*, SIR?
JUST *DO* IT. TRANSPORTER *ROOM*, LISTEN CAREFULLY. HERE'S WHAT YOU'LL DO, AND YOU'LL ONLY HAVE A SECOND OR TWO TO DO IT...
THEY'RE BACKING AWAY FROM US, CAPTAIN, AND...
THEY'VE *DROPPED* THEIR FORWARD SHIELDS!
IT'S A TRICK. HE EXPECTS ME TO COME IN CLOSE TO FINISH HIM.
I'M NOT GOING TO FALL FOR *THAT*. WE CAN DESTROY HIM JUST AS EASILY FROM HERE.
KIRK...
I'M GOING TO *ENJOY* THIS.
SHAAK
SHAAK

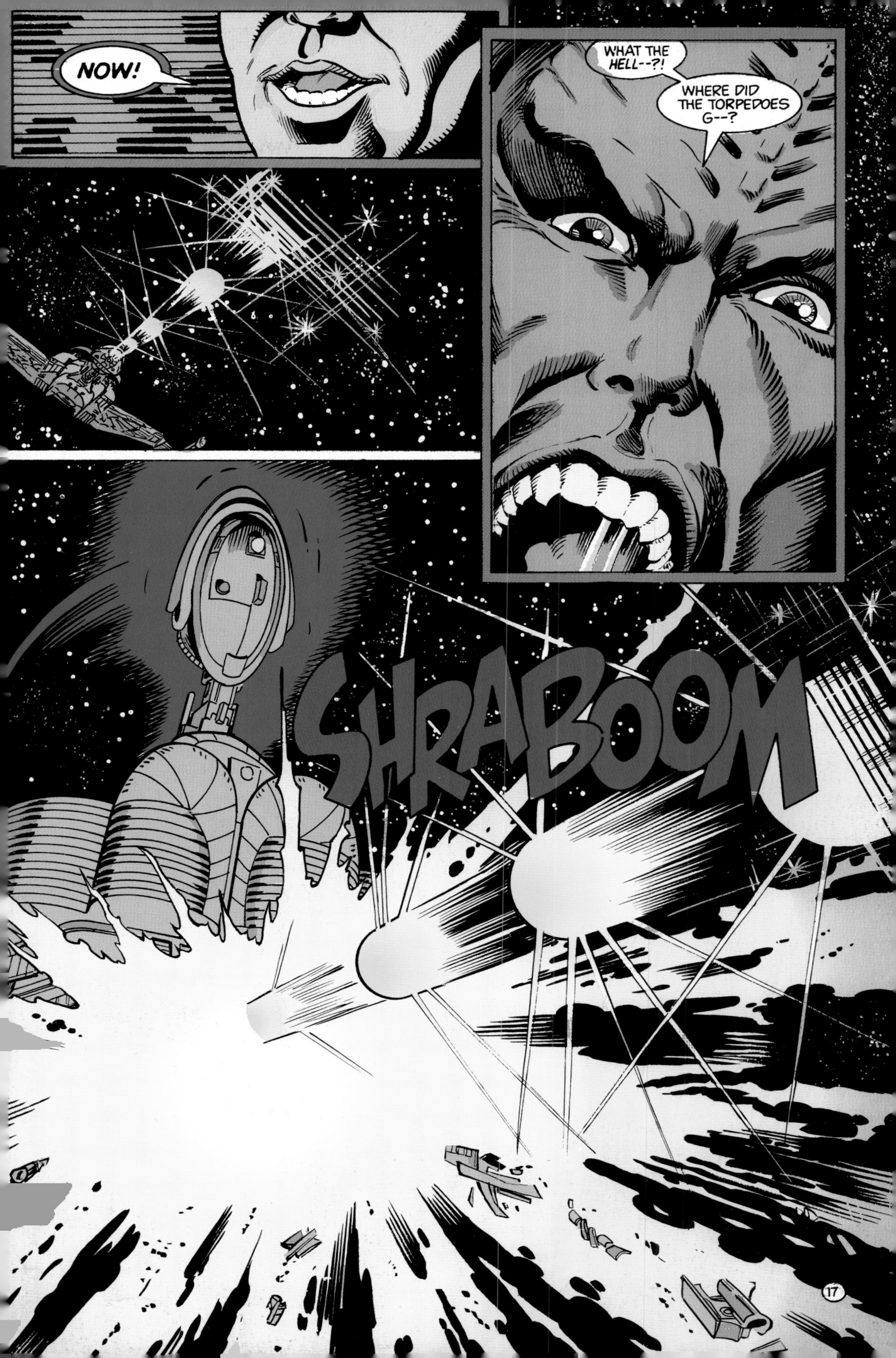
NOW!
WHAT THE HELL--?!
WHERE DID THE TORPEDOES G--?
SHRABOOM

I CAN'T BELIEVE IT WORKED.

MR. SULU, REMIND THEM WE'RE HERE.

SHRABOOM

SHRABOOM

MOVE OFF! ALL SPEED! GET US OUT OF HERE!!

UHURA, GET PALMER'S LAST COORDINATES TO THE TRANSPORTER ROOM AND HAVE HIM BEAMED UP FAST.

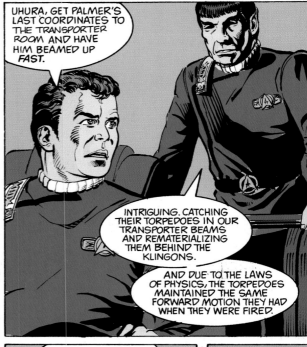

INTRIGUING. CATCHING THEIR TORPEDOES IN OUR TRANSPORTER BEAMS AND REMATERIALIZING THEM BEHIND THE KLINGONS.

AND DUE TO THE LAWS OF PHYSICS, THE TORPEDOES MAINTAINED THE SAME FORWARD MOTION THEY HAD WHEN THEY WERE FIRED.

WERE YOU CERTAIN IT WOULD WORK?

OF COURSE. DESPITE WHAT YOU MAY HAVE HEARD, MR. SPOCK...

I'VE STILL GOT IT.

WELL...

...THERE HAD BEEN RUMORS...

18

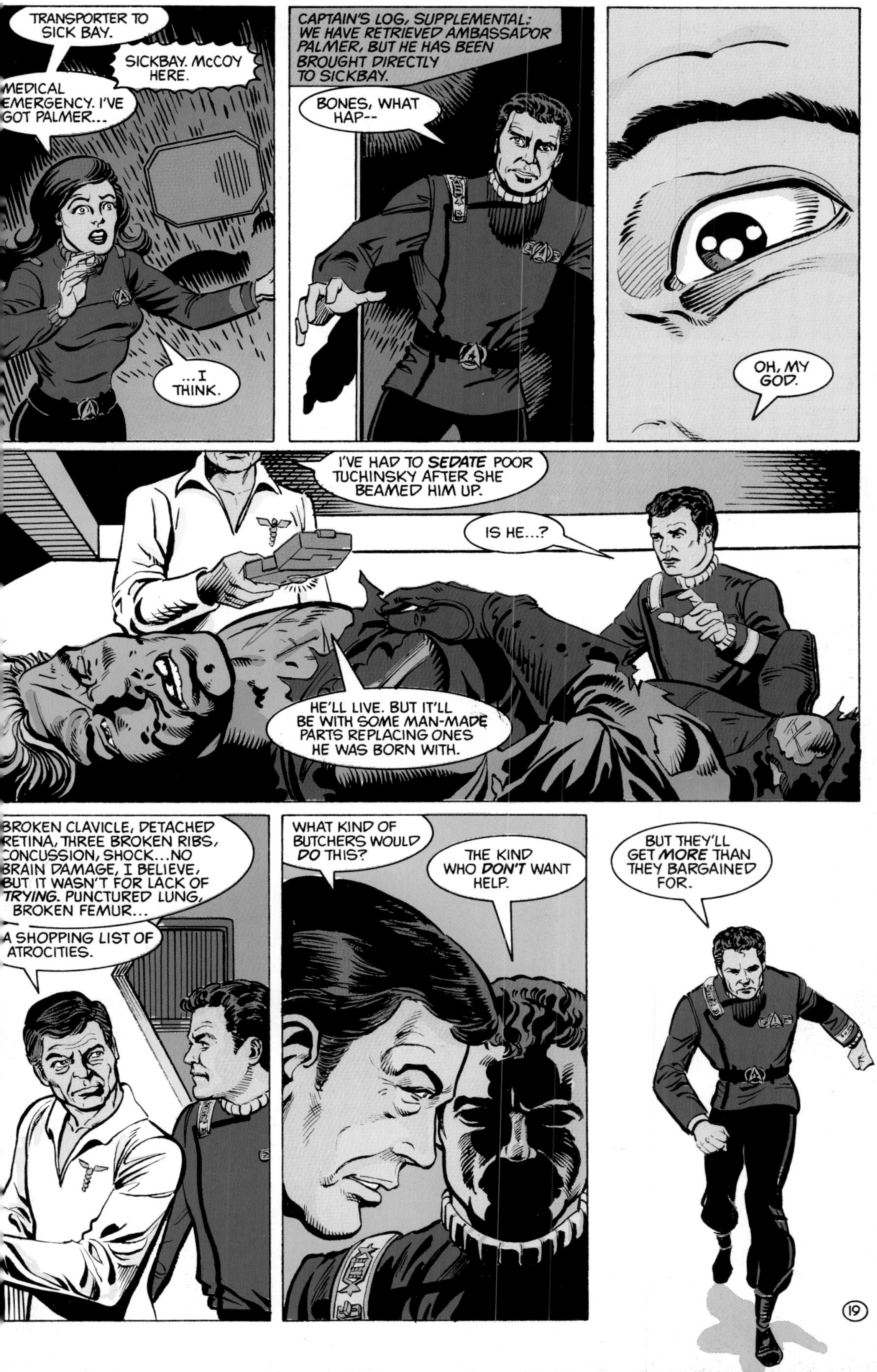

TRANSPORTER TO SICK BAY.
SICKBAY. McCOY HERE.
MEDICAL EMERGENCY. I'VE GOT PALMER...
...I THINK.
CAPTAIN'S LOG, SUPPLEMENTAL: WE HAVE RETRIEVED AMBASSADOR PALMER, BUT HE HAS BEEN BROUGHT DIRECTLY TO SICKBAY.
BONES, WHAT HAP--
OH, MY GOD.
I'VE HAD TO SEDATE POOR TUCHINSKY AFTER SHE BEAMED HIM UP.
IS HE...?
HE'LL LIVE. BUT IT'LL BE WITH SOME MAN-MADE PARTS REPLACING ONES HE WAS BORN WITH.
BROKEN CLAVICLE, DETACHED RETINA, THREE BROKEN RIBS, CONCUSSION, SHOCK...NO BRAIN DAMAGE, I BELIEVE, BUT IT WASN'T FOR LACK OF TRYING. PUNCTURED LUNG, BROKEN FEMUR...
A SHOPPING LIST OF ATROCITIES.
WHAT KIND OF BUTCHERS WOULD DO THIS?
THE KIND WHO DON'T WANT HELP.
BUT THEY'LL GET MORE THAN THEY BARGAINED FOR.

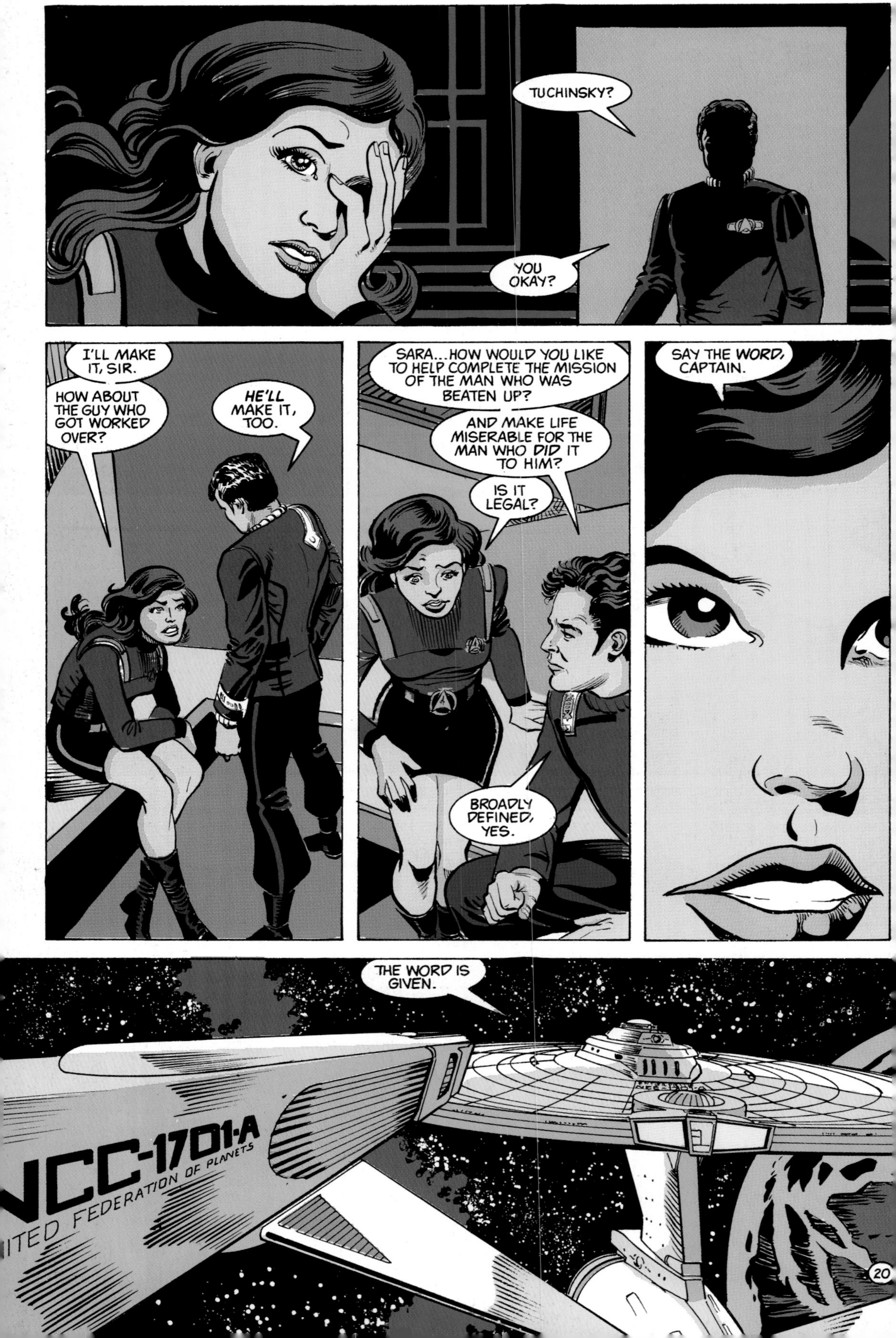
TUCHINSKY?
YOU OKAY?
I'LL MAKE IT, SIR.
HOW ABOUT THE GUY WHO GOT WORKED OVER?
HE'LL MAKE IT, TOO.
SARA...HOW WOULD YOU LIKE TO HELP COMPLETE THE MISSION OF THE MAN WHO WAS BEATEN UP?
AND MAKE LIFE MISERABLE FOR THE MAN WHO DID IT TO HIM?
IS IT LEGAL?
BROADLY DEFINED, YES.
SAY THE WORD, CAPTAIN.
THE WORD IS GIVEN.
NCC-1701-A
UNITED FEDERATION OF PLANETS

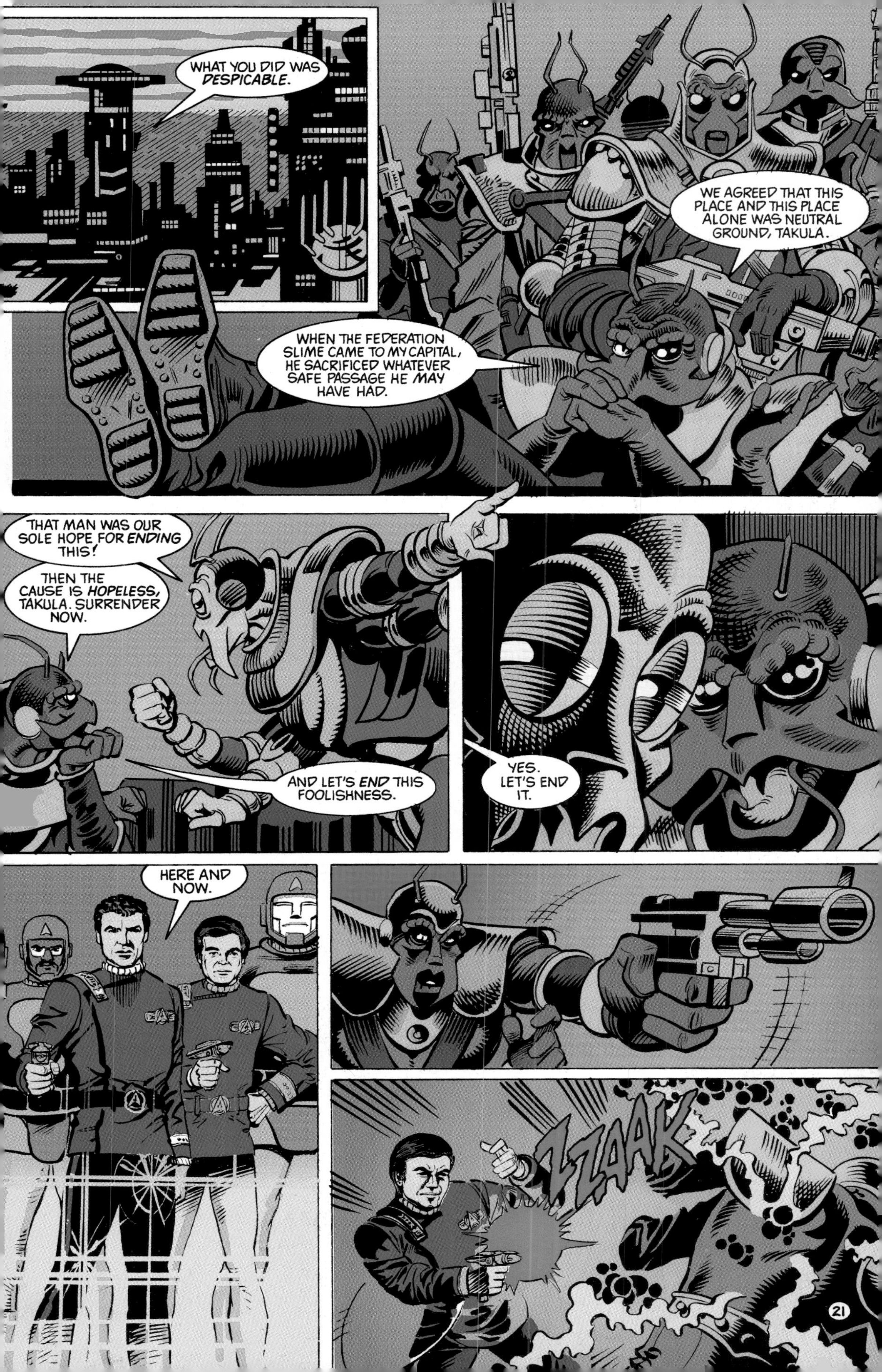
WHAT YOU DID WAS DESPICABLE.
WE AGREED THAT THIS PLACE AND THIS PLACE ALONE WAS NEUTRAL GROUND, TAKULA.
WHEN THE FEDERATION SLIME CAME TO MY CAPITAL, HE SACRIFICED WHATEVER SAFE PASSAGE HE MAY HAVE HAD.
THAT MAN WAS OUR SOLE HOPE FOR ENDING THIS!
THEN THE CAUSE IS HOPELESS, TAKULA. SURRENDER NOW.
AND LET'S END THIS FOOLISHNESS.
YES. LET'S END IT.
HERE AND NOW.
ZZAAK

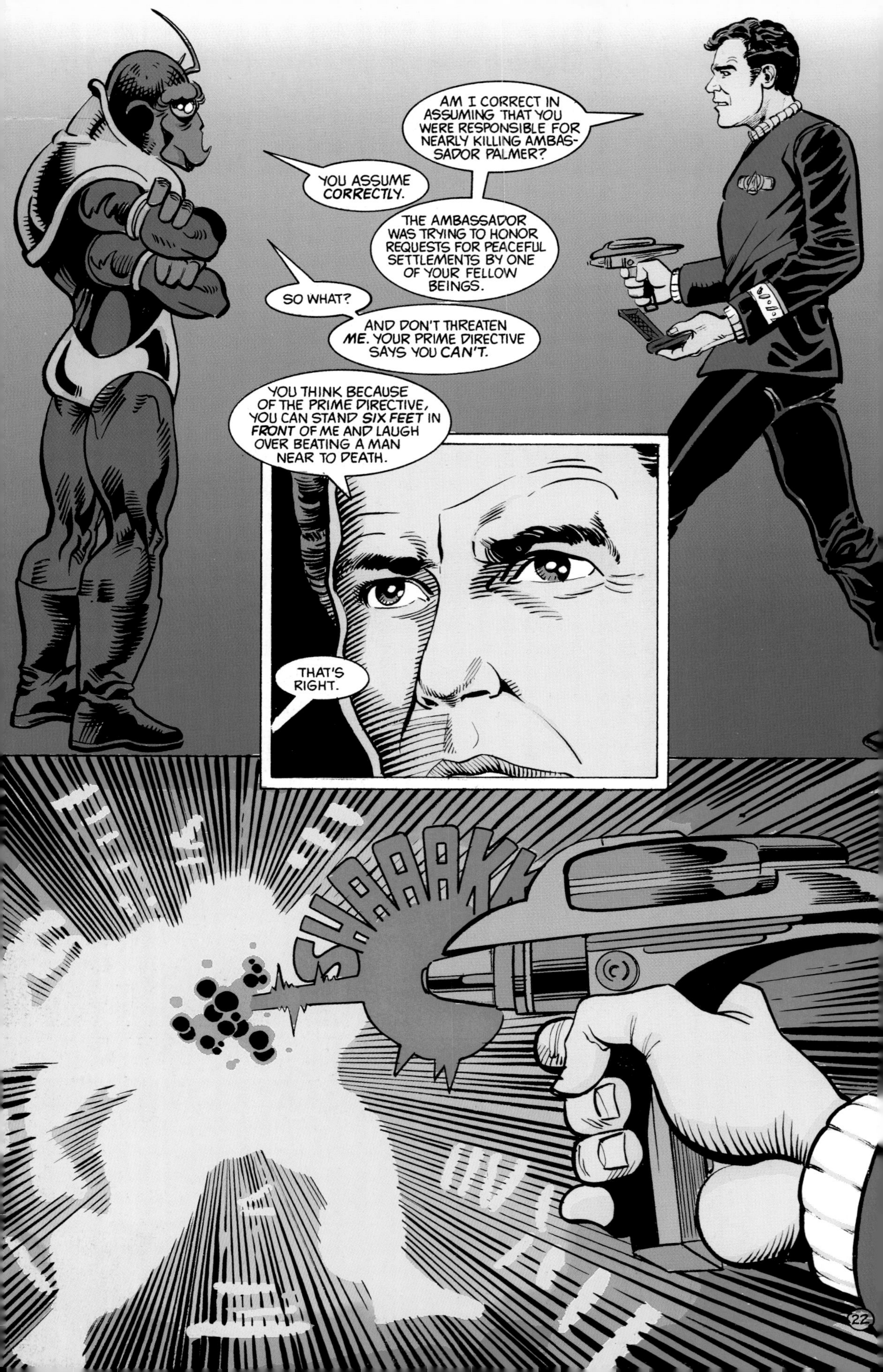
AM I CORRECT IN ASSUMING THAT YOU WERE RESPONSIBLE FOR NEARLY KILLING AMBASSADOR PALMER?
YOU ASSUME *CORRECTLY*.
THE AMBASSADOR WAS TRYING TO HONOR REQUESTS FOR PEACEFUL SETTLEMENTS BY ONE OF YOUR FELLOW BEINGS.
SO WHAT?
AND DON'T THREATEN *ME*. YOUR PRIME DIRECTIVE SAYS YOU *CAN'T*.
YOU THINK BECAUSE OF THE PRIME DIRECTIVE, YOU CAN STAND *SIX FEET* IN *FRONT* OF ME AND LAUGH OVER BEATING A MAN NEAR TO DEATH.
THAT'S RIGHT.
SHAAAKK

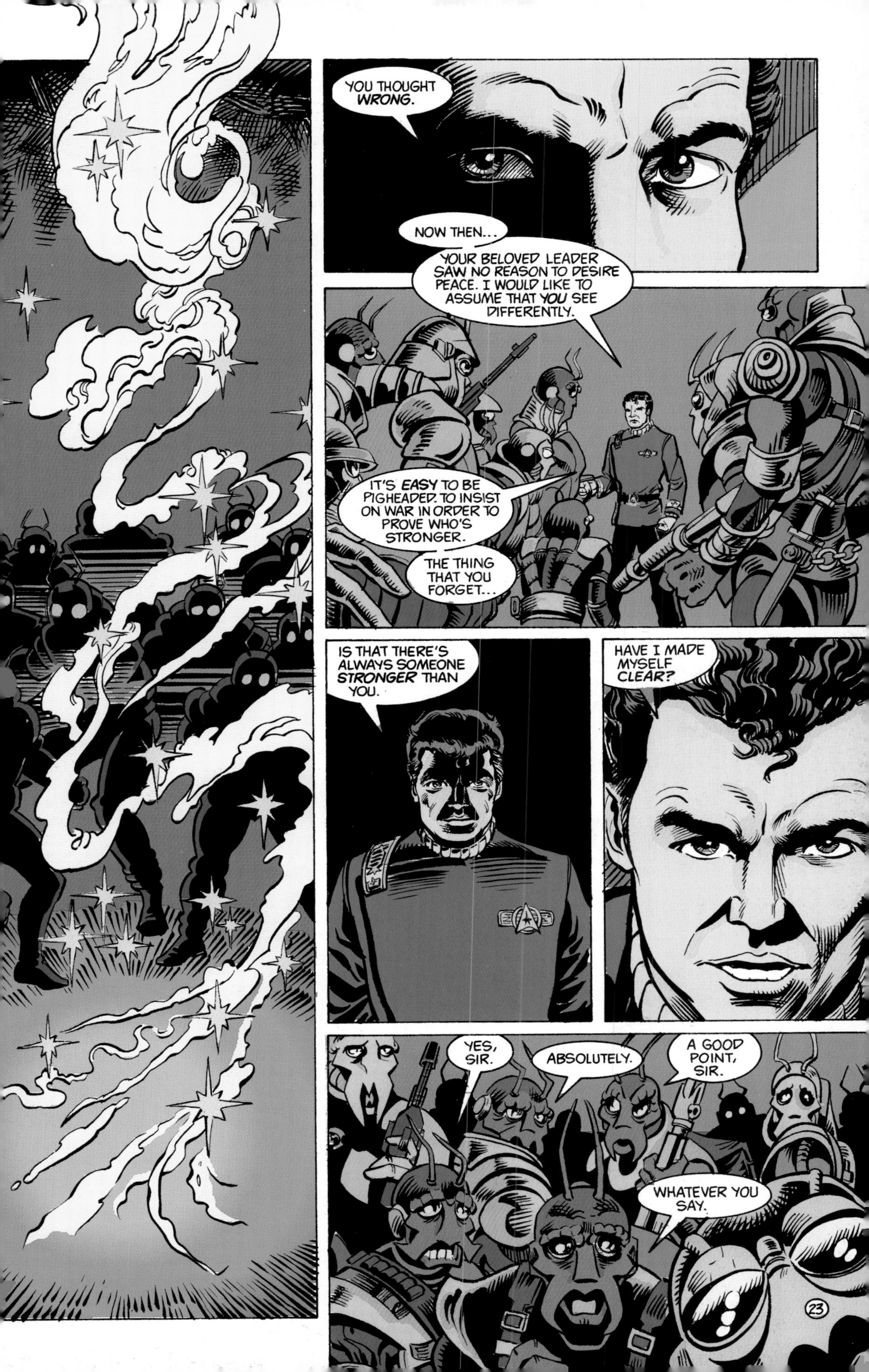

YOU THOUGHT WRONG.
NOW THEN...
YOUR BELOVED LEADER SAW NO REASON TO DESIRE PEACE. I WOULD LIKE TO ASSUME THAT YOU SEE DIFFERENTLY.
IT'S EASY TO BE PIGHEADED. TO INSIST ON WAR IN ORDER TO PROVE WHO'S STRONGER.
THE THING THAT YOU FORGET...
IS THAT THERE'S ALWAYS SOMEONE STRONGER THAN YOU.
HAVE I MADE MYSELF CLEAR?
YES, SIR.
ABSOLUTELY.
A GOOD POINT, SIR.
WHATEVER YOU SAY.
23

A QUESTIONABLE TACTIC, CAPTAIN.

TECHNICALLY, ELIMINATING A HEAD OF STATE CAN BE CONSIDERED INTERFERENCE IN A SOCIETY'S DEVELOPMENT.

THE SOCIETY WAS DEVELOPING TOWARD PEACE, SPOCK. IF *ANYONE* WAS INTERFERING, IT WAS THAT SAME HEAD OF STATE.

BESIDES, HE WASN'T ELIMINATED. HE WAS...SENT ON VACATION.

INDEED.

"ABSOLUTELY, SPOCK. OUR STUDY OF THE ENTIRE PLANET WAS VERY METICULOUS.

"THE AREA HE WAS TRANSPORTED TO IS INHABITED BY A TRIBE OF NOMADS WHO DISDAIN TECHNOLOGY AND VALUE *FRIENDSHIP* ABOVE ALL.

"DESOLATE, BUT RELAXING.

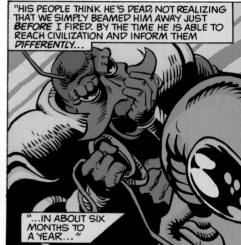

"HIS PEOPLE THINK HE'S DEAD, NOT REALIZING THAT WE SIMPLY BEAMED HIM AWAY JUST *BEFORE* I FIRED. BY THE TIME HE IS ABLE TO REACH CIVILIZATION AND INFORM THEM *DIFFERENTLY...*

"...IN ABOUT SIX MONTHS TO A YEAR..."

...PEACE ON CHRONIAN III SHOULD BE FIRMLY IN PLACE.

WOULDN'T YOU CALL THAT AN *ELEGANT* SOLUTION, MR. SPOCK?

INDEED, CAPTAIN, WHEN I AM REQUIRED TO *TESTIFY* AT A COURT MARTIAL...

I SHALL USE THOSE *VERY* WORDS.

I KNEW I COULD *COUNT* ON YOU, SPOCK.

NEXT: REPERCUSSION!

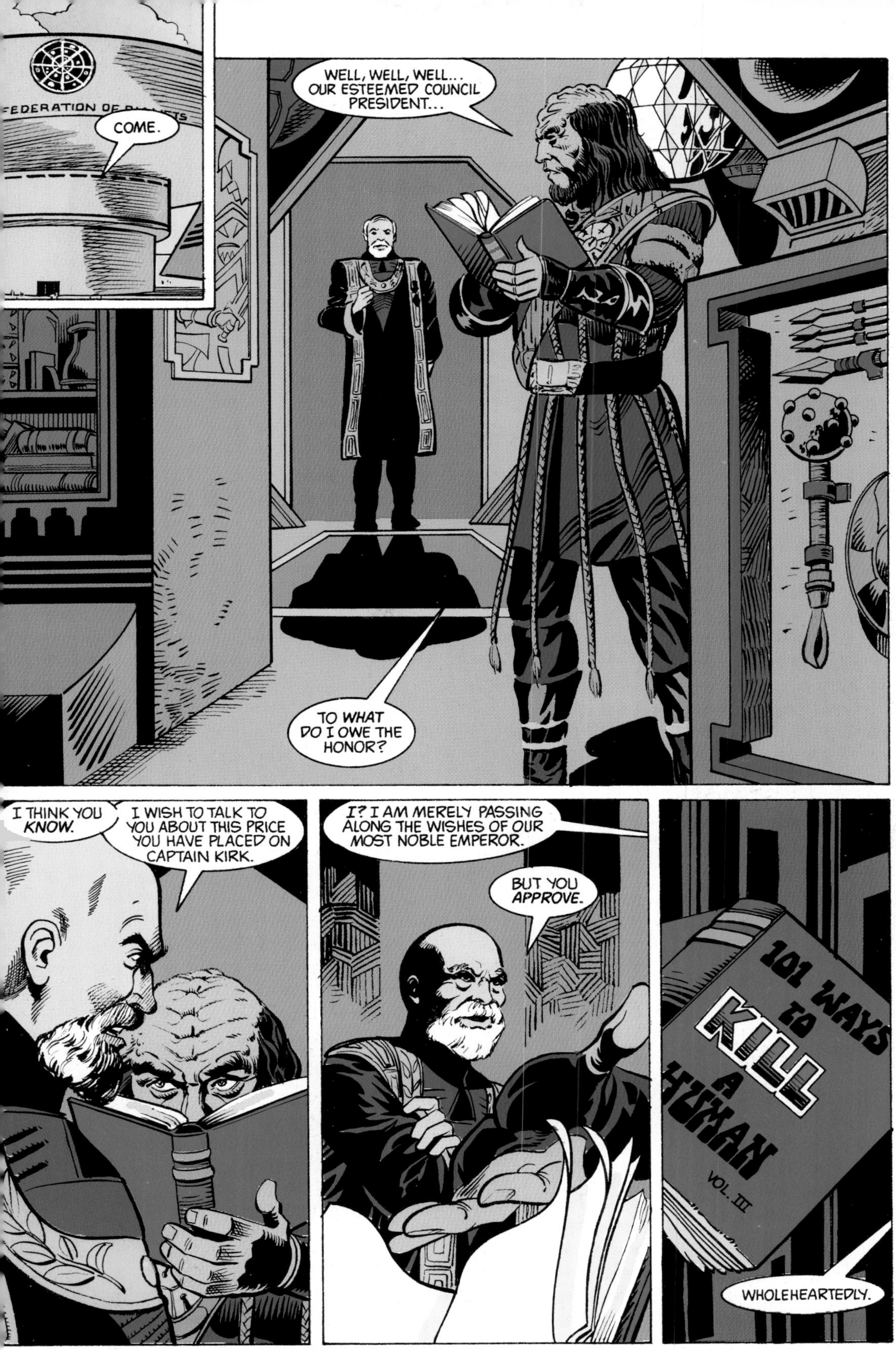
FEDERATION OF PLANETS
COME.
WELL, WELL, WELL... OUR ESTEEMED COUNCIL PRESIDENT...
TO WHAT DO I OWE THE HONOR?
I THINK YOU KNOW.
I WISH TO TALK TO YOU ABOUT THIS PRICE YOU HAVE PLACED ON CAPTAIN KIRK.
I? I AM MERELY PASSING ALONG THE WISHES OF OUR MOST NOBLE EMPEROR.
BUT YOU APPROVE.
101 WAYS TO KILL A HUMAN
VOL. III
WHOLEHEARTEDLY.

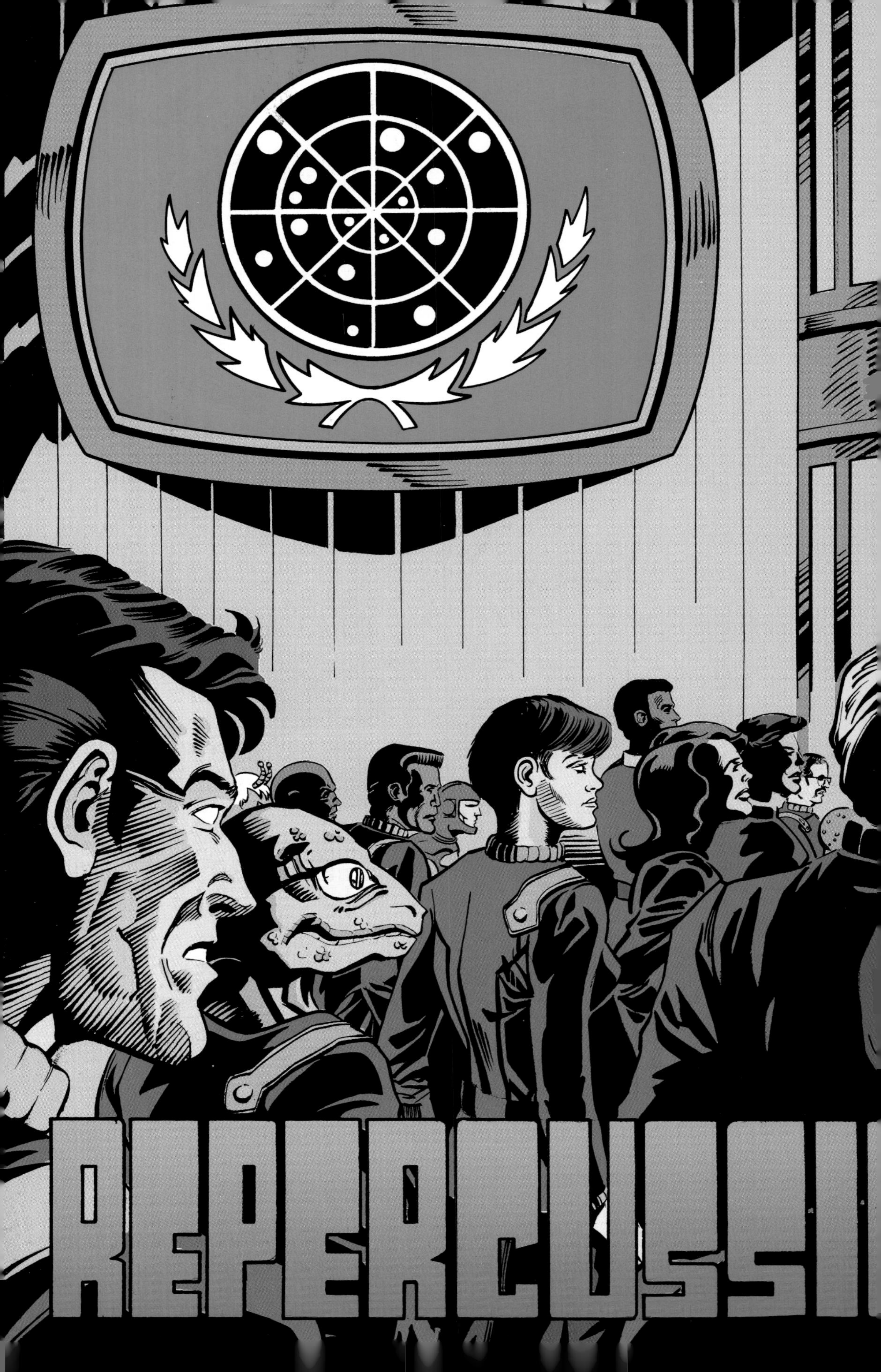
REPERCUSSI

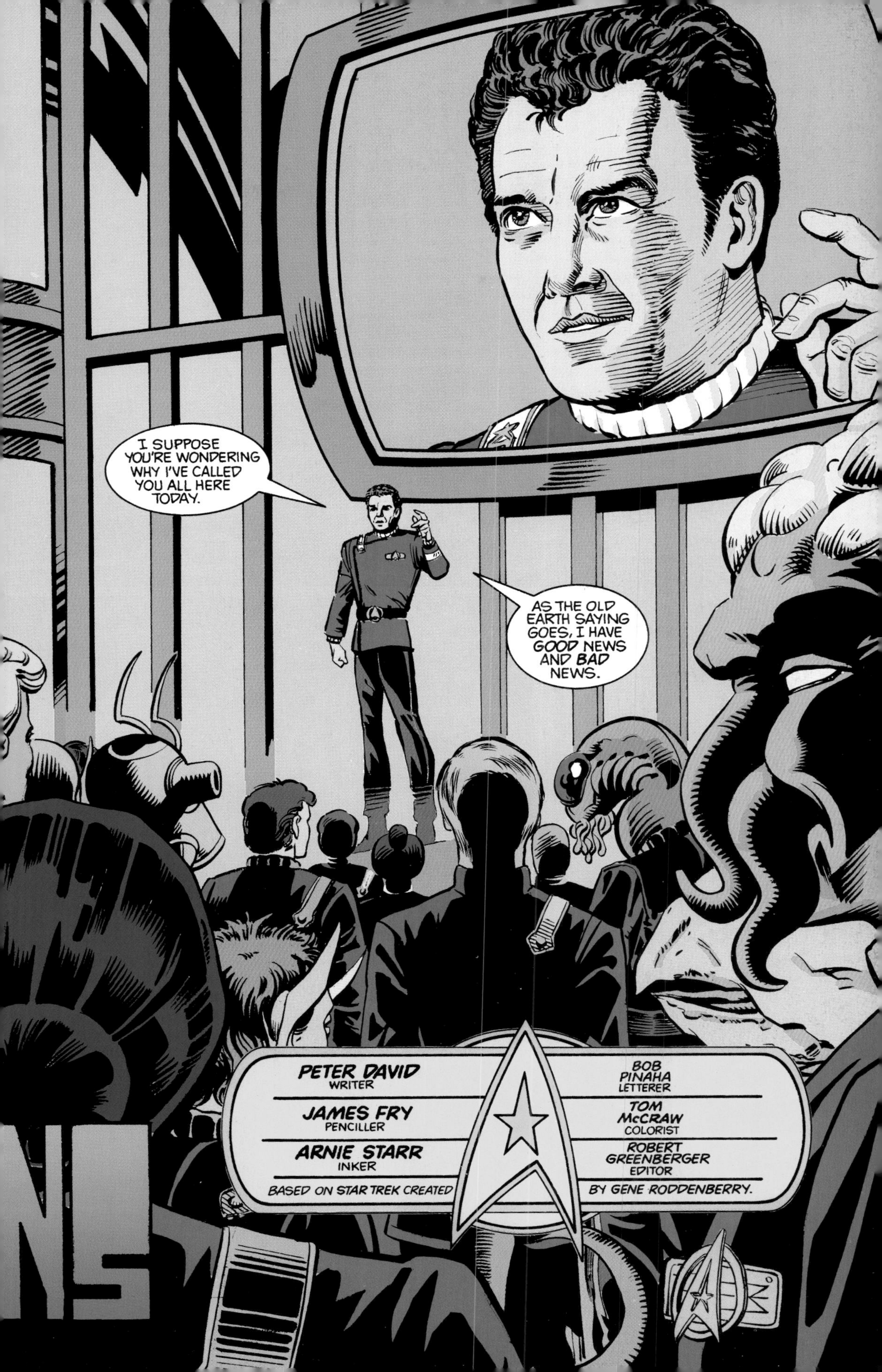
I SUPPOSE YOU'RE WONDERING WHY I'VE CALLED YOU ALL HERE TODAY.
AS THE OLD EARTH SAYING GOES, I HAVE GOOD NEWS AND BAD NEWS.
PETER DAVID WRITER
JAMES FRY PENCILLER
ARNIE STARR INKER
BOB PINAHA LETTERER
TOM McCRAW COLORIST
ROBERT GREENBERGER EDITOR
BASED ON STAR TREK CREATED BY GENE RODDENBERRY.

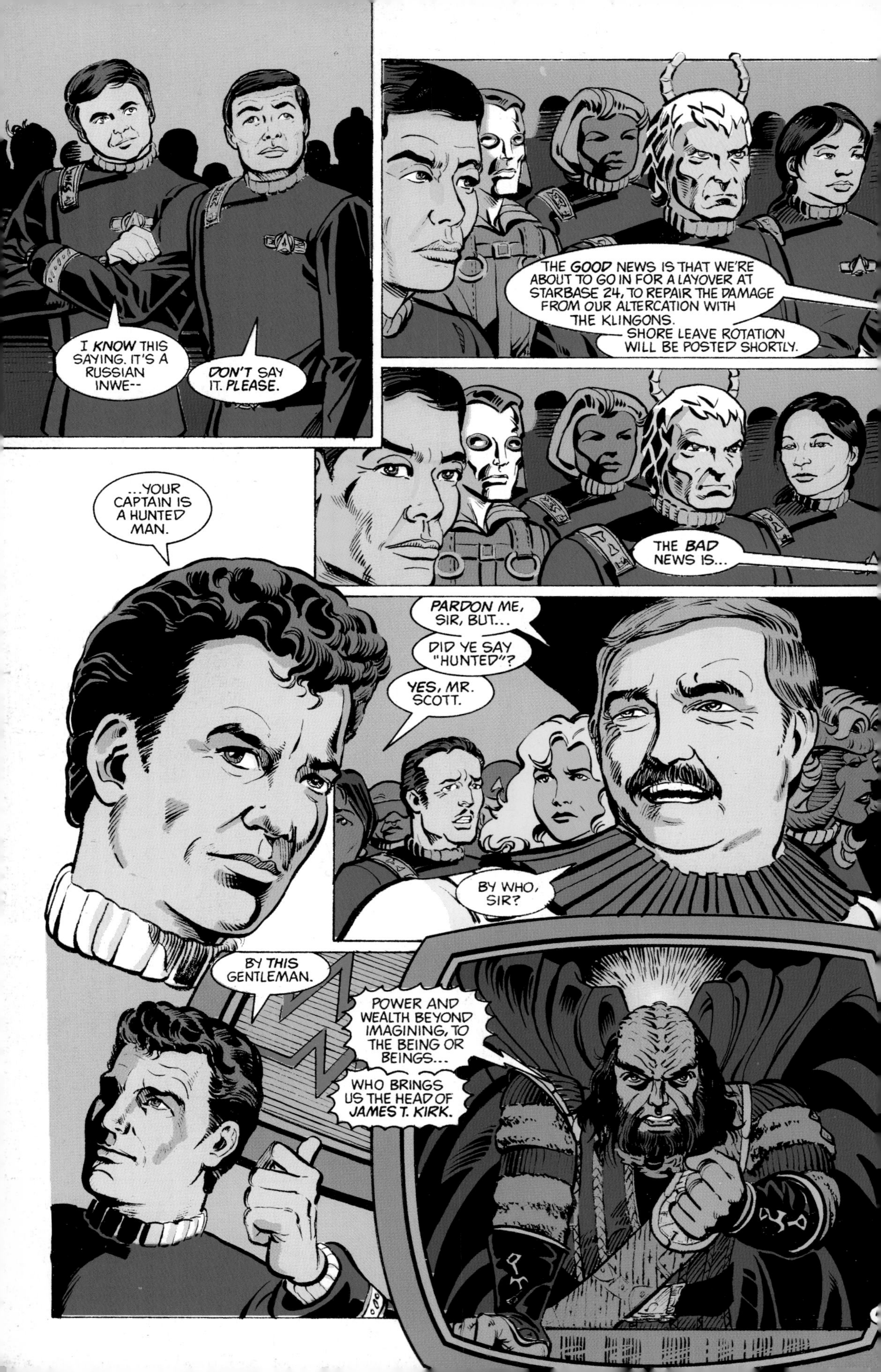
I KNOW THIS SAYING. IT'S A RUSSIAN INWE--
DON'T SAY IT. PLEASE.
THE GOOD NEWS IS THAT WE'RE ABOUT TO GO IN FOR A LAYOVER AT STARBASE 24, TO REPAIR THE DAMAGE FROM OUR ALTERCATION WITH THE KLINGONS.
SHORE LEAVE ROTATION WILL BE POSTED SHORTLY.
THE BAD NEWS IS...
...YOUR CAPTAIN IS A HUNTED MAN.
PARDON ME, SIR, BUT...
DID YE SAY "HUNTED"?
YES, MR. SCOTT.
BY WHO, SIR?
BY THIS GENTLEMAN.
POWER AND WEALTH BEYOND IMAGINING, TO THE BEING OR BEINGS...
WHO BRINGS US THE HEAD OF JAMES T. KIRK.

THE STATEMENT IS CLEAR. BUT THE *MOTIVATION* UTTERLY MYSTIFIES ME.

IT COMES AT A TIME WHEN OUR PEOPLES ARE CLOSER THAN *EVER* TO A LASTING PEACE.

I THOUGHT MY STATEMENT WAS FAIRLY *CLEAR*.

THERE SHALL BE NO PEACE WHILE--

DO YOU SERIOUSLY BELIEVE THAT THE RESCUE OF A BROKEN DOWN, DISGRACED *GENERAL* IS OF SUFFICIENT WEIGHT TO BALANCE THE SCALES...

...FOR THE CREW OF KLINGONS, INCLUDING CAPTAIN KRUGE, THAT KIRK *SLAUGHTERED* ON THE GENESIS PLANET?

FAH. THE ONLY SERVICE *KIRK* COULD HAVE DONE US WOULD HAVE BEEN IF HE HAD LET KORRD DIE SOMETHING VAGUELY RESEMBLING A *NOBLE* DEATH.

KIRK LIVES, YES, SO YOU'VE SAID REPEATEDLY. BUT CERTAINLY WHATEVER GRIEVANCES YOU MAY HAVE HAD WERE LAID TO REST WITH KIRK'S HANDLING OF THE NIMBUS III SITUATION.

HE SAVED ONE OF YOUR *OWN* PEOPLE!

NOW, IF THERE IS NOTHING *ELSE*...

THERE IS A GREAT *DEAL* ELSE THAT I WISH TO--

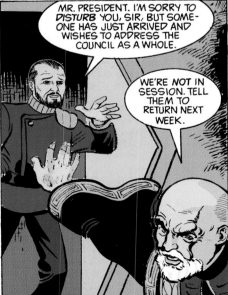

MR. PRESIDENT. I'M SORRY TO *DISTURB* YOU, SIR, BUT SOMEONE HAS JUST ARRIVED AND WISHES TO ADDRESS THE COUNCIL AS A WHOLE.

WE'RE *NOT* IN SESSION. TELL THEM TO RETURN NEXT WEEK.

I DON'T THINK HE'LL *WAIT*, SIR.

IT'S THE SALLA OF THE NASGUL.

5

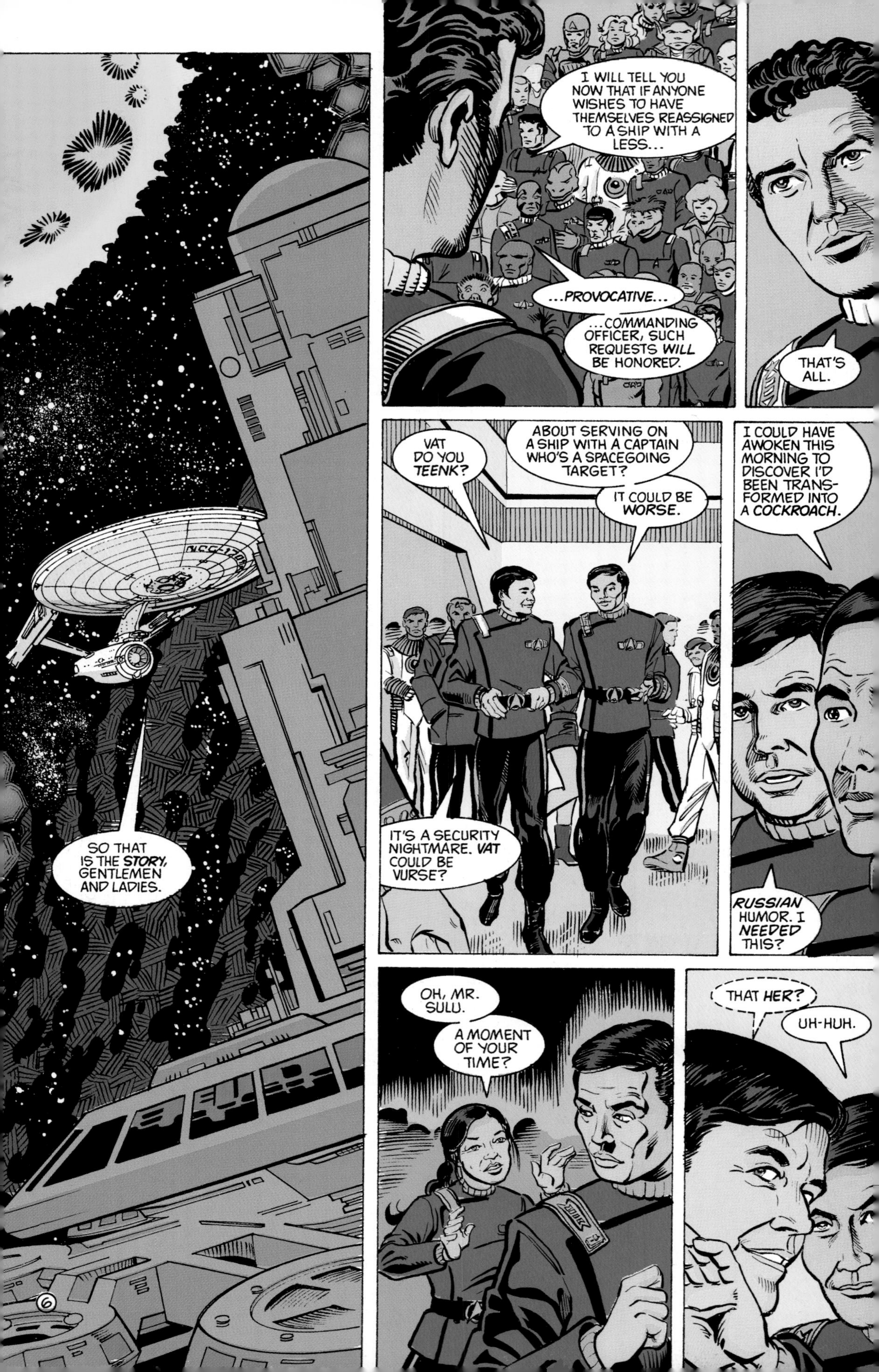

SO THAT IS THE STORY, GENTLEMEN AND LADIES.
I WILL TELL YOU NOW THAT IF ANYONE WISHES TO HAVE THEMSELVES REASSIGNED TO A SHIP WITH A LESS...
...PROVOCATIVE...
...COMMANDING OFFICER, SUCH REQUESTS WILL BE HONORED.
THAT'S ALL.
VAT DO YOU TEENK?
ABOUT SERVING ON A SHIP WITH A CAPTAIN WHO'S A SPACEGOING TARGET?
IT COULD BE WORSE.
IT'S A SECURITY NIGHTMARE. VAT COULD BE VURSE?
I COULD HAVE AWOKEN THIS MORNING TO DISCOVER I'D BEEN TRANSFORMED INTO A COCKROACH.
RUSSIAN HUMOR. I NEEDED THIS?
OH, MR. SULU.
A MOMENT OF YOUR TIME?
THAT HER?
UH-HUH.
6

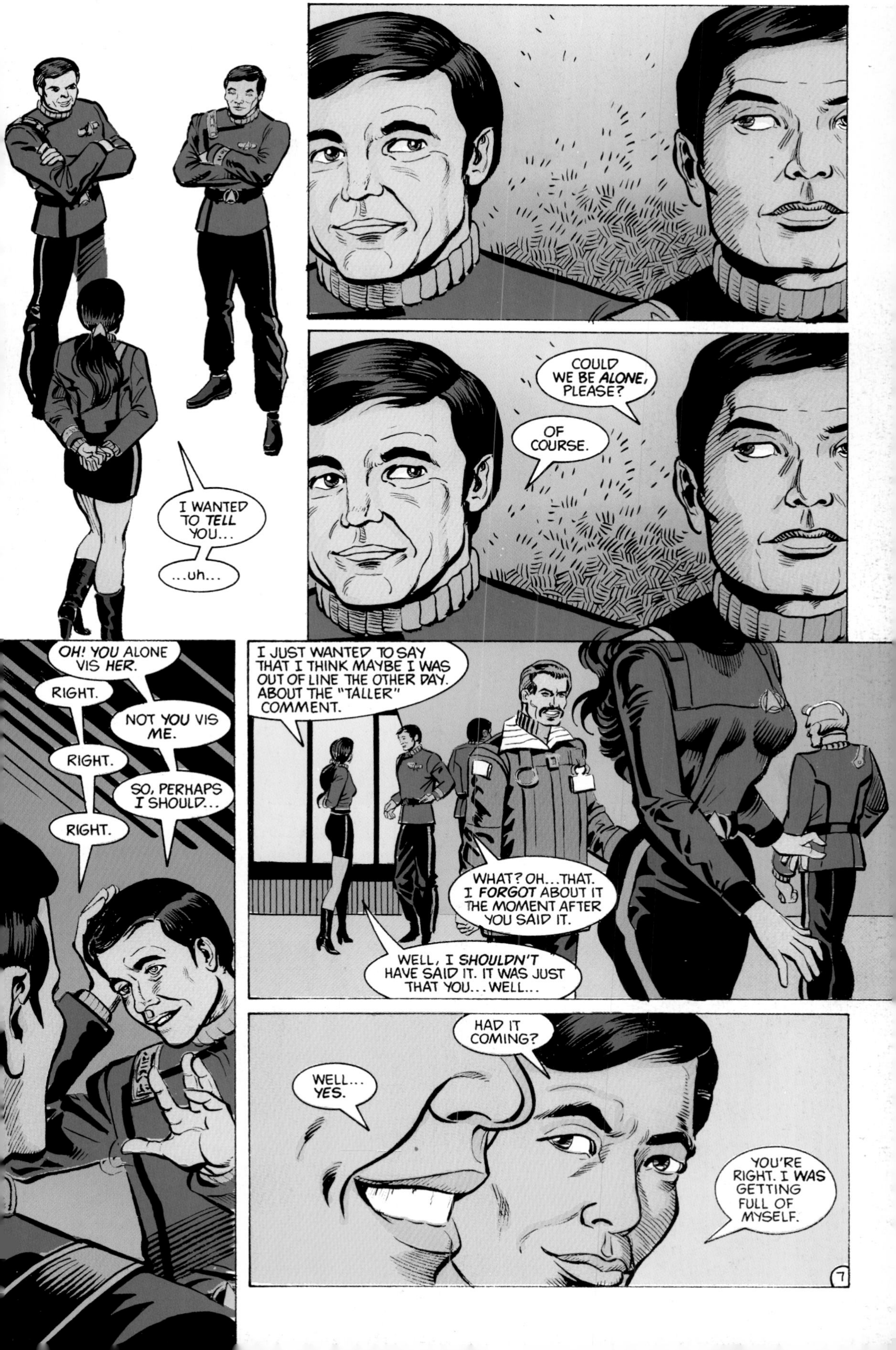
I WANTED TO TELL YOU...
...uh...
COULD WE BE ALONE, PLEASE?
OF COURSE.
OH! YOU ALONE VIS HER.
RIGHT.
NOT YOU VIS ME.
RIGHT.
SO, PERHAPS I SHOULD...
RIGHT.
I JUST WANTED TO SAY THAT I THINK MAYBE I WAS OUT OF LINE THE OTHER DAY. ABOUT THE "TALLER" COMMENT.
WHAT? OH...THAT. I FORGOT ABOUT IT THE MOMENT AFTER YOU SAID IT.
WELL, I SHOULDN'T HAVE SAID IT. IT WAS JUST THAT YOU... WELL...
HAD IT COMING?
WELL... YES.
YOU'RE RIGHT. I WAS GETTING FULL OF MYSELF.
7

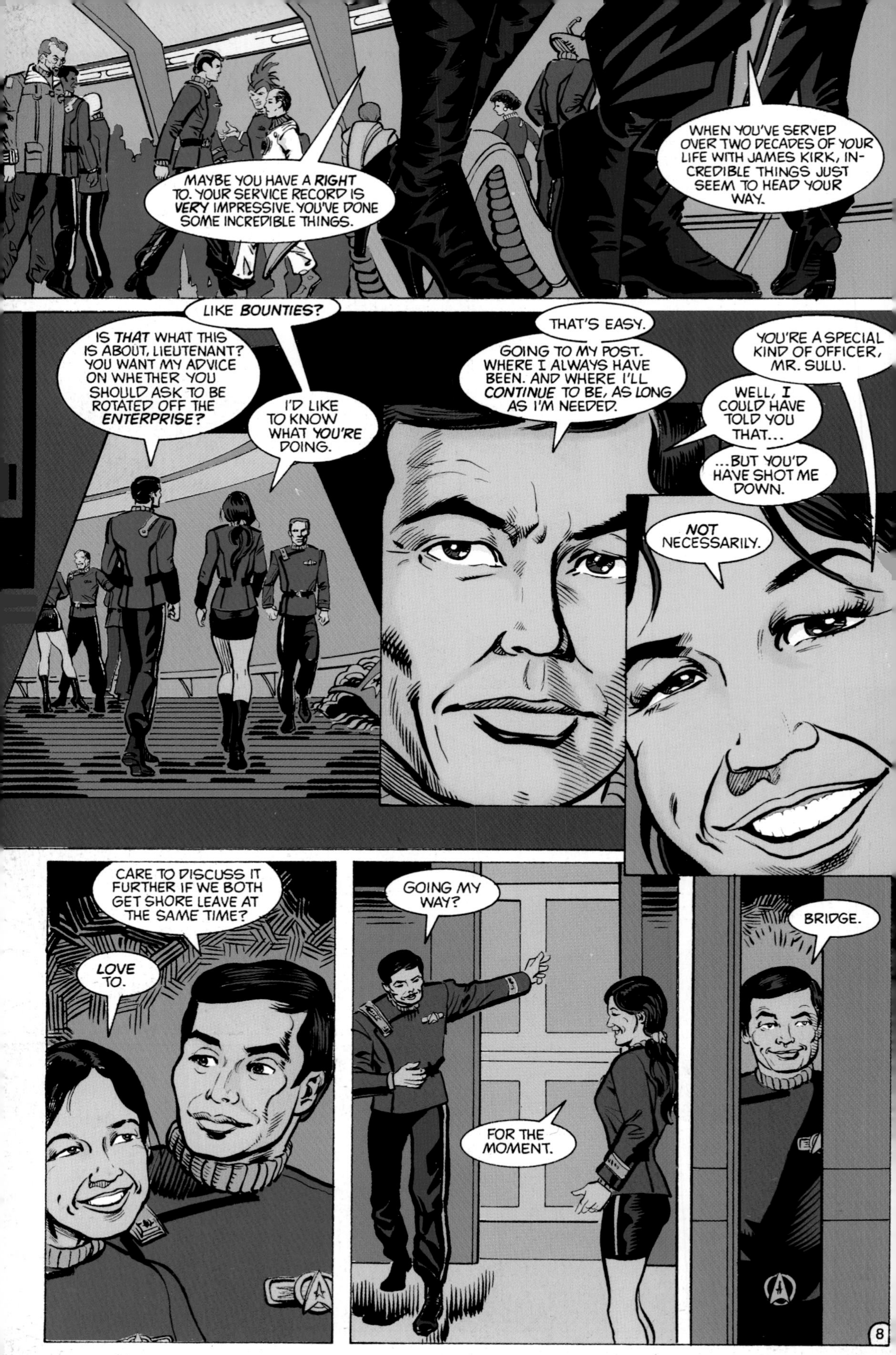
MAYBE YOU HAVE A RIGHT TO. YOUR SERVICE RECORD IS VERY IMPRESSIVE. YOU'VE DONE SOME INCREDIBLE THINGS.
WHEN YOU'VE SERVED OVER TWO DECADES OF YOUR LIFE WITH JAMES KIRK, INCREDIBLE THINGS JUST SEEM TO HEAD YOUR WAY.
LIKE BOUNTIES?
IS THAT WHAT THIS IS ABOUT, LIEUTENANT? YOU WANT MY ADVICE ON WHETHER YOU SHOULD ASK TO BE ROTATED OFF THE ENTERPRISE?
I'D LIKE TO KNOW WHAT YOU'RE DOING.
THAT'S EASY.
GOING TO MY POST. WHERE I ALWAYS HAVE BEEN. AND WHERE I'LL CONTINUE TO BE, AS LONG AS I'M NEEDED.
YOU'RE A SPECIAL KIND OF OFFICER, MR. SULU.
WELL, I COULD HAVE TOLD YOU THAT...
...BUT YOU'D HAVE SHOT ME DOWN.
NOT NECESSARILY.
CARE TO DISCUSS IT FURTHER IF WE BOTH GET SHORE LEAVE AT THE SAME TIME?
LOVE TO.
GOING MY WAY?
FOR THE MOMENT.
BRIDGE.

"CARE TO DISCUSS IT FURTHER..."

"LOVE TO."

PERSONAL LOG, STARDATE 8484.1. THUS FAR, AFTER M'I ANNOUNCEMENT, THERE HAVE BEEN NO REQUESTS FOR TRANSFER OFF THE ENTERPRISE. I'M NOT SURE WHETHER TO BE PLEASED OVER THE LOYALTY OF MY CREW...

...OR CONCERNED THAT THEY DON'T TRULY UNDERSTAND THE GRAVITY OF THE SITUATION.

REPAIR TIME, MR. SCOTT?

GIVE ME SEVENTY-TWO HOURS, CAPTAIN, AND I'LL HAVE HER PURRING LIKE A KITTEN.

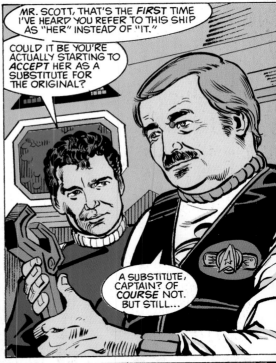

MR. SCOTT, THAT'S THE FIRST TIME I'VE HEARD YOU REFER TO THIS SHIP AS "HER" INSTEAD OF "IT."

COULD IT BE YOU'RE ACTUALLY STARTING TO ACCEPT HER AS A SUBSTITUTE FOR THE ORIGINAL?

A SUBSTITUTE, CAPTAIN? OF COURSE NOT. BUT STILL...

I CAN'T VERY WELL BE WEARING SACK CLOTH AND ASHES THE REST OF M'LIFE, CAN I?

CERTAINLY NOT. CARRY ON, SCOTTY.

I ALWAYS DO, CAPTAIN.

BRIDGE TO CAPTAIN.

9

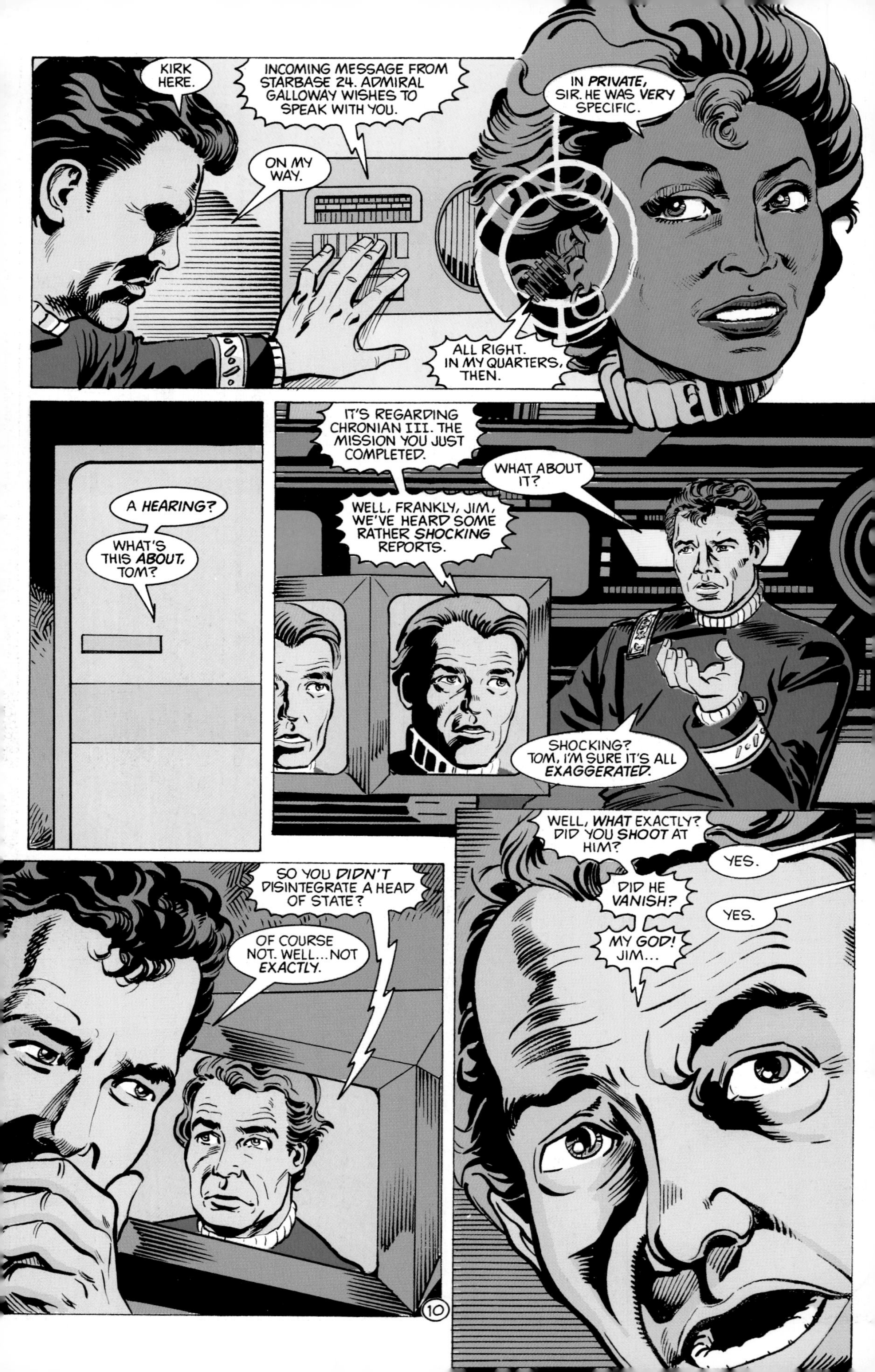
KIRK HERE.
INCOMING MESSAGE FROM STARBASE 24. ADMIRAL GALLOWAY WISHES TO SPEAK WITH YOU.
ON MY WAY.
IN PRIVATE, SIR. HE WAS VERY SPECIFIC.
ALL RIGHT. IN MY QUARTERS, THEN.
A HEARING?
WHAT'S THIS ABOUT, TOM?
IT'S REGARDING CHRONIAN III. THE MISSION YOU JUST COMPLETED.
WHAT ABOUT IT?
WELL, FRANKLY, JIM, WE'VE HEARD SOME RATHER SHOCKING REPORTS.
SHOCKING? TOM, I'M SURE IT'S ALL EXAGGERATED.
SO YOU DIDN'T DISINTEGRATE A HEAD OF STATE?
OF COURSE NOT. WELL...NOT EXACTLY.
WELL, WHAT EXACTLY? DID YOU SHOOT AT HIM?
YES.
DID HE VANISH?
YES.
MY GOD! JIM...

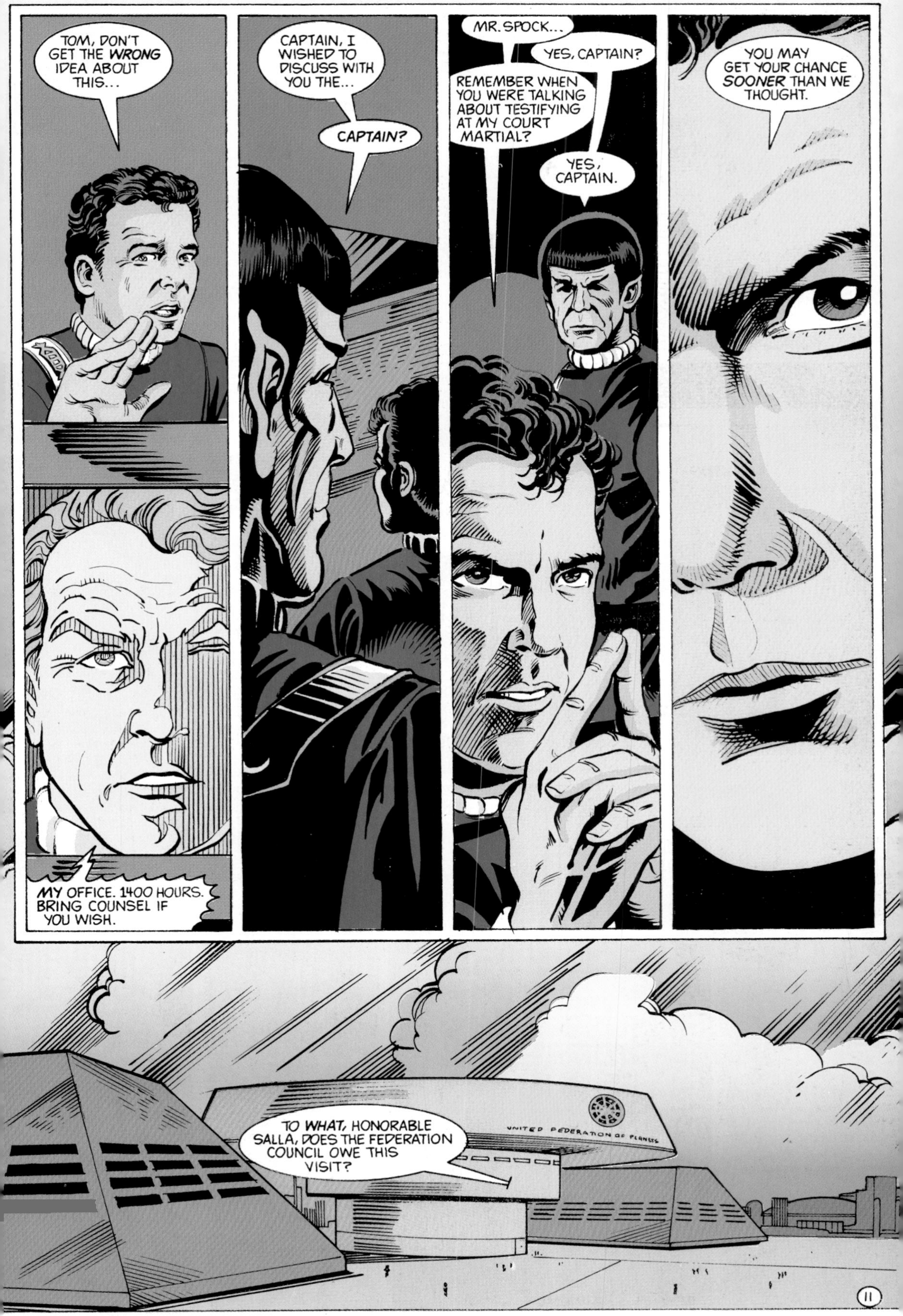

TOM, DON'T GET THE WRONG IDEA ABOUT THIS...
MY OFFICE. 1400 HOURS. BRING COUNSEL IF YOU WISH.
CAPTAIN, I WISHED TO DISCUSS WITH YOU THE...
CAPTAIN?
MR. SPOCK...
YES, CAPTAIN?
REMEMBER WHEN YOU WERE TALKING ABOUT TESTIFYING AT MY COURT MARTIAL?
YES, CAPTAIN.
YOU MAY GET YOUR CHANCE SOONER THAN WE THOUGHT.
UNITED FEDERATION OF PLANETS
TO WHAT, HONORABLE SALLA, DOES THE FEDERATION COUNCIL OWE THIS VISIT?

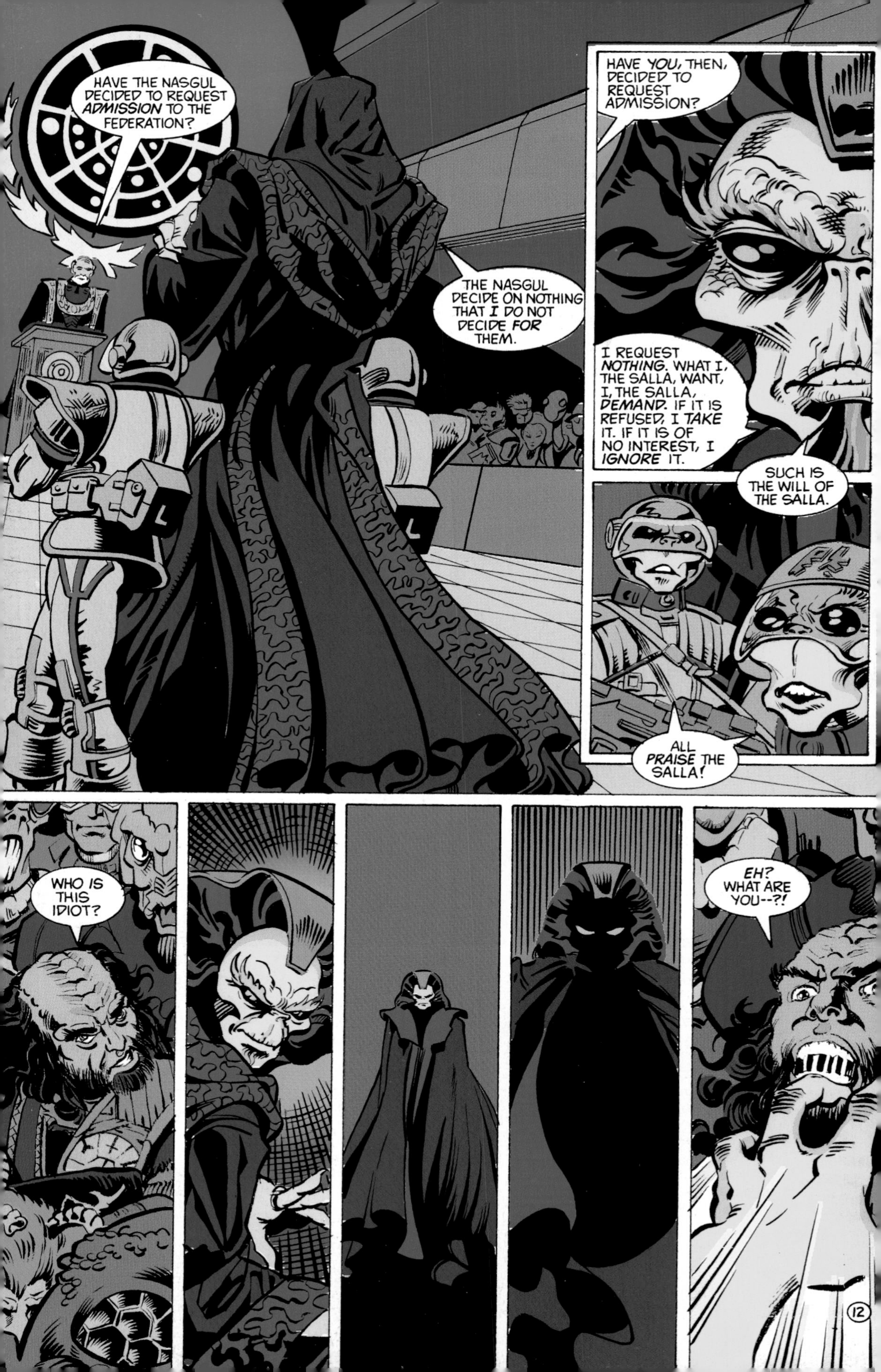
HAVE THE NASGUL DECIDED TO REQUEST ADMISSION TO THE FEDERATION?
THE NASGUL DECIDE ON NOTHING THAT I DO NOT DECIDE FOR THEM.
HAVE YOU, THEN, DECIDED TO REQUEST ADMISSION?
I REQUEST NOTHING. WHAT I, THE SALLA, WANT, I, THE SALLA, DEMAND. IF IT IS REFUSED, I TAKE IT. IF IT IS OF NO INTEREST, I IGNORE IT.
SUCH IS THE WILL OF THE SALLA.
ALL PRAISE THE SALLA!
WHO IS THIS IDIOT?
EH? WHAT ARE YOU--?!

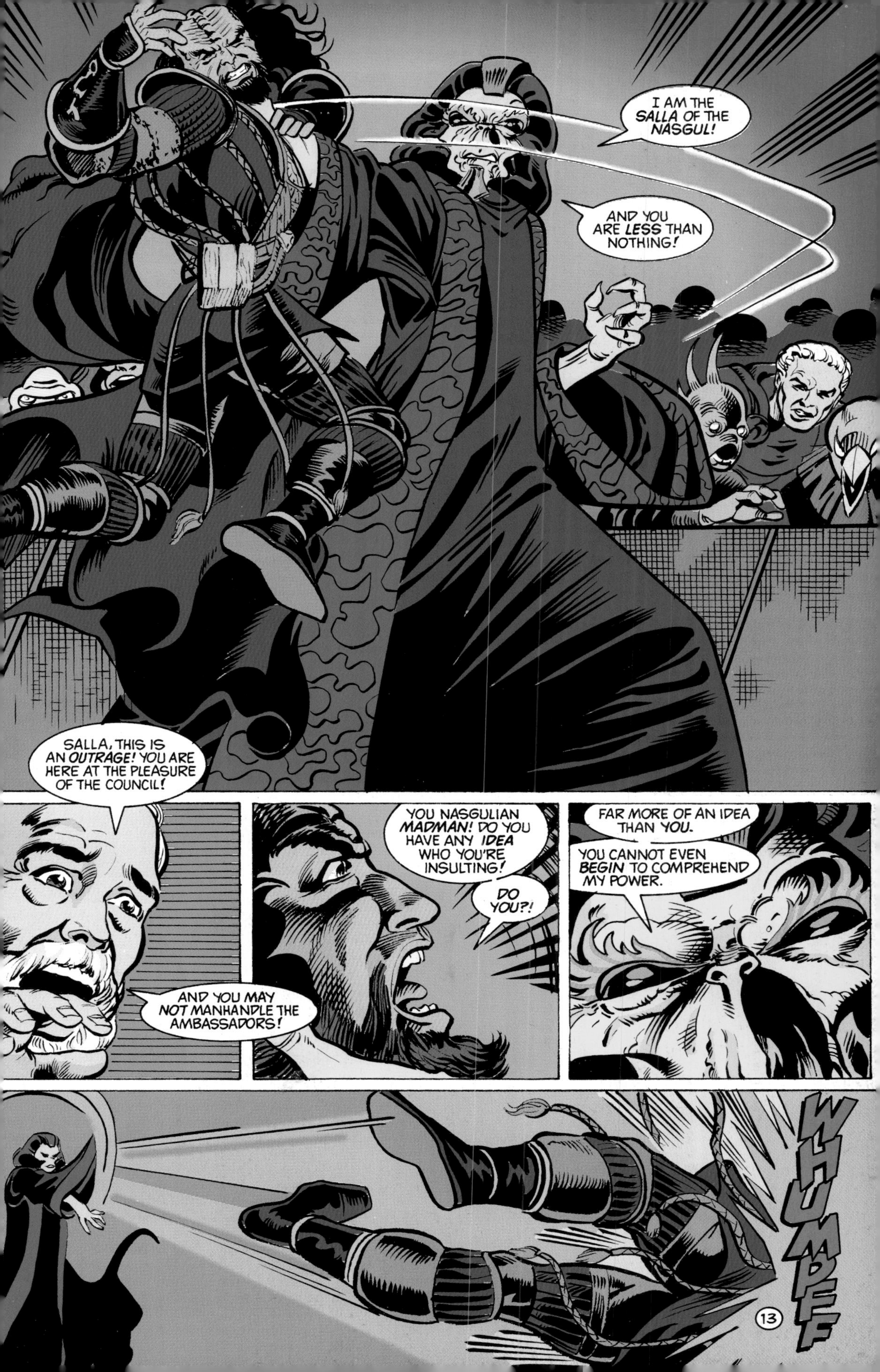
I AM THE SALLA OF THE NASGUL!
AND YOU ARE LESS THAN NOTHING!
SALLA, THIS IS AN OUTRAGE! YOU ARE HERE AT THE PLEASURE OF THE COUNCIL!
AND YOU MAY NOT MANHANDLE THE AMBASSADORS!
YOU NASGULIAN MADMAN! DO YOU HAVE ANY IDEA WHO YOU'RE INSULTING!
DO YOU?!
FAR MORE OF AN IDEA THAN YOU.
YOU CANNOT EVEN BEGIN TO COMPREHEND MY POWER.
WHUMPFF

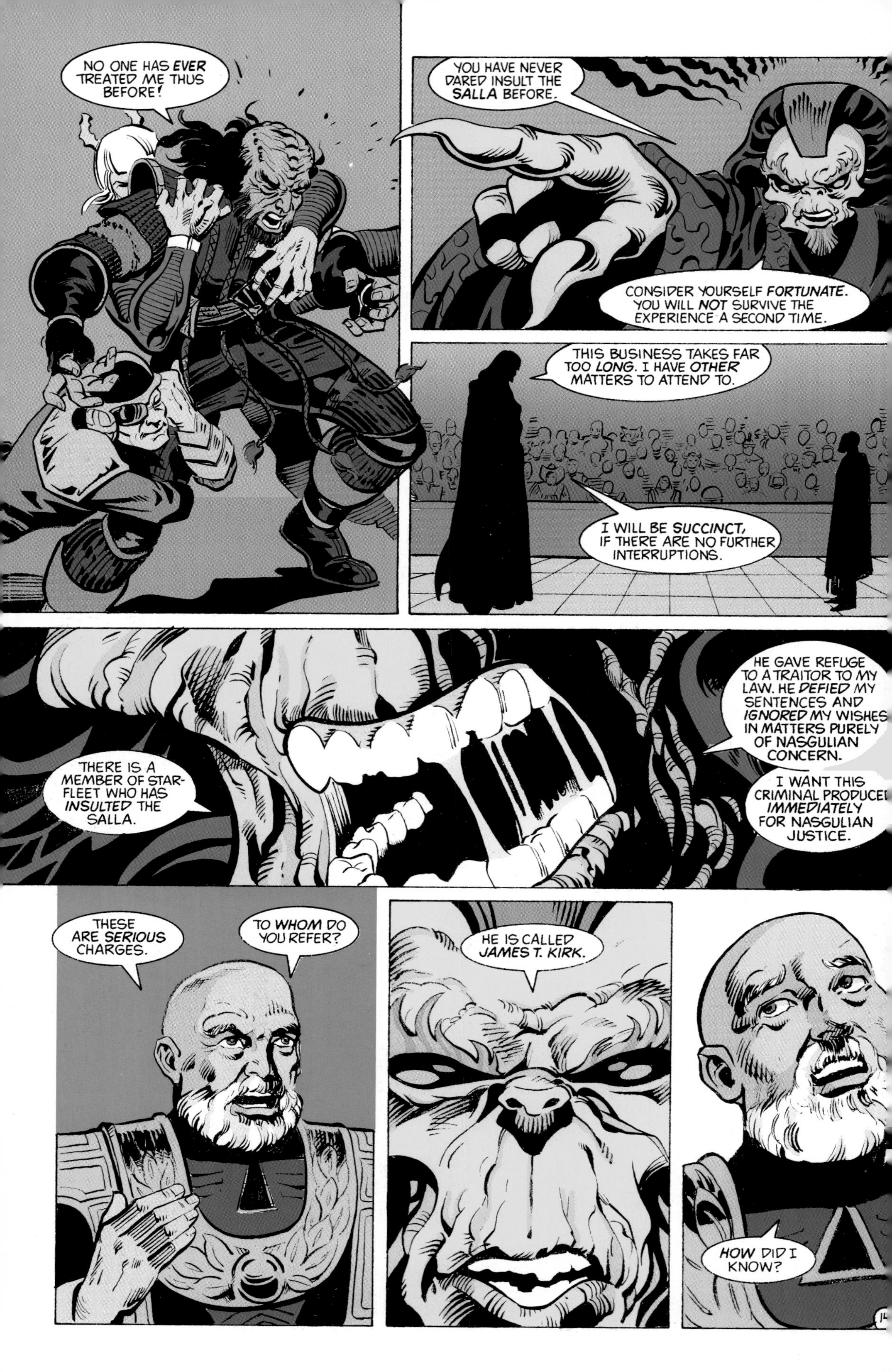

NO ONE HAS EVER TREATED ME THUS BEFORE!
YOU HAVE NEVER DARED INSULT THE SALLA BEFORE.
CONSIDER YOURSELF FORTUNATE. YOU WILL NOT SURVIVE THE EXPERIENCE A SECOND TIME.
THIS BUSINESS TAKES FAR TOO LONG. I HAVE OTHER MATTERS TO ATTEND TO.
I WILL BE SUCCINCT, IF THERE ARE NO FURTHER INTERRUPTIONS.
THERE IS A MEMBER OF STAR-FLEET WHO HAS INSULTED THE SALLA.
HE GAVE REFUGE TO A TRAITOR TO MY LAW. HE DEFIED MY SENTENCES AND IGNORED MY WISHES IN MATTERS PURELY OF NASGULIAN CONCERN.
I WANT THIS CRIMINAL PRODUCED IMMEDIATELY FOR NASGULIAN JUSTICE.
THESE ARE SERIOUS CHARGES.
TO WHOM DO YOU REFER?
HE IS CALLED JAMES T. KIRK.
HOW DID I KNOW?

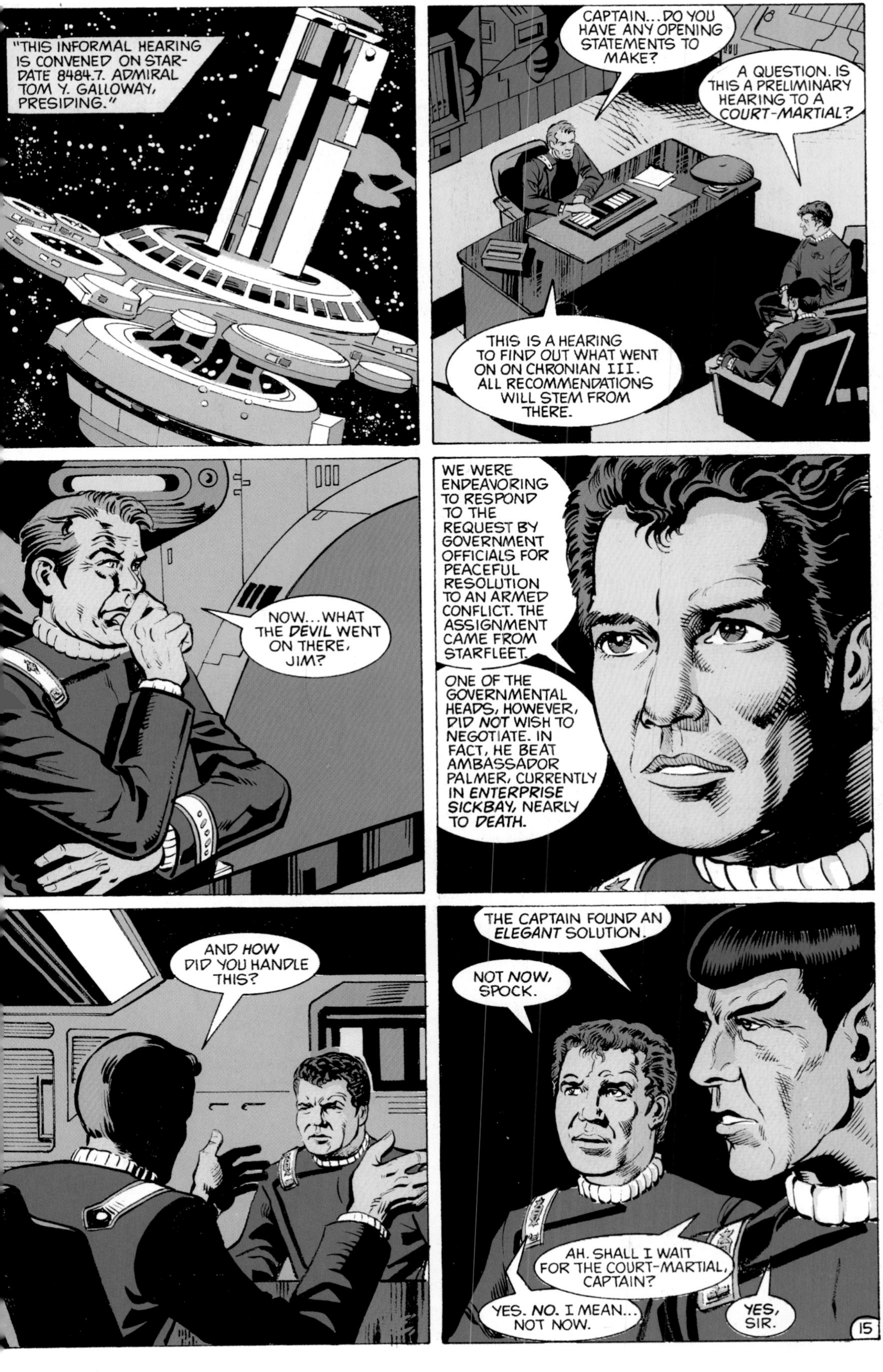
"THIS INFORMAL HEARING IS CONVENED ON STARDATE 8484.7. ADMIRAL TOM Y. GALLOWAY, PRESIDING."
CAPTAIN... DO YOU HAVE ANY OPENING STATEMENTS TO MAKE?
A QUESTION. IS THIS A PRELIMINARY HEARING TO A COURT-MARTIAL?
THIS IS A HEARING TO FIND OUT WHAT WENT ON ON CHRONIAN III. ALL RECOMMENDATIONS WILL STEM FROM THERE.
NOW... WHAT THE *DEVIL* WENT ON THERE, JIM?
WE WERE ENDEAVORING TO RESPOND TO THE REQUEST BY GOVERNMENT OFFICIALS FOR PEACEFUL RESOLUTION TO AN ARMED CONFLICT. THE ASSIGNMENT CAME FROM STARFLEET.
ONE OF THE GOVERNMENTAL HEADS, HOWEVER, *DID NOT* WISH TO NEGOTIATE. IN FACT, HE BEAT AMBASSADOR PALMER, CURRENTLY IN *ENTERPRISE SICKBAY*, NEARLY TO *DEATH*.
AND *HOW* DID YOU HANDLE THIS?
THE CAPTAIN FOUND AN *ELEGANT* SOLUTION.
NOT *NOW*, SPOCK.
AH. SHALL I WAIT FOR THE COURT-MARTIAL, CAPTAIN?
YES. *NO*. I MEAN... NOT NOW.
YES, SIR.

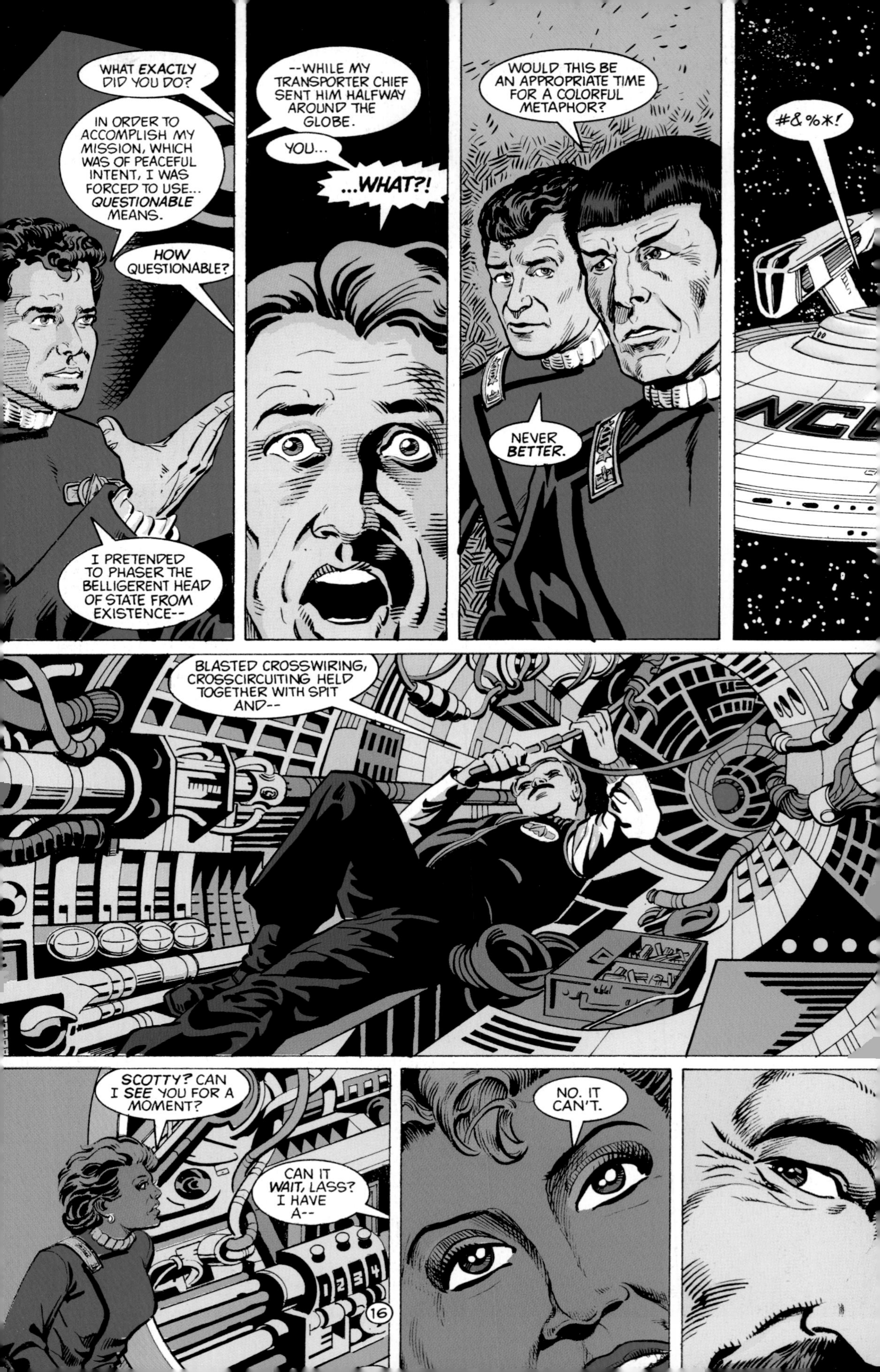
WHAT EXACTLY DID YOU DO?
IN ORDER TO ACCOMPLISH MY MISSION, WHICH WAS OF PEACEFUL INTENT, I WAS FORCED TO USE... QUESTIONABLE MEANS.
HOW QUESTIONABLE?
I PRETENDED TO PHASER THE BELLIGERENT HEAD OF STATE FROM EXISTENCE--
--WHILE MY TRANSPORTER CHIEF SENT HIM HALFWAY AROUND THE GLOBE.
YOU...
...WHAT?!
WOULD THIS BE AN APPROPRIATE TIME FOR A COLORFUL METAPHOR?
NEVER BETTER.
#&%*!
NCC
BLASTED CROSSWIRING, CROSSCIRCUITING HELD TOGETHER WITH SPIT AND--
SCOTTY? CAN I SEE YOU FOR A MOMENT?
CAN IT WAIT, LASS? I HAVE A--
NO. IT CAN'T.
1 2 3 4

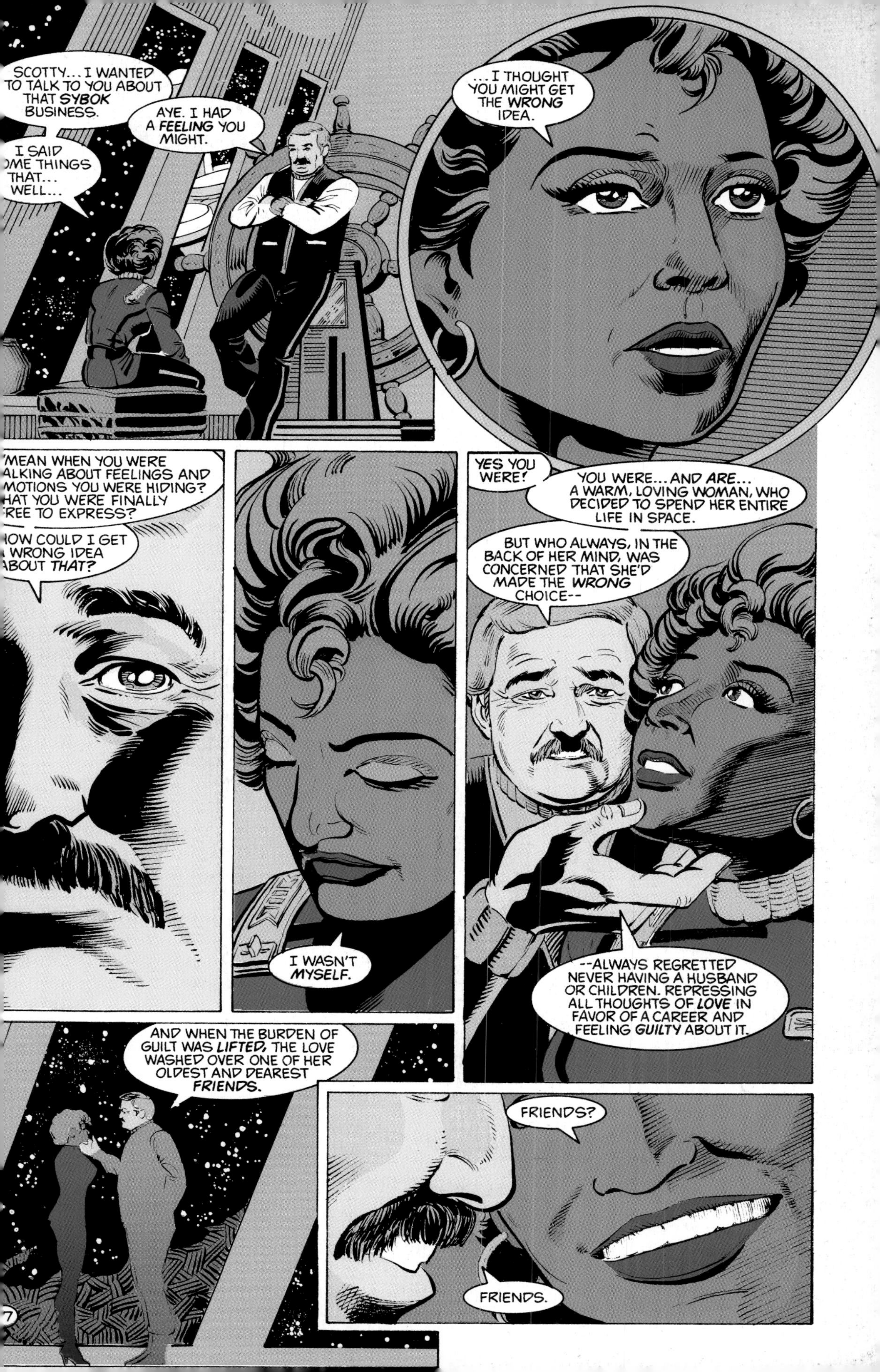
SCOTTY... I WANTED TO TALK TO YOU ABOUT THAT SYBOK BUSINESS.
I SAID OME THINGS THAT... WELL...
AYE. I HAD A FEELING YOU MIGHT.
...I THOUGHT YOU MIGHT GET THE WRONG IDEA.
MEAN WHEN YOU WERE ALKING ABOUT FEELINGS AND MOTIONS YOU WERE HIDING? HAT YOU WERE FINALLY REE TO EXPRESS?
IOW COULD I GET WRONG IDEA ABOUT THAT?
I WASN'T MYSELF.
YES YOU WERE!
YOU WERE... AND ARE... A WARM, LOVING WOMAN, WHO DECIDED TO SPEND HER ENTIRE LIFE IN SPACE.
BUT WHO ALWAYS, IN THE BACK OF HER MIND, WAS CONCERNED THAT SHE'D MADE THE WRONG CHOICE--
--ALWAYS REGRETTED NEVER HAVING A HUSBAND OR CHILDREN. REPRESSING ALL THOUGHTS OF LOVE IN FAVOR OF A CAREER AND FEELING GUILTY ABOUT IT.
AND WHEN THE BURDEN OF GUILT WAS LIFTED, THE LOVE WASHED OVER ONE OF HER OLDEST AND DEAREST FRIENDS.
FRIENDS?
FRIENDS.

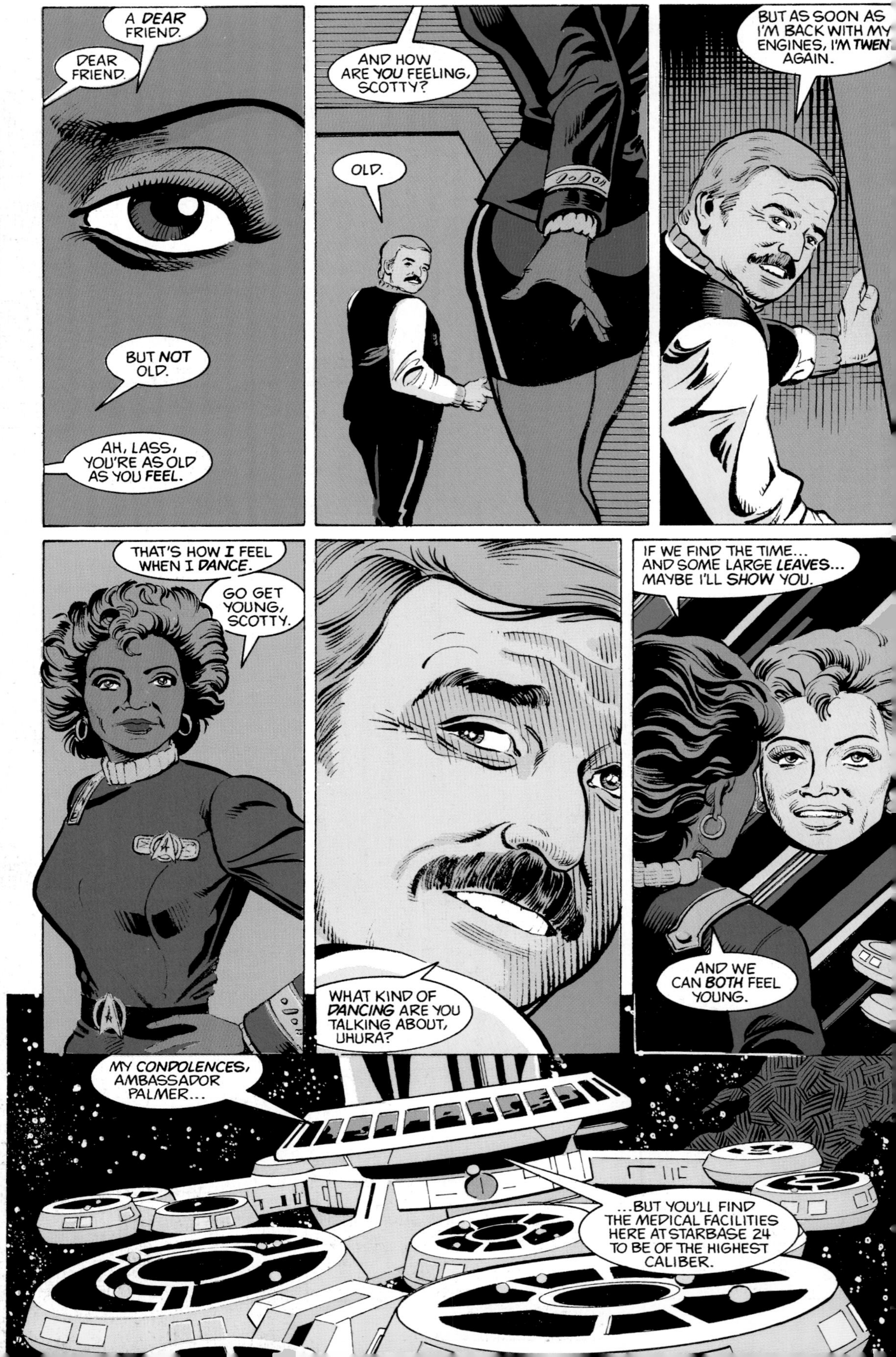

A DEAR FRIEND.
DEAR FRIEND.
BUT NOT OLD.
AH, LASS, YOU'RE AS OLD AS YOU FEEL.
AND HOW ARE YOU FEELING, SCOTTY?
OLD.
BUT AS SOON AS I'M BACK WITH MY ENGINES, I'M TWENT
AGAIN.
THAT'S HOW I FEEL WHEN I DANCE.
GO GET YOUNG, SCOTTY.
WHAT KIND OF DANCING ARE YOU TALKING ABOUT, UHURA?
IF WE FIND THE TIME... AND SOME LARGE LEAVES... MAYBE I'LL SHOW YOU.
AND WE CAN BOTH FEEL YOUNG.
MY CONDOLENCES, AMBASSADOR PALMER...
...BUT YOU'LL FIND THE MEDICAL FACILITIES HERE AT STARBASE 24 TO BE OF THE HIGHEST CALIBER.

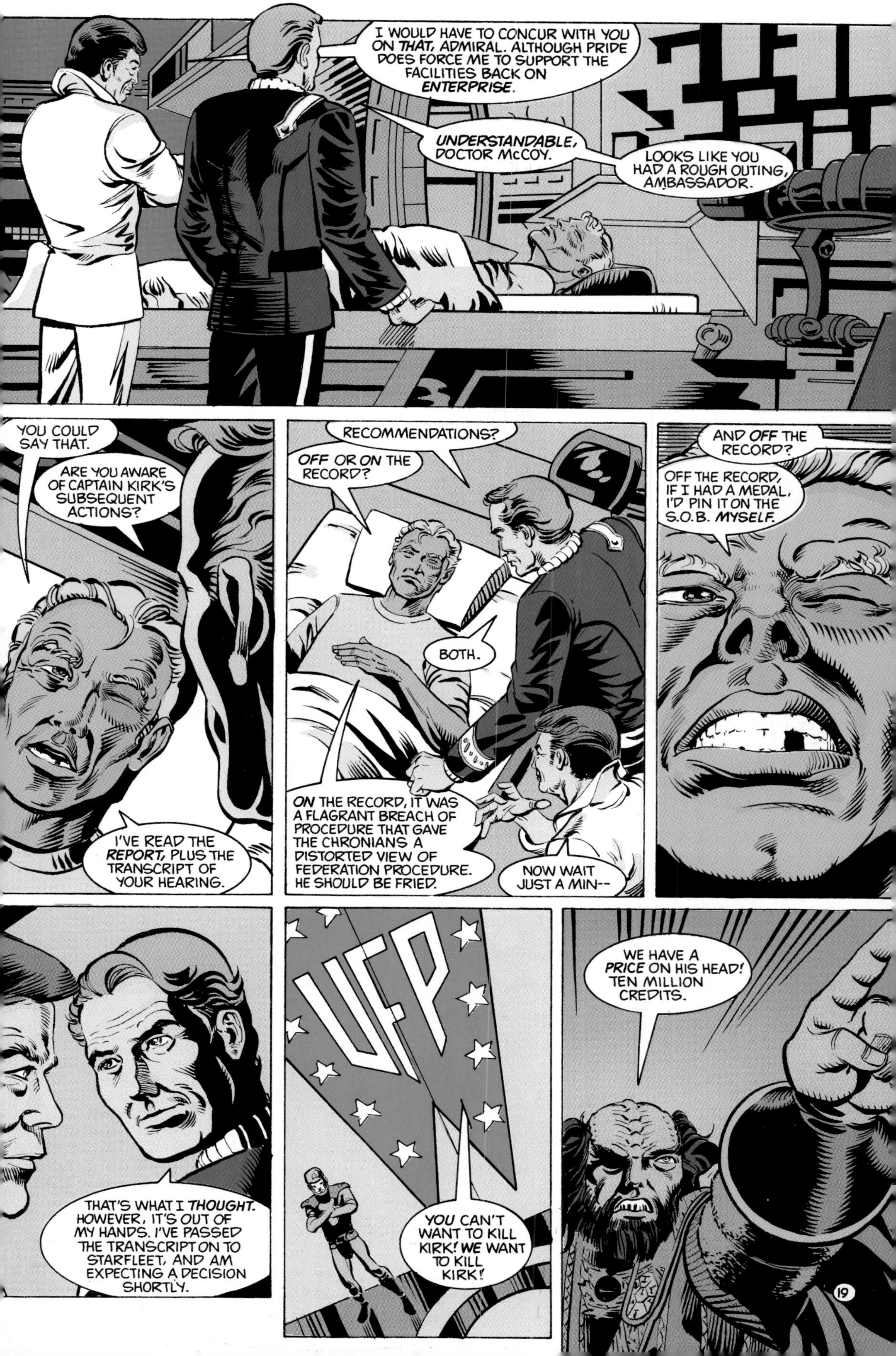

I WOULD HAVE TO CONCUR WITH YOU ON THAT, ADMIRAL. ALTHOUGH PRIDE DOES FORCE ME TO SUPPORT THE FACILITIES BACK ON ENTERPRISE.
UNDERSTANDABLE, DOCTOR McCOY.
LOOKS LIKE YOU HAD A ROUGH OUTING, AMBASSADOR.
YOU COULD SAY THAT.
ARE YOU AWARE OF CAPTAIN KIRK'S SUBSEQUENT ACTIONS?
I'VE READ THE REPORT, PLUS THE TRANSCRIPT OF YOUR HEARING.
RECOMMENDATIONS?
OFF OR ON THE RECORD?
BOTH.
ON THE RECORD, IT WAS A FLAGRANT BREACH OF PROCEDURE THAT GAVE THE CHRONIANS A DISTORTED VIEW OF FEDERATION PROCEDURE. HE SHOULD BE FRIED.
NOW WAIT JUST A MIN--
AND OFF THE RECORD?
OFF THE RECORD, IF I HAD A MEDAL, I'D PIN IT ON THE S.O.B. MYSELF.
THAT'S WHAT I THOUGHT. HOWEVER, IT'S OUT OF MY HANDS. I'VE PASSED THE TRANSCRIPT ON TO STARFLEET, AND AM EXPECTING A DECISION SHORTLY.
UFP
YOU CAN'T WANT TO KILL KIRK! WE WANT TO KILL KIRK!
WE HAVE A PRICE ON HIS HEAD! TEN MILLION CREDITS.

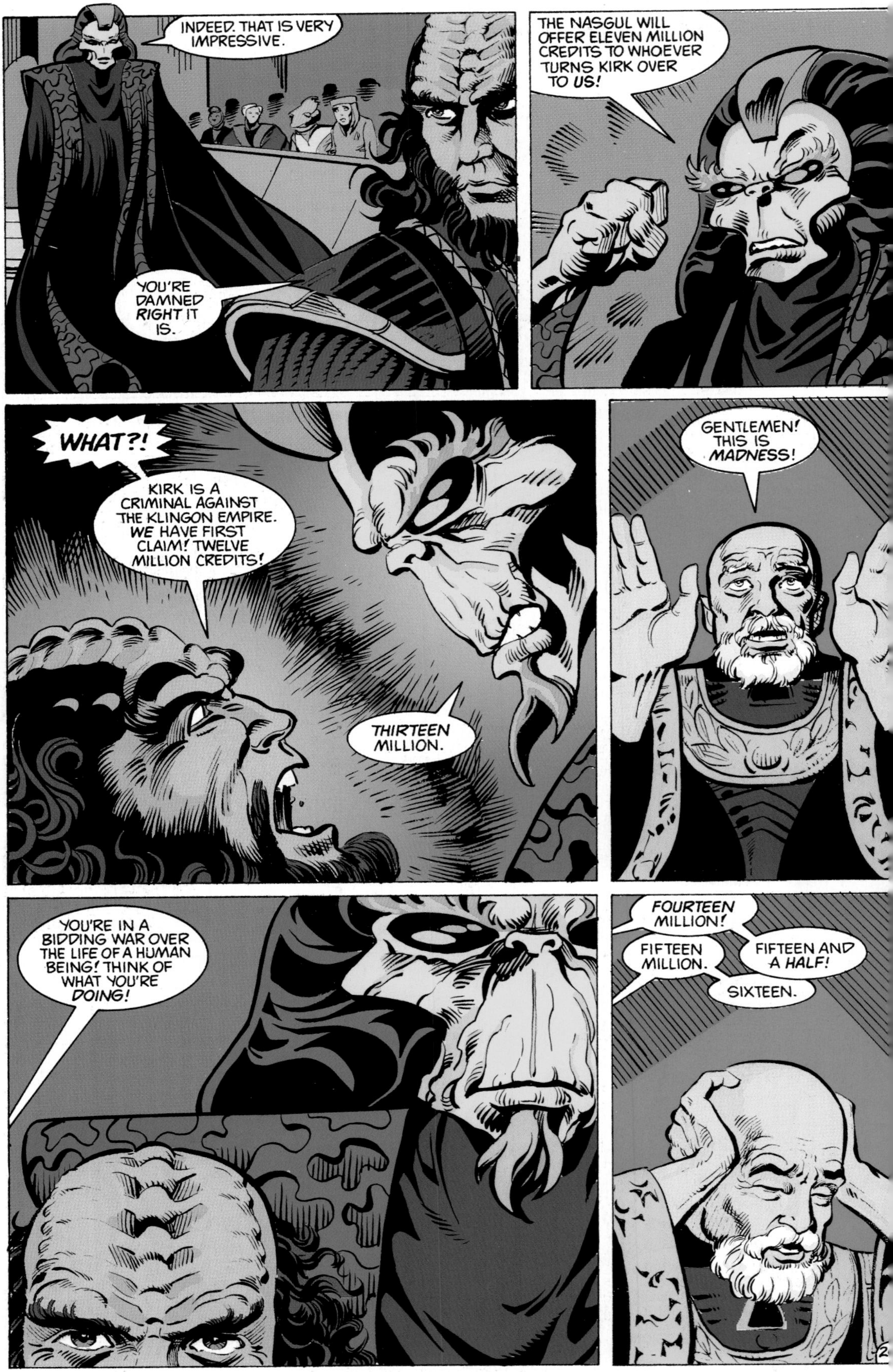
INDEED. THAT IS VERY IMPRESSIVE.
YOU'RE DAMNED RIGHT IT IS.
THE NASGUL WILL OFFER ELEVEN MILLION CREDITS TO WHOEVER TURNS KIRK OVER TO US!
WHAT?!
KIRK IS A CRIMINAL AGAINST THE KLINGON EMPIRE. WE HAVE FIRST CLAIM! TWELVE MILLION CREDITS!
THIRTEEN MILLION.
GENTLEMEN! THIS IS MADNESS!
YOU'RE IN A BIDDING WAR OVER THE LIFE OF A HUMAN BEING! THINK OF WHAT YOU'RE DOING!
FOURTEEN MILLION!
FIFTEEN MILLION.
FIFTEEN AND A HALF!
SIXTEEN.

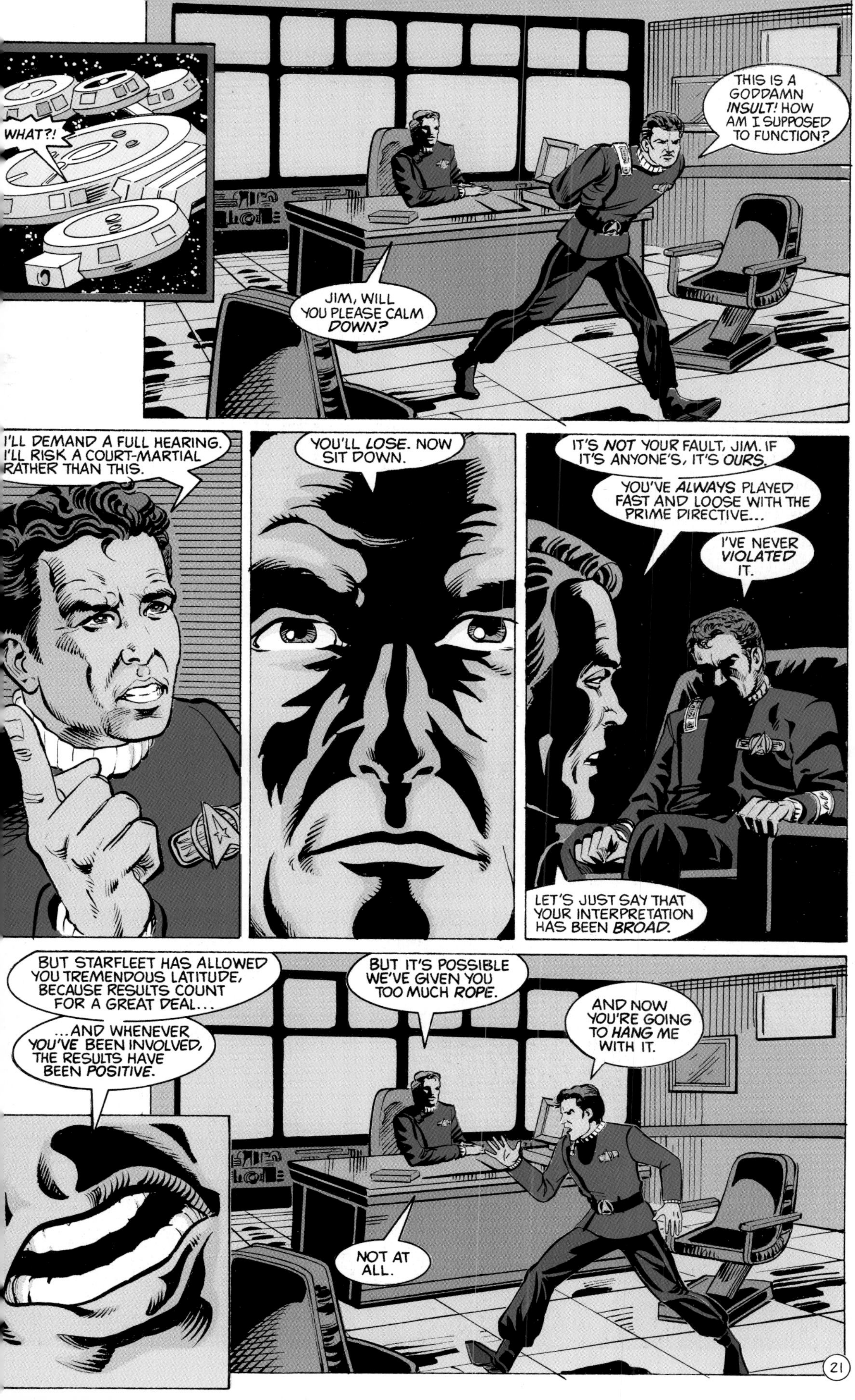
WHAT?!
THIS IS A GODDAMN INSULT! HOW AM I SUPPOSED TO FUNCTION?
JIM, WILL YOU PLEASE CALM DOWN?
I'LL DEMAND A FULL HEARING. I'LL RISK A COURT-MARTIAL RATHER THAN THIS.
YOU'LL LOSE. NOW SIT DOWN.
IT'S NOT YOUR FAULT, JIM. IF IT'S ANYONE'S, IT'S OURS.
YOU'VE ALWAYS PLAYED FAST AND LOOSE WITH THE PRIME DIRECTIVE...
I'VE NEVER VIOLATED IT.
LET'S JUST SAY THAT YOUR INTERPRETATION HAS BEEN BROAD.
BUT STARFLEET HAS ALLOWED YOU TREMENDOUS LATITUDE, BECAUSE RESULTS COUNT FOR A GREAT DEAL...
...AND WHENEVER YOU'VE BEEN INVOLVED, THE RESULTS HAVE BEEN POSITIVE.
BUT IT'S POSSIBLE WE'VE GIVEN YOU TOO MUCH ROPE.
AND NOW YOU'RE GOING TO HANG ME WITH IT.
NOT AT ALL.

BUT THERE'S A NEW *ATTITUDE* SPREADING, JIM. WITH THE POSSIBILITY OF A FEDERATION/KLINGON ALLIANCE, STARFLEET IS TRYING TO BE AS *CAUTIOUS* AS POSSIBLE. AND YOU...

I'M A POLITICAL HOT POTATO, IS THAT IT?

TO BE BLUNT: *YES.*

FACE *FACTS*, JIM. YOU'VE PUT A LOT OF NOSES OUT OF JOINT OVER THE YEARS. NO ONE DENIES THE *QUALITY* OF YOUR WORK, AND IT'S BECAUSE OF THAT THAT YOU HAVE AS MANY *SUPPORTERS* AS YOU DO.

BUT THE FEDERATION IS TRYING TO COVER ITSELF. AND THERE IS CONCERN AMONG SOME QUARTERS THAT YOU'RE A LOOSE CANNON.

THEN PUT ME OUT TO PASTURE. OR BRING ME UP ON CHARGES. BUT NOT *THIS.*

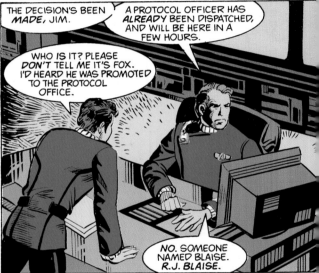

THE DECISION'S BEEN *MADE*, JIM.

A PROTOCOL OFFICER HAS *ALREADY* BEEN DISPATCHED, AND WILL BE HERE IN A FEW HOURS.

WHO IS IT? PLEASE *DON'T* TELL ME IT'S FOX. I'D HEARD HE WAS PROMOTED TO THE PROTOCOL OFFICE.

NO. SOMEONE NAMED BLAISE. R.J. BLAISE.

JIM... PERHAPS IT WILL WORK OUT FOR THE BEST.

SURE.

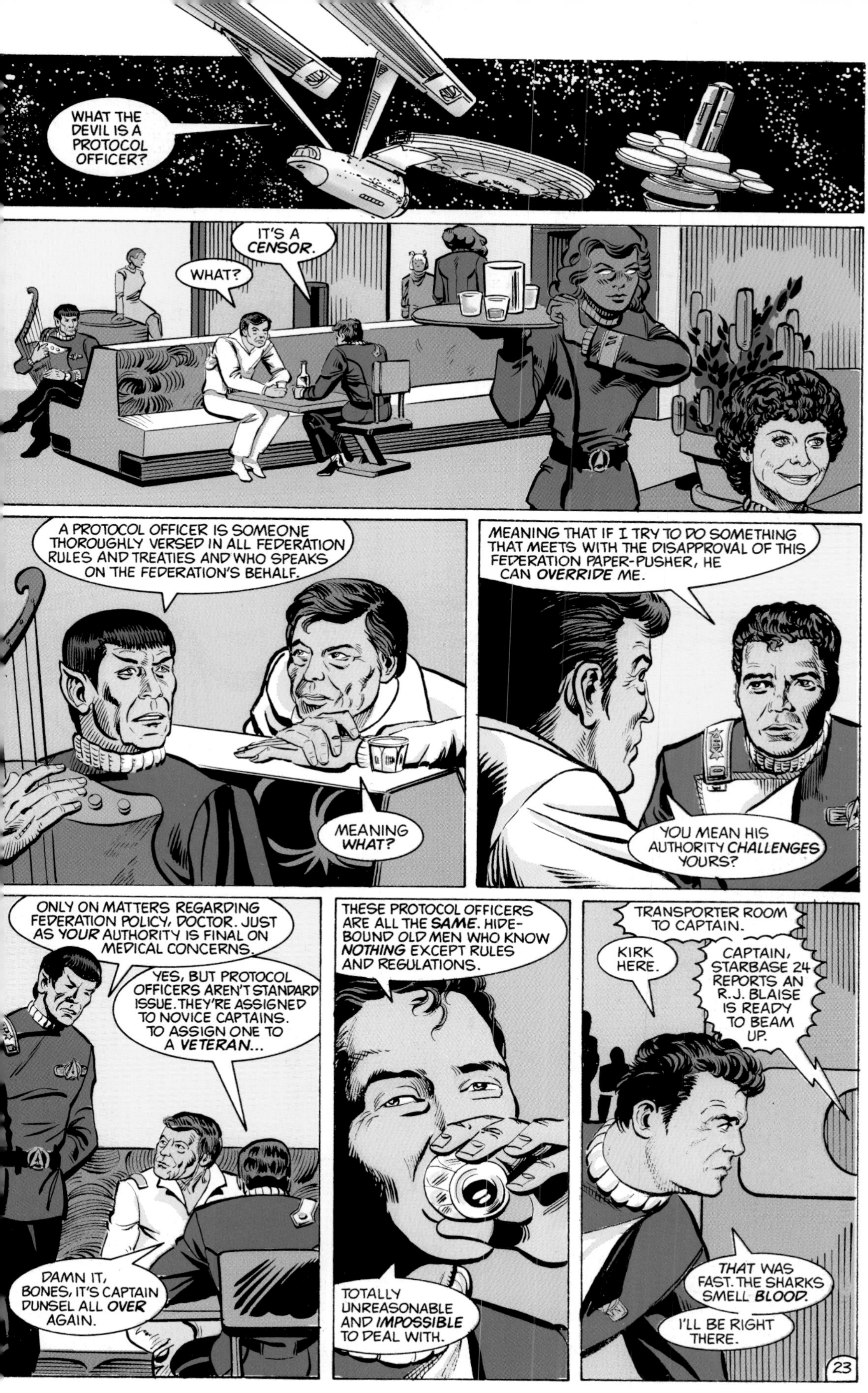
WHAT THE DEVIL IS A PROTOCOL OFFICER?
WHAT?
IT'S A *CENSOR*.
A PROTOCOL OFFICER IS SOMEONE THOROUGHLY VERSED IN ALL FEDERATION RULES AND TREATIES AND WHO SPEAKS ON THE FEDERATION'S BEHALF.
MEANING *WHAT?*
MEANING THAT IF I TRY TO DO SOMETHING THAT MEETS WITH THE DISAPPROVAL OF THIS FEDERATION PAPER-PUSHER, HE CAN *OVERRIDE* ME.
YOU MEAN HIS AUTHORITY *CHALLENGES* YOURS?
ONLY ON MATTERS REGARDING FEDERATION POLICY, DOCTOR. JUST AS *YOUR* AUTHORITY IS FINAL ON MEDICAL CONCERNS.
YES, BUT PROTOCOL OFFICERS AREN'T STANDARD ISSUE. THEY'RE ASSIGNED TO NOVICE CAPTAINS. TO ASSIGN ONE TO A *VETERAN*...
DAMN IT, BONES, IT'S CAPTAIN DUNSEL ALL *OVER* AGAIN.
THESE PROTOCOL OFFICERS ARE ALL THE *SAME*. HIDE-BOUND *OLD* MEN WHO KNOW *NOTHING* EXCEPT RULES AND REGULATIONS.
TOTALLY UNREASONABLE AND *IMPOSSIBLE* TO DEAL WITH.
TRANSPORTER ROOM TO CAPTAIN.
KIRK HERE.
CAPTAIN, STARBASE 24 REPORTS AN R.J. BLAISE IS READY TO BEAM UP.
THAT WAS FAST. THE SHARKS SMELL *BLOOD*.
I'LL BE RIGHT THERE.

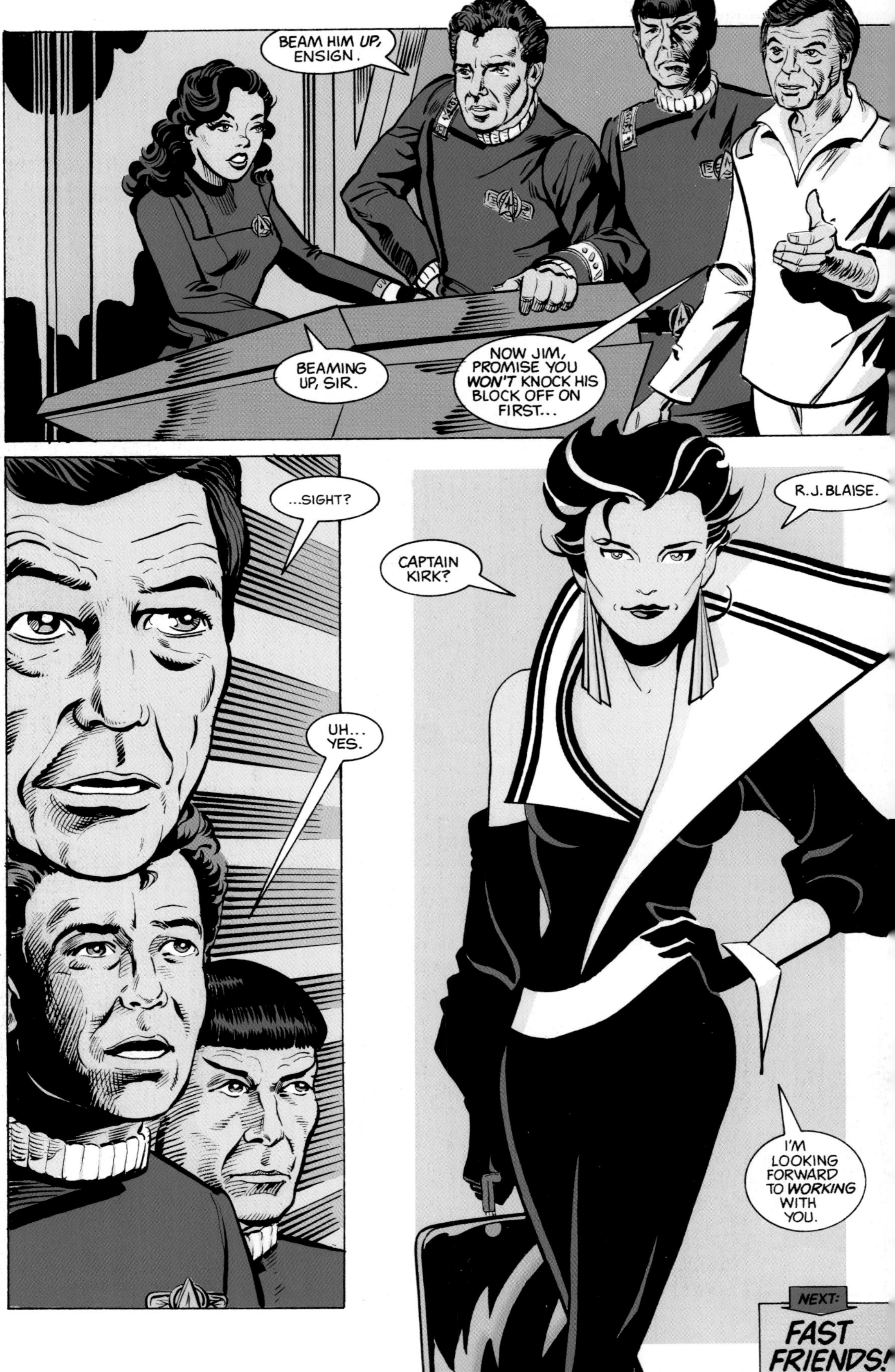
BEAM HIM UP, ENSIGN.
BEAMING UP, SIR.
NOW JIM, PROMISE YOU WON'T KNOCK HIS BLOCK OFF ON FIRST...
...SIGHT?
UH... YES.
R. J. BLAISE.
CAPTAIN KIRK?
I'M LOOKING FORWARD TO WORKING WITH YOU.
NEXT:
FAST FRIENDS!

I DON'T BELIEVE THIS IS HAPPENING!

THAT MEETING OF THE COUNCIL HAD TO BE THE MOST *INSANE* I'VE EVER PRESIDED OVER.

I'M SORRY I *MISSED* IT, SIR.

PURE LUNACY, D'FALCO. IMAGINE THE SALLA AND THE KLINGON AMBASSADOR IN A BIDDING WAR OVER THE RIGHT TO JUDGE, *I.E. EXTERMINATE,* JAMES KIRK.

PERHAPS THE KLINGONS WOULD AT LEAST LISTEN TO *REASON.*

BUT THE NASGUL...THEY'RE *FANATICS.* ONCE THEIR LEADER, THE SALLA, HAS GOTTEN INTO HIS HEAD THAT KIRK MUST DIE...

WELL, FRANKLY, I DON'T SEE HOW IT COULD GET *WORSE.*

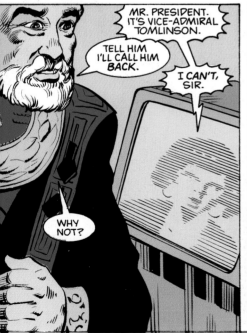

MR. PRESIDENT. IT'S VICE-ADMIRAL TOMLINSON.

TELL HIM I'LL CALL HIM BACK.

I CAN'T, SIR.

WHY NOT?

HE'S HERE IN THE OUTER OFFICE.

WONDERFUL. JUST *WONDERFUL.*

KIRK, WHEREVER YOU ARE...STAY OUT OF *TROUBLE.*

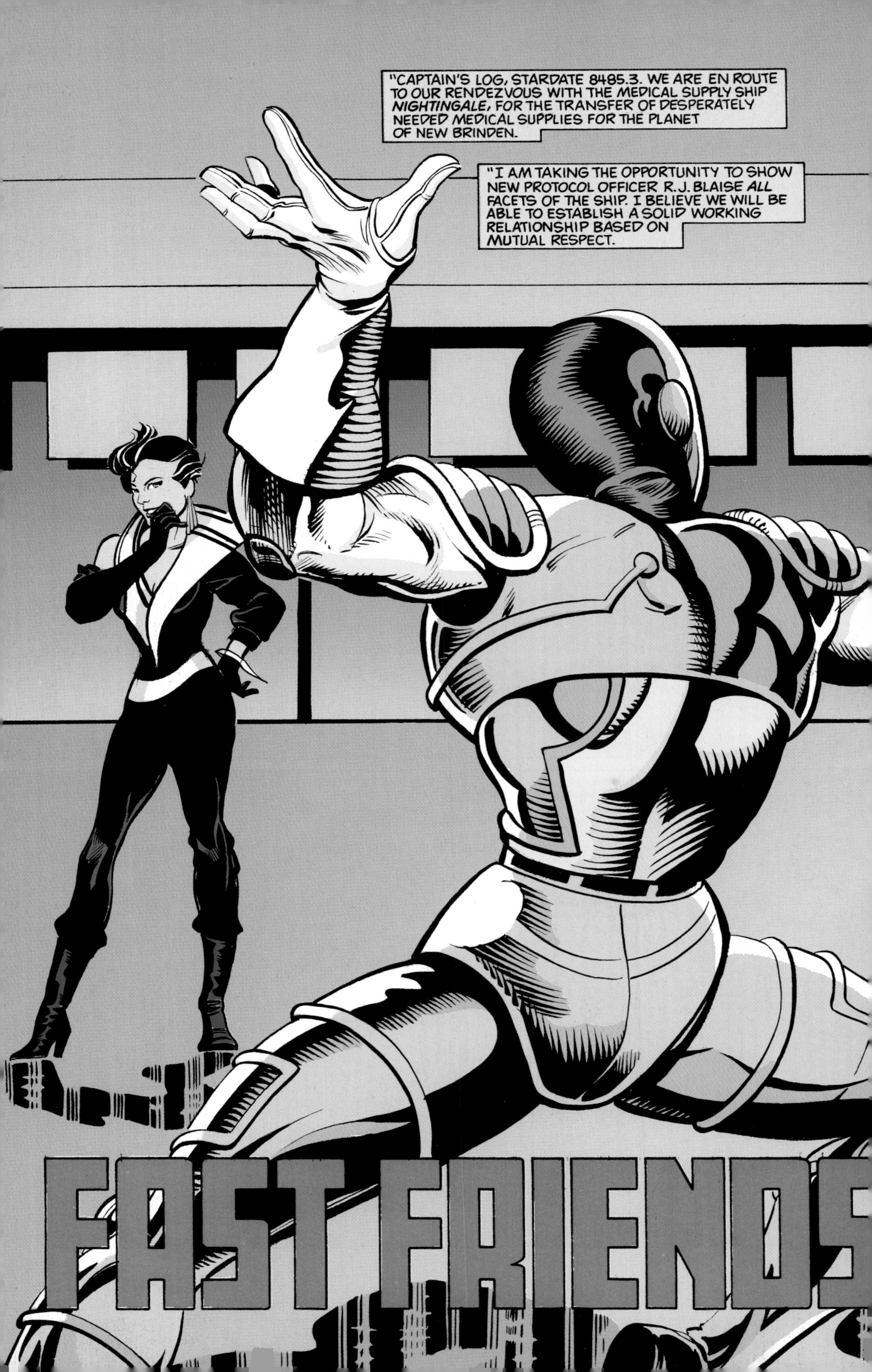
"CAPTAIN'S LOG, STARDATE 8485.3. WE ARE EN ROUTE TO OUR RENDEZVOUS WITH THE MEDICAL SUPPLY SHIP *NIGHTINGALE*, FOR THE TRANSFER OF DESPERATELY NEEDED MEDICAL SUPPLIES FOR THE PLANET OF NEW BRINDEN.
"I AM TAKING THE OPPORTUNITY TO SHOW NEW PROTOCOL OFFICER R.J. BLAISE *ALL* FACETS OF THE SHIP. I BELIEVE WE WILL BE ABLE TO ESTABLISH A SOLID WORKING RELATIONSHIP BASED ON MUTUAL RESPECT.
FAST FRIENDS

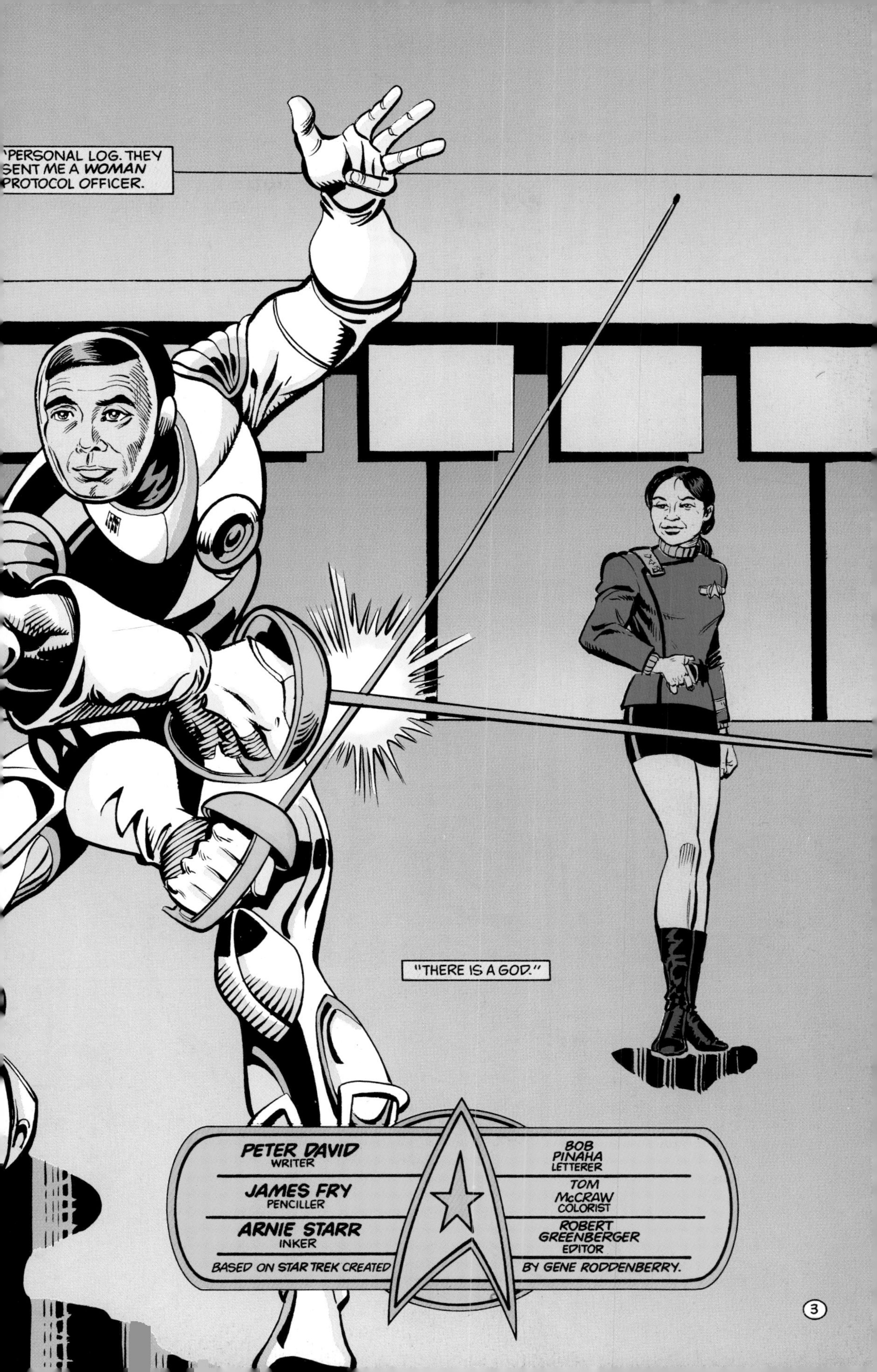
"PERSONAL LOG. THEY SENT ME A *WOMAN* PROTOCOL OFFICER.
"THERE IS A GOD."
PETER DAVID WRITER
JAMES FRY PENCILLER
ARNIE STARR INKER
BOB PINAHA LETTERER
TOM McCRAW COLORIST
ROBERT GREENBERGER EDITOR
BASED ON STAR TREK CREATED BY GENE RODDENBERRY.

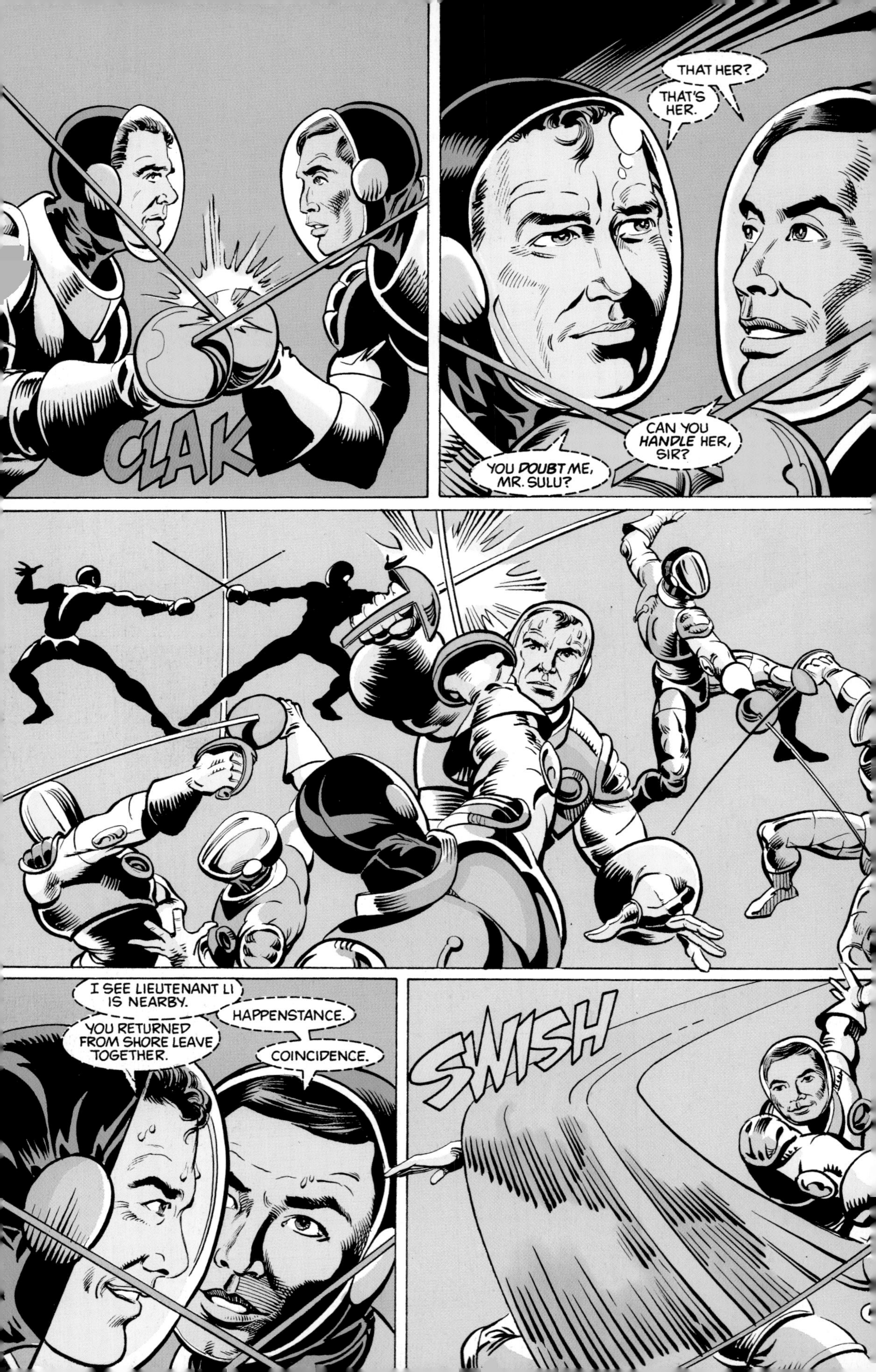
CLAK
THAT HER?
THAT'S HER.
CAN YOU HANDLE HER, SIR?
YOU DOUBT ME, MR. SULU?
I SEE LIEUTENANT LI IS NEARBY.
HAPPENSTANCE.
YOU RETURNED FROM SHORE LEAVE TOGETHER.
COINCIDENCE.
SWISH

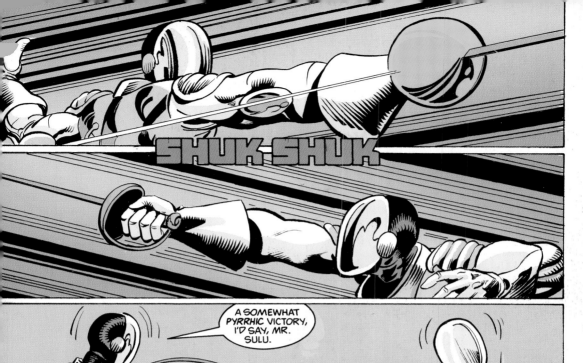

SHUK-SHUK

A SOMEWHAT PYRRHIC VICTORY, I'D SAY, MR. SULU.

CALL IT A DRAW?

THAT WOULD BE FINE BY ME, CAPTAIN.

WE SHOULD DO THIS MORE OFTEN, CAPTAIN.

DOESN'T THE CAPTAIN WORK OUT *REGULARLY*, MR. SULU?

THE CAPTAIN? HEH. WHY, I CAN'T *REMEMBER* THE LAST TIME HE...

UH...

CAN'T REMEMBER THE LAST TIME HE... *MISSED* A WORKOUT!

EVERY DAY, AT LEAST AN HOUR OR MORE, HE'S IN *HERE*. FENCING, LIFTING WEIGHTS, RUNNING.

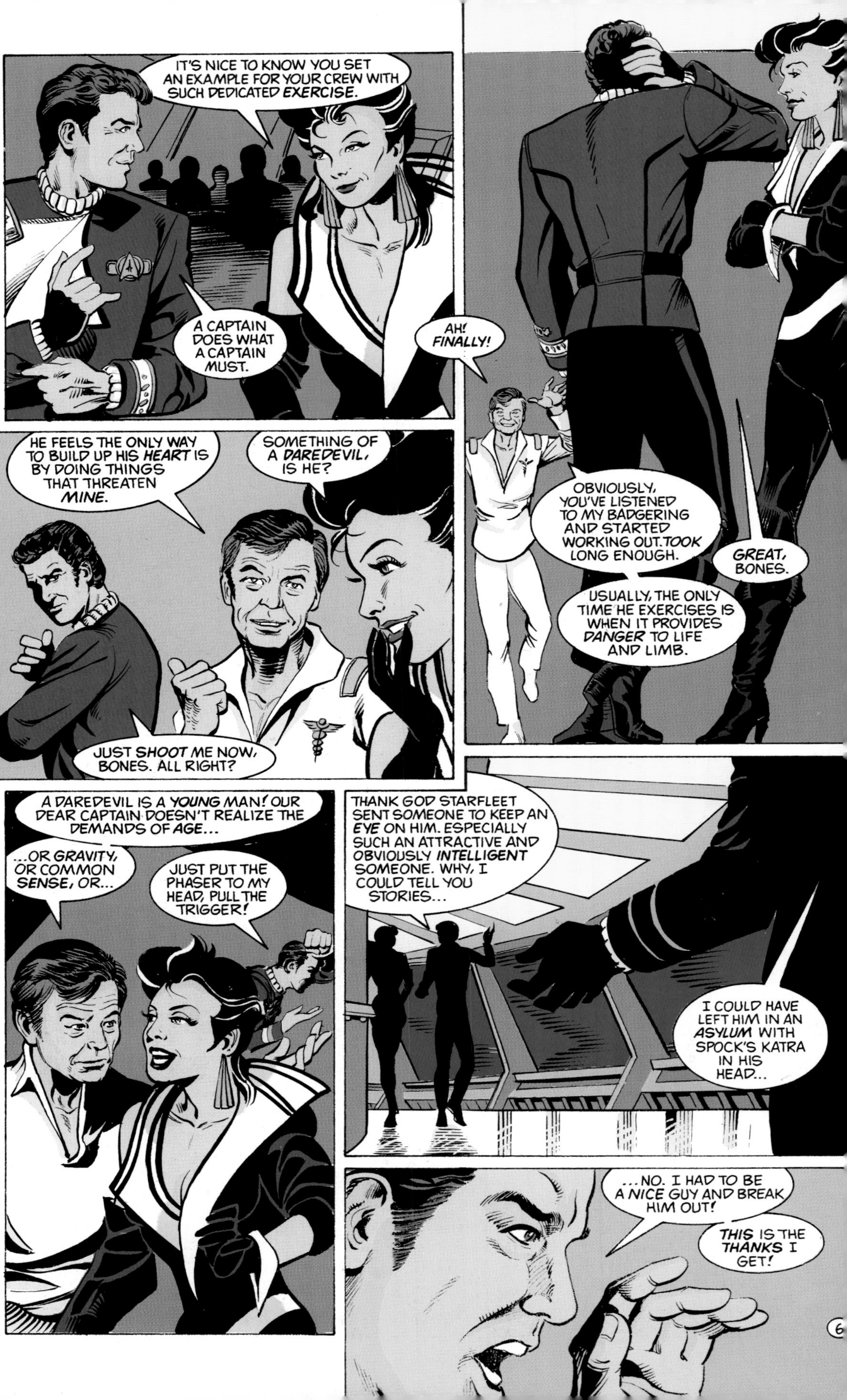

IT'S NICE TO KNOW YOU SET AN EXAMPLE FOR YOUR CREW WITH SUCH DEDICATED EXERCISE.
A CAPTAIN DOES WHAT A CAPTAIN MUST.
AH! FINALLY!
OBVIOUSLY, YOU'VE LISTENED TO MY BADGERING AND STARTED WORKING OUT. TOOK LONG ENOUGH.
GREAT, BONES.
USUALLY, THE ONLY TIME HE EXERCISES IS WHEN IT PROVIDES DANGER TO LIFE AND LIMB.
HE FEELS THE ONLY WAY TO BUILD UP HIS HEART IS BY DOING THINGS THAT THREATEN MINE.
SOMETHING OF A DAREDEVIL, IS HE?
JUST SHOOT ME NOW, BONES. ALL RIGHT?
A DAREDEVIL IS A YOUNG MAN! OUR DEAR CAPTAIN DOESN'T REALIZE THE DEMANDS OF AGE...
...OR GRAVITY, OR COMMON SENSE, OR...
JUST PUT THE PHASER TO MY HEAD, PULL THE TRIGGER!
THANK GOD STARFLEET SENT SOMEONE TO KEEP AN EYE ON HIM. ESPECIALLY SUCH AN ATTRACTIVE AND OBVIOUSLY INTELLIGENT SOMEONE. WHY, I COULD TELL YOU STORIES...
I COULD HAVE LEFT HIM IN AN ASYLUM WITH SPOCK'S KATRA IN HIS HEAD...
...NO. I HAD TO BE A NICE GUY AND BREAK HIM OUT!
THIS IS THE THANKS I GET!

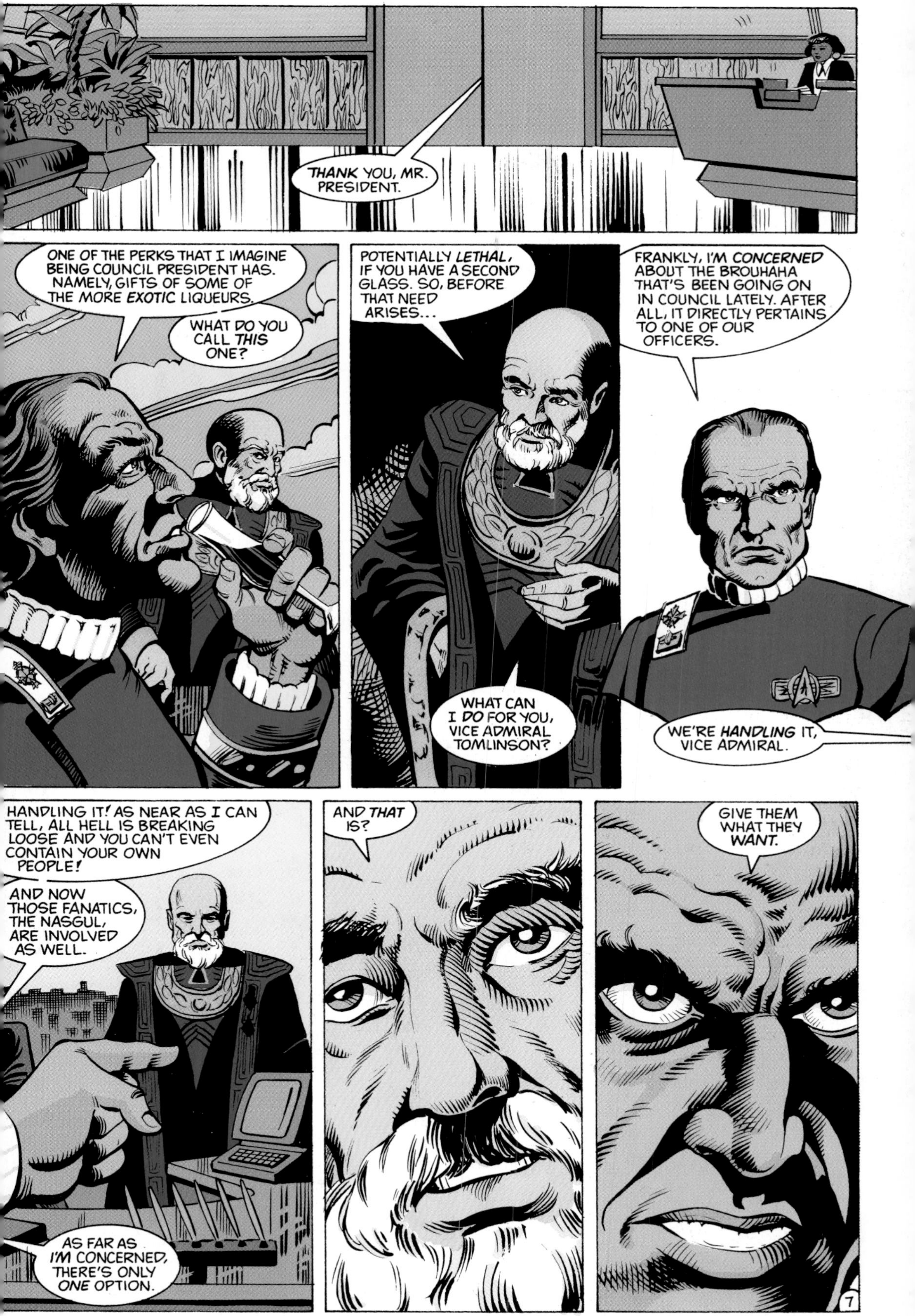
THANK YOU, MR. PRESIDENT.
ONE OF THE PERKS THAT I IMAGINE BEING COUNCIL PRESIDENT HAS. NAMELY, GIFTS OF SOME OF THE MORE EXOTIC LIQUEURS.
WHAT DO YOU CALL THIS ONE?
POTENTIALLY LETHAL, IF YOU HAVE A SECOND GLASS. SO, BEFORE THAT NEED ARISES...
WHAT CAN I DO FOR YOU, VICE ADMIRAL TOMLINSON?
FRANKLY, I'M CONCERNED ABOUT THE BROUHAHA THAT'S BEEN GOING ON IN COUNCIL LATELY. AFTER ALL, IT DIRECTLY PERTAINS TO ONE OF OUR OFFICERS.
WE'RE HANDLING IT, VICE ADMIRAL.
HANDLING IT! AS NEAR AS I CAN TELL, ALL HELL IS BREAKING LOOSE AND YOU CAN'T EVEN CONTAIN YOUR OWN PEOPLE!
AND NOW THOSE FANATICS, THE NASGUL, ARE INVOLVED AS WELL.
AS FAR AS I'M CONCERNED, THERE'S ONLY ONE OPTION.
AND THAT IS?
GIVE THEM WHAT THEY WANT.
7

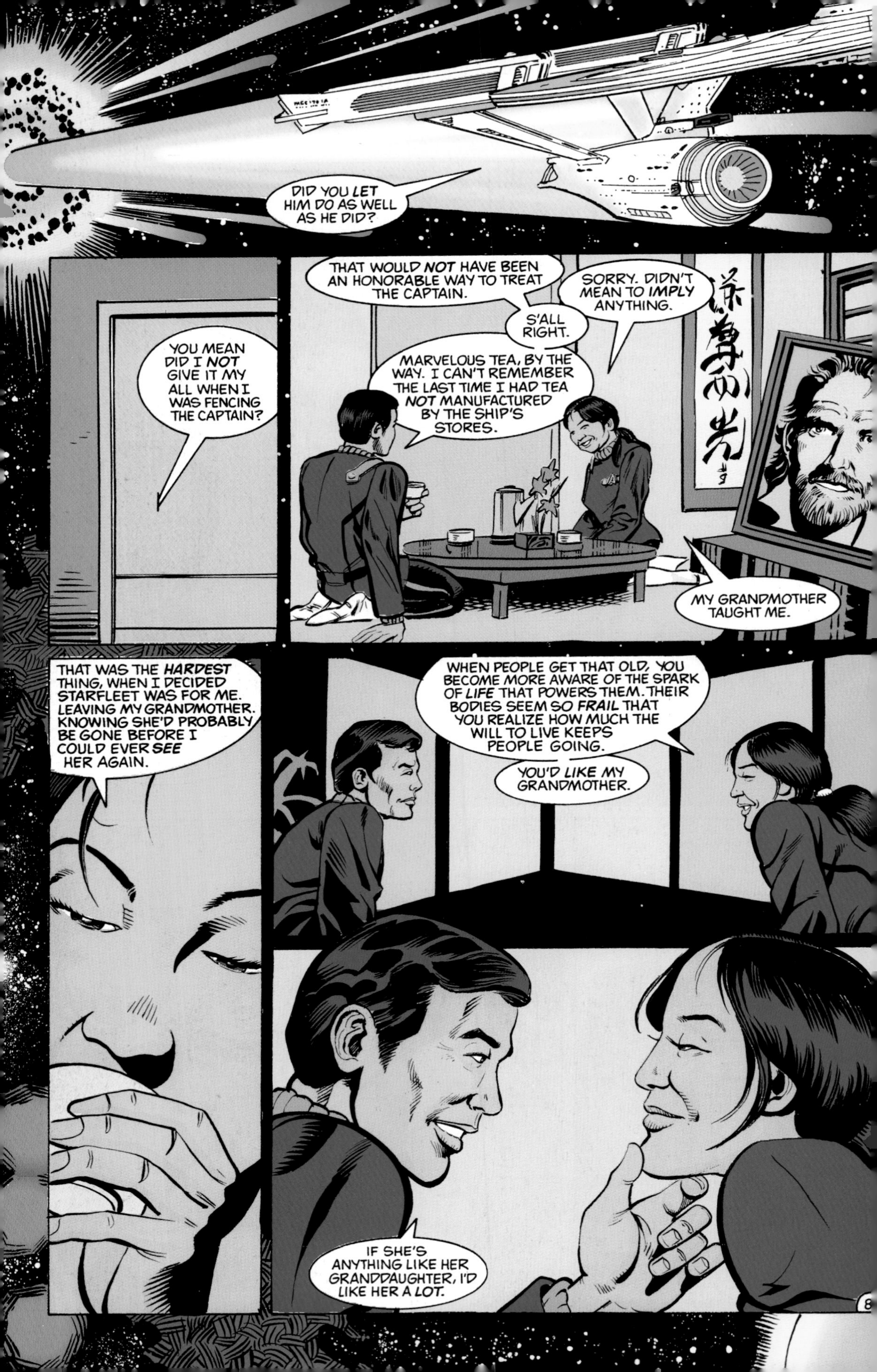
DID YOU LET HIM DO AS WELL AS HE DID?
YOU MEAN DID I NOT GIVE IT MY ALL WHEN I WAS FENCING THE CAPTAIN?
THAT WOULD NOT HAVE BEEN AN HONORABLE WAY TO TREAT THE CAPTAIN.
SORRY. DIDN'T MEAN TO IMPLY ANYTHING.
S'ALL RIGHT.
MARVELOUS TEA, BY THE WAY. I CAN'T REMEMBER THE LAST TIME I HAD TEA NOT MANUFACTURED BY THE SHIP'S STORES.
MY GRANDMOTHER TAUGHT ME.
THAT WAS THE HARDEST THING, WHEN I DECIDED STARFLEET WAS FOR ME. LEAVING MY GRANDMOTHER. KNOWING SHE'D PROBABLY BE GONE BEFORE I COULD EVER SEE HER AGAIN.
WHEN PEOPLE GET THAT OLD, YOU BECOME MORE AWARE OF THE SPARK OF LIFE THAT POWERS THEM. THEIR BODIES SEEM SO FRAIL THAT YOU REALIZE HOW MUCH THE WILL TO LIVE KEEPS PEOPLE GOING.
YOU'D LIKE MY GRANDMOTHER.
IF SHE'S ANYTHING LIKE HER GRANDDAUGHTER, I'D LIKE HER A LOT.

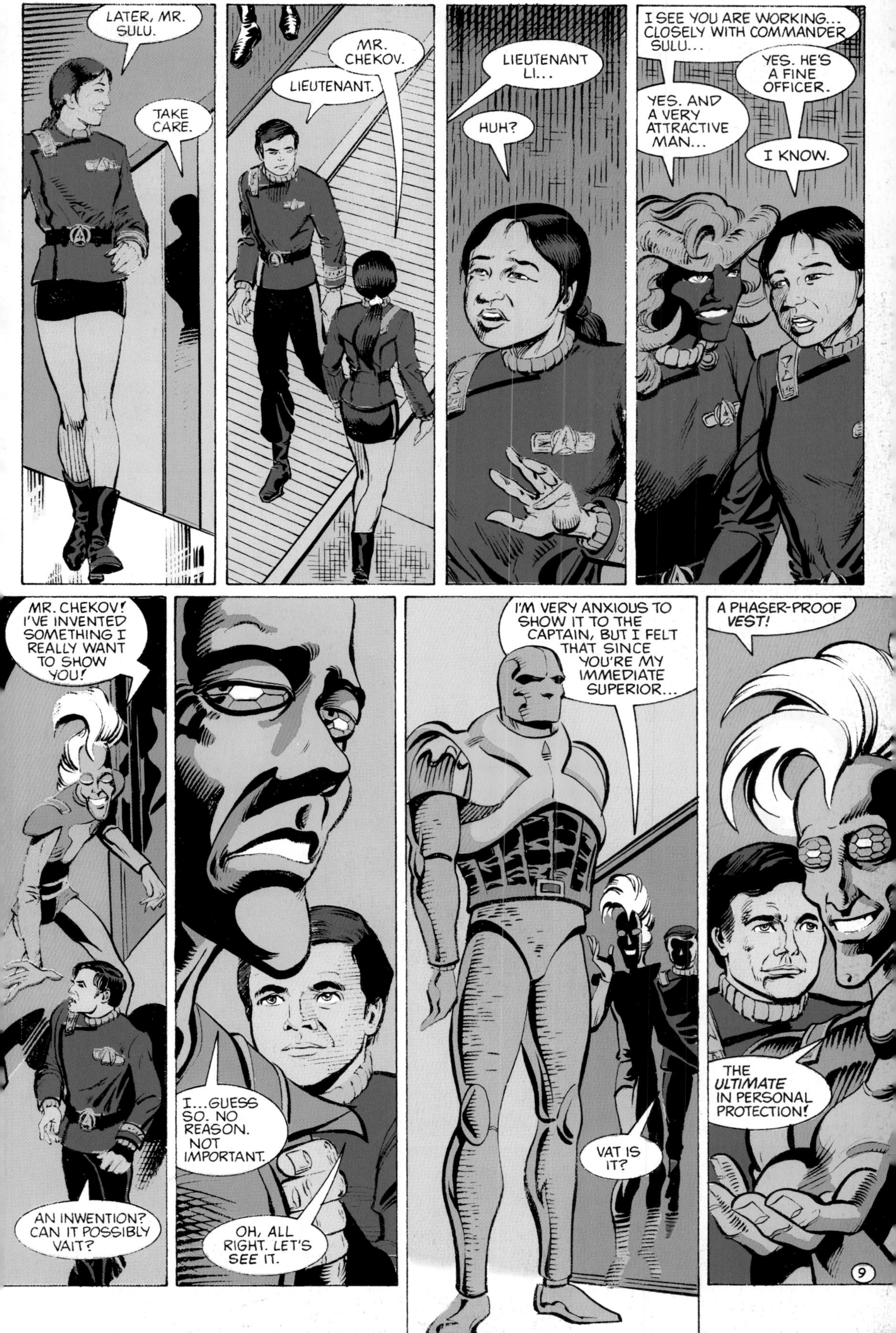
LATER, MR. SULU.
TAKE CARE.
MR. CHEKOV.
LIEUTENANT.
LIEUTENANT LI...
HUH?
I SEE YOU ARE WORKING... CLOSELY WITH COMMANDER SULU...
YES. HE'S A FINE OFFICER.
YES. AND A VERY ATTRACTIVE MAN...
I KNOW.
MR. CHEKOV! I'VE INVENTED SOMETHING I REALLY WANT TO SHOW YOU!
AN INWENTION? CAN IT POSSIBLY VAIT?
I...GUESS SO. NO REASON. NOT IMPORTANT.
OH, ALL RIGHT. LET'S SEE IT.
I'M VERY ANXIOUS TO SHOW IT TO THE CAPTAIN, BUT I FELT THAT SINCE YOU'RE MY IMMEDIATE SUPERIOR...
VAT IS IT?
A PHASER-PROOF VEST!
THE ULTIMATE IN PERSONAL PROTECTION!
9

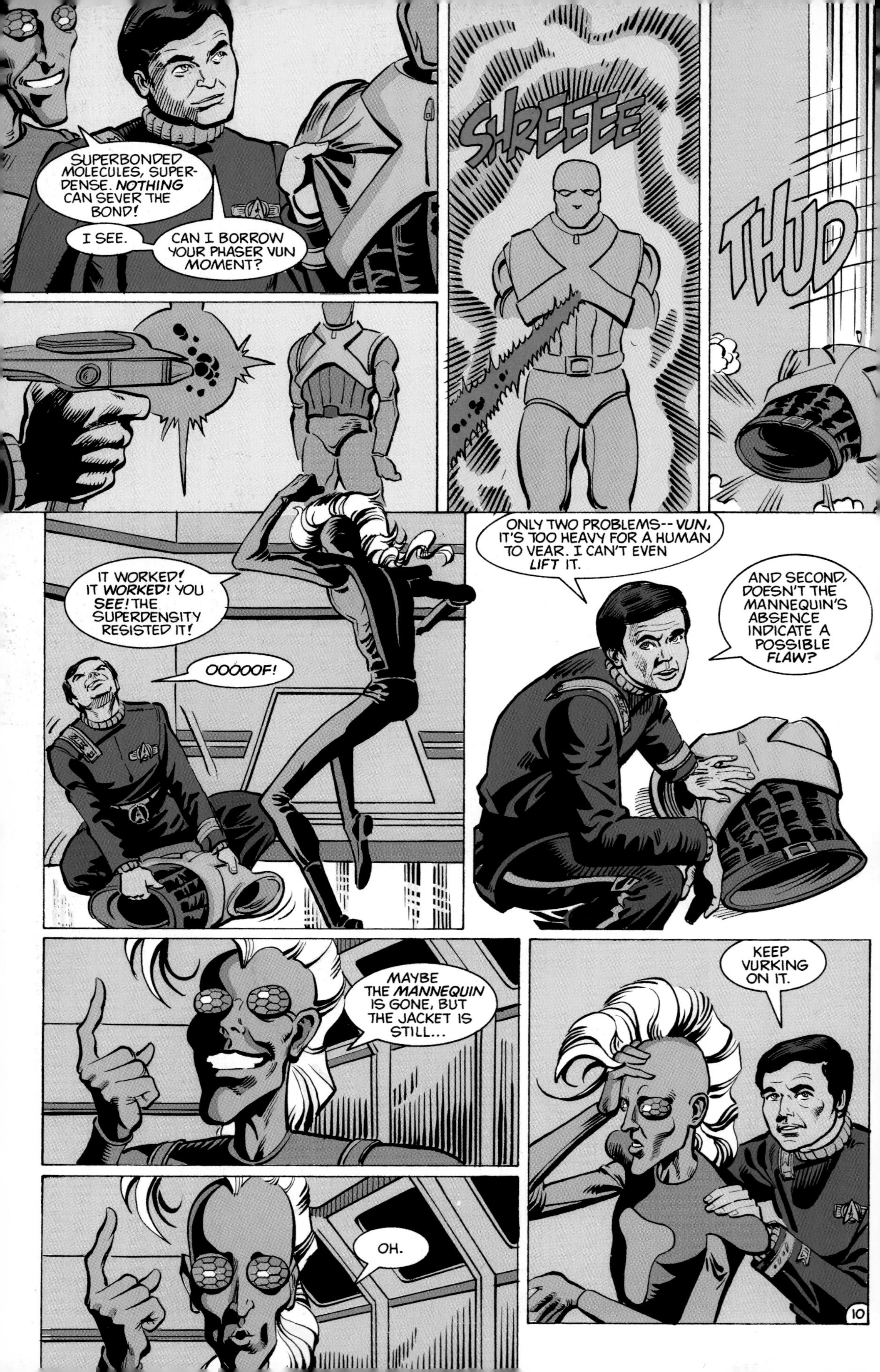

SUPERBONDED MOLECULES, SUPER-DENSE. NOTHING CAN SEVER THE BOND!
I SEE.
CAN I BORROW YOUR PHASER VUN MOMENT?
SHREEEE
THUD
IT WORKED! IT WORKED! YOU SEE! THE SUPERDENSITY RESISTED IT!
OOOOOF!
ONLY TWO PROBLEMS-- VUN, IT'S TOO HEAVY FOR A HUMAN TO VEAR. I CAN'T EVEN LIFT IT.
AND SECOND, DOESN'T THE MANNEQUIN'S ABSENCE INDICATE A POSSIBLE FLAW?
MAYBE THE MANNEQUIN IS GONE, BUT THE JACKET IS STILL...
OH.
KEEP VURKING ON IT.

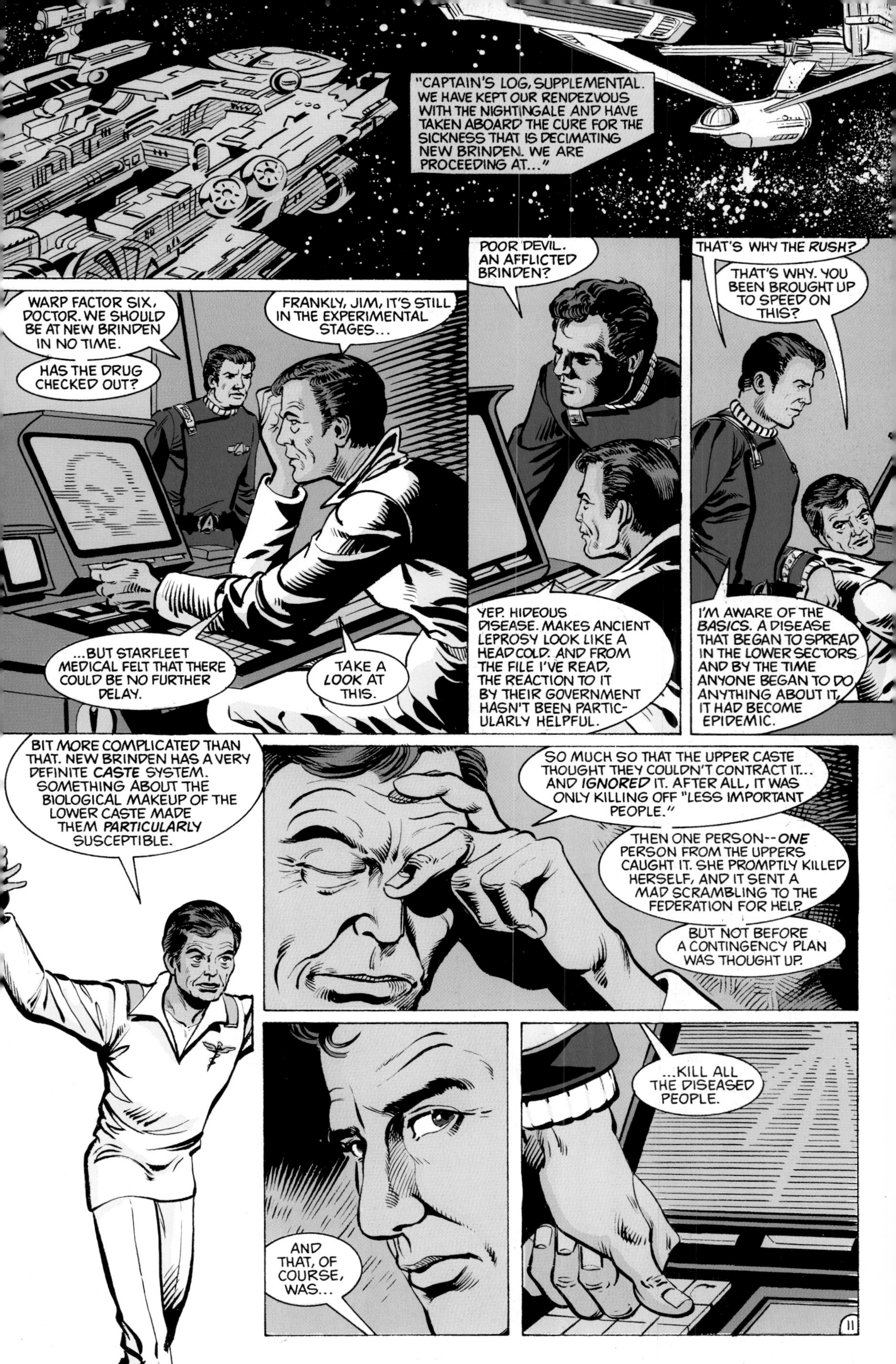
"CAPTAIN'S LOG, SUPPLEMENTAL. WE HAVE KEPT OUR RENDEZVOUS WITH THE NIGHTINGALE AND HAVE TAKEN ABOARD THE CURE FOR THE SICKNESS THAT IS DECIMATING NEW BRINDEN. WE ARE PROCEEDING AT..."
WARP FACTOR SIX, DOCTOR. WE SHOULD BE AT NEW BRINDEN IN NO TIME.
HAS THE DRUG CHECKED OUT?
FRANKLY, JIM, IT'S STILL IN THE EXPERIMENTAL STAGES...
...BUT STARFLEET MEDICAL FELT THAT THERE COULD BE NO FURTHER DELAY.
TAKE A LOOK AT THIS.
POOR DEVIL. AN AFFLICTED BRINDEN?
YEP. HIDEOUS DISEASE. MAKES ANCIENT LEPROSY LOOK LIKE A HEAD COLD. AND FROM THE FILE I'VE READ, THE REACTION TO IT BY THEIR GOVERNMENT HASN'T BEEN PARTIC-ULARLY HELPFUL.
THAT'S WHY THE RUSH?
THAT'S WHY. YOU BEEN BROUGHT UP TO SPEED ON THIS?
I'M AWARE OF THE BASICS. A DISEASE THAT BEGAN TO SPREAD IN THE LOWER SECTORS AND BY THE TIME ANYONE BEGAN TO DO ANYTHING ABOUT IT, IT HAD BECOME EPIDEMIC.
BIT MORE COMPLICATED THAN THAT. NEW BRINDEN HAS A VERY DEFINITE CASTE SYSTEM. SOMETHING ABOUT THE BIOLOGICAL MAKEUP OF THE LOWER CASTE MADE THEM PARTICULARLY SUSCEPTIBLE.
SO MUCH SO THAT THE UPPER CASTE THOUGHT THEY COULDN'T CONTRACT IT... AND IGNORED IT. AFTER ALL, IT WAS ONLY KILLING OFF "LESS IMPORTANT PEOPLE."
THEN ONE PERSON--ONE PERSON FROM THE UPPERS CAUGHT IT. SHE PROMPTLY KILLED HERSELF, AND IT SENT A MAD SCRAMBLING TO THE FEDERATION FOR HELP.
BUT NOT BEFORE A CONTINGENCY PLAN WAS THOUGHT UP.
AND THAT, OF COURSE, WAS...
...KILL ALL THE DISEASED PEOPLE.
11

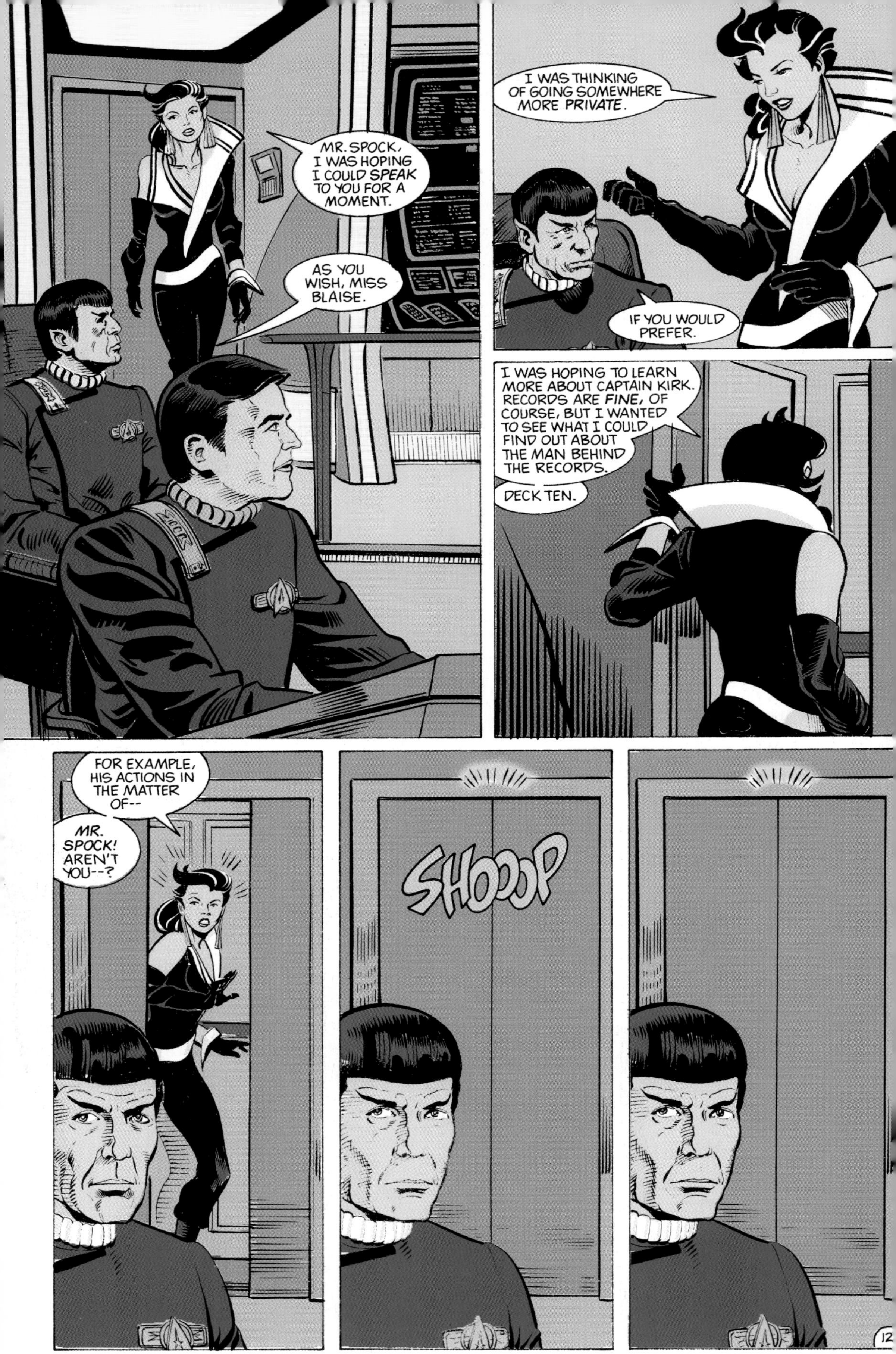
MR. SPOCK, I WAS HOPING I COULD SPEAK TO YOU FOR A MOMENT.
AS YOU WISH, MISS BLAISE.
I WAS THINKING OF GOING SOMEWHERE MORE PRIVATE.
IF YOU WOULD PREFER.
I WAS HOPING TO LEARN MORE ABOUT CAPTAIN KIRK. RECORDS ARE FINE, OF COURSE, BUT I WANTED TO SEE WHAT I COULD FIND OUT ABOUT THE MAN BEHIND THE RECORDS.
DECK TEN.
FOR EXAMPLE, HIS ACTIONS IN THE MATTER OF--
MR. SPOCK! AREN'T YOU--?
SHOOOP

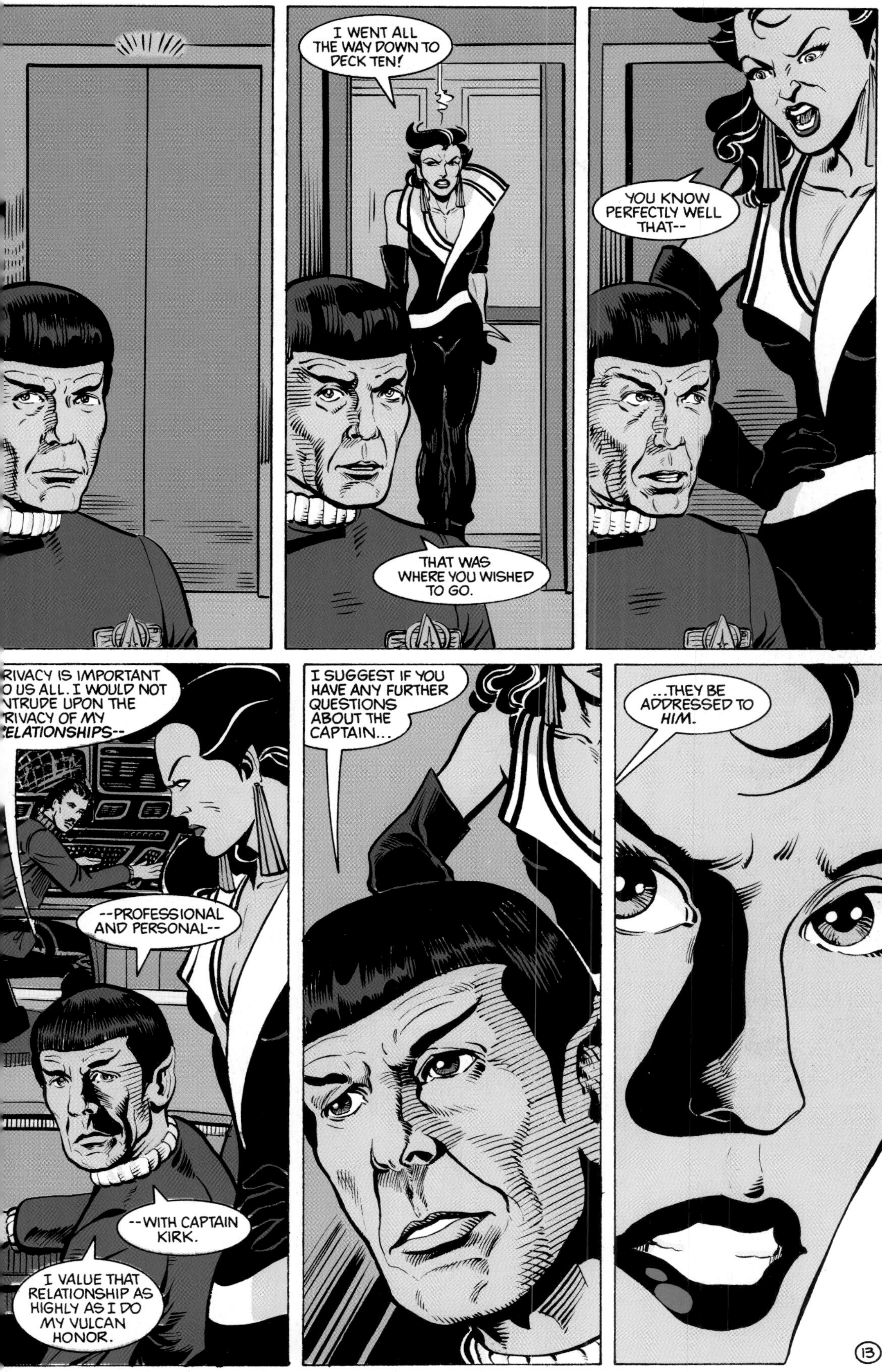
I WENT ALL THE WAY DOWN TO DECK TEN!
THAT WAS WHERE YOU WISHED TO GO.
YOU KNOW PERFECTLY WELL THAT--
RIVACY IS IMPORTANT O US ALL. I WOULD NOT NTRUDE UPON THE RIVACY OF MY RELATIONSHIPS--
--PROFESSIONAL AND PERSONAL--
--WITH CAPTAIN KIRK.
I VALUE THAT RELATIONSHIP AS HIGHLY AS I DO MY VULCAN HONOR.
I SUGGEST IF YOU HAVE ANY FURTHER QUESTIONS ABOUT THE CAPTAIN...
...THEY BE ADDRESSED TO HIM.

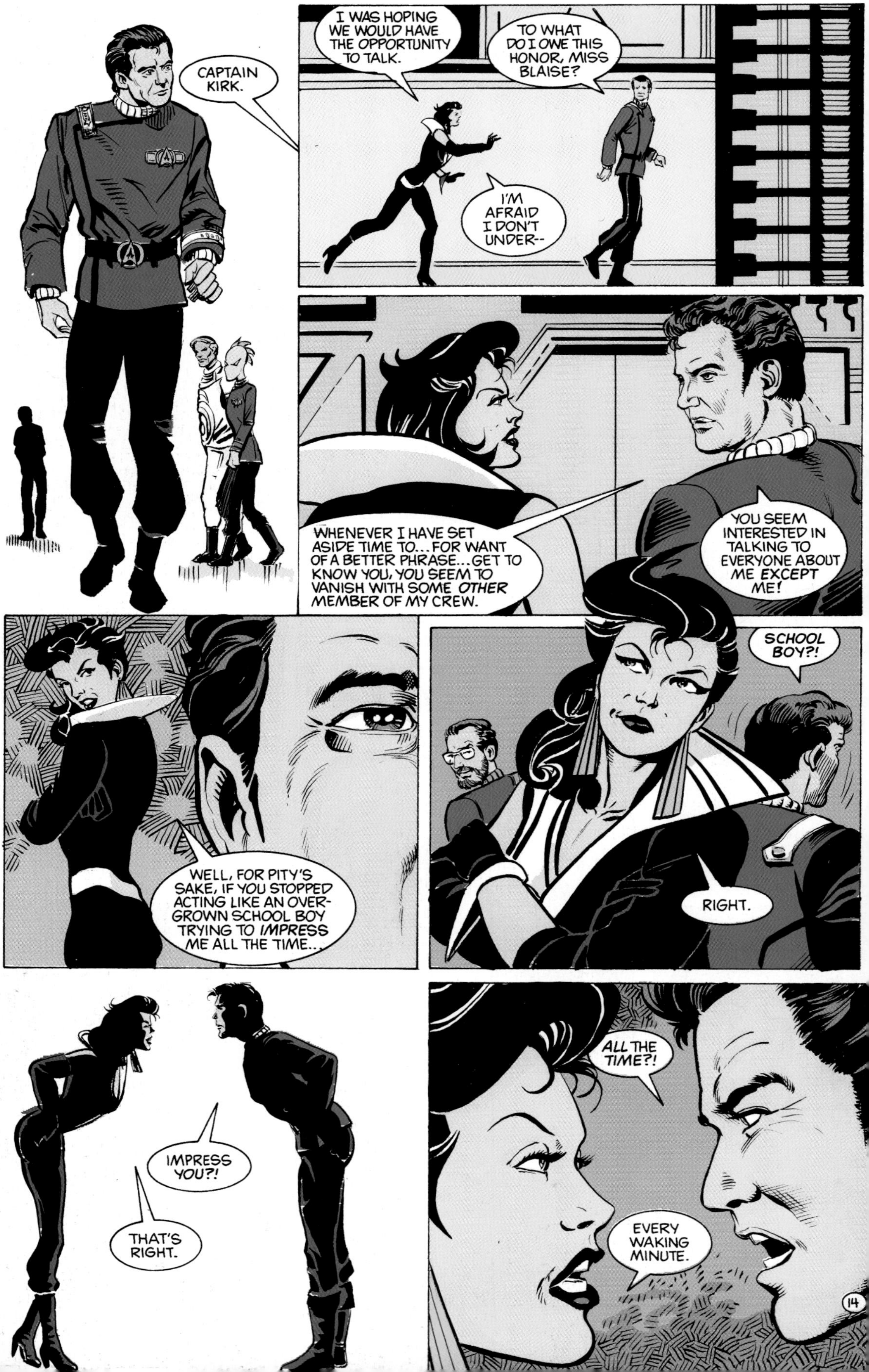
CAPTAIN KIRK.
I WAS HOPING WE WOULD HAVE THE OPPORTUNITY TO TALK.
TO WHAT DO I OWE THIS HONOR, MISS BLAISE?
I'M AFRAID I DON'T UNDER--
WHENEVER I HAVE SET ASIDE TIME TO... FOR WANT OF A BETTER PHRASE... GET TO KNOW YOU, YOU SEEM TO VANISH WITH SOME OTHER MEMBER OF MY CREW.
YOU SEEM INTERESTED IN TALKING TO EVERYONE ABOUT ME EXCEPT ME!
WELL, FOR PITY'S SAKE, IF YOU STOPPED ACTING LIKE AN OVER-GROWN SCHOOL BOY TRYING TO IMPRESS ME ALL THE TIME...
SCHOOL BOY?!
RIGHT.
IMPRESS YOU?!
THAT'S RIGHT.
ALL THE TIME?!
EVERY WAKING MINUTE.
14

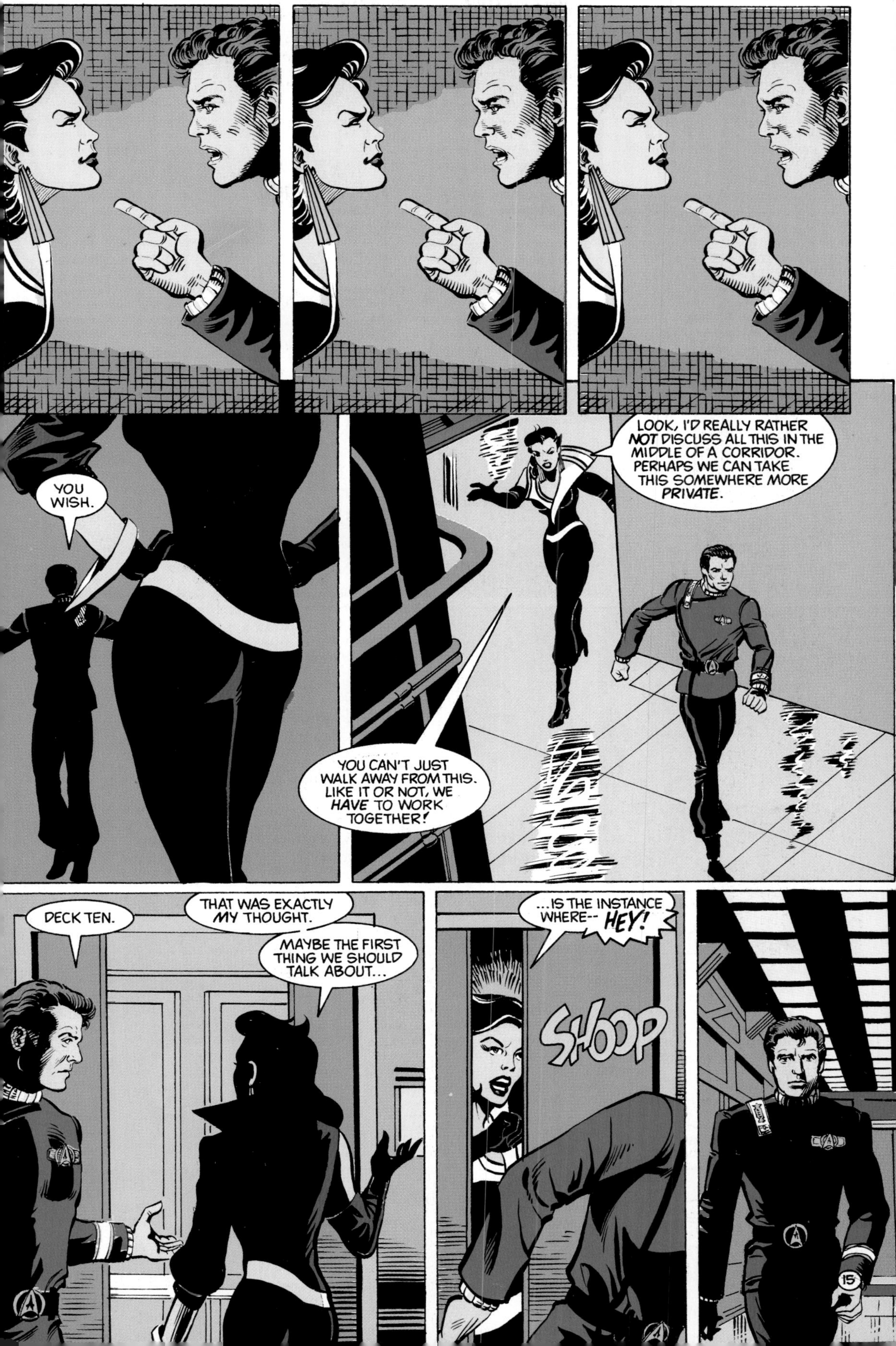
YOU WISH.
LOOK, I'D REALLY RATHER NOT DISCUSS ALL THIS IN THE MIDDLE OF A CORRIDOR. PERHAPS WE CAN TAKE THIS SOMEWHERE MORE PRIVATE.
YOU CAN'T JUST WALK AWAY FROM THIS. LIKE IT OR NOT, WE HAVE TO WORK TOGETHER!
DECK TEN.
THAT WAS EXACTLY MY THOUGHT.
MAYBE THE FIRST THING WE SHOULD TALK ABOUT...
...IS THE INSTANCE WHERE-- HEY!
SHOOP
15

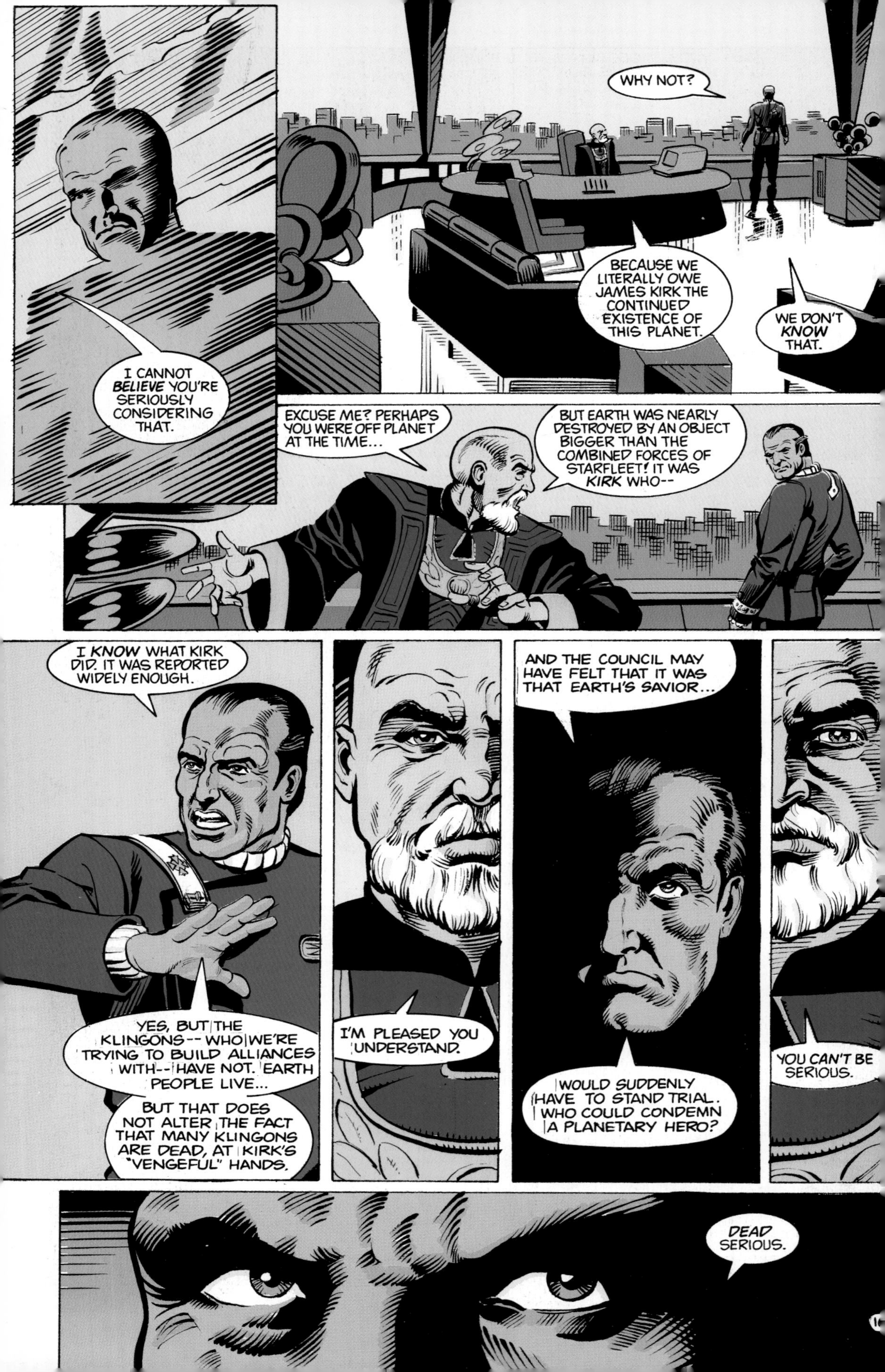
I CANNOT BELIEVE YOU'RE SERIOUSLY CONSIDERING THAT.
WHY NOT?
BECAUSE WE LITERALLY OWE JAMES KIRK THE CONTINUED EXISTENCE OF THIS PLANET.
WE DON'T KNOW THAT.
EXCUSE ME? PERHAPS YOU WERE OFF PLANET AT THE TIME...
BUT EARTH WAS NEARLY DESTROYED BY AN OBJECT BIGGER THAN THE COMBINED FORCES OF STARFLEET! IT WAS KIRK WHO--
I KNOW WHAT KIRK DID. IT WAS REPORTED WIDELY ENOUGH.
YES, BUT THE KLINGONS-- WHO WE'RE TRYING TO BUILD ALLIANCES WITH-- HAVE NOT. EARTH PEOPLE LIVE...
BUT THAT DOES NOT ALTER THE FACT THAT MANY KLINGONS ARE DEAD, AT KIRK'S "VENGEFUL" HANDS.
I'M PLEASED YOU UNDERSTAND.
AND THE COUNCIL MAY HAVE FELT THAT IT WAS THAT EARTH'S SAVIOR...
WOULD SUDDENLY HAVE TO STAND TRIAL. WHO COULD CONDEMN A PLANETARY HERO?
YOU CAN'T BE SERIOUS.
DEAD SERIOUS.

THE SUGGESTION THAT KIRK IS SOME SORT OF MAD DOG KILLER IS LUDICROUS.

BUT IMPOSSIBLE?

NOT IMPOSSIBLE, NO, BUT UTTERLY--

POSSIBLE.

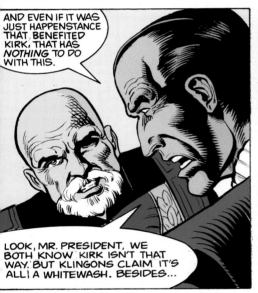

AND EVEN IF IT WAS JUST HAPPENSTANCE THAT BENEFITED KIRK, THAT HAS NOTHING TO DO WITH THIS.

LOOK, MR. PRESIDENT, WE BOTH KNOW KIRK ISN'T THAT WAY. BUT KLINGONS CLAIM IT'S ALL A WHITEWASH. BESIDES...

...SOONER OR LATER... PROBABLY SOONER... IT WILL COME TO WAR.

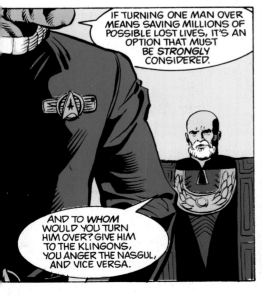

IF TURNING ONE MAN OVER MEANS SAVING MILLIONS OF POSSIBLE LOST LIVES, IT'S AN OPTION THAT MUST BE STRONGLY CONSIDERED.

AND TO WHOM WOULD YOU TURN HIM OVER? GIVE HIM TO THE KLINGONS, YOU ANGER THE NASGUL, AND VICE VERSA.

WE MAY HAVE TO CUT HIM IN HALF.

.17

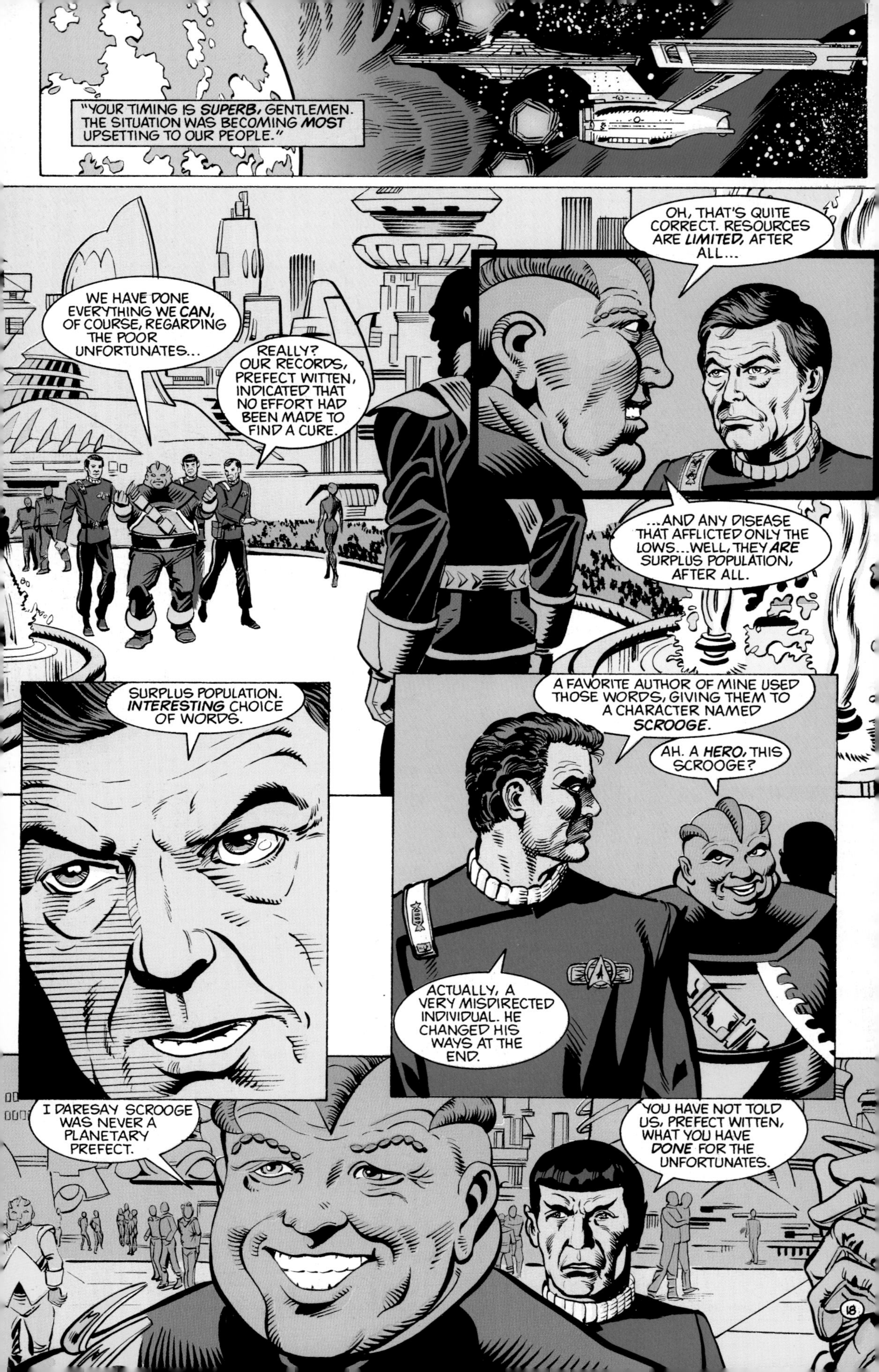
"YOUR TIMING IS SUPERB, GENTLEMEN. THE SITUATION WAS BECOMING MOST UPSETTING TO OUR PEOPLE."
WE HAVE DONE EVERYTHING WE CAN, OF COURSE, REGARDING THE POOR UNFORTUNATES...
REALLY? OUR RECORDS, PREFECT WITTEN, INDICATED THAT NO EFFORT HAD BEEN MADE TO FIND A CURE.
OH, THAT'S QUITE CORRECT. RESOURCES ARE LIMITED, AFTER ALL...
...AND ANY DISEASE THAT AFFLICTED ONLY THE LOWS...WELL, THEY ARE SURPLUS POPULATION, AFTER ALL.
SURPLUS POPULATION. INTERESTING CHOICE OF WORDS.
A FAVORITE AUTHOR OF MINE USED THOSE WORDS, GIVING THEM TO A CHARACTER NAMED SCROOGE.
AH. A HERO, THIS SCROOGE?
ACTUALLY, A VERY MISDIRECTED INDIVIDUAL. HE CHANGED HIS WAYS AT THE END.
I DARESAY SCROOGE WAS NEVER A PLANETARY PREFECT.
YOU HAVE NOT TOLD US, PREFECT WITTEN, WHAT YOU HAVE DONE FOR THE UNFORTUNATES.

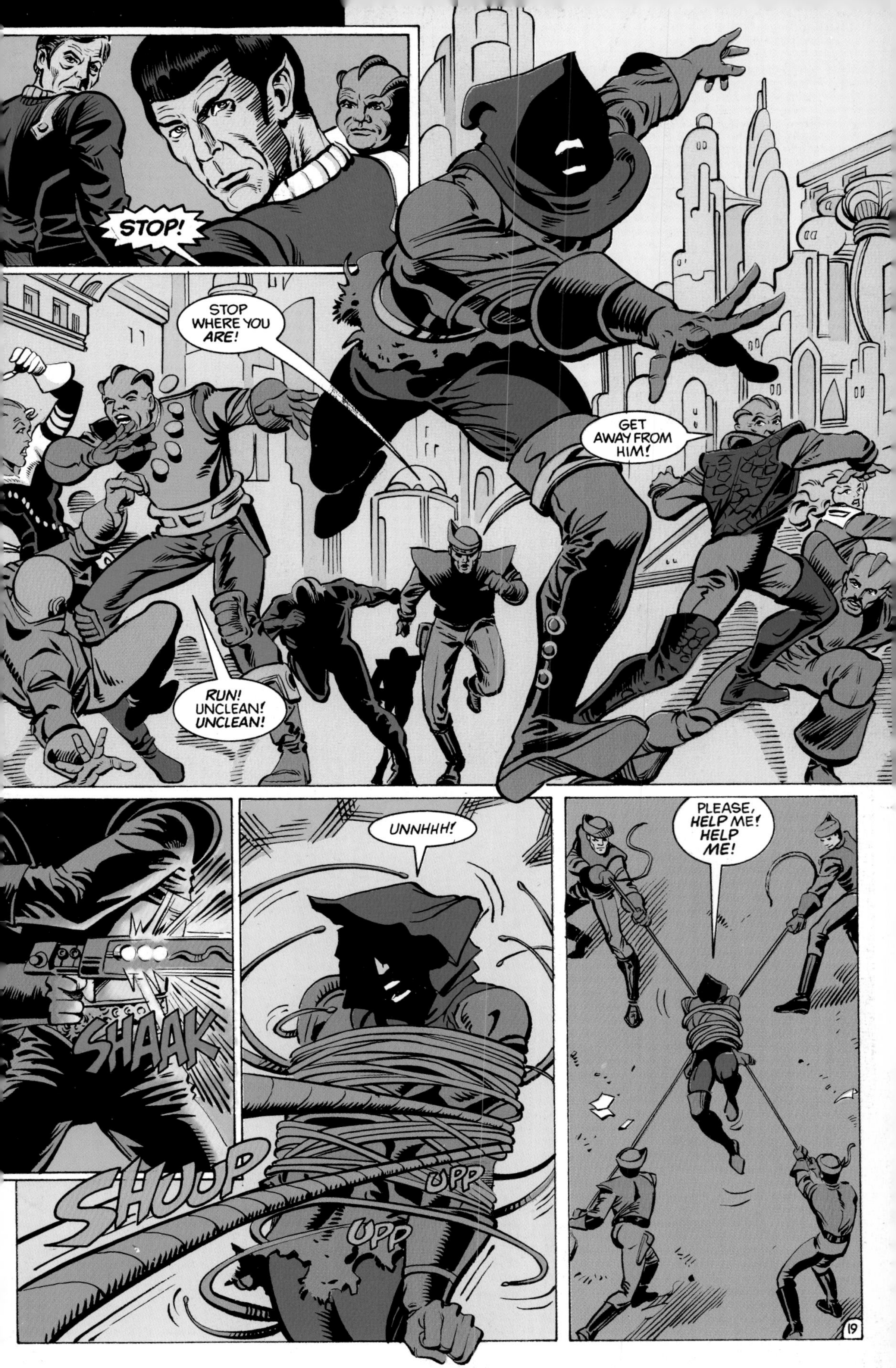
STOP!
STOP WHERE YOU ARE!
GET AWAY FROM HIM!
RUN! UNCLEAN! UNCLEAN!
SHAAK
SHOOP
UNNHHH!
UPP
UPP
PLEASE, HELP ME! HELP ME!
19

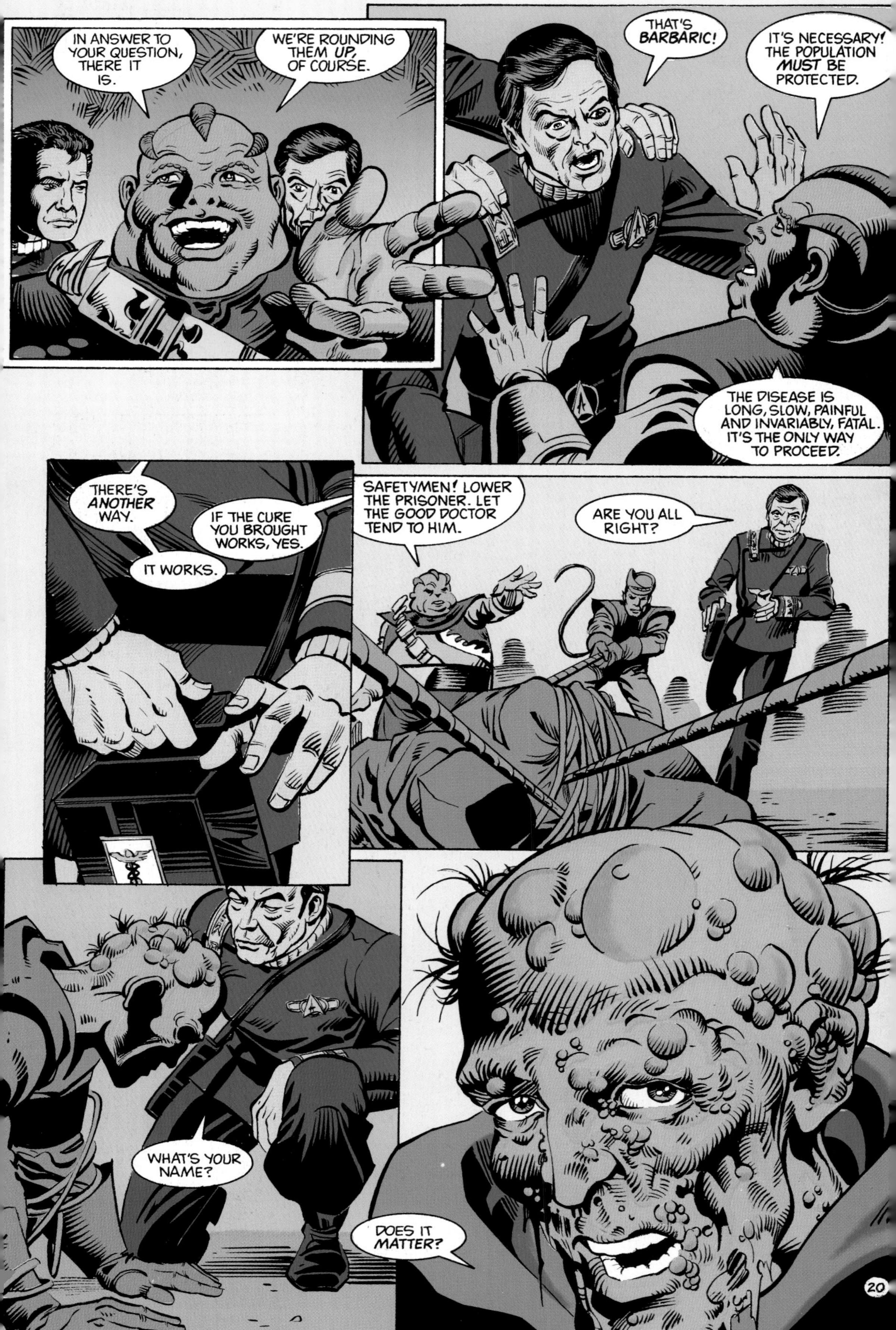

IN ANSWER TO YOUR QUESTION, THERE IT IS.
WE'RE ROUNDING THEM UP, OF COURSE.
THAT'S BARBARIC!
IT'S NECESSARY! THE POPULATION MUST BE PROTECTED.
THE DISEASE IS LONG, SLOW, PAINFUL AND INVARIABLY, FATAL. IT'S THE ONLY WAY TO PROCEED.
THERE'S ANOTHER WAY.
IF THE CURE YOU BROUGHT WORKS, YES.
IT WORKS.
SAFETYMEN! LOWER THE PRISONER. LET THE GOOD DOCTOR TEND TO HIM.
ARE YOU ALL RIGHT?
WHAT'S YOUR NAME?
DOES IT MATTER?

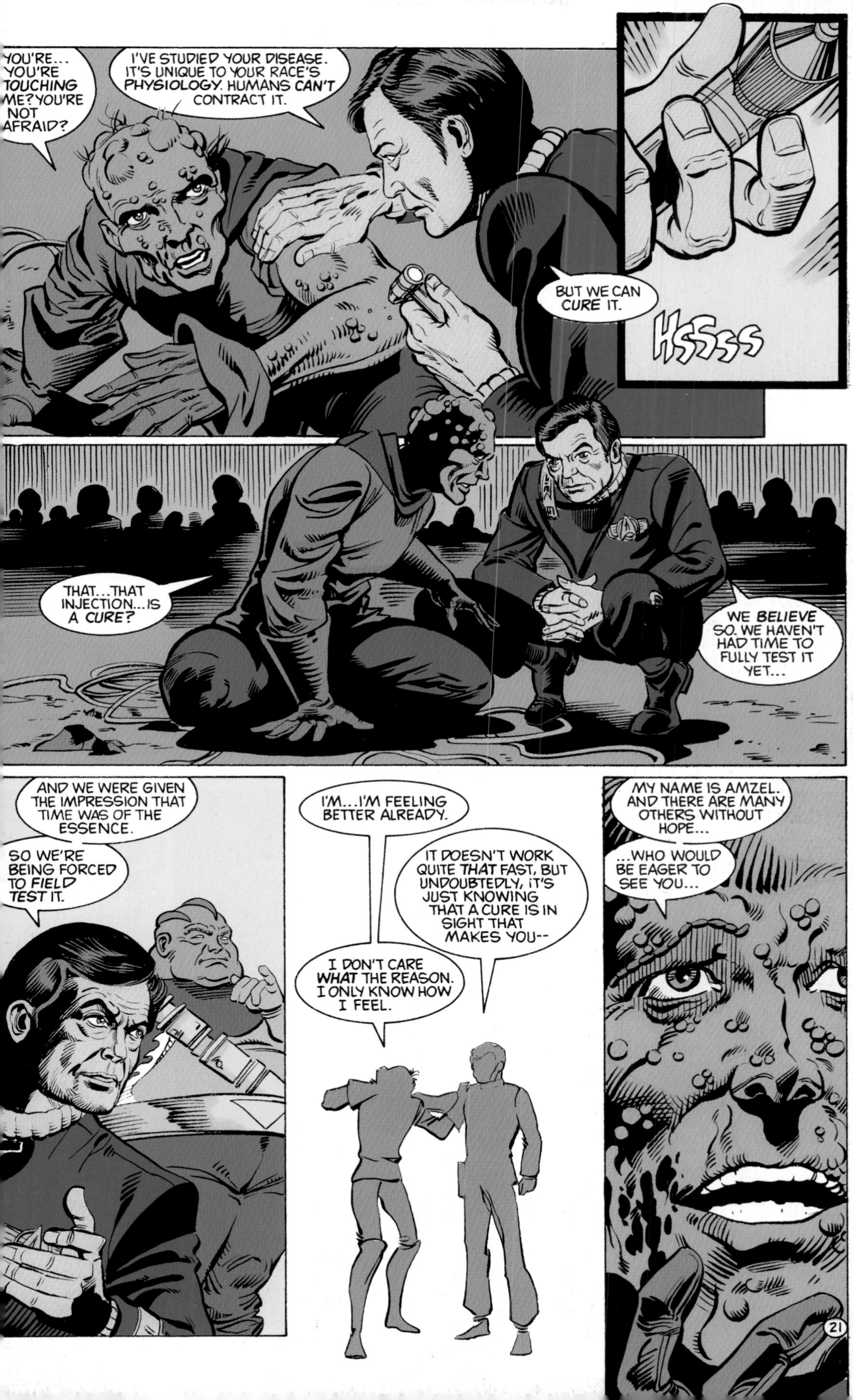
YOU'RE... YOU'RE TOUCHING ME? YOU'RE NOT AFRAID?
I'VE STUDIED YOUR DISEASE. IT'S UNIQUE TO YOUR RACE'S PHYSIOLOGY. HUMANS CAN'T CONTRACT IT.
BUT WE CAN CURE IT.
HSSSS
THAT... THAT INJECTION... IS A CURE?
WE BELIEVE SO. WE HAVEN'T HAD TIME TO FULLY TEST IT YET...
AND WE WERE GIVEN THE IMPRESSION THAT TIME WAS OF THE ESSENCE.
SO WE'RE BEING FORCED TO FIELD TEST IT.
I'M... I'M FEELING BETTER ALREADY.
IT DOESN'T WORK QUITE THAT FAST, BUT UNDOUBTEDLY, IT'S JUST KNOWING THAT A CURE IS IN SIGHT THAT MAKES YOU--
I DON'T CARE WHAT THE REASON. I ONLY KNOW HOW I FEEL.
MY NAME IS AMZEL. AND THERE ARE MANY OTHERS WITHOUT HOPE...
...WHO WOULD BE EAGER TO SEE YOU...
21

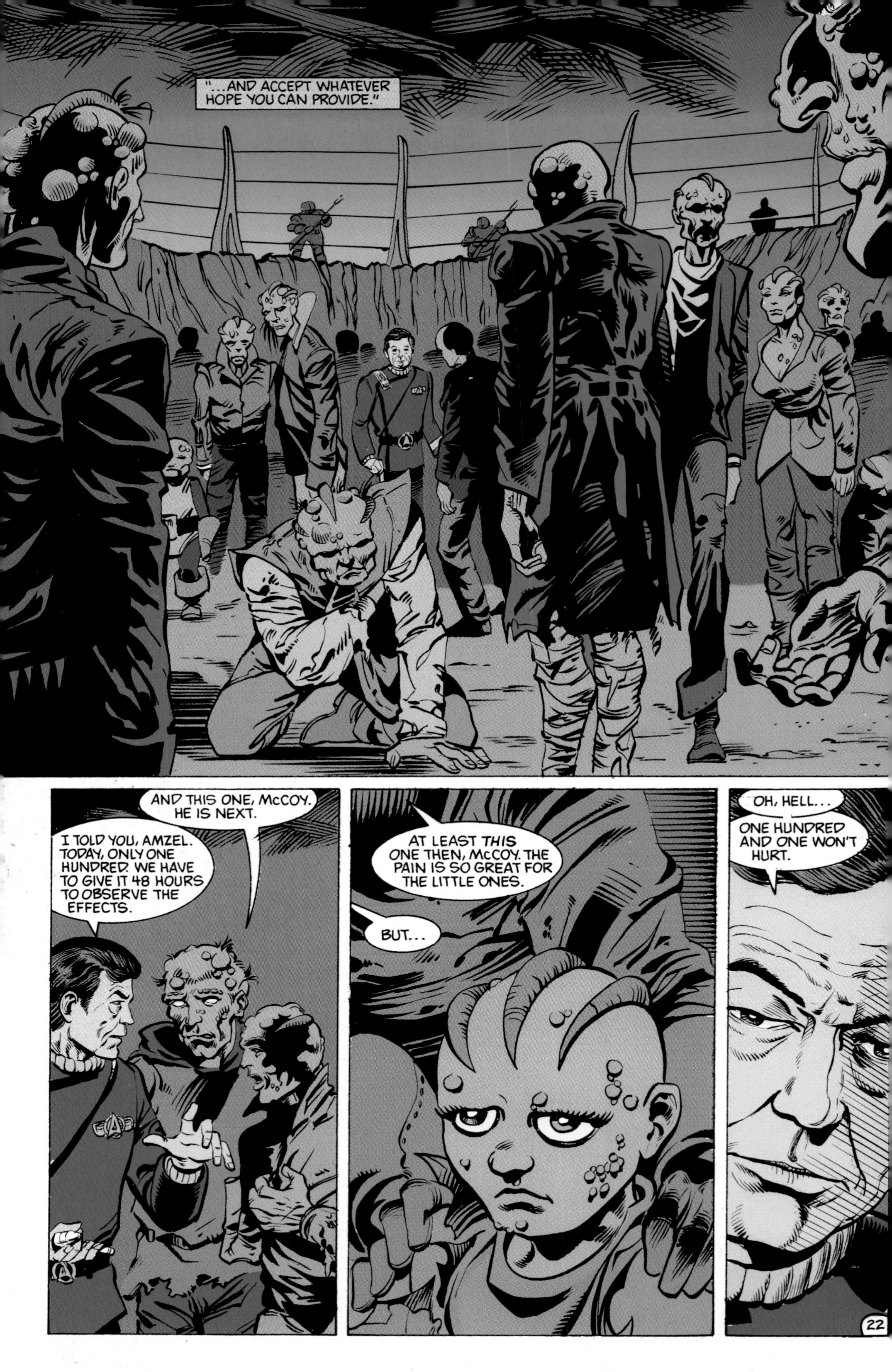
"...AND ACCEPT WHATEVER HOPE YOU CAN PROVIDE."
AND THIS ONE, McCOY. HE IS NEXT.
I TOLD YOU, AMZEL. TODAY, ONLY ONE HUNDRED. WE HAVE TO GIVE IT 48 HOURS TO OBSERVE THE EFFECTS.
AT LEAST THIS ONE THEN, McCOY. THE PAIN IS SO GREAT FOR THE LITTLE ONES.
BUT...
OH, HELL...
ONE HUNDRED AND ONE WON'T HURT.
22

TWELVE HOURS GONE. HOW'S IT LOOKING, BONES?

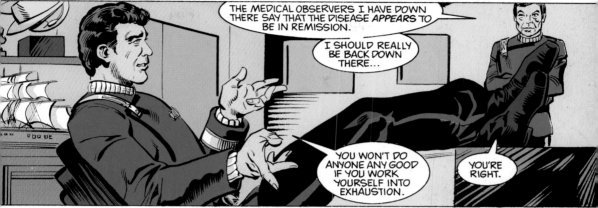

THE MEDICAL OBSERVERS I HAVE DOWN THERE SAY THAT THE DISEASE *APPEARS* TO BE IN REMISSION.

I SHOULD REALLY BE BACK DOWN THERE...

YOU WON'T DO ANYONE ANY GOOD IF YOU WORK YOURSELF INTO EXHAUSTION.

YOU'RE RIGHT.

SEE? UNLIKE *SOME* PEOPLE I KNOW, I CAN TAKE REASONABLE ADVICE.

OH, GIVE IT A *REST*, BONES.

COME IN.

CAPTAIN KIRK, I THINK WE SHOULD GET SOME- THING STRAIGHT.

OH, GOD.

ARE YOU *LISTENING*? BECAUSE I WANT TO BE *CLEAR* ON THIS.

YEEEESS, I'M LISTENING.

GOOD. BECAUSE HERE IT COMES...

NO ONE CALLS ME *MISS* BLAISE. I'M R.J., IS THAT CLEAR? GOOD.

23

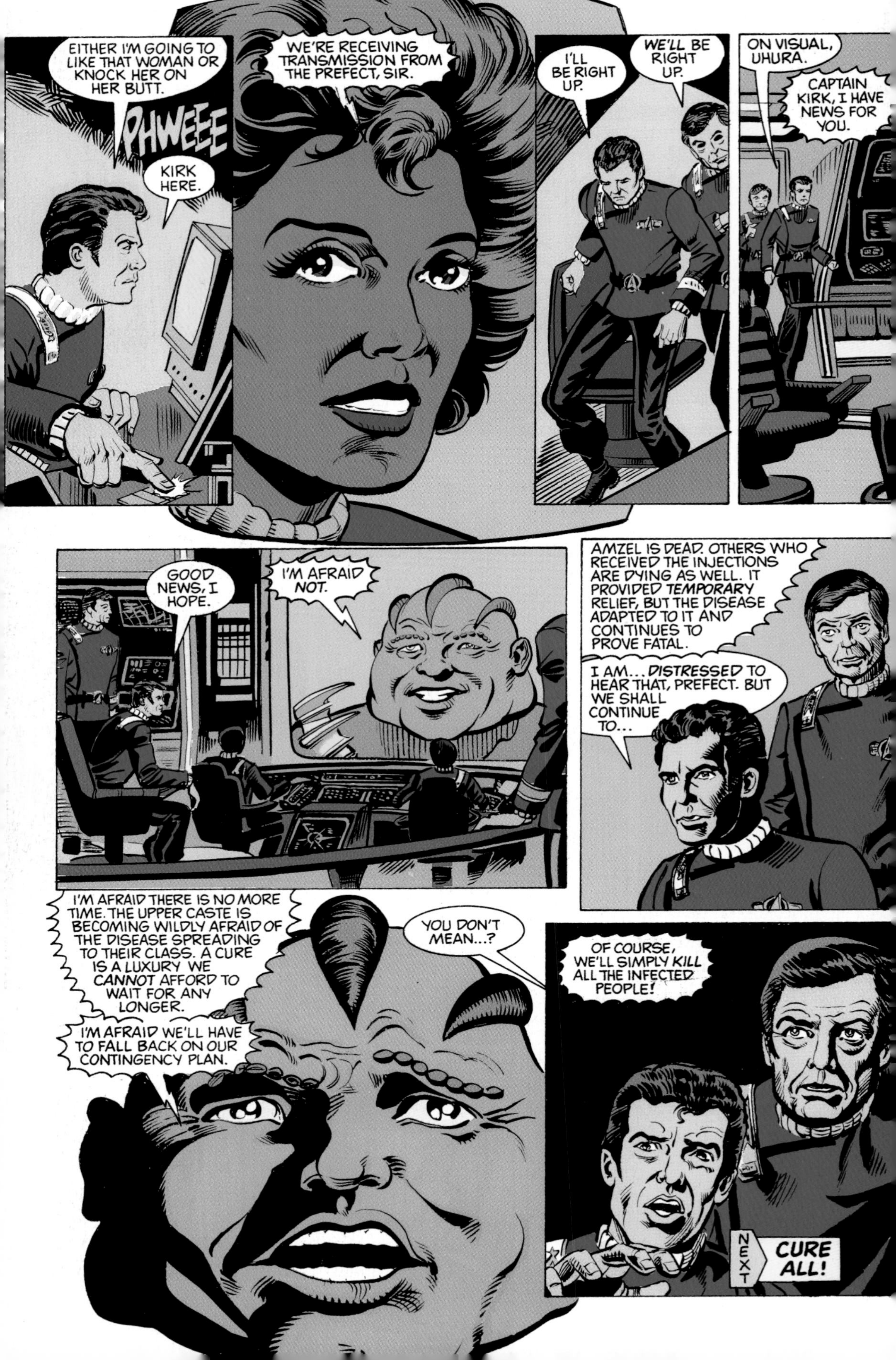
EITHER I'M GOING TO LIKE THAT WOMAN OR KNOCK HER ON HER BUTT.
PHWEEE
KIRK HERE.
WE'RE RECEIVING TRANSMISSION FROM THE PREFECT, SIR.
I'LL BE RIGHT UP.
WE'LL BE RIGHT UP.
ON VISUAL, UHURA.
CAPTAIN KIRK, I HAVE NEWS FOR YOU.
GOOD NEWS, I HOPE.
I'M AFRAID NOT.
AMZEL IS DEAD. OTHERS WHO RECEIVED THE INJECTIONS ARE DYING AS WELL. IT PROVIDED TEMPORARY RELIEF, BUT THE DISEASE ADAPTED TO IT AND CONTINUES TO PROVE FATAL.
I AM... DISTRESSED TO HEAR THAT, PREFECT. BUT WE SHALL CONTINUE TO...
I'M AFRAID THERE IS NO MORE TIME. THE UPPER CASTE IS BECOMING WILDLY AFRAID OF THE DISEASE SPREADING TO THEIR CLASS. A CURE IS A LUXURY WE CANNOT AFFORD TO WAIT FOR ANY LONGER.
I'M AFRAID WE'LL HAVE TO FALL BACK ON OUR CONTINGENCY PLAN.
YOU DON'T MEAN...?
OF COURSE, WE'LL SIMPLY KILL ALL THE INFECTED PEOPLE!
NEXT
CURE ALL!

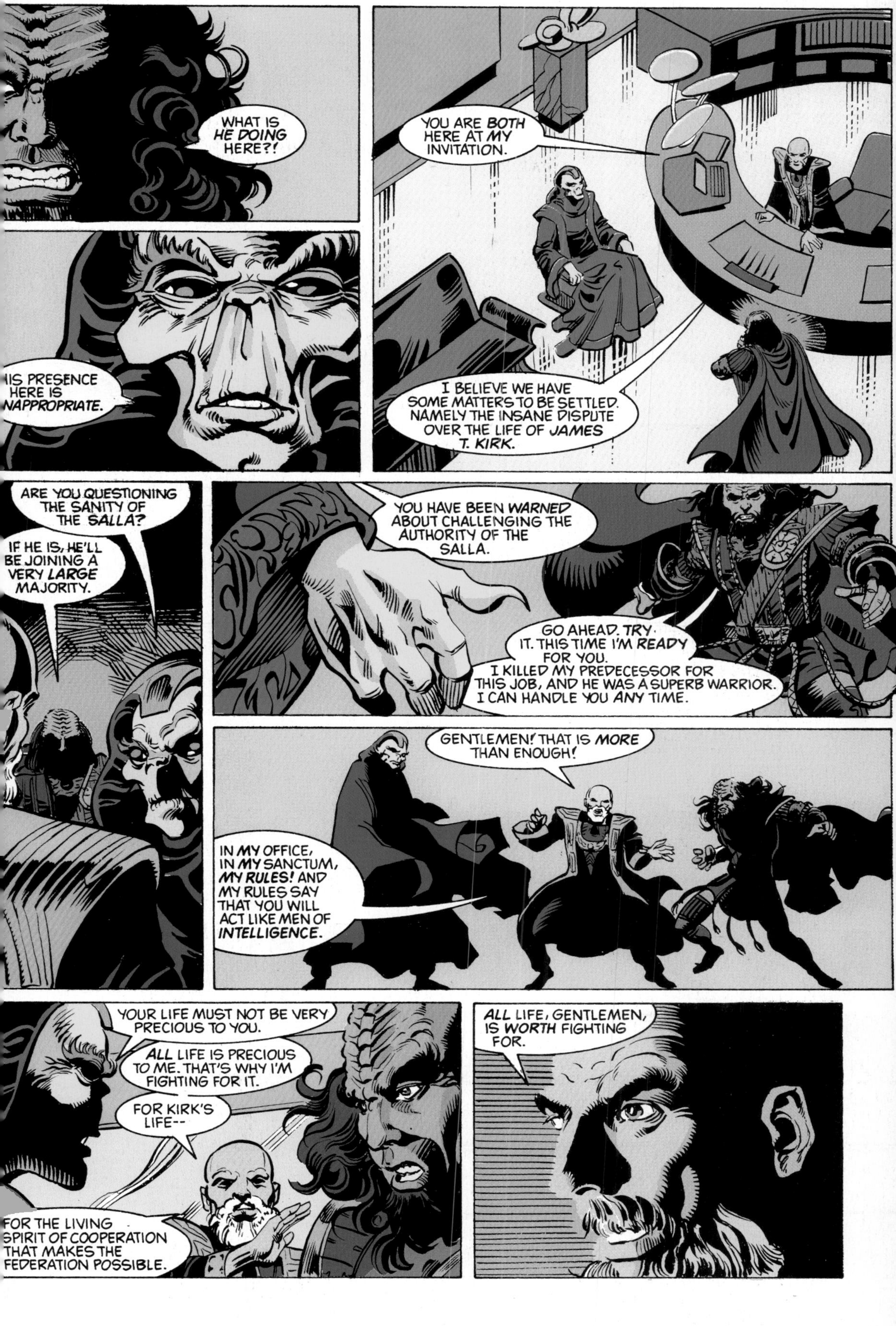
WHAT IS HE DOING HERE?!
YOU ARE BOTH HERE AT MY INVITATION.
IIS PRESENCE HERE IS NAPPROPRIATE.
I BELIEVE WE HAVE SOME MATTERS TO BE SETTLED. NAMELY THE INSANE DISPUTE OVER THE LIFE OF JAMES T. KIRK.
ARE YOU QUESTIONING THE SANITY OF THE SALLA?
IF HE IS, HE'LL BE JOINING A VERY LARGE MAJORITY.
YOU HAVE BEEN WARNED ABOUT CHALLENGING THE AUTHORITY OF THE SALLA.
GO AHEAD. TRY IT. THIS TIME I'M READY FOR YOU.
I KILLED MY PREDECESSOR FOR THIS JOB, AND HE WAS A SUPERB WARRIOR. I CAN HANDLE YOU ANY TIME.
GENTLEMEN! THAT IS MORE THAN ENOUGH!
IN MY OFFICE, IN MY SANCTUM, MY RULES! AND MY RULES SAY THAT YOU WILL ACT LIKE MEN OF INTELLIGENCE.
YOUR LIFE MUST NOT BE VERY PRECIOUS TO YOU.
ALL LIFE IS PRECIOUS TO ME. THAT'S WHY I'M FIGHTING FOR IT.
FOR KIRK'S LIFE--
FOR THE LIVING SPIRIT OF COOPERATION THAT MAKES THE FEDERATION POSSIBLE.
ALL LIFE, GENTLEMEN, IS WORTH FIGHTING FOR.

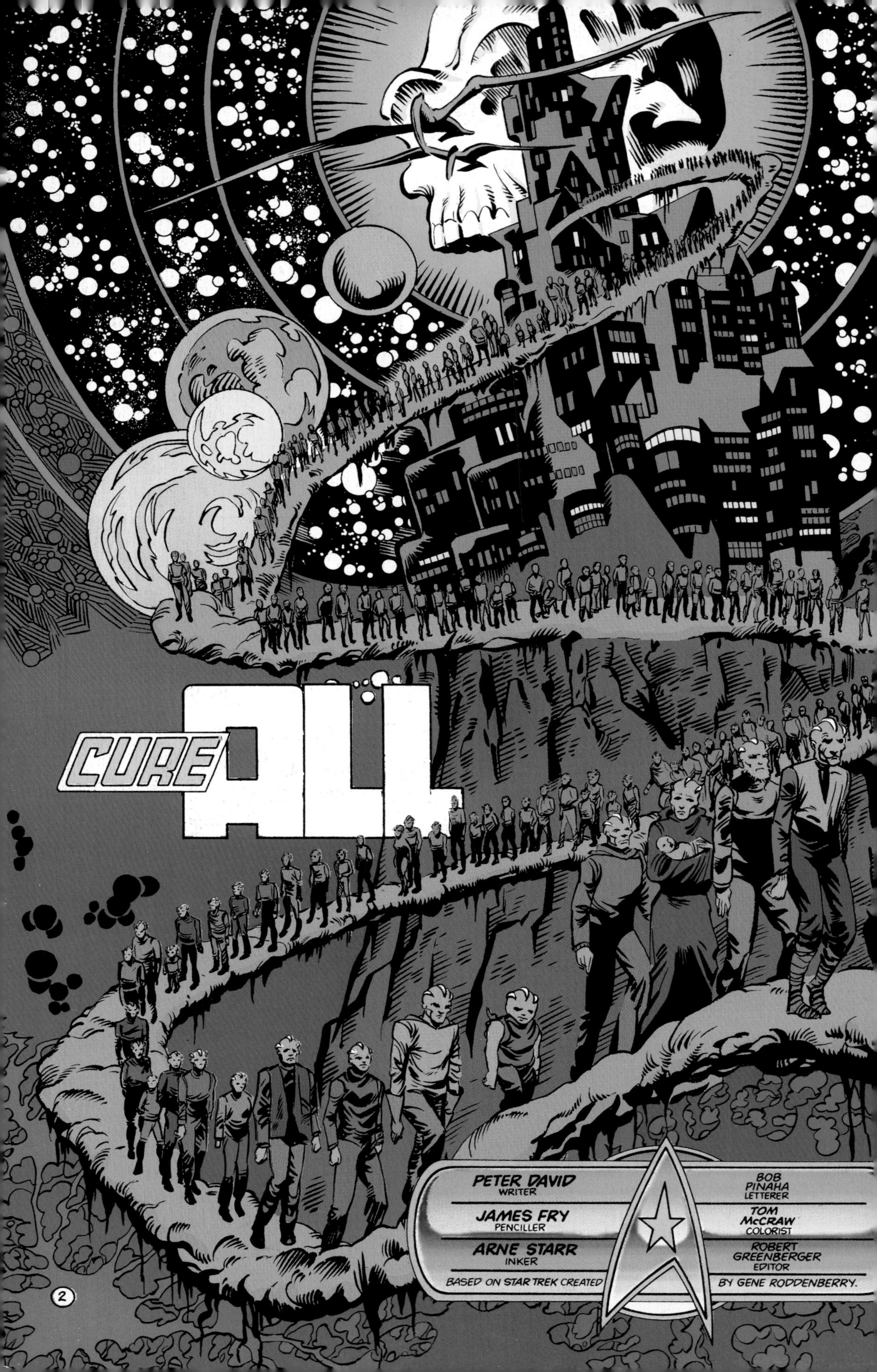

CURE ALL
PETER DAVID
WRITER
JAMES FRY
PENCILLER
ARNE STARR
INKER
BOB PINAHA
LETTERER
TOM McCRAW
COLORIST
ROBERT GREENBERGER
EDITOR
BASED ON STAR TREK CREATED BY GENE RODDENBERRY.

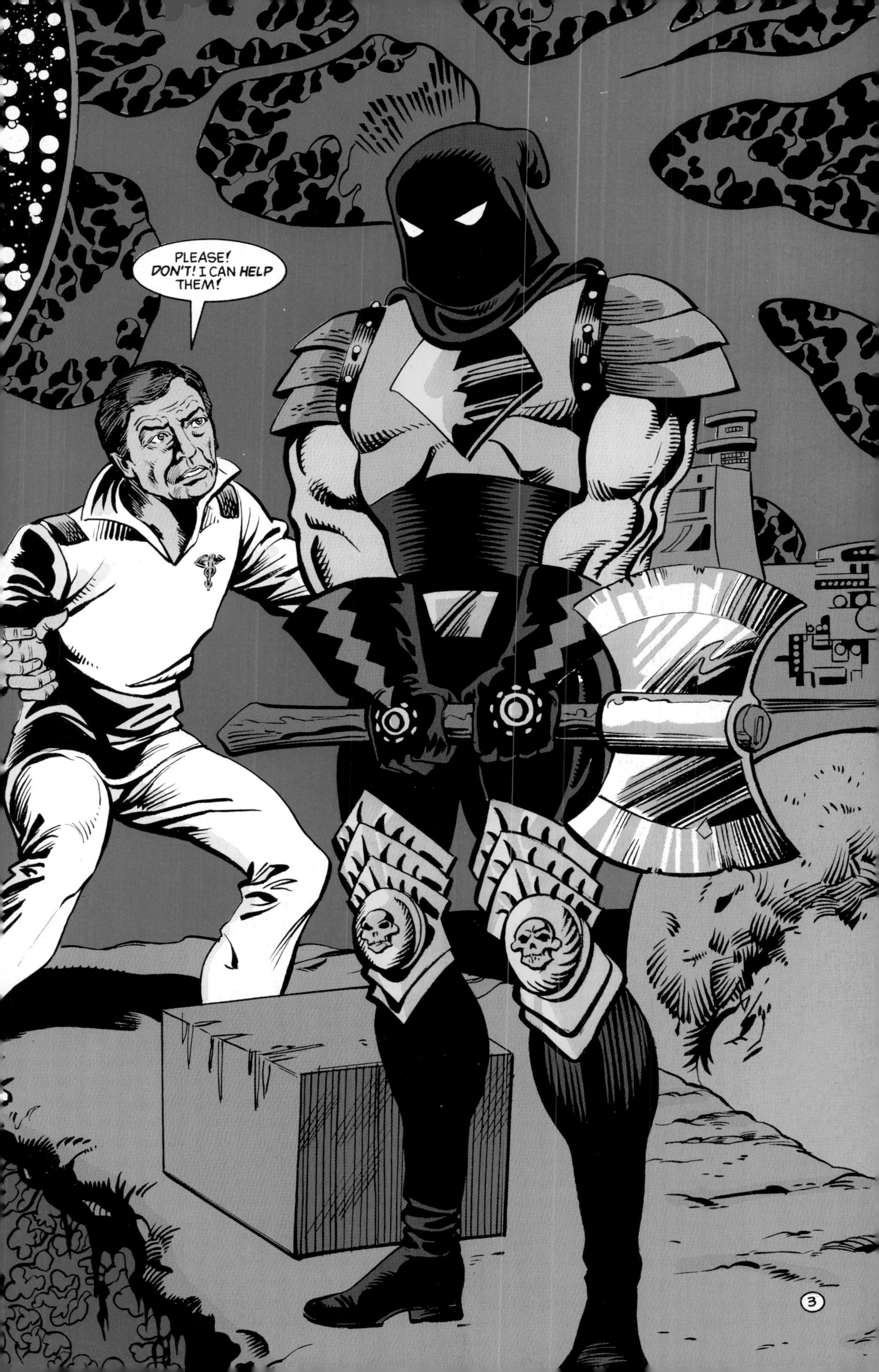
PLEASE! DON'T! I CAN HELP THEM!

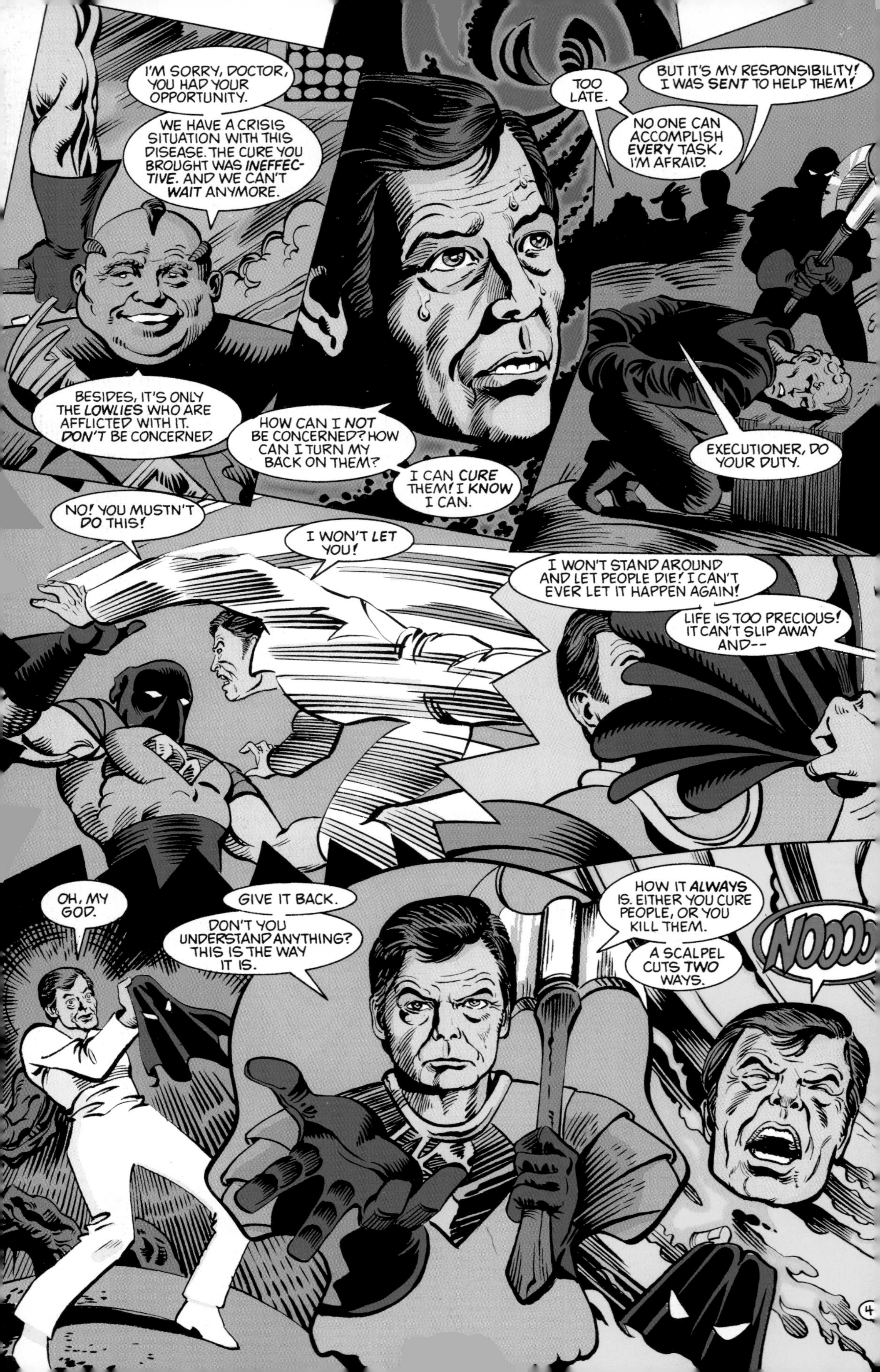
I'M SORRY, DOCTOR, YOU HAD YOUR OPPORTUNITY.
WE HAVE A CRISIS SITUATION WITH THIS DISEASE. THE CURE YOU BROUGHT WAS INEFFECTIVE. AND WE CAN'T WAIT ANYMORE.
BESIDES, IT'S ONLY THE LOWLIES WHO ARE AFFLICTED WITH IT. DON'T BE CONCERNED.
HOW CAN I NOT BE CONCERNED? HOW CAN I TURN MY BACK ON THEM?
I CAN CURE THEM! I KNOW I CAN.
TOO LATE.
BUT IT'S MY RESPONSIBILITY! I WAS SENT TO HELP THEM!
NO ONE CAN ACCOMPLISH EVERY TASK, I'M AFRAID.
EXECUTIONER, DO YOUR DUTY.
NO! YOU MUSTN'T DO THIS!
I WON'T LET YOU!
I WON'T STAND AROUND AND LET PEOPLE DIE! I CAN'T EVER LET IT HAPPEN AGAIN!
LIFE IS TOO PRECIOUS! IT CAN'T SLIP AWAY AND--
OH, MY GOD.
GIVE IT BACK.
DON'T YOU UNDERSTAND ANYTHING? THIS IS THE WAY IT IS.
HOW IT ALWAYS IS. EITHER YOU CURE PEOPLE, OR YOU KILL THEM.
A SCALPEL CUTS TWO WAYS.
NOOOO

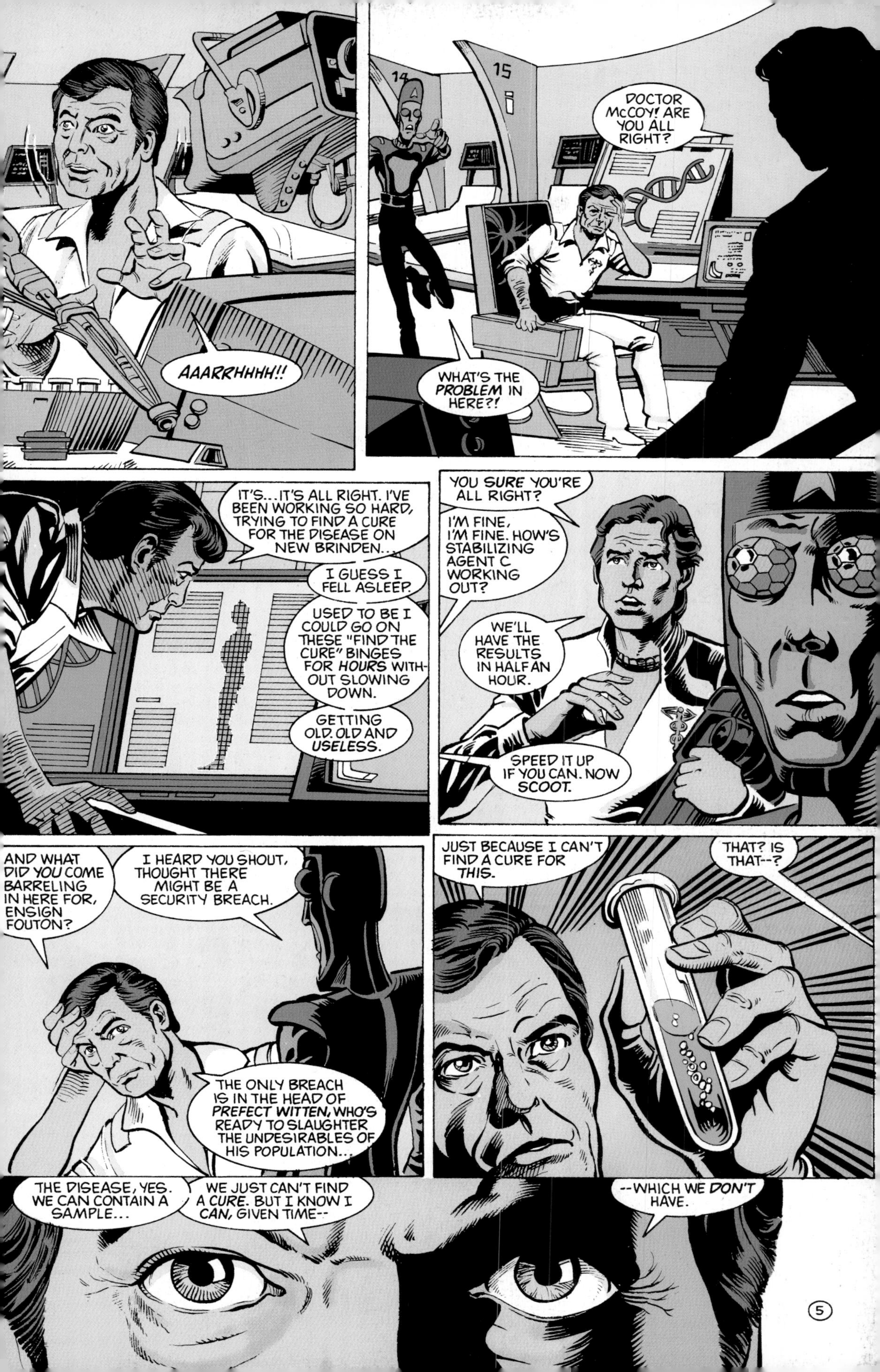
AAARRHHHH!!
DOCTOR McCOY! ARE YOU ALL RIGHT?
WHAT'S THE PROBLEM IN HERE?!
IT'S...IT'S ALL RIGHT. I'VE BEEN WORKING SO HARD, TRYING TO FIND A CURE FOR THE DISEASE ON NEW BRINDEN...
I GUESS I FELL ASLEEP.
USED TO BE I COULD GO ON THESE "FIND THE CURE" BINGES FOR HOURS WITHOUT SLOWING DOWN.
GETTING OLD. OLD AND USELESS.
YOU SURE YOU'RE ALL RIGHT?
I'M FINE, I'M FINE. HOW'S STABILIZING AGENT C WORKING OUT?
WE'LL HAVE THE RESULTS IN HALF AN HOUR.
SPEED IT UP IF YOU CAN. NOW SCOOT.
AND WHAT DID YOU COME BARRELING IN HERE FOR, ENSIGN FOUTON?
I HEARD YOU SHOUT, THOUGHT THERE MIGHT BE A SECURITY BREACH.
THE ONLY BREACH IS IN THE HEAD OF PREFECT WITTEN, WHO'S READY TO SLAUGHTER THE UNDESIRABLES OF HIS POPULATION...
JUST BECAUSE I CAN'T FIND A CURE FOR THIS.
THAT? IS THAT--?
THE DISEASE, YES. WE CAN CONTAIN A SAMPLE...
WE JUST CAN'T FIND A CURE. BUT I KNOW I CAN, GIVEN TIME--
--WHICH WE DON'T HAVE.

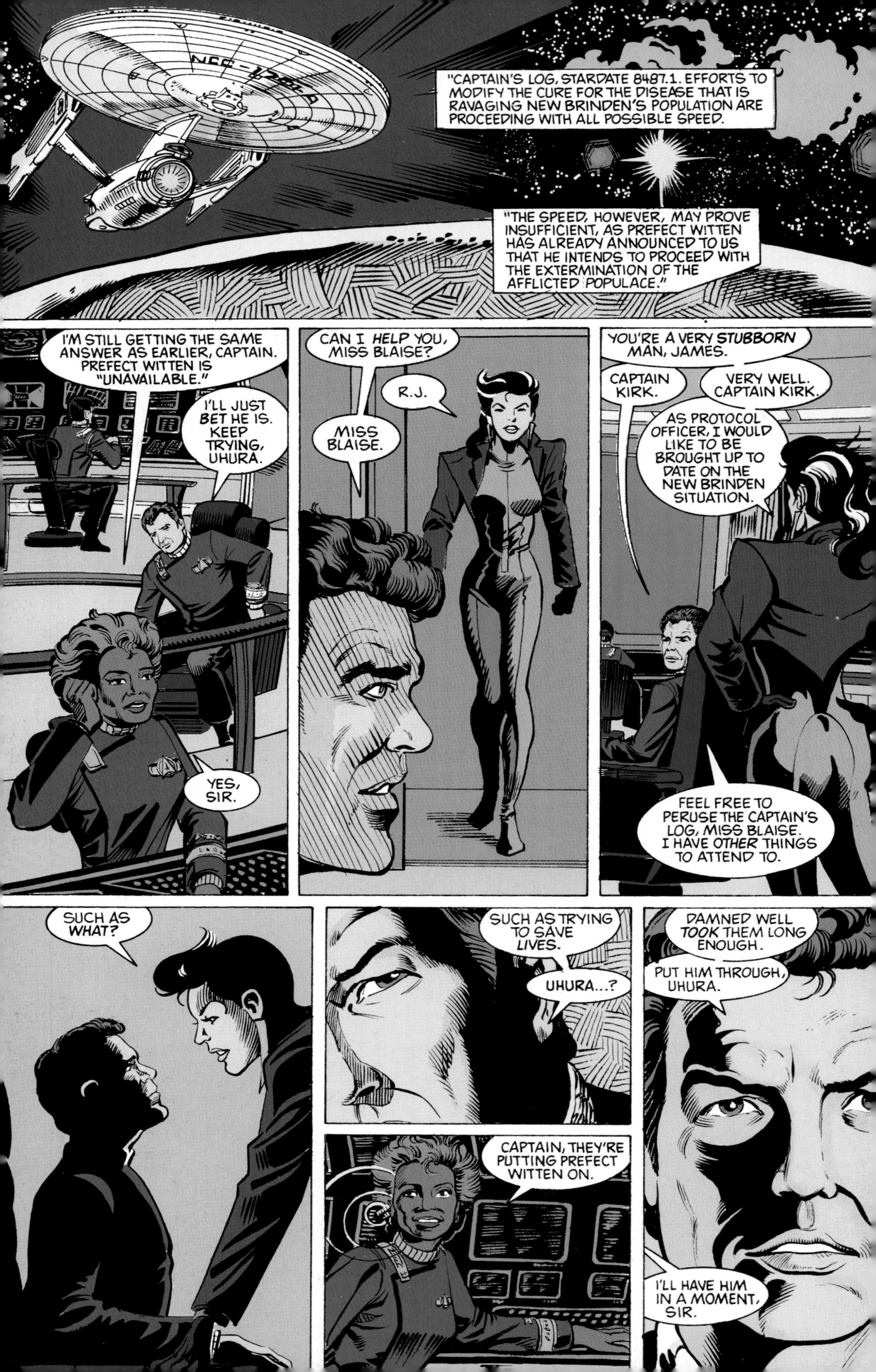

"CAPTAIN'S LOG, STARDATE 8487.1. EFFORTS TO MODIFY THE CURE FOR THE DISEASE THAT IS RAVAGING NEW BRINDEN'S POPULATION ARE PROCEEDING WITH ALL POSSIBLE SPEED.
"THE SPEED, HOWEVER, MAY PROVE INSUFFICIENT, AS PREFECT WITTEN HAS ALREADY ANNOUNCED TO US THAT HE INTENDS TO PROCEED WITH THE EXTERMINATION OF THE AFFLICTED POPULACE."
I'M STILL GETTING THE SAME ANSWER AS EARLIER, CAPTAIN. PREFECT WITTEN IS "UNAVAILABLE."
I'LL JUST BET HE IS. KEEP TRYING, UHURA.
YES, SIR.
CAN I HELP YOU, MISS BLAISE?
R.J.
MISS BLAISE.
YOU'RE A VERY STUBBORN MAN, JAMES.
CAPTAIN KIRK.
VERY WELL. CAPTAIN KIRK.
AS PROTOCOL OFFICER, I WOULD LIKE TO BE BROUGHT UP TO DATE ON THE NEW BRINDEN SITUATION.
FEEL FREE TO PERUSE THE CAPTAIN'S LOG, MISS BLAISE. I HAVE OTHER THINGS TO ATTEND TO.
SUCH AS WHAT?
SUCH AS TRYING TO SAVE LIVES.
UHURA...?
CAPTAIN, THEY'RE PUTTING PREFECT WITTEN ON.
DAMNED WELL TOOK THEM LONG ENOUGH.
PUT HIM THROUGH, UHURA.
I'LL HAVE HIM IN A MOMENT, SIR.

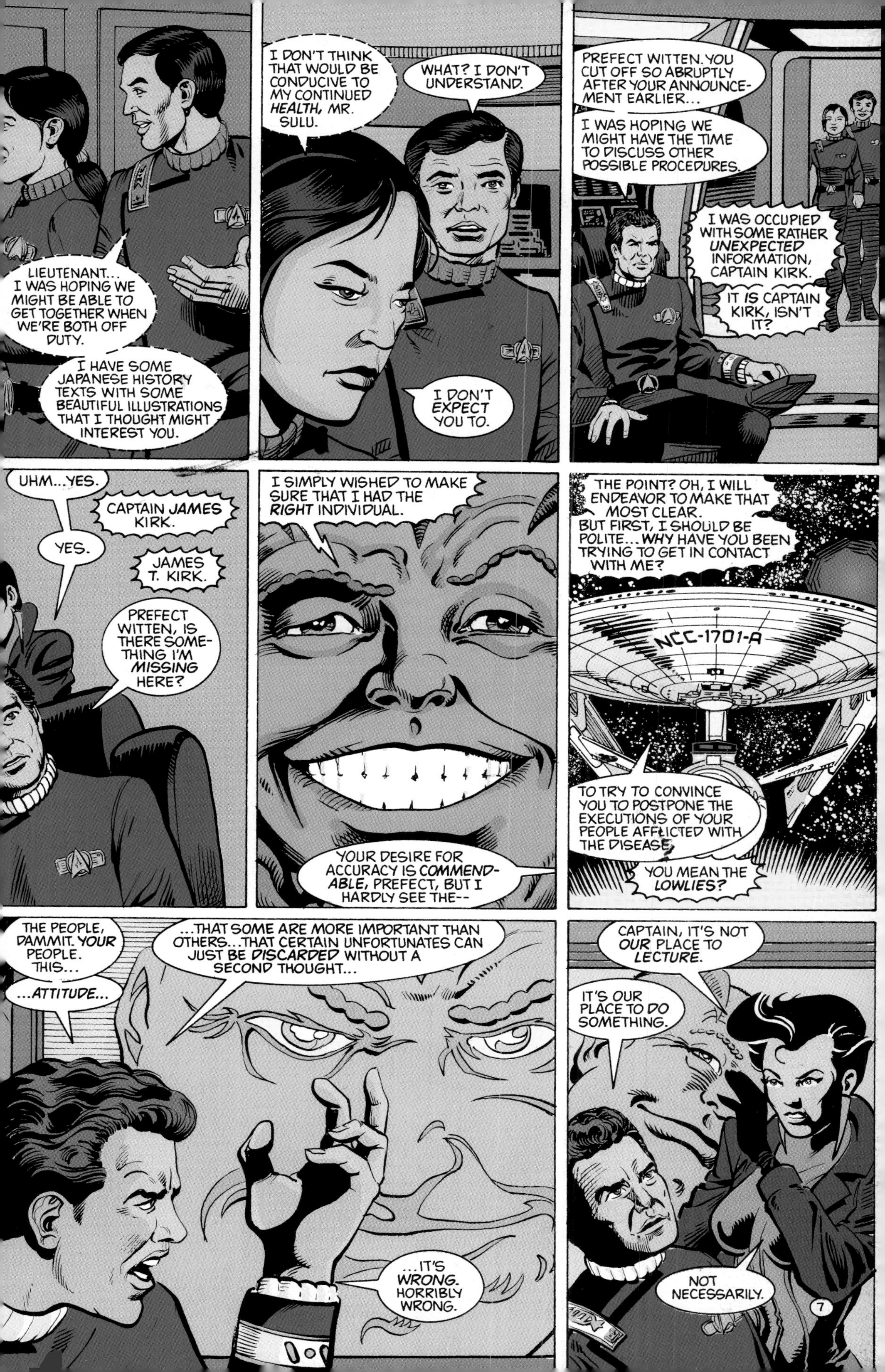
LIEUTENANT... I WAS HOPING WE MIGHT BE ABLE TO GET TOGETHER WHEN WE'RE BOTH OFF DUTY.
I HAVE SOME JAPANESE HISTORY TEXTS WITH SOME BEAUTIFUL ILLUSTRATIONS THAT I THOUGHT MIGHT INTEREST YOU.
I DON'T THINK THAT WOULD BE CONDUCIVE TO MY CONTINUED HEALTH, MR. SULU.
WHAT? I DON'T UNDERSTAND.
I DON'T EXPECT YOU TO.
PREFECT WITTEN. YOU CUT OFF SO ABRUPTLY AFTER YOUR ANNOUNCEMENT EARLIER...
I WAS HOPING WE MIGHT HAVE THE TIME TO DISCUSS OTHER POSSIBLE PROCEDURES.
I WAS OCCUPIED WITH SOME RATHER UNEXPECTED INFORMATION, CAPTAIN KIRK.
IT IS CAPTAIN KIRK, ISN'T IT?
UHM...YES.
CAPTAIN JAMES KIRK.
YES.
JAMES T. KIRK.
PREFECT WITTEN, IS THERE SOMETHING I'M MISSING HERE?
I SIMPLY WISHED TO MAKE SURE THAT I HAD THE RIGHT INDIVIDUAL.
YOUR DESIRE FOR ACCURACY IS COMMENDABLE, PREFECT, BUT I HARDLY SEE THE--
THE POINT? OH, I WILL ENDEAVOR TO MAKE THAT MOST CLEAR. BUT FIRST, I SHOULD BE POLITE... WHY HAVE YOU BEEN TRYING TO GET IN CONTACT WITH ME?
NCC-1701-A
TO TRY TO CONVINCE YOU TO POSTPONE THE EXECUTIONS OF YOUR PEOPLE AFFLICTED WITH THE DISEASE.
YOU MEAN THE LOWLIES?
THE PEOPLE, DAMMIT. YOUR PEOPLE. THIS...
...ATTITUDE...
...THAT SOME ARE MORE IMPORTANT THAN OTHERS...THAT CERTAIN UNFORTUNATES CAN JUST BE DISCARDED WITHOUT A SECOND THOUGHT...
...IT'S WRONG. HORRIBLY WRONG.
CAPTAIN, IT'S NOT OUR PLACE TO LECTURE.
IT'S OUR PLACE TO DO SOMETHING.
NOT NECESSARILY.

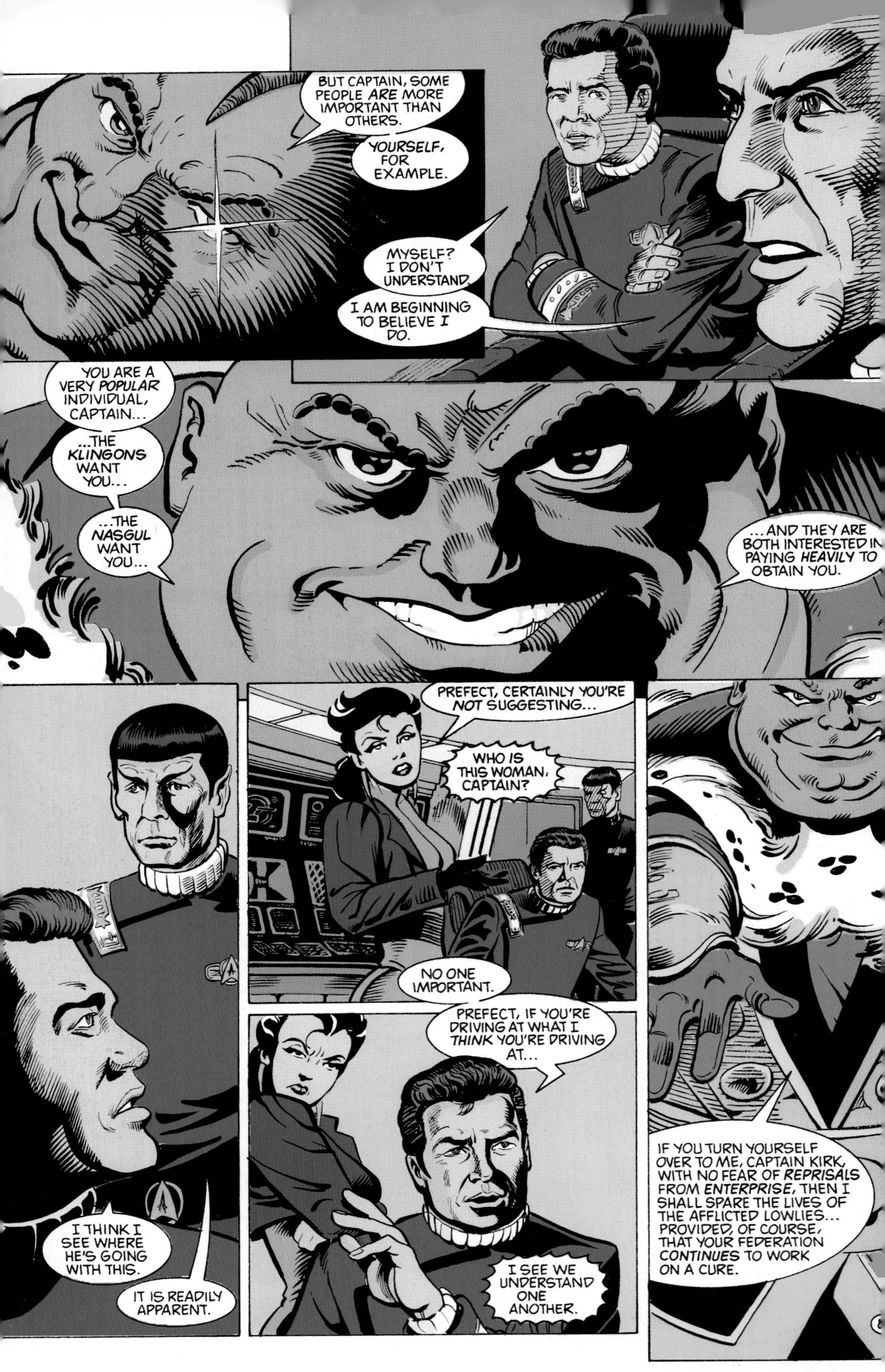
BUT CAPTAIN, SOME PEOPLE ARE MORE IMPORTANT THAN OTHERS.
YOURSELF, FOR EXAMPLE.
MYSELF? I DON'T UNDERSTAND.
I AM BEGINNING TO BELIEVE I DO.
YOU ARE A VERY POPULAR INDIVIDUAL, CAPTAIN...
...THE KLINGONS WANT YOU...
...THE NASGUL WANT YOU...
...AND THEY ARE BOTH INTERESTED IN PAYING HEAVILY TO OBTAIN YOU.
I THINK I SEE WHERE HE'S GOING WITH THIS.
IT IS READILY APPARENT.
PREFECT, CERTAINLY YOU'RE NOT SUGGESTING...
WHO IS THIS WOMAN, CAPTAIN?
NO ONE IMPORTANT.
PREFECT, IF YOU'RE DRIVING AT WHAT I THINK YOU'RE DRIVING AT...
I SEE WE UNDERSTAND ONE ANOTHER.
IF YOU TURN YOURSELF OVER TO ME, CAPTAIN KIRK, WITH NO FEAR OF REPRISALS FROM ENTERPRISE, THEN I SHALL SPARE THE LIVES OF THE AFFLICTED LOWLIES... PROVIDED, OF COURSE, THAT YOUR FEDERATION CONTINUES TO WORK ON A CURE.

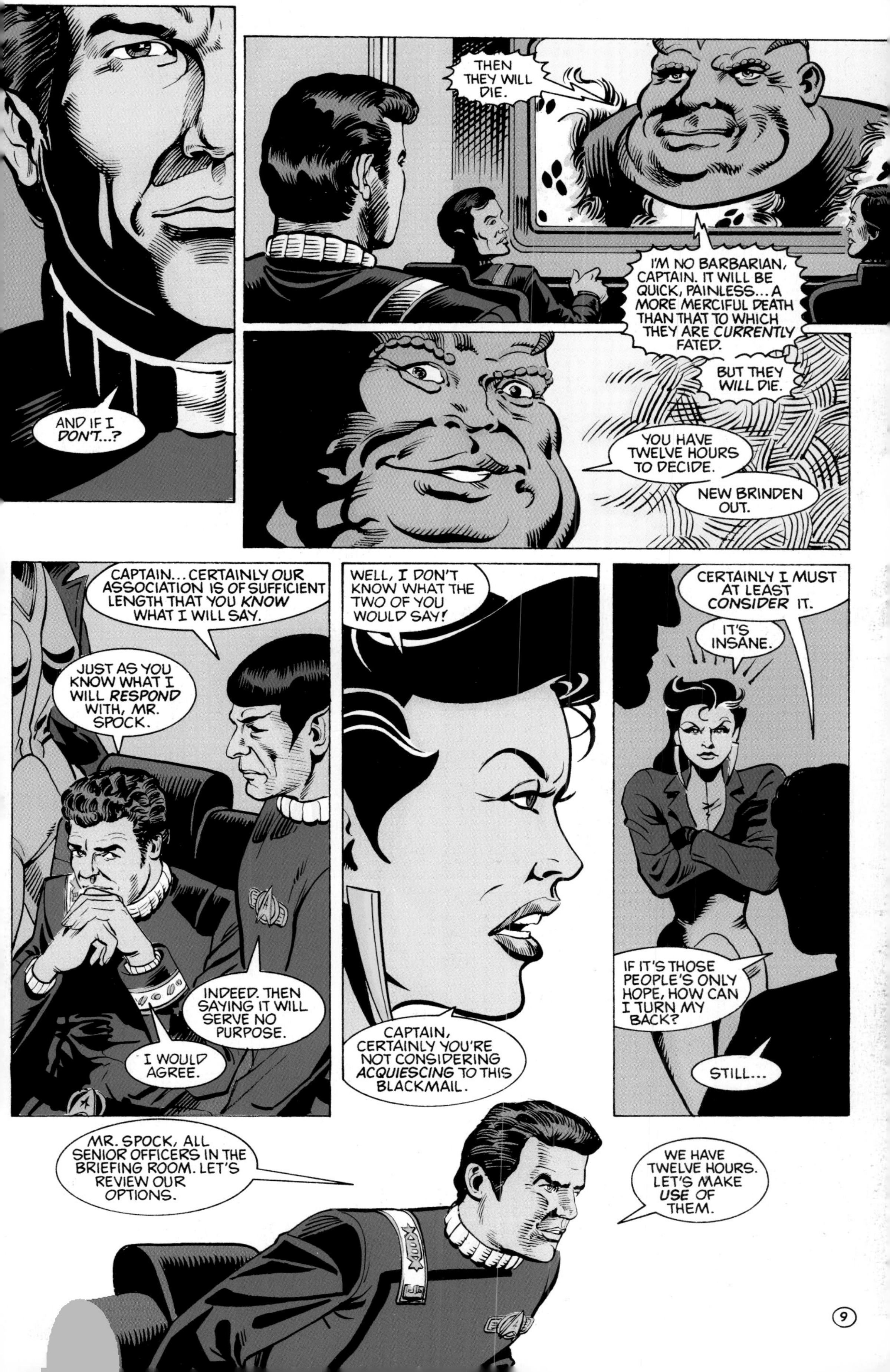
AND IF I DON'T...?
THEN THEY WILL DIE.
I'M NO BARBARIAN, CAPTAIN. IT WILL BE QUICK, PAINLESS... A MORE MERCIFUL DEATH THAN THAT TO WHICH THEY ARE CURRENTLY FATED.
BUT THEY WILL DIE.
YOU HAVE TWELVE HOURS TO DECIDE.
NEW BRINDEN OUT.
CAPTAIN... CERTAINLY OUR ASSOCIATION IS OF SUFFICIENT LENGTH THAT YOU KNOW WHAT I WILL SAY.
JUST AS YOU KNOW WHAT I WILL RESPOND WITH, MR. SPOCK.
INDEED. THEN SAYING IT WILL SERVE NO PURPOSE.
I WOULD AGREE.
WELL, I DON'T KNOW WHAT THE TWO OF YOU WOULD SAY!
CAPTAIN, CERTAINLY YOU'RE NOT CONSIDERING ACQUIESCING TO THIS BLACKMAIL.
CERTAINLY I MUST AT LEAST CONSIDER IT.
IT'S INSANE.
IF IT'S THOSE PEOPLE'S ONLY HOPE, HOW CAN I TURN MY BACK?
STILL...
MR. SPOCK, ALL SENIOR OFFICERS IN THE BRIEFING ROOM. LET'S REVIEW OUR OPTIONS.
WE HAVE TWELVE HOURS. LET'S MAKE USE OF THEM.

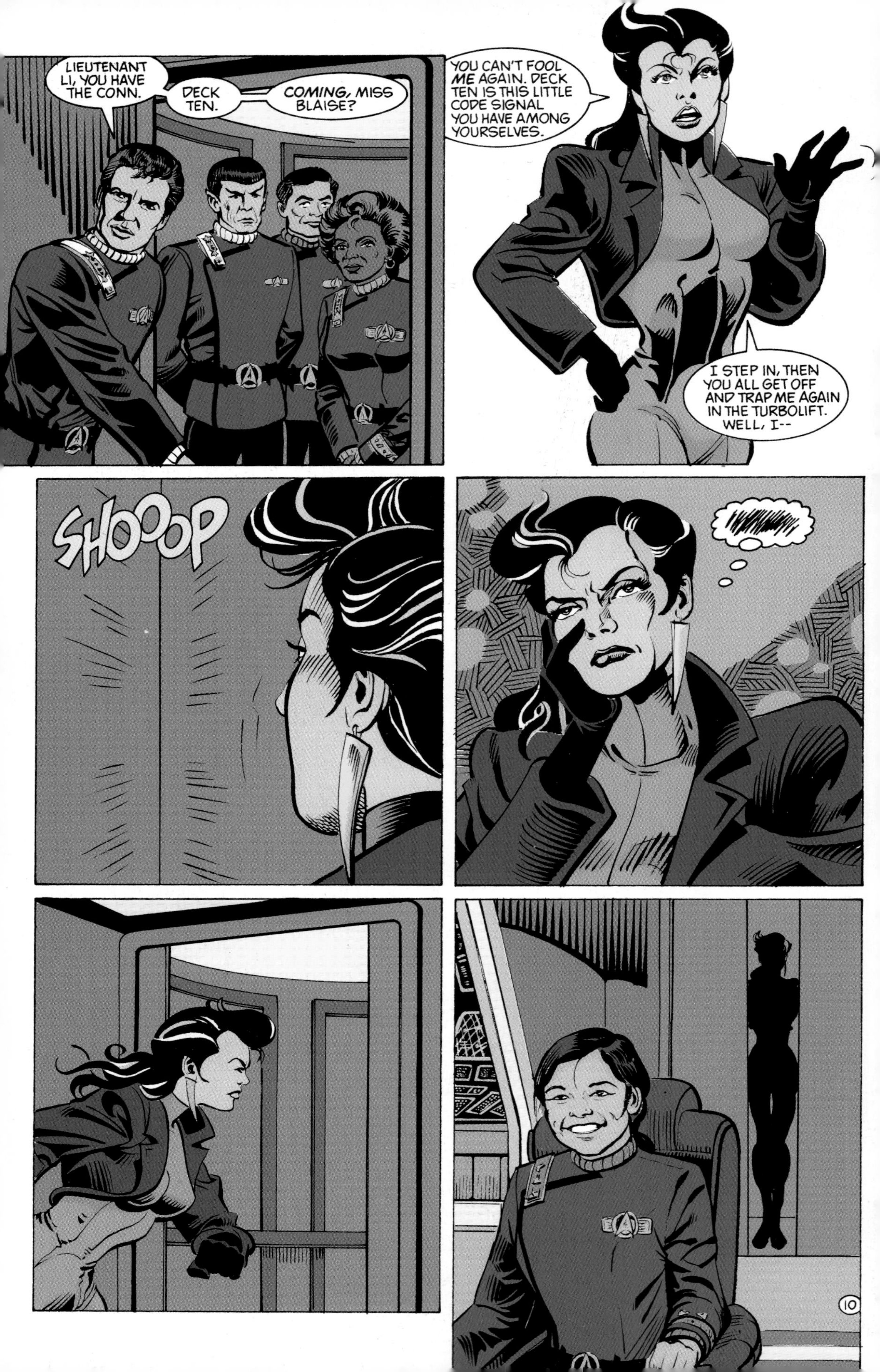
LIEUTENANT LI, YOU HAVE THE CONN.
DECK TEN.
COMING, MISS BLAISE?
YOU CAN'T FOOL ME AGAIN. DECK TEN IS THIS LITTLE CODE SIGNAL YOU HAVE AMONG YOURSELVES.
I STEP IN, THEN YOU ALL GET OFF AND TRAP ME AGAIN IN THE TURBOLIFT. WELL, I--
SHOOOP
10

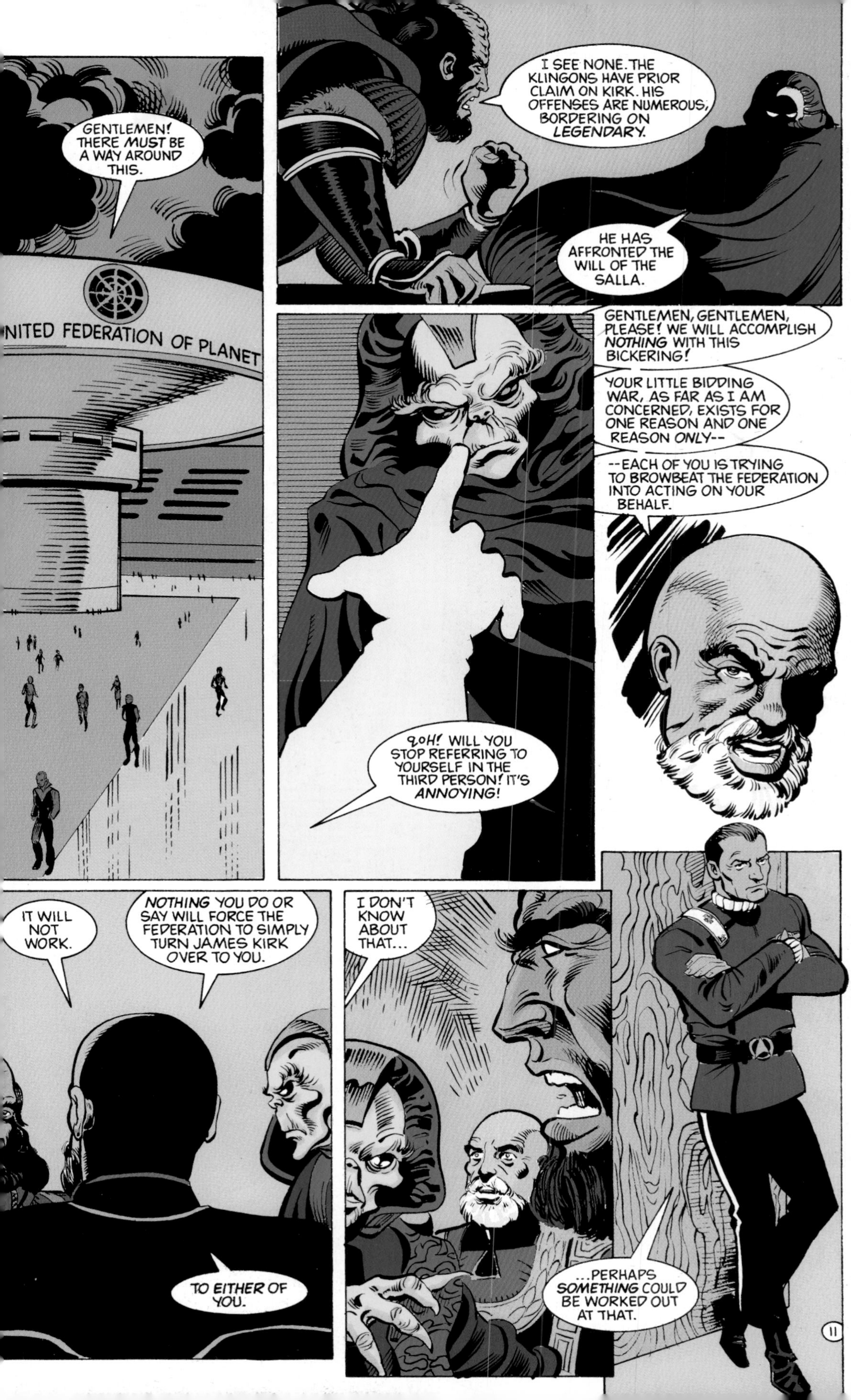
GENTLEMEN! THERE MUST BE A WAY AROUND THIS.
NITED FEDERATION OF PLANET
I SEE NONE. THE KLINGONS HAVE PRIOR CLAIM ON KIRK. HIS OFFENSES ARE NUMEROUS, BORDERING ON LEGENDARY.
HE HAS AFFRONTED THE WILL OF THE SALLA.
GENTLEMEN, GENTLEMEN, PLEASE! WE WILL ACCOMPLISH NOTHING WITH THIS BICKERING!
YOUR LITTLE BIDDING WAR, AS FAR AS I AM CONCERNED, EXISTS FOR ONE REASON AND ONE REASON ONLY--
--EACH OF YOU IS TRYING TO BROWBEAT THE FEDERATION INTO ACTING ON YOUR BEHALF.
QOH! WILL YOU STOP REFERRING TO YOURSELF IN THE THIRD PERSON! IT'S ANNOYING!
IT WILL NOT WORK.
NOTHING YOU DO OR SAY WILL FORCE THE FEDERATION TO SIMPLY TURN JAMES KIRK OVER TO YOU.
TO EITHER OF YOU.
I DON'T KNOW ABOUT THAT...
...PERHAPS SOMETHING COULD BE WORKED OUT AT THAT.

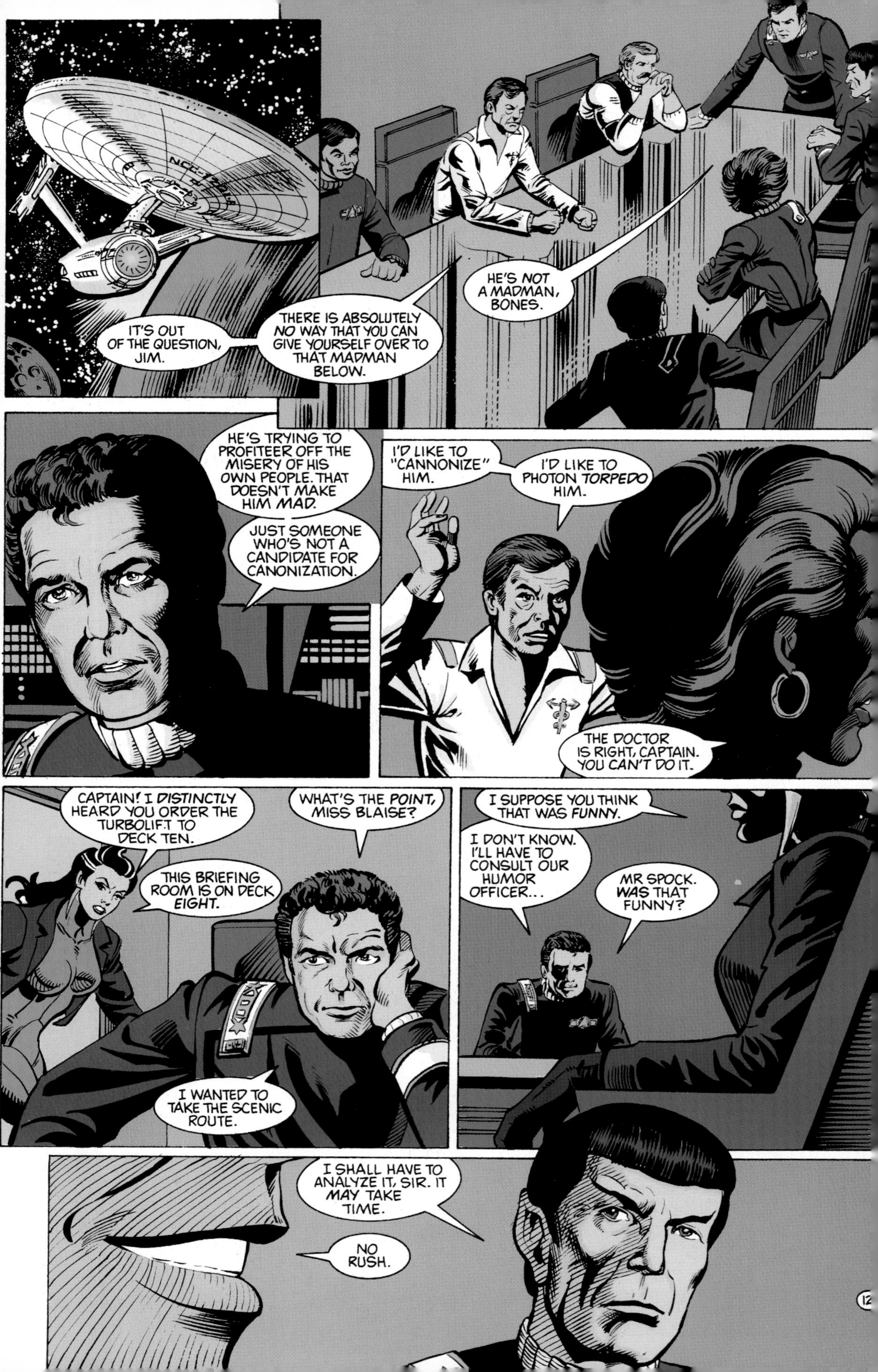

IT'S OUT OF THE QUESTION, JIM.
THERE IS ABSOLUTELY NO WAY THAT YOU CAN GIVE YOURSELF OVER TO THAT MADMAN BELOW.
HE'S NOT A MADMAN, BONES.
HE'S TRYING TO PROFITEER OFF THE MISERY OF HIS OWN PEOPLE. THAT DOESN'T MAKE HIM MAD.
JUST SOMEONE WHO'S NOT A CANDIDATE FOR CANONIZATION.
I'D LIKE TO "CANNONIZE" HIM.
I'D LIKE TO PHOTON TORPEDO HIM.
THE DOCTOR IS RIGHT, CAPTAIN. YOU CAN'T DO IT.
CAPTAIN! I DISTINCTLY HEARD YOU ORDER THE TURBOLIFT TO DECK TEN.
THIS BRIEFING ROOM IS ON DECK EIGHT.
WHAT'S THE POINT, MISS BLAISE?
I WANTED TO TAKE THE SCENIC ROUTE.
I SUPPOSE YOU THINK THAT WAS FUNNY.
I DON'T KNOW. I'LL HAVE TO CONSULT OUR HUMOR OFFICER...
MR SPOCK. WAS THAT FUNNY?
I SHALL HAVE TO ANALYZE IT, SIR. IT MAY TAKE TIME.
NO RUSH.

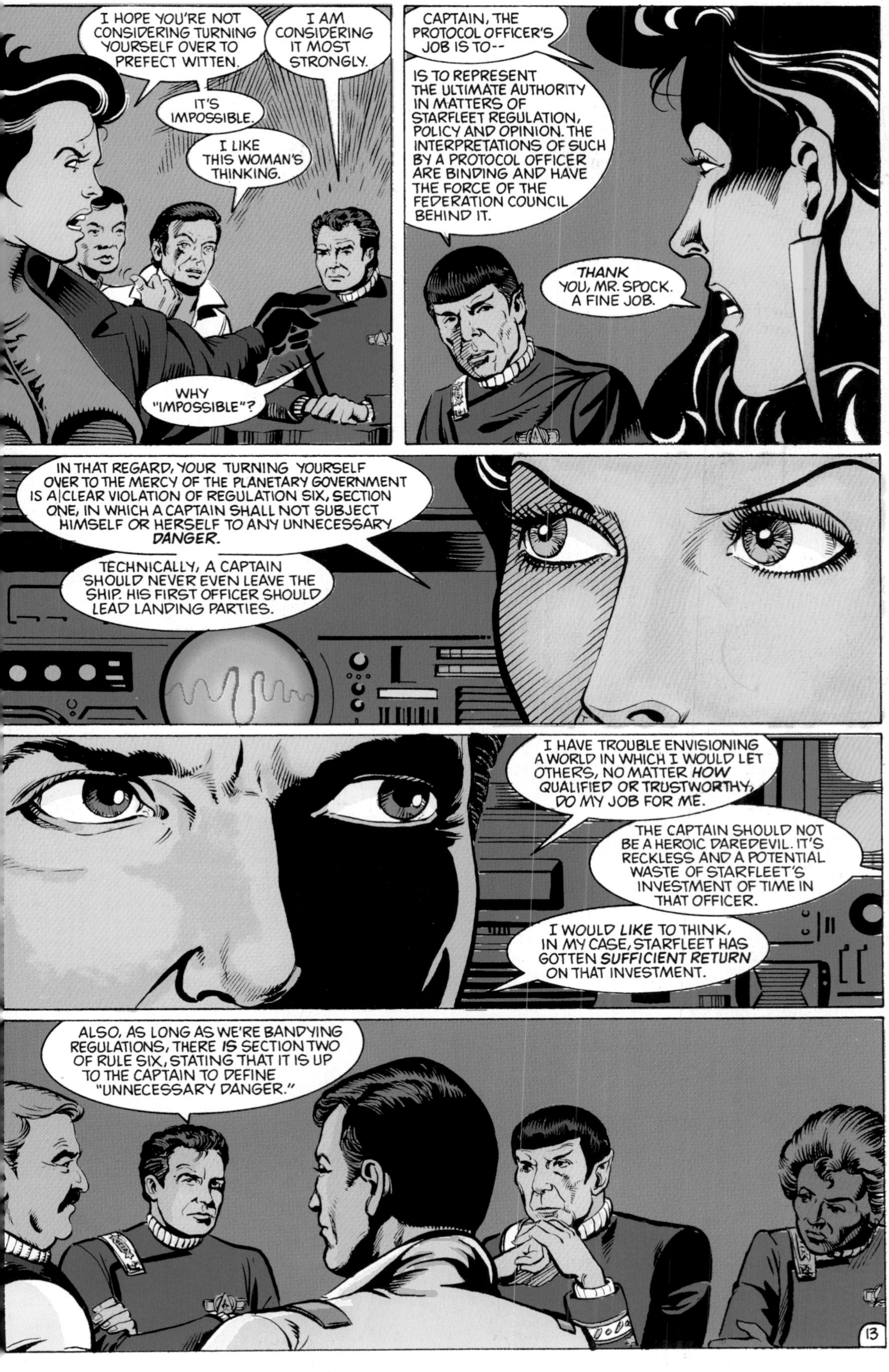

I HOPE YOU'RE NOT CONSIDERING TURNING YOURSELF OVER TO PREFECT WITTEN.
I AM CONSIDERING IT MOST STRONGLY.
IT'S IMPOSSIBLE.
I LIKE THIS WOMAN'S THINKING.
WHY "IMPOSSIBLE"?
CAPTAIN, THE PROTOCOL OFFICER'S JOB IS TO--
IS TO REPRESENT THE ULTIMATE AUTHORITY IN MATTERS OF STARFLEET REGULATION, POLICY AND OPINION. THE INTERPRETATIONS OF SUCH BY A PROTOCOL OFFICER ARE BINDING AND HAVE THE FORCE OF THE FEDERATION COUNCIL BEHIND IT.
THANK YOU, MR. SPOCK. A FINE JOB.
IN THAT REGARD, YOUR TURNING YOURSELF OVER TO THE MERCY OF THE PLANETARY GOVERNMENT IS A CLEAR VIOLATION OF REGULATION SIX, SECTION ONE, IN WHICH A CAPTAIN SHALL NOT SUBJECT HIMSELF OR HERSELF TO ANY UNNECESSARY DANGER.
TECHNICALLY, A CAPTAIN SHOULD NEVER EVEN LEAVE THE SHIP. HIS FIRST OFFICER SHOULD LEAD LANDING PARTIES.
I HAVE TROUBLE ENVISIONING A WORLD IN WHICH I WOULD LET OTHERS, NO MATTER HOW QUALIFIED OR TRUSTWORTHY, DO MY JOB FOR ME.
THE CAPTAIN SHOULD NOT BE A HEROIC DAREDEVIL. IT'S RECKLESS AND A POTENTIAL WASTE OF STARFLEET'S INVESTMENT OF TIME IN THAT OFFICER.
I WOULD LIKE TO THINK, IN MY CASE, STARFLEET HAS GOTTEN SUFFICIENT RETURN ON THAT INVESTMENT.
ALSO, AS LONG AS WE'RE BANDYING REGULATIONS, THERE IS SECTION TWO OF RULE SIX, STATING THAT IT IS UP TO THE CAPTAIN TO DEFINE "UNNECESSARY DANGER."

IS THERE ANYONE AT THIS TABLE WHO *DOES* FEEL THAT I SHOULD GIVE MYSELF UP TO THE PREFECT?

ABSOLUTELY NOT.

A *WERY* BAD MISTAKE, SIR.

MOST UNWISE, CAPTAIN.

MR. SPOCK? YOU MIGHT AS WELL SAY IT.

OR OF THE ONE.

LOGICALLY, CAPTAIN, THERE WOULD SEEM NO ALTERNATIVE. THAT IS, IF YOU ARE WEIGHING THE NEEDS OF THE *MANY* AGAINST THE NEEDS OF THE FEW.

NEVERTHELESS... *THIS "ONE"* WOULD FIND YOUR SACRIFICE...

...UNFORTUNATE.

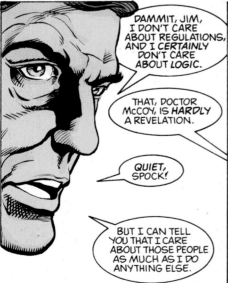

DAMMIT, JIM, I DON'T CARE ABOUT REGULATIONS, AND I *CERTAINLY* DON'T CARE ABOUT *LOGIC*.

THAT, DOCTOR McCOY, IS *HARDLY* A REVELATION.

QUIET, SPOCK!

BUT I CAN TELL YOU THAT I CARE ABOUT THOSE PEOPLE AS MUCH AS I DO ANYTHING ELSE.

WE HAVE TWELVE MORE HOURS, BY WITTEN'S DEADLINE. I *KNOW* I CAN FIND A CURE, GIVEN ENOUGH TIME.

HELL, MOST OF THE WORK IS ALREADY DONE. I JUST HAVE TO FIND THE PROPER REAGENT TO MAKE IT *PERMANENT*.

14

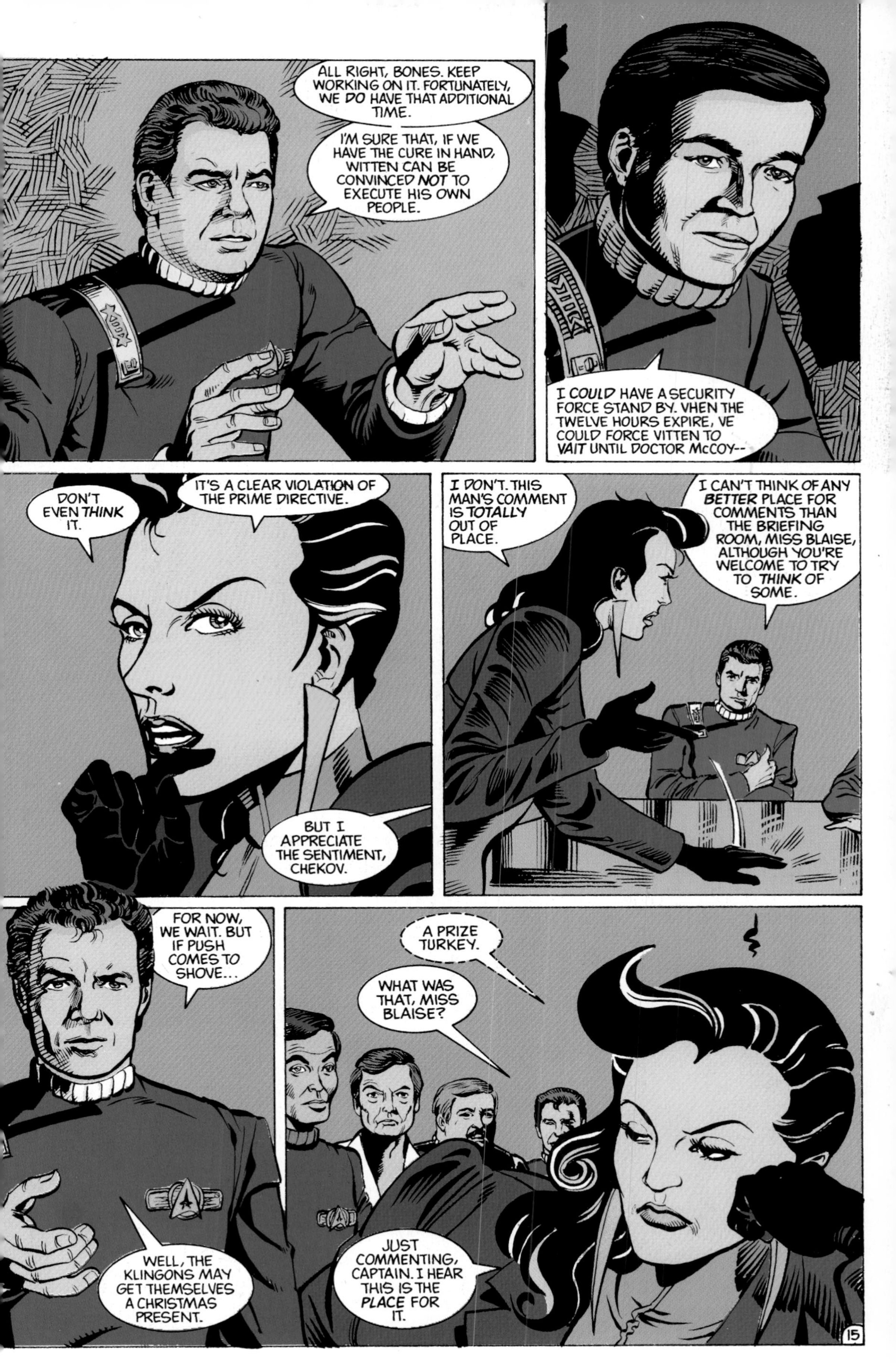
ALL RIGHT, BONES. KEEP WORKING ON IT. FORTUNATELY, WE DO HAVE THAT ADDITIONAL TIME.
I'M SURE THAT, IF WE HAVE THE CURE IN HAND, WITTEN CAN BE CONVINCED NOT TO EXECUTE HIS OWN PEOPLE.
I COULD HAVE A SECURITY FORCE STAND BY. VHEN THE TWELVE HOURS EXPIRE, VE COULD FORCE VITTEN TO VAIT UNTIL DOCTOR McCOY--
DON'T EVEN THINK IT.
IT'S A CLEAR VIOLATION OF THE PRIME DIRECTIVE.
BUT I APPRECIATE THE SENTIMENT, CHEKOV.
I DON'T. THIS MAN'S COMMENT IS TOTALLY OUT OF PLACE.
I CAN'T THINK OF ANY BETTER PLACE FOR COMMENTS THAN THE BRIEFING ROOM, MISS BLAISE, ALTHOUGH YOU'RE WELCOME TO TRY TO THINK OF SOME.
FOR NOW, WE WAIT. BUT IF PUSH COMES TO SHOVE...
WELL, THE KLINGONS MAY GET THEMSELVES A CHRISTMAS PRESENT.
A PRIZE TURKEY.
WHAT WAS THAT, MISS BLAISE?
JUST COMMENTING, CAPTAIN. I HEAR THIS IS THE PLACE FOR IT.

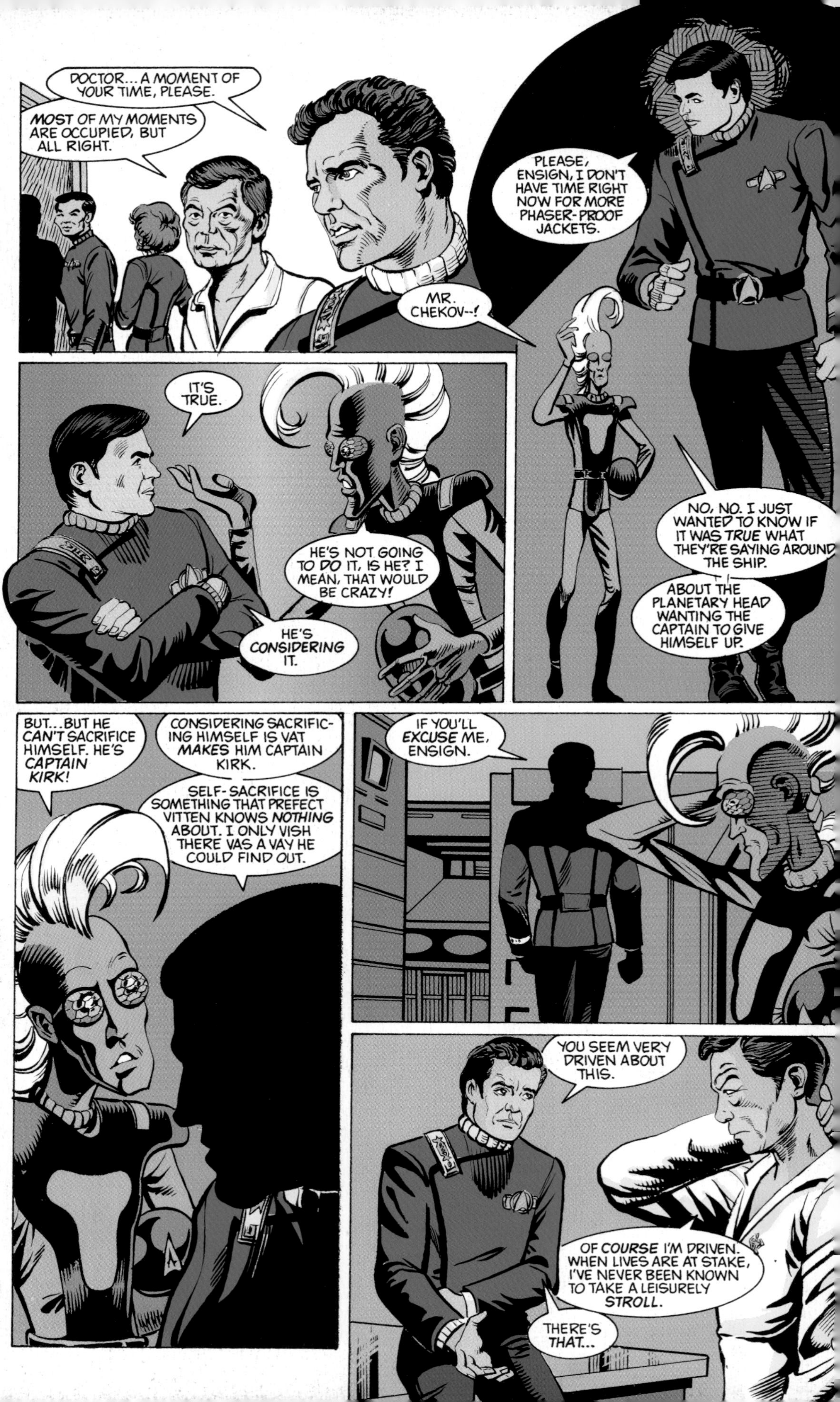
DOCTOR... A MOMENT OF YOUR TIME, PLEASE.
MOST OF MY MOMENTS ARE OCCUPIED, BUT ALL RIGHT.
PLEASE, ENSIGN, I DON'T HAVE TIME RIGHT NOW FOR MORE PHASER-PROOF JACKETS.
MR. CHEKOV--!
NO, NO. I JUST WANTED TO KNOW IF IT WAS TRUE WHAT THEY'RE SAYING AROUND THE SHIP.
ABOUT THE PLANETARY HEAD WANTING THE CAPTAIN TO GIVE HIMSELF UP.
IT'S TRUE.
HE'S NOT GOING TO DO IT, IS HE? I MEAN, THAT WOULD BE CRAZY!
HE'S CONSIDERING IT.
BUT...BUT HE CAN'T SACRIFICE HIMSELF. HE'S CAPTAIN KIRK!
CONSIDERING SACRIFICING HIMSELF IS VAT MAKES HIM CAPTAIN KIRK.
SELF-SACRIFICE IS SOMETHING THAT PREFECT VITTEN KNOWS NOTHING ABOUT. I ONLY VISH THERE VAS A VAY HE COULD FIND OUT.
IF YOU'LL EXCUSE ME, ENSIGN.
YOU SEEM VERY DRIVEN ABOUT THIS.
OF COURSE I'M DRIVEN. WHEN LIVES ARE AT STAKE, I'VE NEVER BEEN KNOWN TO TAKE A LEISURELY STROLL.
THERE'S THAT...

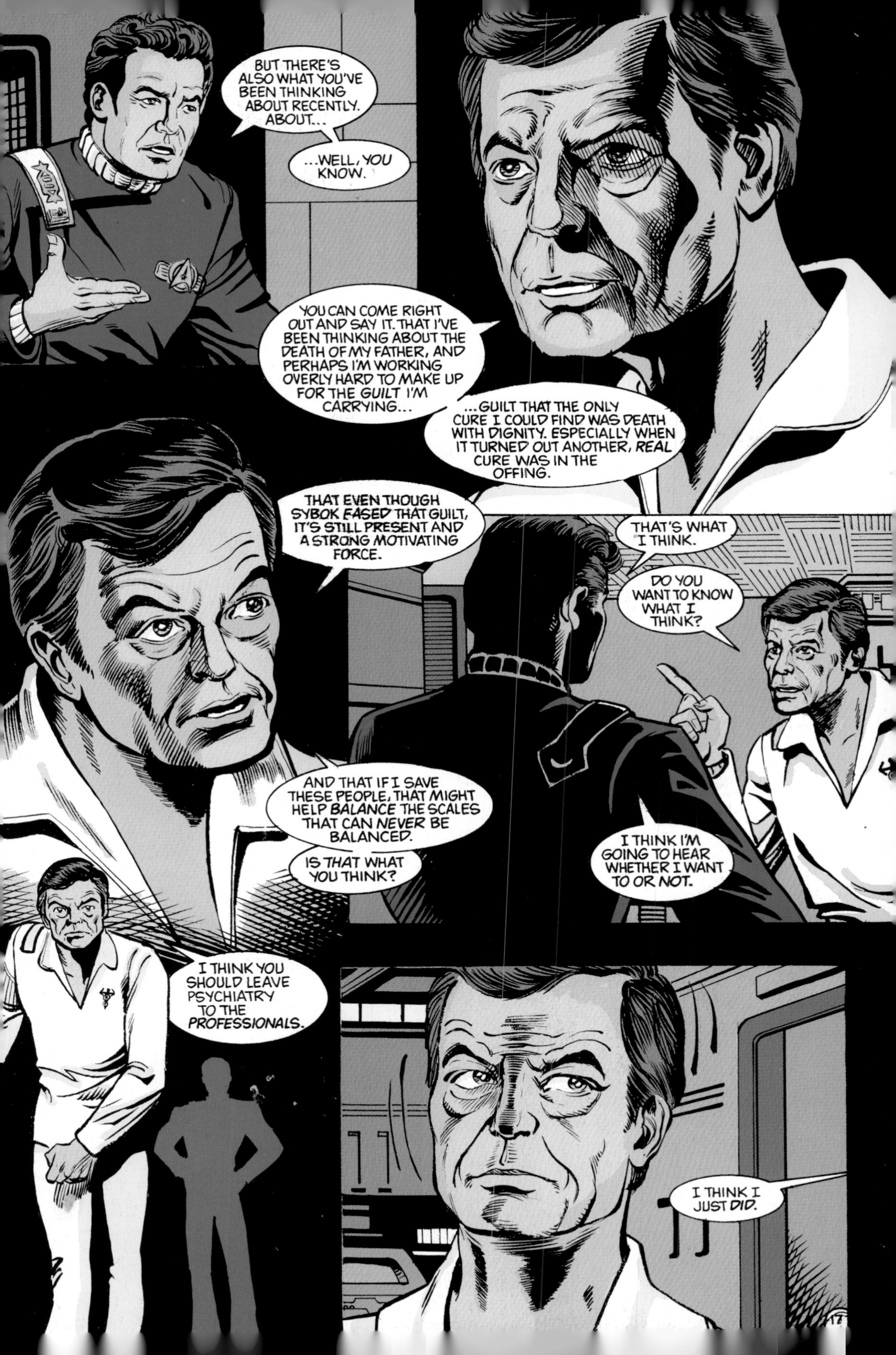
BUT THERE'S ALSO WHAT YOU'VE BEEN THINKING ABOUT RECENTLY. ABOUT...
...WELL, YOU KNOW.
YOU CAN COME RIGHT OUT AND SAY IT. THAT I'VE BEEN THINKING ABOUT THE DEATH OF MY FATHER, AND PERHAPS I'M WORKING OVERLY HARD TO MAKE UP FOR THE GUILT I'M CARRYING...
...GUILT THAT THE ONLY CURE I COULD FIND WAS DEATH WITH DIGNITY. ESPECIALLY WHEN IT TURNED OUT ANOTHER, REAL CURE WAS IN THE OFFING.
THAT EVEN THOUGH SYBOK EASED THAT GUILT, IT'S STILL PRESENT AND A STRONG MOTIVATING FORCE.
AND THAT IF I SAVE THESE PEOPLE, THAT MIGHT HELP BALANCE THE SCALES THAT CAN NEVER BE BALANCED.
IS THAT WHAT YOU THINK?
THAT'S WHAT I THINK.
DO YOU WANT TO KNOW WHAT I THINK?
I THINK I'M GOING TO HEAR WHETHER I WANT TO OR NOT.
I THINK YOU SHOULD LEAVE PSYCHIATRY TO THE PROFESSIONALS.
I THINK I JUST DID.
17

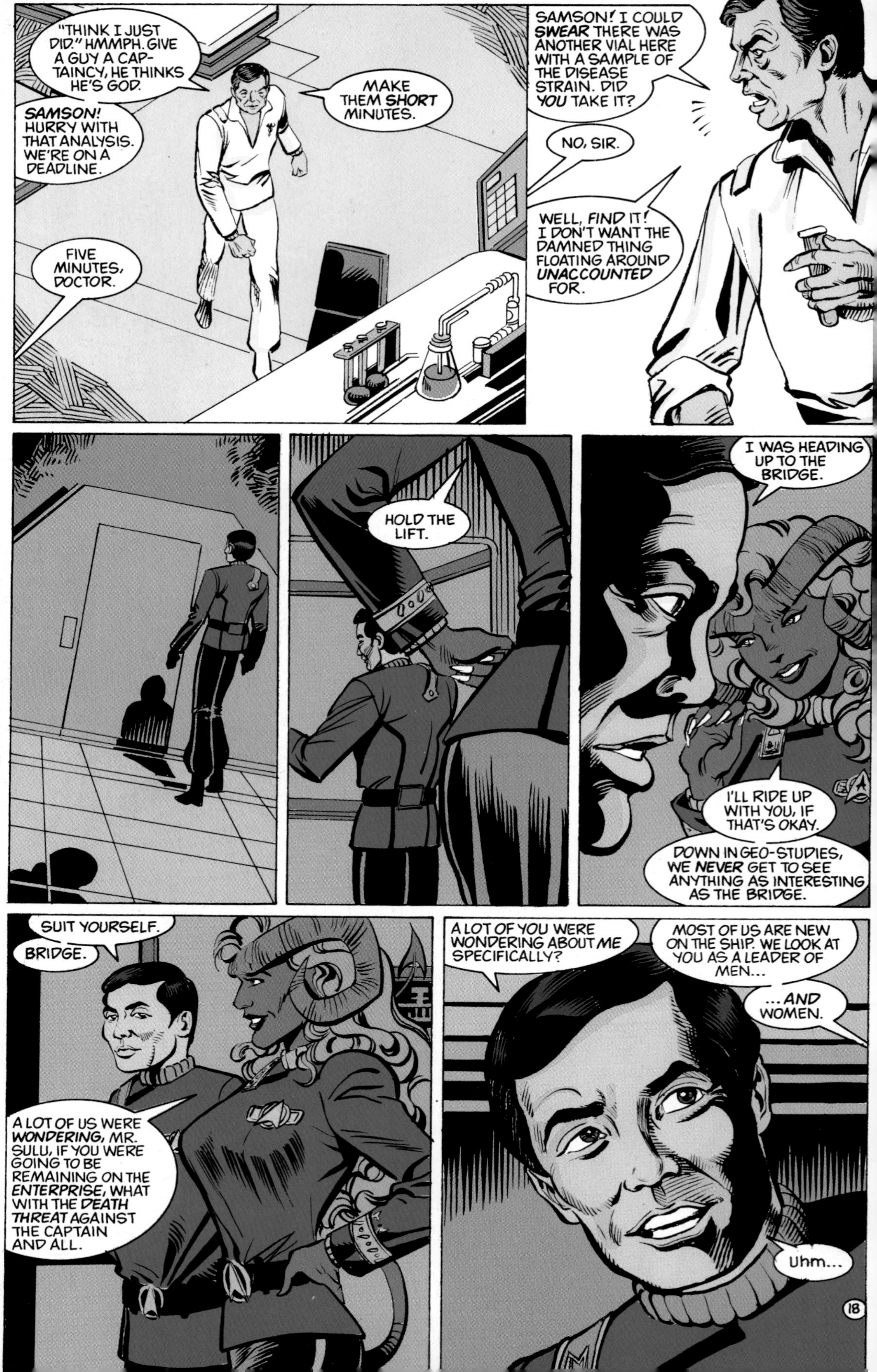
"THINK I JUST DID." HMMPH. GIVE A GUY A CAPTAINCY, HE THINKS HE'S GOD.
SAMSON! HURRY WITH THAT ANALYSIS. WE'RE ON A DEADLINE.
FIVE MINUTES, DOCTOR.
MAKE THEM SHORT MINUTES.
SAMSON! I COULD SWEAR THERE WAS ANOTHER VIAL HERE WITH A SAMPLE OF THE DISEASE STRAIN. DID YOU TAKE IT?
NO, SIR.
WELL, FIND IT! I DON'T WANT THE DAMNED THING FLOATING AROUND UNACCOUNTED FOR.
HOLD THE LIFT.
I WAS HEADING UP TO THE BRIDGE.
I'LL RIDE UP WITH YOU, IF THAT'S OKAY.
DOWN IN GEO-STUDIES, WE NEVER GET TO SEE ANYTHING AS INTERESTING AS THE BRIDGE.
SUIT YOURSELF.
BRIDGE.
A LOT OF US WERE WONDERING, MR. SULU, IF YOU WERE GOING TO BE REMAINING ON THE ENTERPRISE, WHAT WITH THE DEATH THREAT AGAINST THE CAPTAIN AND ALL.
A LOT OF YOU WERE WONDERING ABOUT ME SPECIFICALLY?
MOST OF US ARE NEW ON THE SHIP. WE LOOK AT YOU AS A LEADER OF MEN...
...AND WOMEN.
Uhm...
18

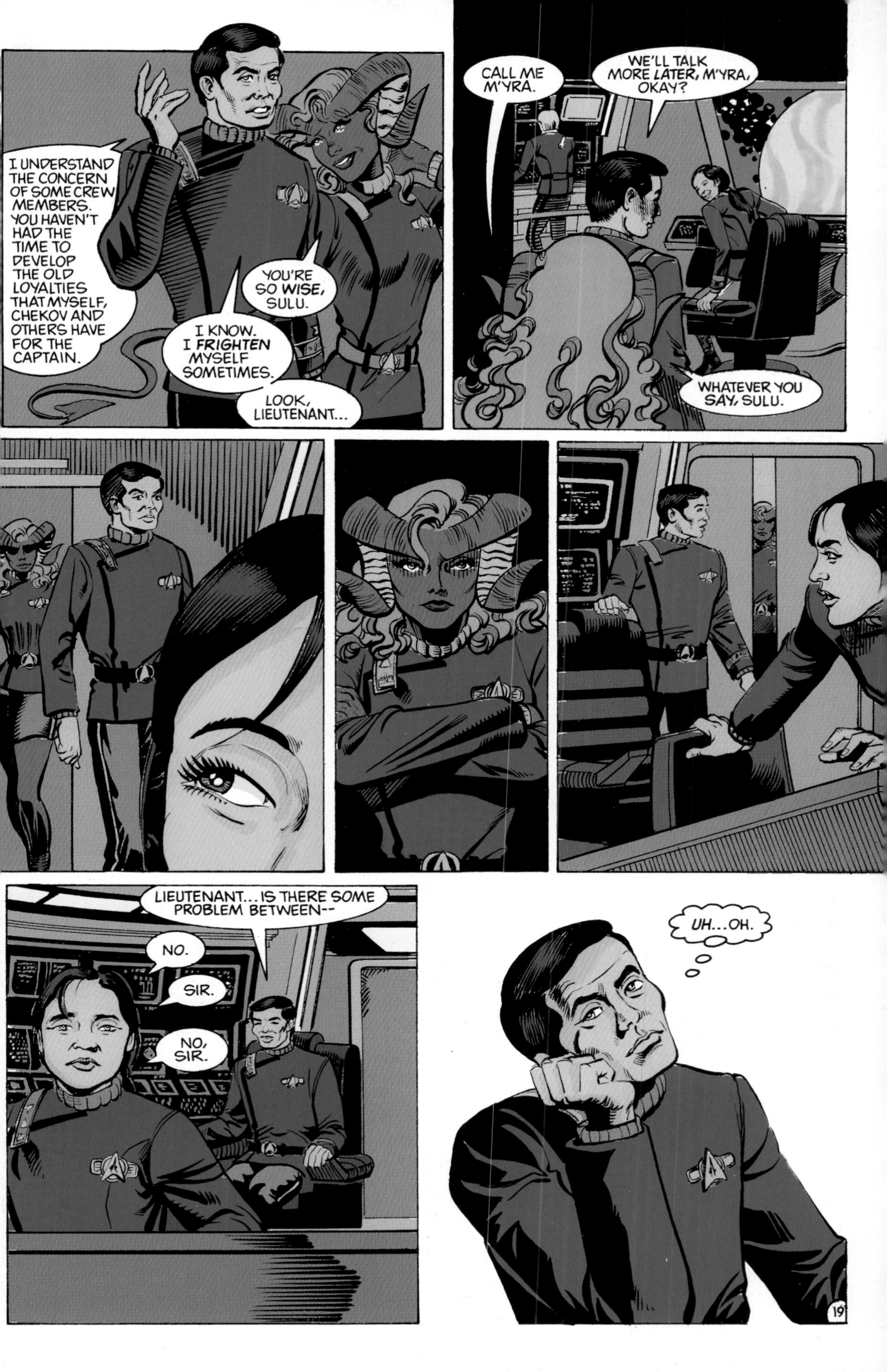

I UNDERSTAND THE CONCERN OF SOME CREW MEMBERS. YOU HAVEN'T HAD THE TIME TO DEVELOP THE OLD LOYALTIES THAT MYSELF, CHEKOV AND OTHERS HAVE FOR THE CAPTAIN.
YOU'RE SO WISE, SULU.
I KNOW. I FRIGHTEN MYSELF SOMETIMES.
LOOK, LIEUTENANT...
CALL ME M'YRA.
WE'LL TALK MORE LATER, M'YRA, OKAY?
WHATEVER YOU SAY, SULU.
LIEUTENANT... IS THERE SOME PROBLEM BETWEEN--
NO.
SIR.
NO, SIR.
UH... OH.

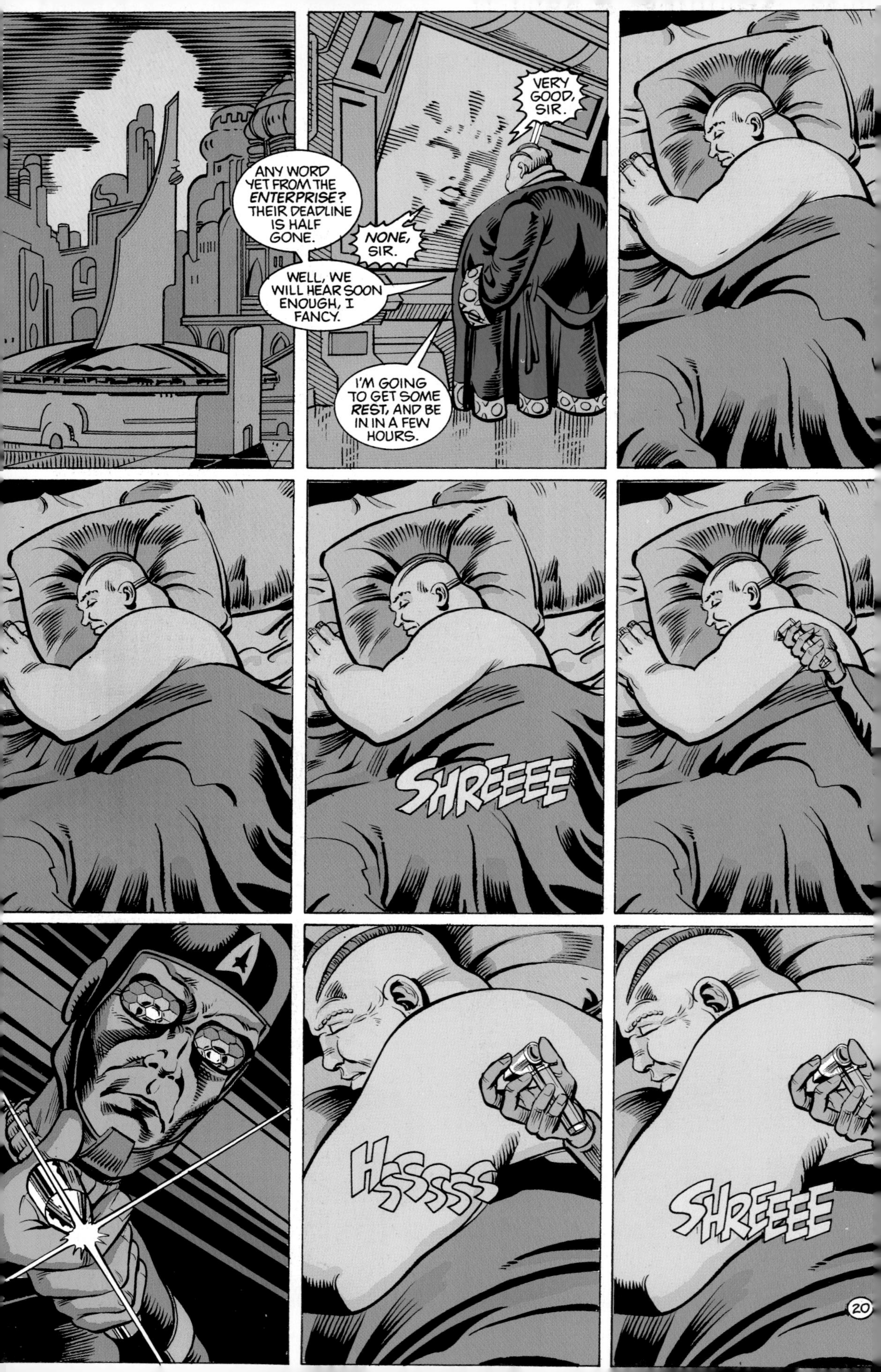
ANY WORD YET FROM THE ENTERPRISE? THEIR DEADLINE IS HALF GONE.
NONE, SIR.
WELL, WE WILL HEAR SOON ENOUGH, I FANCY.
I'M GOING TO GET SOME REST, AND BE IN IN A FEW HOURS.
VERY GOOD, SIR.
SHREEEE
HSSSSS
SHREEEE
20

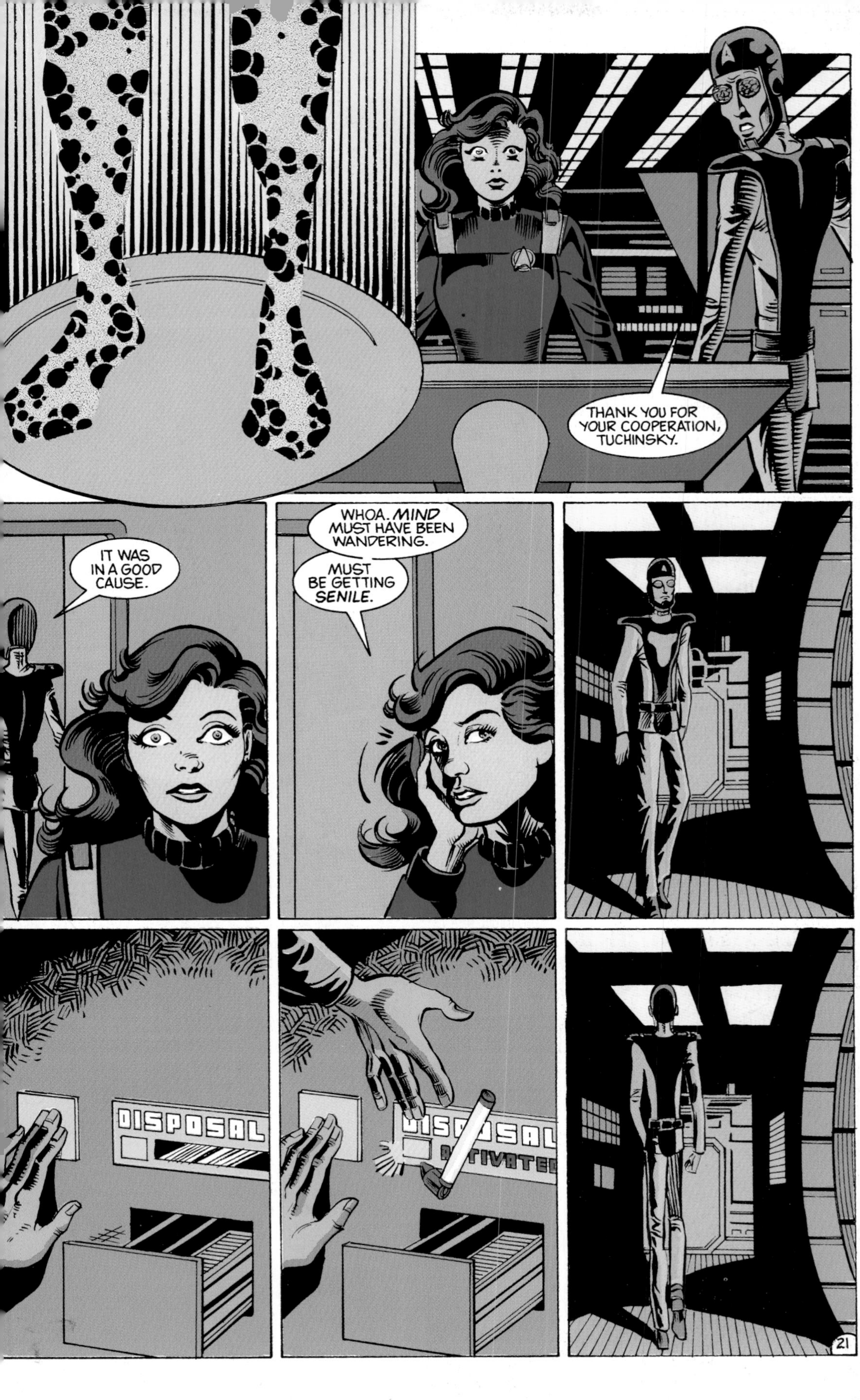

THANK YOU FOR YOUR COOPERATION, TUCHINSKY.
IT WAS IN A GOOD CAUSE.
WHOA. MIND MUST HAVE BEEN WANDERING.
MUST BE GETTING SENILE.
DISPOSAL
DISPOSAL ACTIVATED

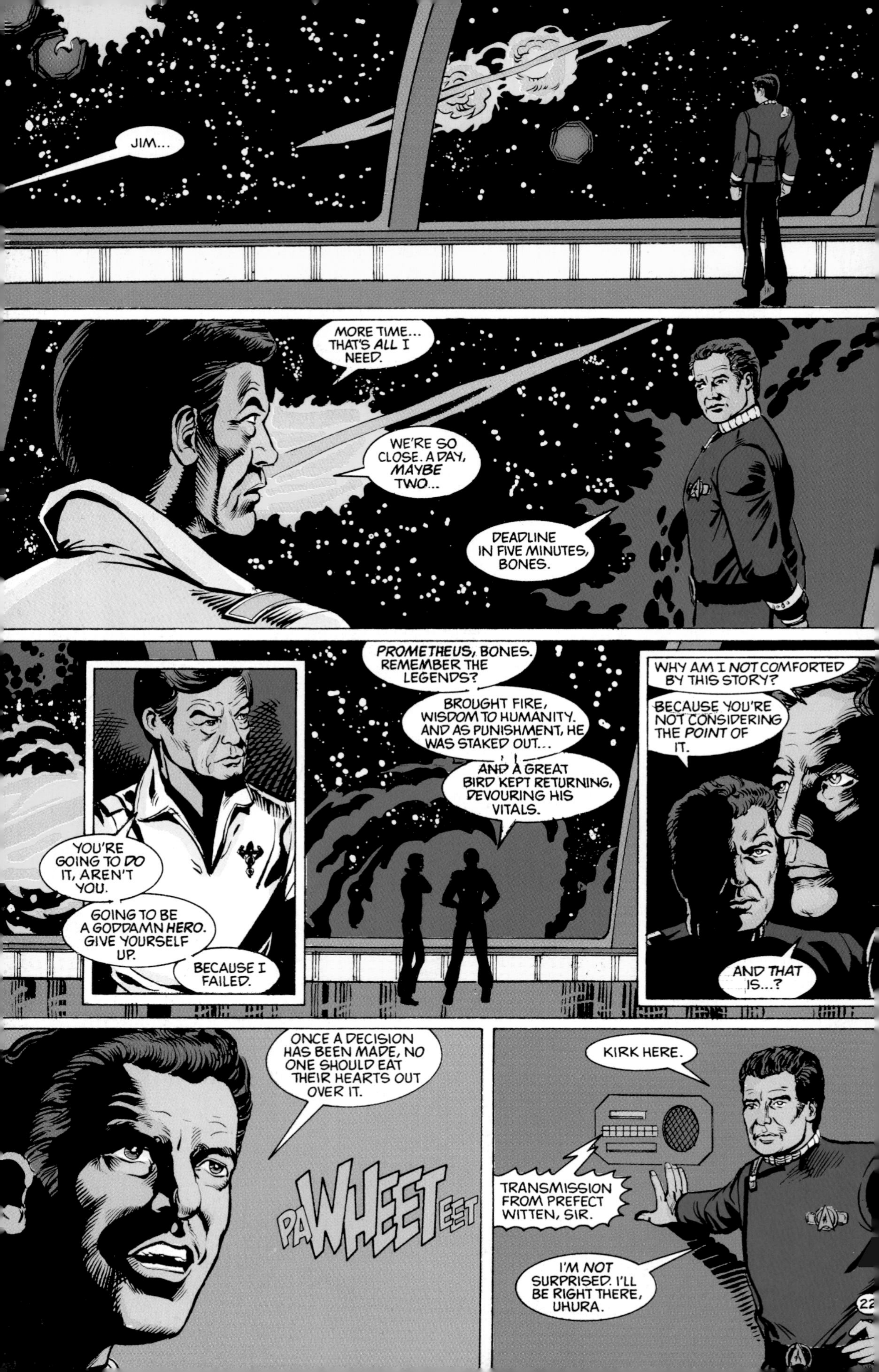
JIM...
MORE TIME... THAT'S ALL I NEED.
WE'RE SO CLOSE. A DAY, MAYBE TWO...
DEADLINE IN FIVE MINUTES, BONES.
PROMETHEUS, BONES. REMEMBER THE LEGENDS?
BROUGHT FIRE, WISDOM TO HUMANITY. AND AS PUNISHMENT, HE WAS STAKED OUT...
AND A GREAT BIRD KEPT RETURNING, DEVOURING HIS VITALS.
YOU'RE GOING TO DO IT, AREN'T YOU.
GOING TO BE A GODDAMN HERO. GIVE YOURSELF UP.
BECAUSE I FAILED.
WHY AM I NOT COMFORTED BY THIS STORY?
BECAUSE YOU'RE NOT CONSIDERING THE POINT OF IT.
AND THAT IS...?
ONCE A DECISION HAS BEEN MADE, NO ONE SHOULD EAT THEIR HEARTS OUT OVER IT.
PAWHEETEET
KIRK HERE.
TRANSMISSION FROM PREFECT WITTEN, SIR.
I'M NOT SURPRISED. I'LL BE RIGHT THERE, UHURA.
22

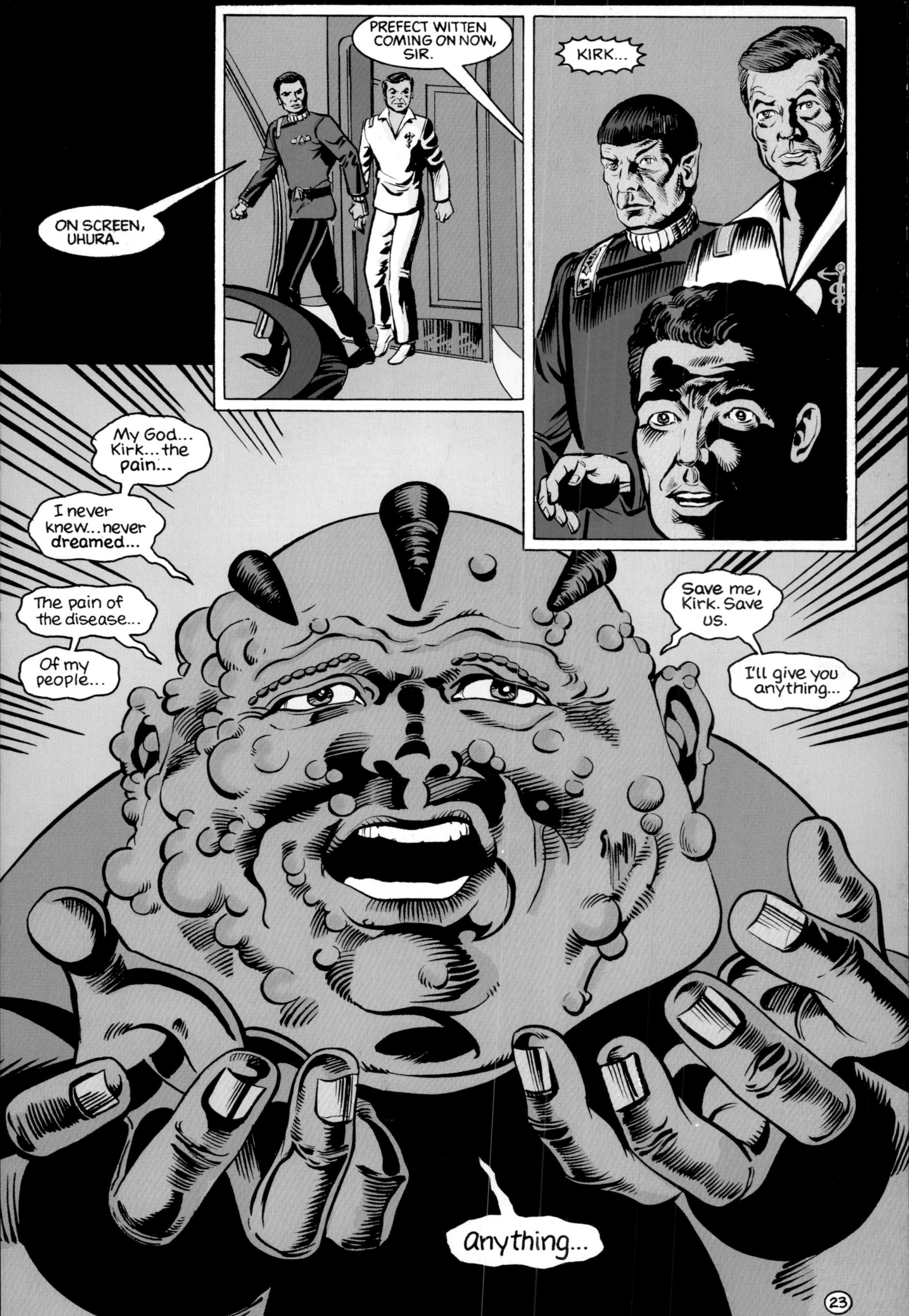
ON SCREEN, UHURA.
PREFECT WITTEN COMING ON NOW, SIR.
KIRK...
My God... Kirk... the pain...
I never knew... never dreamed...
The pain of the disease...
Of my people...
Save me, Kirk. Save us.
I'll give you anything...
anything...

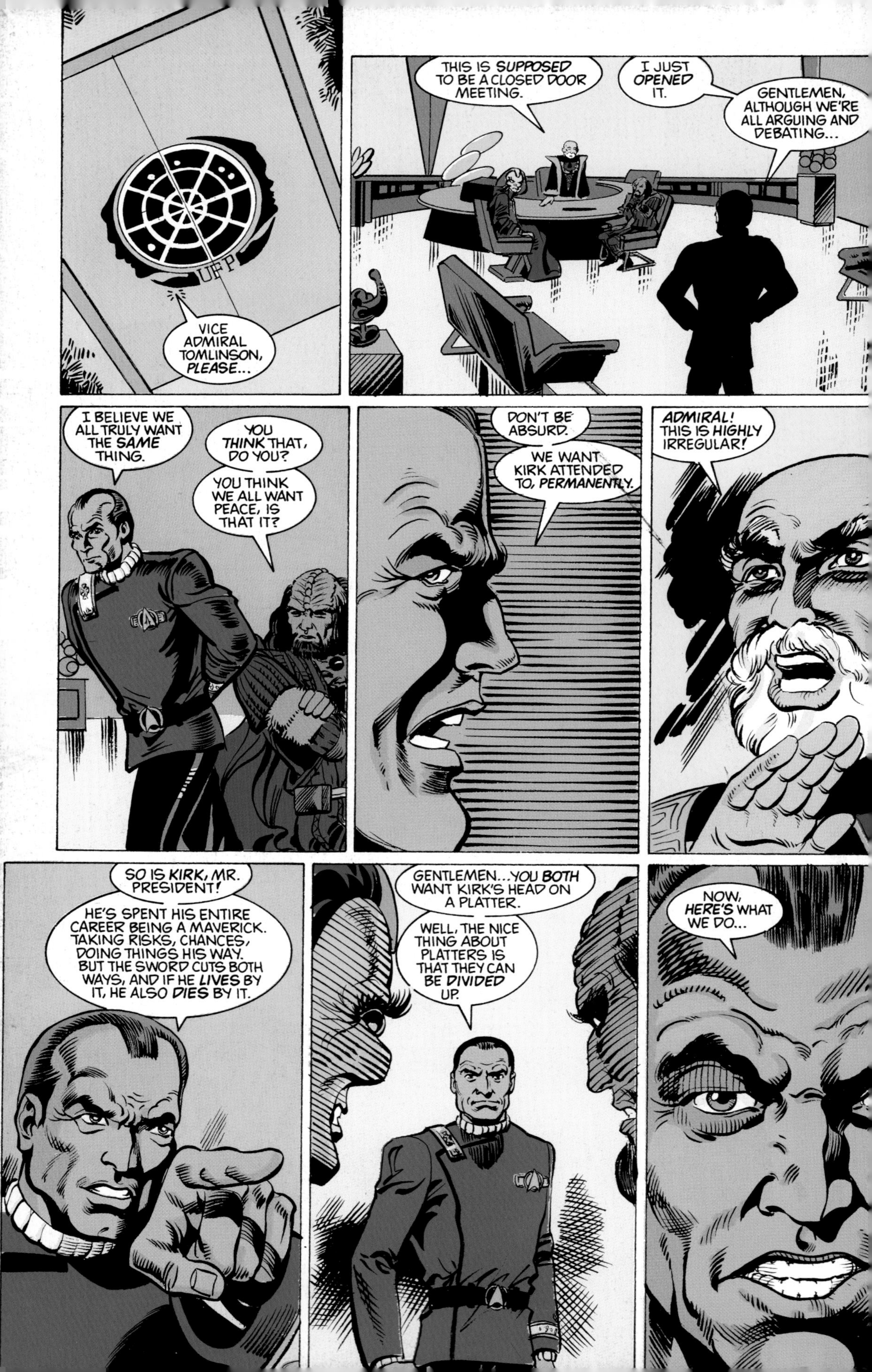
UFP
VICE ADMIRAL TOMLINSON, PLEASE...
THIS IS SUPPOSED TO BE A CLOSED DOOR MEETING.
I JUST OPENED IT.
GENTLEMEN, ALTHOUGH WE'RE ALL ARGUING AND DEBATING...
I BELIEVE WE ALL TRULY WANT THE SAME THING.
YOU THINK THAT, DO YOU?
YOU THINK WE ALL WANT PEACE, IS THAT IT?
DON'T BE ABSURD.
WE WANT KIRK ATTENDED TO, PERMANENTLY.
ADMIRAL! THIS IS HIGHLY IRREGULAR!
SO IS KIRK, MR. PRESIDENT!
HE'S SPENT HIS ENTIRE CAREER BEING A MAVERICK. TAKING RISKS, CHANCES, DOING THINGS HIS WAY. BUT THE SWORD CUTS BOTH WAYS, AND IF HE LIVES BY IT, HE ALSO DIES BY IT.
GENTLEMEN...YOU BOTH WANT KIRK'S HEAD ON A PLATTER.
WELL, THE NICE THING ABOUT PLATTERS IS THAT THEY CAN BE DIVIDED UP.
NOW, HERE'S WHAT WE DO...

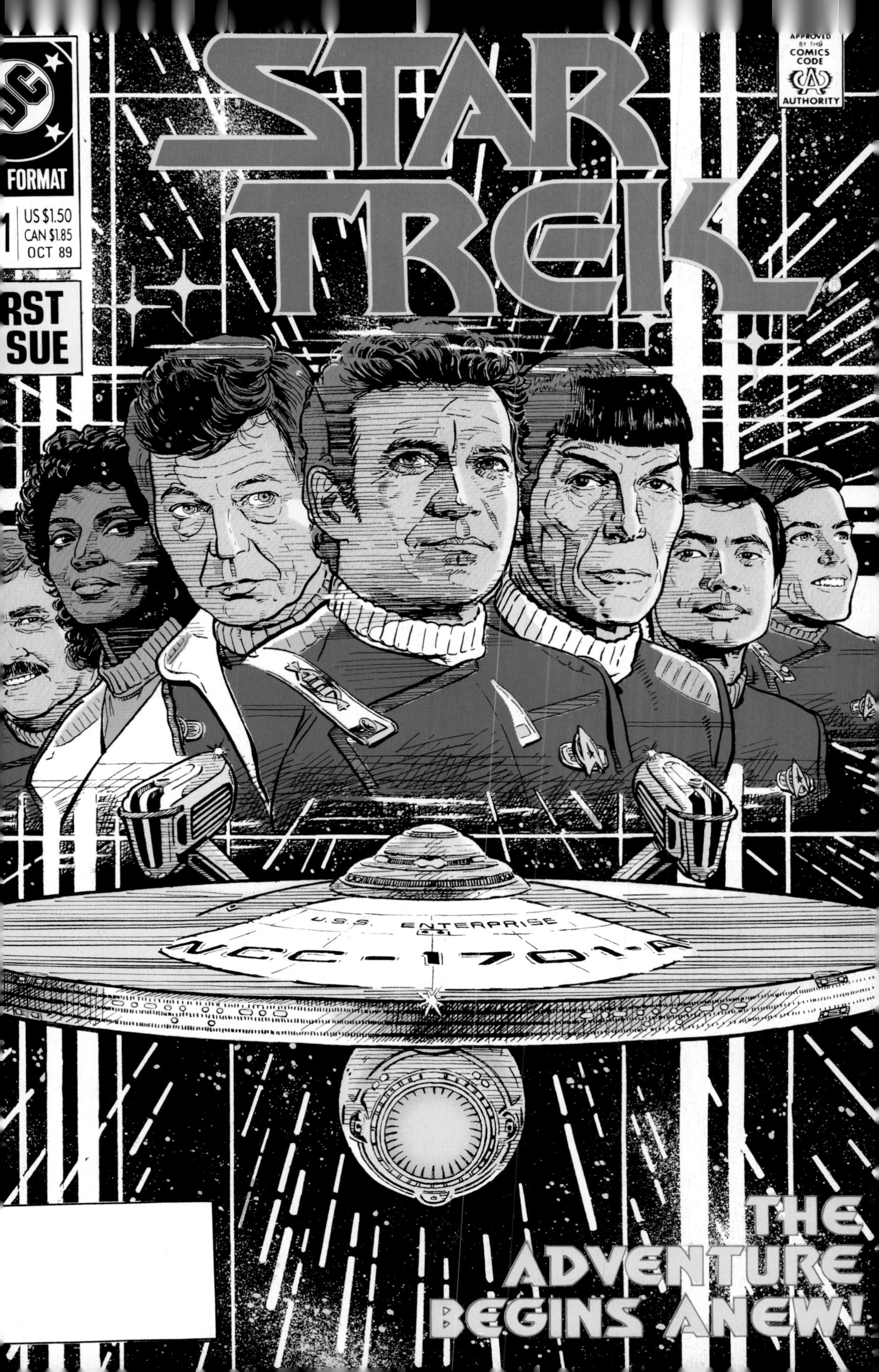
FORMAT
1
US $1.50
CAN $1.85
OCT 89
RST
SUE
STAR TREK
APPROVED BY THE COMICS CODE AUTHORITY
U.S.S. ENTERPRISE
NCC-1701-A
THE ADVENTURE BEGINS ANEW!

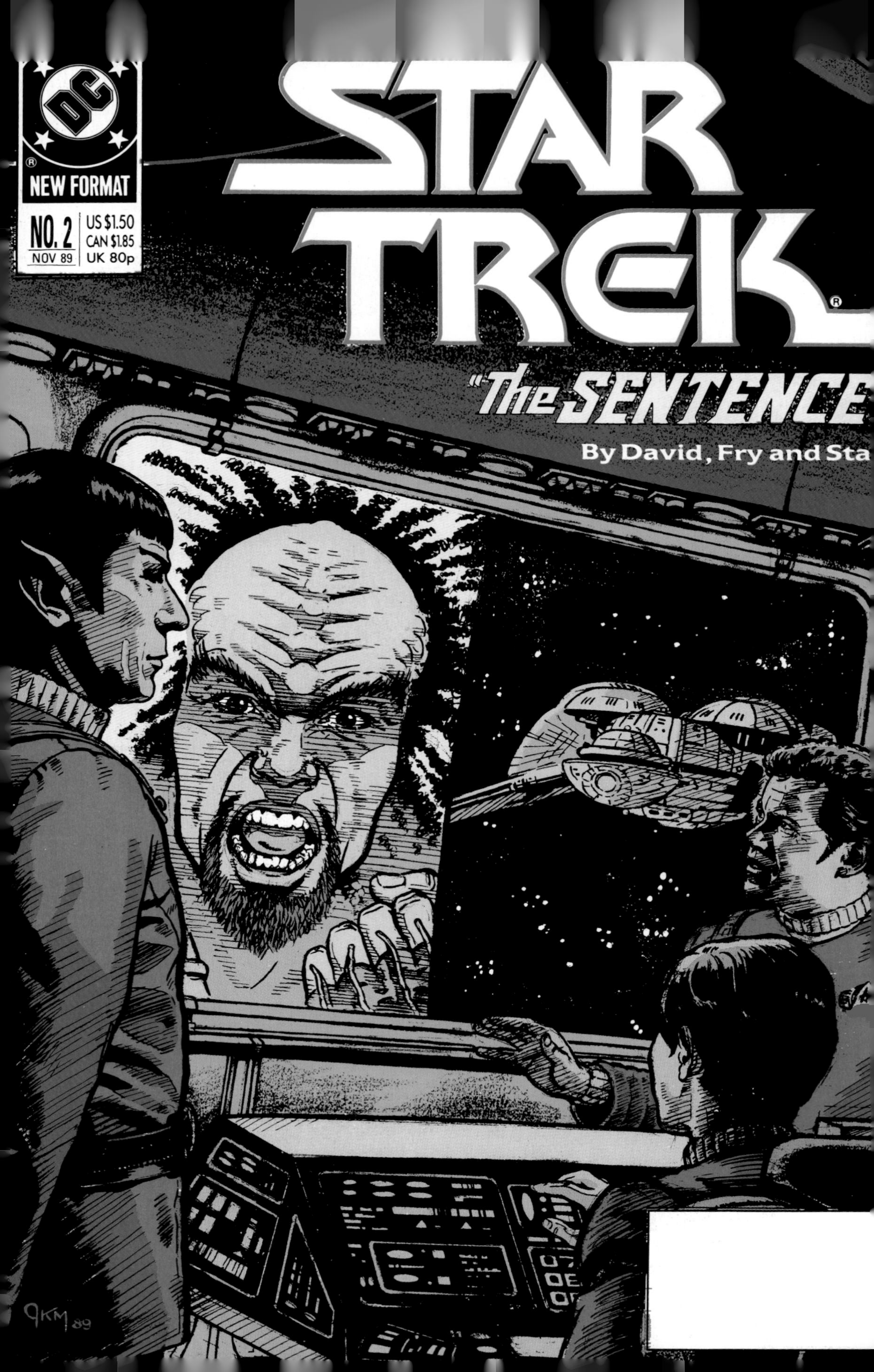
NEW FORMAT
NO. 2
NOV 89
US $1.50
CAN $1.85
UK 80p
STAR TREK
"The SENTENCE
By David, Fry and Sta

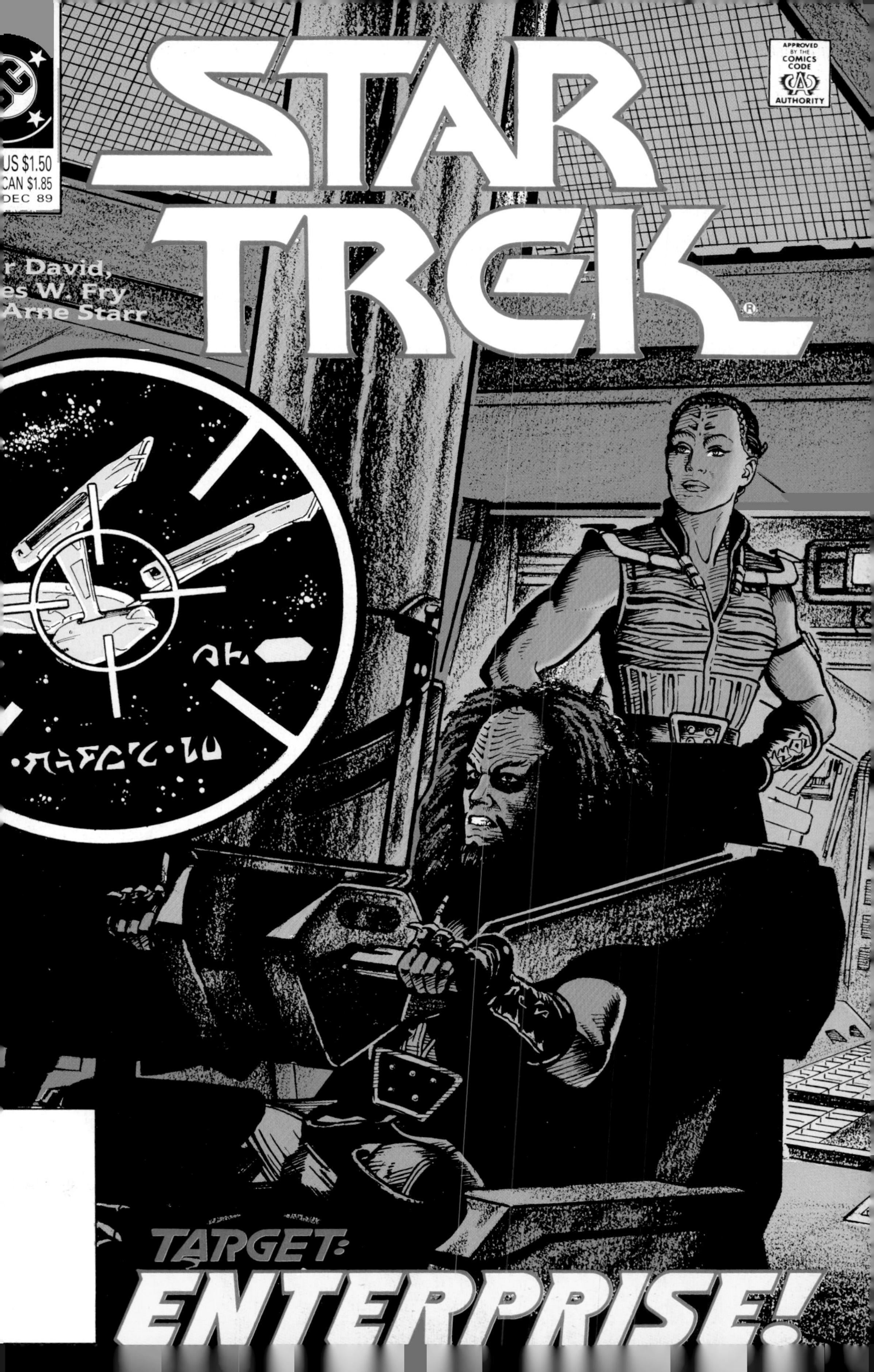

STAR TREK®
US $1.50
CAN $1.85
DEC 89
APPROVED BY THE COMICS CODE AUTHORITY
r David,
es W. Fry
Arne Starr
TARGET:
ENTERPRISE!

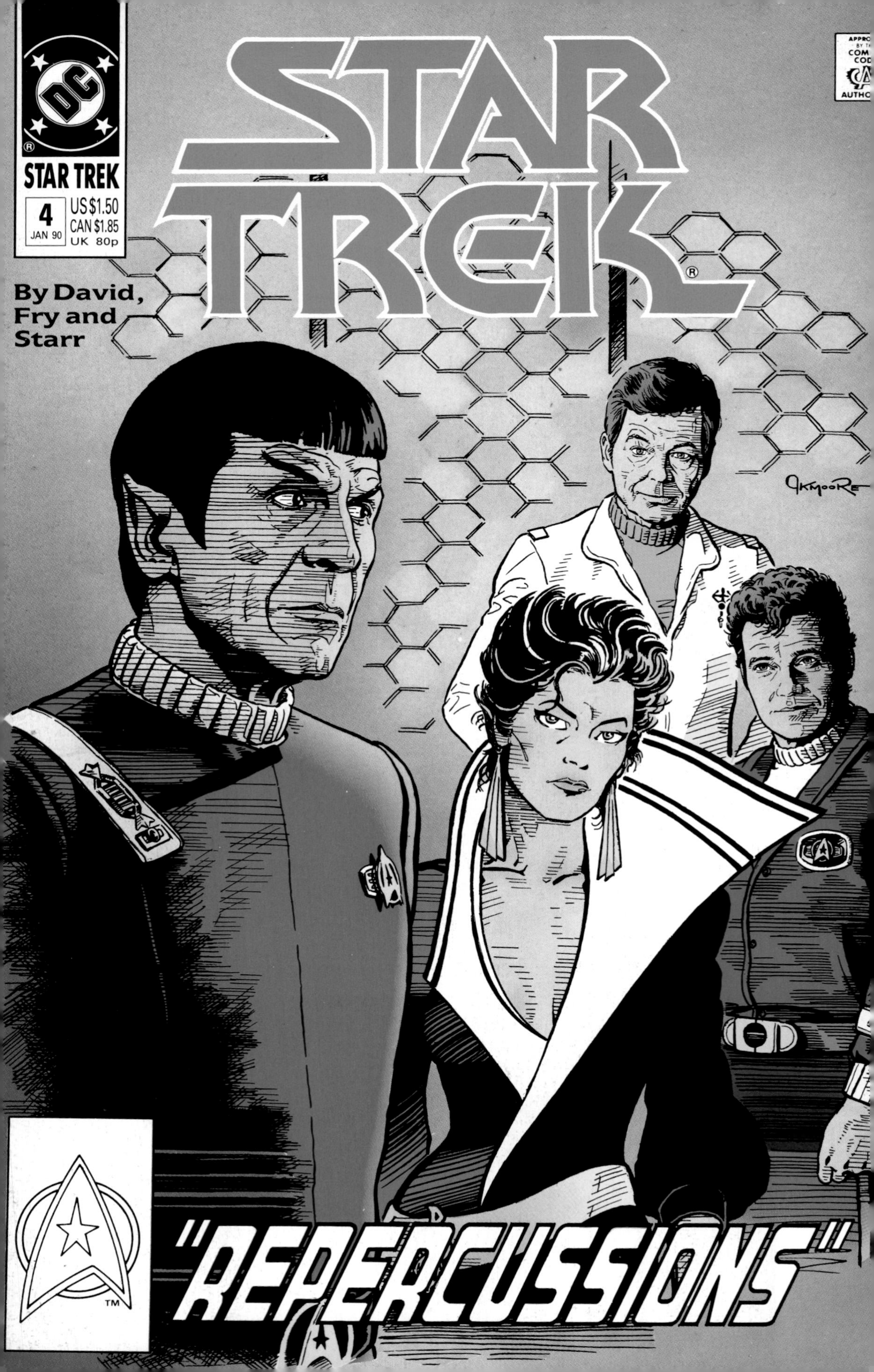

DC
STAR TREK
4
JAN 90
US $1.50
CAN $1.85
UK 80p
STAR TREK
By David, Fry and Starr
JKMOORE
"REPERCUSSIONS"

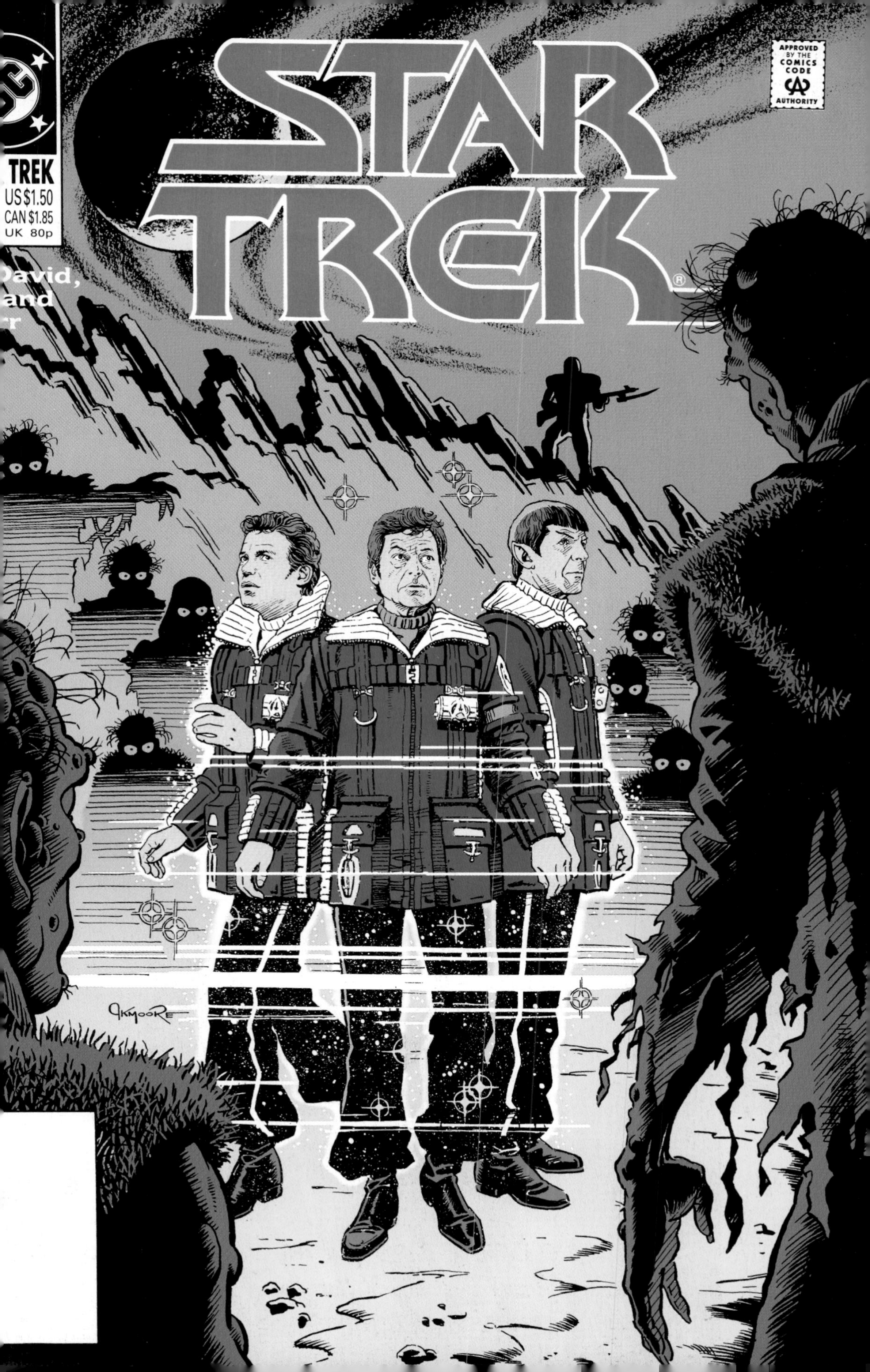

STAR TREK®
TREK
US $1.50
CAN $1.85
UK 80p
APPROVED BY THE COMICS CODE AUTHORITY
David,
and
r
GKMOORE

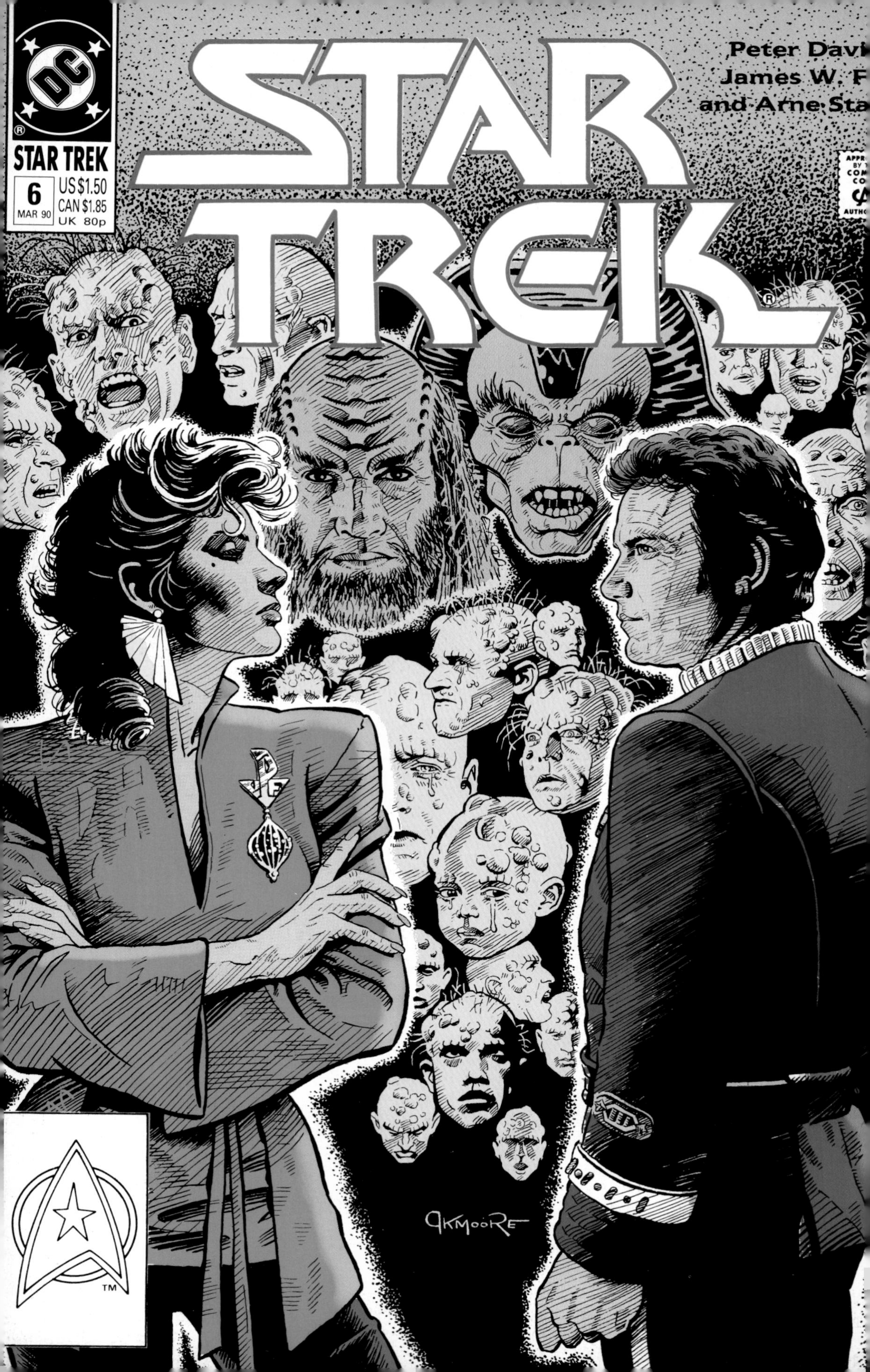
DC
STAR TREK
6
MAR 90
US$1.50
CAN $1.85
UK 80p
STAR TREK
Peter Davi
James W. F
and Arne Sta
AKMOORE

CREATOR BIOGRAPHIES

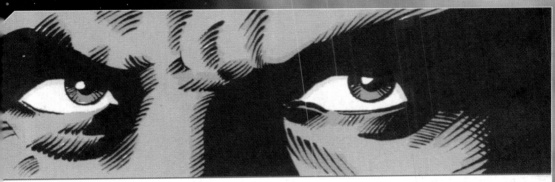

PETER DAVID is a multiple award-winning author whose career spans nearly two decades. David has had over fifty novels published, including *Sir Apropos of Nothing*, the *Psi-Man* adventure series and the bestselling *Star Trek: New Frontier* series. He has also written such *Trek* novels as *Q-Squared*, *The Siege*, and *Vendetta*. David's comics resumé includes a definitive run on *The Incredible Hulk*, as well as *Aquaman*, *Sachs & Violens*, *Soulsearchers and Company*, *Spider-Man*, *Supergirl*, *Wolverine*, *X-Factor*, *Young Justice* and many others. David is also the co-creator of the science fiction series *Space Cases*, and has written scripts for *Babylon 5*, *Crusade*, and several films. He is currently writing a new run of *The Incredible Hulk*.

JAMES W. FRY has pencilled *Avengers*, *Birds of Prey*, *Captain Marvel*, *Doom Patrol*, *Excalibur*, *Liberty Project*, *Marvel Comics Presents*, *Nomad*, *Slapstick*, *Sonic the Hedgehog*, *Spider-Man* and *X-Factor*. He is currently working on a freelance basis, teaching the art of comics illustration.

ARNE STARR'S twenty-five-year-plus career has seen him work across a wide range of commercial media and print projects. Perhaps best known for creating more art for *Star Trek* comics than any other artist, he has also produced uncredited co-inking on *Crisis on Infinite Earths*, *Booster Gold* and *Batman*, followed by credited stints on *Firestorm*, *Power Girl*, *Legion of Super-Heroes* and *Unknown Soldier*. His work also includes *The Black Tiger*, *Nexus* and *Spider-Man*. His first graphic novel, an adaptation of *War Of The Worlds*, is now available.

CONFLICT AND CRISIS!

STAR TREK
THE NEXT GENERATION™

THE BATTLE WITHIN

ISBN 1 84576 155 3

BEAMING UP SOON!